Best Wishes to

Mary Hoffauer

Carrie B. LeNoir

1/27/99

JEVAN β KLEIN

BEYOND REASONABLE DOUBT

BY

CARRIE BAKER LENOIR

BEYOND REASONABLE DOUBT

BY

CARRIE BAKER LeNOIR

Printed in the United States of America

DEDICATED

To the memory of my loving parents, William Frank and May Hatfield Baker, who, at a very early age, taught me a deep, abiding Faith in God; and to my dear Husband of fifty three years, a true Christian Gentleman, Samuel Gaillard LeNoir.

ACKNOWLEDGMENTS

I express hereby my deep gratitude for any and all support given me during the difficult years — the "Seventies and Eighties", and especially the news media, which kept the public informed of developments. The Charlotte Observer, The Atlanta Constitution, and The Columbia Record and State did an outstanding job; but most of all, The Sumter Daily Item gave very fair, accurate, and impartial coverage to the tragic death of Margaret "Peg" Cuttino, and the bizarre chain of events which followed during one of Sumter County's darkest period of history.

Once to ev'ry man and nation
Comes the moment to decide,
In the strife of truth with falsehood,
For the good or evil side;

Some great cause, God's new Messiah,
Off'ring each the bloom or blight,
And the choice goes by for ever
'Twixt that darkness and that light.

Then to side with truth is noble,
When we share her wretched crust,
Ere her cause bring fame and profit
And 'tis prosp'rous to be just;

Then it is the brave man chooses,
While the coward stands aside
Till the multitude make virtue
Of the faith they had denied.

By the light of burning martyrs
Jesus' bleeding feet I track,
Toiling up new Calvaries ever
With the cross that turns not back;

New occasions teach new duties,
Time makes ancient good uncouth;
They must upward still and onward
Who would keep abreast of truth.

Though the cause of evil prosper,
Yet 'tis truth alone is strong;
Though her portion be the scaffold,
And upon the throne be wrong,

Yet that scaffold sways the future,
And, behind the dim unknown,
Standeth God within the shadow
Keeping watch above his own.

— *James Russell Lowell, 1845*

BEYOND REASONABLE DOUBT

TABLE OF CONTENTS

CHAPTER 1	PEG CUTTINO DISAPPEARS	PAGE	1
CHAPTER 2	WILLIAM "JUNIOR" PIERCE, JR., CONFESSES	PAGE	15
CHAPTER 3	THE PIERCE TRIAL	PAGE	21
CHAPTER 4	APPEAL FOR NEW TRIAL	PAGE	43
CHAPTER 5	THE CONCERNED CITIZENS COMMITTEE	PAGE	71
CHAPTER 6	SOLICITOR R. KIRK MCLEOD DEFENDS LAW ENFORCEMENT OFFICERS	PAGE	79
CHAPTER 7	ITEM EDITOR, HUBERT D. OSTEEN, JR., DEFENDS NEWS MEDIA	PAGE	87
CHAPTER 8	THE GRAND JURY INVESTIGATION	PAGE	101
CHAPTER 9	CORONER HOWARD PARNELL ARRESTED	PAGE	113
CHAPTER 10	CORONER HOWARD PARNELL RESIGNS	PAGE	123
CHAPTER 11	APPEAL TO SOUTH CAROLINA STATE ATTORNEY GENERAL DANIEL R. MCLEOD	PAGE	129
CHAPTER 12	APPEAL TO THE UNITED STATES JUSTICE DEPARTMENT	PAGE	131
CHAPTER 13	"PEE WEE" GASKINS CONFESSES	PAGE	133
CHAPTER 14	THE CITIZENS FOR JUSTICE	PAGE	143
CHAPTER 15	THE SECOND GRAND JURY HEARING	PAGE	147
CHAPTER 16	MRS. LENOIR GOES TO JAIL	PAGE	165
CHAPTER 17	THE OSCEOLA INVESTIGATION AND REPORTS	PAGE	179
CHAPTER 18	THE THREE MILLION DOLLAR LAWSUIT	PAGE	209
CHAPTER 19	SHERIFF PARNELL DEFEATED	PAGE	229
CHAPTER 20	OTHER OFFICIALS FALL	PAGE	243
CHAPTER 21	PIERCE'S APPEAL FILED	PAGE	253
CHAPTER 22	PIERCE FINALLY GETS A HEARING	PAGE	259
CHAPTER 23	"PEE WEE" GASKINS' LAST DAYS	PAGE	273
CHAPTER 24	END OF AN ERA	PAGE	279
CHAPTER 25	HOW INVOLVED WAS GASKINS?	PAGE	287
CHAPTER 26	EARL WILLIAMS	PAGE	295
CHAPTER 27	THE "PEG" COAT	PAGE	297
CHAPTER 28	UPDATE ON CHIEF CHARACTERS AND EVENTS	PAGE	301
CHAPTER 29	LOSING FAITH IN OUR FELLOW MAN	PAGE	307
CHAPTER 30	INSPIRATION AND ENCOURAGEMENT FROM MANY SOURCES	PAGE	311
CHAPTER 31	IN RETROSPECT	PAGE	315
CHAPTER 32	IN DEEP GRATITUDE	PAGE	317

PREFACE

"Now in this particular case the State indicted William J. Pierce, Jr., for committing this offense on December 18th, 1970, in Sumter County. So the burden was, therefore, on the State to prove beyond a reasonable doubt that the offense was committed on December 18th, 1970." "No argument, no argument about that. No argument about that at all", Presiding Judge Louis Rosen assured Attorney James M. Connor on March 19th, 1973 at a hearing of a motion for a new trial, held in Kingstree, South Carolina, on Pierce's conviction for the Peg Cuttino murder.

This hearing was continued on April 5, 1973 in Sumter, South Carolina. Toward the end of the hearing, by Attorney Joseph McElveen: "If the Court please, there's been a right severe attack on the LeNoirs here today. If this is the position that law enforcement takes, if a person presents evidence in every way trying to help law enforcement, and be put through this harassment; then we can never hope to have people attempt to help law enforcement. These people — By the Court: Mr. McElveen, I don't agree with you at all in that statement, and I'm going to have to interrupt you from time to time. This thing is difficult for me too. I'm satisfied that during the investigation of this case nobody was under more pressure than the sheriff of this county; and, I mean, he would have been glad to get, I can only conclude he would have been happy to receive the most minute clue into the death of the young girl. I know that you don't contradict that it has been testified to he must have run down, I said three thousand, it may have been more leads than that; so I can't imagine law enforcement officers of Sumter County disregarding evidence that would have led to the murderer of this young girl. That's difficult for me to believe. By Mr. McElveen: We don't contend that. By the Court: I thought that's what you said. By Mr. McElveeen: I didn't mean that if that's the way it came across. The inference was from all our witnesses why didn't you contact somebody at the time of the trial. The confession was never published in the newspapers until after the trial. There was nothing to make anyone doubt anything like that the State had an ironclad case against this man. Furthermore when a citizen reports an incident to the police, this is his duty, and as a responsible citizen, he's not going to further hinder the work of law enforcement by calling, and calling, and calling. These people did their duty and they have sworn affidavits saying that they have made a positive identification of the person."

Several years ago a Ghost Writer prepared the first nineteen chapters for this book; but, because of failing eyesight, had to abandon the project. He presented his transcript to me, with the request that I complete it. Therefore, the writing in Chapter Twenty changes from third person to first person. I have searched my soul, and prayed to God for the answer — should I publish the book? The answer always comes back "Yes". I know it will open wounds for some, which I regret; but I feel a deep obligation to William J. Pierce, Jr., as The Concerned Citizens and Citizens for Justice feel that The State of South Carolina has failed to prove, Beyond Reasonable Doubt, that he is guilty of the Cuttino murder.

CHAPTER ONE

"PEG" CUTTINO DISAPPEARS
DECEMBER 18, 1970

Friday, December 18, 1970. It was the last day of school before the Christmas holidays and thousands of young people tensely struggled through their mid-term exams.

Much of the nation was covered with snow and battered by extremely cold winds and temperatures at this time of the year; but, down here in the South - in the quiet little town of Sumter, South Carolina - the weather was mild, even for this part of the country that year. Temperatures had dropped to 31 degrees during the prior night; but, by the middle of the day, had risen to a comfortable 65 degrees. The sun shown brightly through partly cloudy skies and a light coat felt good.

Shopkeepers were busily stocking their shelves with every toy and gift that could be imagined, in eager anticipation of the inevitable rush of shoppers in the coming week before Christmas day.

All was peaceful Day-to-day activities continued as the people went about their business in the knowledge that all was safe and that peace-on-earth, at least here in Sumter, was a reality.

But, as fate would have it, this was no ordinary day. The events of this day would forever change the history of Sumter and Sumter County. Families would turn against families and friends against friends — citizens against their public officials and law enforcement officials against the people. Under oath, in open and closed courts, officials would give contradictory testimony in an unbelievable chain of events that seemed to have no end.

Could it be that some prominent families, fearing social disgrace if the truth were revealed, would use their wealth, position and influence to gain the cooperation and assistance of noted public officials to shift the blame on less fortunate members of society — somehow convincing themselves that it was best for all concerned.

At first, their seemingly insignificant little "white lies" and deeds appeared to them to be harmless; but they found that — to cover up one lie, you had to tell another — and the lies and deeds increased in size and complexity until they reached levels that could no longer be controlled. Respectable citizens, seeking only to do their civic duty in testifying of things that they had seen, were pressured and confused, degraded and treated worse than common criminals, even to the point of imprisonment, by desperate and overzealous public officials in an effort to get out of the "corner" that they found they had worked themselves into.

Torture and threats against lives were employed by officials and condoned by others, reputations were marred, lives shattered and enormous lawsuits lodged against those who tried to expose them and some against those who only sympathized with the oppressed.

The effects of this day would reach to state levels here in South Carolina, involve Georgia, North Carolina, and eventually the U.S. Justice Department, in Washington D.C.

Yes, it all began here in the quiet and peaceful little city of Sumter, South Carolina. And it's not over yet. We don't yet know the truth about the events of December 18, 1970, and the days that followed...(and we possibly never will).

This was a dark period in the history of Sumter County and one that is hoped will never recur. Unless we learn from this experience and take definite actions to see that it cannot happen again...it may.

In the 1960's and early 1970's, a wave of disturbances swept across the United States, stemming from the activities of the youth of our nation.

It was the era of the flower children — the beatniks — the youth demonstrations. The free flow of various forms of drugs were discovered to be rampant in this country. The news was full of rebellious actions against our society by these groups of young people.

The adult population, who had formed, and were quite pleased with our society — in fact, very proud of it — was shocked and sickened by these "social misfits" who spanned the very elements of society which assured them the wealth and freedoms to which they were accustomed.

This alarming news was, at first, just something that was happening "out in California" but, by the late 1960's, Sumter County parents were stunned by the sudden realization that our own city and county schools were infiltrated with drugs.

Marijuana was being smoked freely by the young people and could be easily obtained by any young person, right on the school grounds. And pills of every description were available everywhere.

A whole new language of illegal narcotics were painfully taught to the shocked and disbelieving parents through police reports and news coverage of the new-found menace to our way of life.

Many parents read, listened to and watched these reports, but refused to believe, or even think of the possible involvement in drug usage by their own children. They were often brokenhearted and disillusioned when their child was found in some ally, or deserted house on the wrong side of the tracks and rushed to the hospital, at the point of death from an overdose, or from a bad batch of dope.

Or, they would receive a call, late at night, from the police station with news that their child had been arrested for possession, under the influence, or distribution of the illegal substance.

Children became addicted and because of the obsession and need for dope, they turned against their parents and their way of life — left home — often disappearing without a trace — leaving brokenhearted parents wondering "where they went wrong."

Pushers of the illegal pills and cigarettes would often contact children whose parents were wealthy or public officials — politicians, judges, lawyers, school teachers, even clergymen — people who could not afford a scandal if the child was caught and who had enough influence in their communities to "hush it up" if necessary.

It has been rumored that, right here in Sumter, in the early 1970's there was a studio where unscrupulous men used teenage girls and boys in the production of pornographic movies. They produced the films here and shipped them to the west coast to supply the growing and profitable, demand from perverted men who would pay large sums of money for them.

In order to get the teenage girls and boys to participate in these films, the children would be contacted and provided with whatever drugs were popular at the time on campus. For awhile, the pusher would simply deal with the child through the dope business. But, eventually, the pusher would blackmail the child, with threats of exposure - or worse, into participating in pornographic movies.

Perhaps it was true — perhaps it was not — but whatever was going on in Sumter at that time, we know now was not a healthy environment for our young people.

Missing persons reports for teenagers were common in those unstable days. Children ran off and joined the communes of the flower children frequently. It seemed that they just wanted to tune the whole world out and get away from it all. They resented any parental authority. Seemingly in defiance of their parents, young men grew long, straggly, unkempt heads of hair and grew mustaches and beards — oh, and they spoke a language of their own, which was alien and utterly repulsive to their parents and other adults. It seemed that the young people, girls and boys, tried to see just how filthy and unkempt they could be. Their clothes were totally unacceptable to their parents.

These clashes between the generations led to many of the disappearances of young people during that period. Some of them got along all right, for a few years, came to their senses and returned to the love and guidance of their parents and got back into the mainstream of our society.

However, many of them have never been heard from again. We have learned of the fate of some, but there are others that perhaps we will never know what fate befell them.

Police and law enforcement agencies did the best they could, in most instances, and honestly endeavored to locate and return these missing children. But, because of the vastness of the problem, the lack of information to go on, the lack of funds to do extensive investigations into each disappearance and, of course, the civil rights of the child, which was becoming an issue of the day, there was only so much that they could do.

Bear these things in mind as you read through the pages of this book. Some things are not "black" or "white" sometimes. There is a vast area that is simply "gray."

Be careful not to judge any of the persons too harshly on the basis of what is written here. We only have what was written, spoken or imagined to consider and it is possible that, had you been the person involved, citizen, law officer, law official, accused, parent of the missing or murdered child, judge, elected official, news person, writer, or whatever,—you might have done exactly what each person in this bizarre case did.

Although the sands of time continually wear away at the chronicle reality of this tragedy, it will live in the minds and hearts of those who were actually involved, as long as God lends them breath — and will have affects on their descendants for untold centuries to come.

At about 12:00 p.m., pretty, 13-year-old Margaret Edwards Cuttino, the daughter of then South Carolina State Representative, James C. Cuttino, left her home at 45 Mason Croft Drive, walking north on Winn Street. According to her mother, she planned to walk the several blocks to Willow Drive School, on Willow Drive, and to have lunch with her younger sister, Pamela, who was a student there.

Peg, as she was known to her family and friends, was a student at nearby Alice Drive Junior High School and had completed her school activities by about 11:30 a.m. that day and was free for the holidays.

She walked down Willow Drive, passed in front of the new Y.M.C.A. building on the lot beside the school her sister attended.

But, she never arrived.

A classmate of Peg's, Jerry Artrip, finished his exams and other activities at about 12 o'clock, left the school grounds shortly after, and walked the two blocks to his home at 106 Reynolds Road.

He got on his bicycle and peddled to a friend's house to have lunch with him. When he arrived, he discovered that he had left his wallet at home and rode back to his home and got it.

On the way back to the friend's house, near the intersection of Phelps and Wren Streets, a car approached and took a left turn on Phelps Street.

Jerry saw Peg sitting in the back seat of the car and waved to her, but she did not wave back. He had no classes with her, but did know her and had on occasion spoken with her. Maybe she just didn't see him. It was then about 1:00 p.m., and Jerry, thinking no more about the incident, continued to his friend's house for lunch.

Around 2:30 p.m., Mr. and Mrs. Cuttino reported to the Sumter police that Peg was missing and the search for her began.

The local radio stations were provided a description of the missing girl, and they began immediately to broadcast the information, in hopes that someone had seen her.

Within hours, perhaps the most massive search ever launched in South Carolina began.

At his home, Jerry Artrip was listening to the radio and heard the bulletin on Peg. Recalling the earlier incident, he told his father that he had seen her, and his father immediately called the city police.

Early Saturday morning, December 19, a large group of friends of the family organized a search party, under the direction of George James, a local attorney. The helicopter was still searching the area and Sumter County Sheriff, I. Byrd Parnell, was on board.

A communications truck, equipped with radio facilities, maintained constant contact with the helicopter and other search parties.

The police department sent out a nationwide all points bulletin, and reports were issued to television stations, radio stations and newspapers in South Carolina.

Under the direction of Chief of Police, Leslie W. Griffin, the city police department began to contact close friends of the missing girl, in hopes of gaining more information.

Chief Griffin told the press, "All efforts are being made by the various law enforcement agencies and interested citizens in the area to locate Peggy Cuttino."

Jerry Artrip was asked to come to the police station and he went to the sheriff's department and told several officers what he had seen.

"There was a man driving the car with dark colored hair, with glasses. He was between 30 and 35 years of age. A woman was sitting in the front passenger seat. I could not see her face. I am positive Peg Cuttino was in the back seat of the car, on the right side. I saw her face and her eyes were open. I waved to her, but she did not wave back."

Mrs. Carrie LeNoir, Postmaster in the little town of Horatio, in the upper western section of Sumter County, first became aware of Peg's disappearance about 9:30 Saturday morning, when a relative phoned and told her of it. However, she was so busy that morning that she barely had time to take note of it and immediately returned to her work.

Mr. S.G. LeNoir owned and operated a general store, there in Horatio, that had been in the LeNoir family continually since before the year 1800. LeNoirs had owned and operated it for six generations, in fact, it was the only remaining store in what was once a good sized little town, boasting several stores and other businesses. The Post Office was located immediately upon entering and to the left side, as you walked into the store, and the counter where Mr. LeNoir spent most of his time was across the back of the store some distance from the post office, where Mrs. LeNoir spent most of her time. On very busy days, sometimes, they would work there all day without having time for more than a few words between them. The LeNoir home is next door to the store and, when there was not much traffic, Mrs. LeNoir would go over to the house and prepare dinner and eat, then come back and operate the store and Post Office while her husband went to the house and ate. However, when they were too busy, as they were Saturday, December 19, 1970, they grabbed a snack and a drink there in the store and never left except to run to the house for a minute to use the bathroom, which the store did not have.

Around 2:30 that day, things slowed down a little, and Mrs. LeNoir took about a five-minute break and went to the house. On her way back, she noticed a strange, brownish-yellow car sitting in front of the store. As she approached, two boys and a girl came out of the store and entered the car. The boys got into the front seat and the girl got into the back.

Mrs. LeNoir did not see the girl's face clearly, but she knew that she did not know the boys. She intended to ask Gaillard if he knew them.

Horatio is located on a farm-to-market road, a few miles off the main road from Stateburg to Camden, and there is very seldom any traffic "just passing through." So, since the LeNoirs have spent their entire lives there in the community, operating the store and post office and active in social, religious and political affairs, they know everyone, black and white, for many miles around. "When you see a stranger in Horatio," Mrs. LeNoir says, "you just naturally are curious as to who they are and why they are visiting in our town."

Well, she intended to ask her husband, but barely got in the front door before she found herself up to her elbows in work in the Post Office again. And there she stayed until she finished around 4:45 p.m.

As she left the Post Office area and was walking back into the area where the store counter was, the two boys that she had seen earlier getting into the car with the girl came in, handed her three dollars and said they had put in three dollars worth of gasoline. Most people pump their own gas at the LeNoir store.

"The boys seemed real excited, " Mrs. LeNoir said. They had handed her the money, turned and hurried out before she had a chance to say anything to them. She followed them to the front door and watched as they got into the same car they had been in earlier and drove off and turned down the Claremont Road, just as they had done the first time. The girl was not with them. She did not think much about the incident, however, they were just kids enjoying the first day of Christmas holidays, so she returned to the counter at the back of the store and began to assist her husband with the customers.

When the afternoon newspaper, *The Sumter Daily Item*, was delivered a short time later, Mr. LeNoir noticed the picture of Peggy Cuttino on the front. "That girl was in the store today," he exclaimed.

"Are you sure?" Mrs. LeNoir asked him.

"Yes, I'm sure," he assured her. "She stood right there and I handed her a Coca-Cola and looked right in her face. She looked sad."

A discussion between the two followed and Mrs. LeNoir started recalling things about the girl she'd seen getting into the car in comparison with the Peggy Cuttino that she remembered from a few years earlier when Peggy was with her father, there at the Horatio community Center for a campaign supper and speeches. It was customary, prior to elections, to have all of the candidates come up and speak. Mrs. LeNoir could recall vividly how Peggy had walked around, passing out her father's campaign cards and saying, "Please vote for my daddy."

But, she remembered Peggy with longer hair and the girl that she had seen that day had shoulder length hair. The picture in the paper showed her with medium length hair, and Mrs. LeNoir wondered if she should call the police or the family or what. The paper reporting her missing had been printed early that morning and surely she had contacted her parents and they knew where she was. She did not want to get involved in what appeared to be a family matter.

The LeNoirs finally got through with their day's work about 9:30 that night, went on to the house and ate supper. There was no discussion between them about the Cuttino girl, and they went to bed at 11 o'clock. But, neither of them slept much that night. They tossed and turned all night.

Next morning, in discussion of the restless night, Mrs. Carrie told her husband that she had dreamed throughout the night of the girl she had seen getting into the car. Mr. LeNoir revealed that he had seemed to see the sad little girl standing in the store, reaching out for the Coke, all during the long restless night.

Mrs. Carrie got up at 8 o'clock and called the residence of Mr. Cuttino's sister, Mrs. W.C. (Lucy Anne) Eldridge. She was still wondering about the length of the girl's hair.

Mrs. Eldridge's son, Jamie, answered the phone and Mrs. Carrie identified herself and told him that she had called to check the length of Peg's hair at present.

"Shoulder length," Jamie told her.

"That confirms our belief that she was in our store yesterday," she told him and went on to relate the events of the day before.

He said that he would notify the police for them and she hung up and went about getting ready for church.

They attended church services at the Church of the Ascension, in the nearby little town of Hagood, where they had been lifelong members and, as was often their custom, drove into Sumter and had dinner at a restaurant.

The church was having it's Christmas pageant that evening and since Mrs. Carrie was to play the organ for the pageant, she returned that afternoon to practice. About 4:30, she was sitting at the organ practicing the carols while the children were in the Parish House getting on their costumes, when John Brabham, another member of the church, came in and told her that two men were waiting to see her. As she walked into the sacristy, there stood Detectives Hugh Mathis and Tommy Mims.

"Mrs. LeNoir," Detective Mathis began with a smile, "I've come to tell you that I expect that J. Edgar Hoover will be drafting you 'most any time to serve with the F.B.I." They all laughed — the reason for this remark being that Mrs. Carrie had helped them solve the mystery of 'who wrecked the train in Horatio' the Monday night before.

He then told her that they had received their message and had been by the house and talked to Mr. LeNoir. He had told them where to find her.

Mrs. Carrie related to them the events of the previous day, and they left.

Prayers went up from churches throughout the Sumter area on Sunday morning, December 20, for the welfare and safe return of the Cuttino child.

In the early afternoon, a horseback search was begun by 17 people, led by City Detective Jearl F. Wheat that would continue to cover a four square mile area of the wooded areas in the western part of Sumter, until dark.

Another 20 people combed the area on foot, but no evidence was turned up, which might shed light on the case.

The vigorous search continued on Monday, December 21. The newspaper and three radio stations in Sumter encouraged the community to join in a moment of silent prayer at 6 p.m. that night, for the safety of the child. All three radio stations observed the moment by airing a prayer by the Reverend Murray Shull, President of the Sumter County Ministers Association, which, along with Sumter Mayor Robert E. Graham, had proposed this plea.

In a news release that day, Chief Griffin said, "We have not been able to discern any evidence which might indicate foul play here, but we have found no evidence to rule out a kidnapping."

"Our men are following up every possible lead, but the concentrated search in this area has been called off for all practical purposes. We are going under the assumption that she was kidnapped and have released all-points bulletins throughout the United States."

Griffin also disclosed that the girl's parents had received no communication from anyone who might have taken her.

He also referred to the statement made by Jerry Artrip, who had reported seeing Peggy in a car with two other people on the day she disappeared. "The boy is sure it was Margaret. He says a couple was in the front seat and he saw them about 15 minutes after she left her house. We've questioned him twice and there is no doubting his sincerity."

Tuesday, as the search moved into the fifth day, law enforcement officers admitted to the increasingly concerned people of the city and county that not much headway had been made.

According to various officials, interviewed by *Item* Staff Writer, Van King, no helpful leads had developed, although tips had been coming in from many quarters.

The public was reassured that the several state and local law enforcement agencies were working day and night to find the missing child. Officials were reported to be working on the assumption that a kidnap case was involved.

"This is the biggest kidnap case I can recall since I've been in law enforcement work," remarked Police Chief Griffin.

By this time, The Federal Bureau of Investigation was observing the case closely and assisting in the coverage of out-of-state leads.

Chief Griffin revealed that a number of leads had been coming from out-of-state sources, mainly police stations from across the country, which had been alerted in the nationwide bulletin.

"We're getting all kinds of information, but nothing is panning out," he said. "We have all our detectives and youth officers working on the case. The sheriff and most of his force are working on it and SLED has been here since Friday. We've got enough available manpower for the operation here and the police agencies throughout the nation are making an effort to help. We've gotten a number of long distance calls from police agencies across the nation, giving us bits of information that might tie in, but none of them have. They tell us things like 'we've got this person missing in our state and we think this may tie in.'"

Slowly, as the reality of Peg's disappearance sank in, a deep, terrifying helplessness engulfed the people of Sumter and Sumter County.

Nervous and fearful parents panicked if a child was overdue at some point or could not be accounted for, even for a few minutes. Children, who do not see danger as vividly as their parents, disliked and resented this close supervision, even knowing that it was for their own good.

To make matters even worse, just across the river, in West Columbia, 17 year old Kathy Jo Anderson left the drive-in restaurant where she worked, after her shift was over, and disappeared. Her abandoned car was later found with a flat tire.

Wednesday, December 23, a $5,000.00 reward was announced in an article in *The Sumter Daily Item*. According to the authorities, the money for the reward was offered by persons whose identity was not to be disclosed and was for the safe return of the missing child. No leads had yet developed which could point to the circumstances surrounding her disappearance.

It was stressed that the reward was not being offered by law enforcement agencies. The reward offer was made voluntarily and no calls or letters requesting any kind of ransom had been received. The authorities had only been authorized, at the request of the unidentified individuals, to offer the reward hoping that the offer may lead to the child's safe return.

No evidence of foul play had been indicated by any of the leads followed up on so far and the local search had been called off on the assumption that she was the victim of kidnappers.

Although several calls had been received from various cities, none of the leads offered indicated any relation to the Cuttino girl's case.

Reward posters were authorized and distributed, listing the missing girl and describing her as white, female, age: 13 years, 5 feet 2 inches tall, weighing 130 pounds, with blue eyes and brown shoulder length hair. She was last seen wearing a blue blouse, white skirt and polka dot belt.

Thursday, December 24 — Christmas Eve Day found the weary law enforcement officers still busily checking out the seemingly endless flow of leads that consumed their time but always led nowhere.

"If something doesn't break on this case today, there's going to be a cloud over the whole city for Christmas," Chief Griffin predicted.

The feelings of that day were perhaps best expressed in an editorial in *The Sumter Daily Item*, entitled "Hope for Peggy."

It read "On the eve of Christmas, normally a time of joy and thanksgiving, a heavy cloud hangs over this city following the disappearance of 13-year-old Peggy Cuttino.

In spite of a massive, around-the-clock search, no clue as to her whereabouts has turned up. Law enforcement agencies, local, state and federal, have worked diligently and tirelessly to find this child and return her safely to her stricken family. The offering of a reward for her safe return, hopefully, will bring some results.

One of the greatest blessing of Christmas is that of hope and optimism. It is our fervent prayer — and that of many others who've followed the plight of the Cuttino family — that Peggy will be reunited with her parents and their Christmas will be one of joy rather than sorrow.

Let us be thankful for our blessings on Christmas Day, and also hopeful that a distraught family will once again be happy and whole."

But, the day ended — and there was no word from Peggy.

And Christmas day was indeed a sad day in Sumter and Sumter County. Families gathered as usual for the traditional dinner and exchange of gifts, but Peggy Cuttino's fate was the predominant topic of conversation.

Rumors abounded and various opinions, expressed solely as one's opinion, would later be repeated as the 'gospel truth.'

The authorities had ceased to release any information about the various leads being investigated, but bits and pieces of what was happening at the Sheriff's Office and City Police Headquarters leaked out. There were so many officers, investigators and authorities working on the case that it was impossible to keep the whole thing contained.

Just as abruptly as it had begun, the long, frustrating search came to an end on Wednesday afternoon around 3 o'clock, December 30.

Captains Gregory Dorsey and Paul Nowak, from Shaw Air Force Base, were trail riding in the vast wooded area near Sumter, known as Manchester State Forest.

"I thought it was a manikin at first," Captain Dorsey said. "Then I noticed the polka dot belt and something just clicked in my head — this could be the girl. We determined it was the body and drove to a store up the road and called the Highway Patrol and the Sheriff's office."

They ran into Game Warden Gene Jackson as they left the store, and the three of them returned to the scene and waited for the arrival of Sheriff Parnell.

"I knew right away it was her, from the description I had been given and from her clothes," warden Jackson said later.

She had on the same clothes that she had been wearing when she disappeared thirteen days ago: a blue blouse, white skirt and polka dot sash belt.

When the news had been received at the Sheriff's office, Sheriff Parnell, Coroner Howard Parnell, SLED Chief J.P. Strom, Police Chief L.W. Griffin, and SLED agents quickly converged on the scene and sealed off the area.

"It's her!" said a grim-faced Sheriff Byrd Parnell, as he drove out of a wooded area about 2.5 miles south of Wedgefield, off Highway 261, after he had been to the scene and had looked for himself. He said it appeared that an attempt had been made to conceal the body with leaves and moss, and assured the public that all efforts to locate suspects in the slaying were being made by local and state law enforcement agencies.

Three criminal pathologists from the Medical University of South Carolina at Charleston — Drs. Charles Garrett, Joel S. Sexton and Ervin B. Shaw, Jr. — were brought to the scene to examine the body and determine the cause of death and how long the child had been dead.

The body was later removed to Charleston for further examination.

The story of Peg's tragic end and plans for her funeral appeared in *The Sumter Daily Item* on Thursday afternoon, December 31 — leaving it's readers relieved that the long search was over, but brokenhearted for the Cuttino family in their loss. People who had never seen any member of the Cuttino family wept openly when the subject came up. The melancholy cloud of sadness that hung over Sumter and Sumter County for the next few days amply demonstrated the feelings and emotions of a people who cared deeply for their fellow man and shared in the loss of Peg Cuttino, as if she were their own child.

Peg was the typical teenager — typically every parent's teenage daughter. She was born in Sumter September 30, 1957, an eighth grade student at Alice Drive Junior High School, a member of the first string girls varsity basketball team, a member of the Youth Choir of First Presbyterian Church, the Pioneer Sunday School Class and the Pioneer Youth Fellowship.

Because of the tragedy of the events — because of the publicity that it had received and because every parent and every child realized that 'It could have been me,' Sumter and Sumter County citizens had become a real, caring, feeling part of the Cuttino family's misfortune.

Rumors ran wildly throughout the county in the next few days. There were several versions of stories that the killer had been captured. Several versions claimed that a man had been arrested, he was believed to be the killer and was being investigated further.

It seemed that everyone had heard about the trailer found near Wedgefield. It was all bloody inside and believed to be the place where Peg was killed. But, no one was sure of anything.

The mobile home was owned by Mrs. Edward (Martha Pauline) Garber (now Mrs. Casey) who was away in England, since September of that year. She had listed the mobile home "for rent" with a local real estate firm, but had not received any rent. On the day Peg's body was found, only a few miles away, it was discovered by an employee of the real estate firm that the mobile home had been entered and apparently used for parties. There were beer cans all over, and it was covered with blood in places.

The police were picking up certain people and interrogating them for various reasons, and this, perhaps, prompted the various rumors about someone being arrested and charged.

Numerous calls to the Police Department inquired about the trailer, but the police would neither confirm nor deny it's existence. There was never anything released to the papers and the news of Peg's unfortunate end overshadowed the discovery, and it was soon forgotten.

Most people, when later asked "What did they ever find out about that trailer?" would answer that they didn't believe there ever was a trailer. "If there had been," they would say, "you would have seen something about it in *The Item*."

Thursday, January 7, 1971. Sheriff I. Byrd Parnell refuted a number of rumors currently being circulated with regard to alleged arrests made in connection with the slaying, according to an article in *The Item*.

"No one has been apprehended or charged with the offense," Parnell said, "and we have received no hot leads in the case. Our local investigators are still working on the case and we are not trying to hide anything from anybody."

He stated that several persons were questioned yesterday with regard to the case, but the results of the lie detector proved to be negative.

In another article, on Friday, January 8, Chief Investigator T.L. McJunkin, of the Sumter County Sheriff's Department, said the investigation was continuing at "full speed."

"No arrest warrants have been issued so far in the case," he added, "but we are still questioning people every day. Our investigators along with all other persons working on the case are checking out every possible lead that turns up."

The article also stated that "Although no conclusive proof was established from the autopsy, the pathologists theorized that Peg Cuttino was probably slain the day she disappeared, December 18."

Monday, January 11, was the same. Chief McJunkin said, "All tips are being checked out and all possibilities are being looked into."

Then, on Tuesday, January 12, a small article appeared entitled "Reward Offered In Death." It stated that "A $5,000.00 reward is being offered for information leading to the apprehension and conviction of persons responsible for the death of Margaret 'Peg' Cuttino."

The announcement was released jointly by Sheriff Parnell and City Police Chief Griffin. It stated that the reward was being offered by concerned citizens.

Rumors again raged throughout the area, fanned daily by the picking up and questioning of various people in connection with the case and the sheriff took the opportunity of this article to try to quiet them.

"All rumors currently being circulated — many of them vicious — concerning arrests, are false. I hope that persons responsible for starting and circulating these rumors will refrain from making these groundless accusations."

On Thursday, January 14, it seemed that a ray of hope may have finally shown through the cloud that hung over the long investigation, when a composite drawing of a man appeared in The Item. The picture was made up by State Law Enforcement Division Lt. Laney Talbert from information furnished by 'a reliable source' who had seen the suspect in the area where the body had been found. He was described as being between 25 and 30 years of age, 5-8 to 5-10 in height, 160 to 170 pounds, with brown hair and a medium build.

By Saturday, however, though officials had received what they described as 'a good response' from citizens who were trying to help identify the suspect, no positive identification had been made.

"A lot of them tell us he looks like somebody they know or have seen but we haven't gotten any definite identification on him yet," Police Chief Griffin reported.

By February 10, 1971, more than 50 days after Peg was first reported missing, investigators still had not identified or apprehended her slayer, but *Item* Staff Writer Tom Prewett reported that the case was far from being cold."

"Approximately 30 leads are currently being worked on by city detectives, Sumter County Sheriff's deputies and State Law Enforcement Division (SLED) officers.

"Investigators from these three law enforcement divisions meet three times a week in the small courtroom of the Sumter County Courthouse to rehash old leads, share information on new leads and in general, stay on top of the situation.

"Since the outset of the investigation, investigators from all law enforcement agencies involved have questioned 1,465 persons on the Cuttino case.

"During the same period of time, they have tracked down 242 local leads, 27 out-of-county leads and five out-of-state leads.

"Agents of the Federal Bureau of Investigation have been instrumental in checking out-of-state leads throughout the investigation.

"In all, a total of 274 leads have been checked out by investigators, including those which led to polygraph (lie detector) tests for 24 suspects, not all of whom have been able to prove their activities on the eighteenth of December, the day Peg Cuttino disappeared."

"While many leads have proved to a dead end, some of them have led us to other leads which our investigators are still working on," Chief Griffin said. "There are certain aspects of the investigation which the authorities have not released to the public, because if some facts were made public information, the guilty party might be alerted and this would impede our investigation." Chief Griffin and Sheriff Parnell felt at that time that the prospects were good for finding the killer and bringing him (or her) to justice.

They said that response from the public had been "very encouraging."

"I feel that this indicates that the public is behind us 100 percent of the way as far as the investigation," Chief Griffin said.

Sheriff Parnell indicated that the Cuttino case had resulted in definite steps toward tightening up of safety practices by parents with regard to their children.

"It is unfortunate that it took a tragic incident like the death of Peg Cuttino to bring about these precautionary measures."

He indicated that since the Cuttino incident, there had been reports made to police concerning attempts made by unknown persons to pick up children in the city prior to December 18, which were not reported to police until after the Cuttino girl's disappearance became public information.

On February 19, 1971, a body was found in a shallow grave in a wooded area of Lexington County and was identified as that of 17-year-old Kathy Jo Anderson, who disappeared on December 22 of 1970.

CHAPTER TWO

WILLIAM "JUNIOR" PIERCE, JR., CONFESSES
APRIL 29, 1971

In a bulletin, appearing in *The Item* on Thursday, April 29, 1971, it was disclosed that South Carolina Solicitor John Ford, of Columbia, had revealed that an arrest had been made in Georgia, in the death of Peggy Cuttino of Sumter. He said that the arrest was made somewhere in Georgia, but he had no further information at press time.

Next day, *Item* Staff Writer Tom Prewett's article disclosed the following details:

"Prayers, perseverance and cooperation" were credited today by Sumter County Sheriff I. Byrd Parnell as the key factors leading to the apprehension of a 40-year-old Swainsboro, Georgia, man who has been formally charged with murder in the December 18, 1970, death of 13-year-old Margaret "Peg" Cuttino.

Identified as William J. Pierce, Jr., an unmarried service station attendant who is being held in the Baxley, Georgia, jail, charged with the murder of three women, five armed robberies and three assaults, the suspect was interviewed extensively yesterday by City Police Chief L.W. Griffin, Sheriff Parnell and Lt. Leon Dollard of the State Law Enforcement Division (SLED).

"Enough facts were established during the interrogation to constitute the signing of a warrant in connection with Peg Cuttino's slaying," Parnell said this morning at a joint news conference with Chief Griffin and Lt. Dollard.

We had determined from the beginning of this investigation over four months ago that we were going to keep working on this case until it was solved," Chief Griffin stated.

"We knew that the safety and the peace of mind of this community would not be insured until we apprehended Peg Cuttino's slayer," Griffin said.

Both Griffin and Parnell agreed that the evidence they gleaned during their interrogation of Pierce in Baxley, yesterday, gives a strong indication that the Cuttino girl was picked up at gun point somewhere between her home at 45 Mason Croft Drive and Broad Street on the day she disappeared. They also said they had reason to believe that she was probably killed within an hour after she was abducted.

"Local law enforcement officers have put between 8,000 and 10,000 man hours into the investigation since the girl's disappearance was first reported," Griffin stated.

Appling County Sheriff J.B. "Red" Carter, of Baxley, Georgia, who describes himself as "just an old country boy" has been credited with playing a key role in singling out Pierce as Peg Cuttino's suspected slayer during an investigation of a series of five murders.

William Joseph Pierce, Jr., had been in prison before. He had been serving a sentence in Georgia State Prison, at Reidsville, Georgia, for burglary; but was paroled on May 25, 1970.

After he was paroled, a string of seemingly disconnected murders occurred in

South Carolina and Georgia, which had one similarity — there were no witnesses, except in one case.

The first of these was 18-year-old Ann Goodwin, of North Augusta, South Carolina, who was shot on June 27, 1970, while babysitting at the home of W.E. Pooser. When the Poosers returned home, they found Ann partially clad and lying across the bed in an upstairs bedroom, blood streaming from a bullet wound in the head. She died three days later. There were no witnesses.

Police said the killer apparently forced the rear door of the house open with a screwdriver. Four other houses had been entered that night, by the same method, and were within a block and a half of each other.

Margaret "Peg" Cuttino disappeared about 12:30 p.m. on Friday, December 18, 1970. She was found slain and there were no witnesses.

Early on the morning of Sunday, December 20, 1970, Joe Fletcher, a 59-year-old traveling salesman, was shot and killed at a Vidalia, Georgia, service station, where he worked between traveling jobs. Seventy-eight dollars was missing from a cash register. Again, there were no witnesses.

Kathy Jo Anderson, a 17-year-old employee of a West Columbia, South Carolina, drive-in restaurant, finished her shift, got into her car and left for home. Her abandoned car was later found with a flat tire; but Miss Anderson disappeared. She was found slain and there were no witnesses. She disappeared on December 22, 1970.

On January 12, 1971, Mrs. Lacy Thigpen, the 51-year-old operator of a country store near Soperton, Georgia, was shot and killed during an apparent robbery. There were no witnesses.

On January 22, 1971, Helen Wilcox, a shapely 32-year-old mother of four, disappeared from a small grocery store which she operated near Hazelhurst, Georgia. Her body, nude from the waist down, was eventually found buried in a wooded area near the swamps.

On January 28, 1971, 60-year-old Vivian Miles, who operated a country store near Baxley, Georgia, was killed during an apparent robbery. Her 5-year-old granddaughter Rhonda Ussery was severely beaten, but later recovered.

This time, there was a witness. A bread truck driver, Joe Overstreet, was shot at twice by the robber as he fled the scene. The robber missed Overstreet both times, and Overstreet later identified William Pierce, Jr. as the man that shot at him.

William Pierce is referred to in the various articles by the nicknames of "Bill" and the most common "Junior." He was born in Swainsboro, Georgia, where his father lived on a farm and ran a country store. The depression came, and the family store went broke, so the Pierce family moved to Savannah, Georgia, when "Junior" was nine years old.

A few years later, when he was 13, his mother left his father, took him and returned to Swainsboro, where she later remarried.

"Junior" and his stepfather did not get along, and "Junior" left home. He dropped out of the tenth grade at Oconee High School and got a job in a grocery store as "a package boy — sweeping the floor and stocking, just a regular worker."

He was drafted when he was 19 and was shipped to Ft. Jackson, South Carolina, but only stayed there a few months and he was given a medical discharge. "Mama got me a medical discharge," he said, "there wasn't anything wrong with me — just knew the right people."

He was married in 1951, for the first time, and was divorced that same year. In 1953, he married again and had a son by that marriage. He reportedly lived with a couple of other women, from time to time, but never married any of them.

While in prison at Reidsville, it is reported that his mother badgered and bombarded the Parole Board there until they sent him, in March, 1970, to the prison's diagnostic center for evaluation for possible parole. He went through several tests and psychological examinations. One psychologist wrote that the tests revealed him possibly "sociopathic" and warned that he "may be dangerous to himself and others." He also warned that Pierce "has little or no feelings for the misfortunes and suffering of others."

A classification officer warned that he was "emotionally unstable" and that "he will probably continue to lead a life of crime."

Prison records show he has an I.Q. of 74 — a "borderline" score just above the 70 considered retarded, and below the 90-110 average range, according to an article in *The Item* on May 17, 1971, written by UPI writer Bob Miller.

If these facts are accurate, whether "Junior" Pierce committed the crimes that he has been accused of since his parole or not, one certainly wonders why he was ever released back into society in that condition.

Pierce seems to be the typical "good ole boy who went bad," from all that has been written about him. Bob Miller summarized him as follows: "The story of William Joseph Pierce, Jr. — the good ole boy who went bad — is rooted in the rural poverty of the depression, where he spent his boyhood in the south Georgia swamps, making meals out of berries and squirrel meat, with stretches through a series of unsuccessful marriages, scrapes with the law and low-paying jobs."

"Pierce will tell you he's smarter than most of the people he meets. He claims to speak several languages — Spanish, German, French, Russian, Libyan and Apache."

Miller wrote that Pierce had said, "Some people are ignorant, but I've got a psychic magnet, clairvoyance, telepathy, a sixth sense. When everybody started asking me about all these murders, I told them exactly how each one occurred, all the details they wanted, where to find bodies, and all that. But I never did 'em. Well, maybe I did. I either did it or dreamed it."

One of Pierce's employers, at a car rental agency in Savannah, Nathan Portman remembered him as "sort of scary." "He was always over-polite to everybody. You talk the least bit stern to him and he'd jump 12 feet."

Another ex-boss, Vernon Gillis, manager of a gasoline station at Waycross, remembered him as a good worker. "He'd spend five minutes wiping a windshield, particularly if there was a pretty girl in the car."

One of the jobs that he had held was driving a truck for the Georgia Highway Department where he was struck in the head by a 700-pound attachment to a truck. "That put me out," Pierce said, "I was out for more than two and a half hours. They said it was a concussion. Ever since that time things have been going foul for me. My brain vitality cells were damaged. But I ain't crazy. I'm just like Einstein. My brains are stimulated by — I can't pronounce this word, but I can spell it — it's h-y-p-e-r-t-h-y-r-o-i-d-i-s-m."

Pierce was not arrested for any of the murders, however. On the afternoon of March 8, 1971, Baxley police chased down an old blue car, after a service station complained that its driver had failed to pay for $1.37 worth of gasoline. The driver was Pierce. After intense questioning and fitting together scores of pieces — some of them supplied by the single witness — he was charged with six murders, according to the article by Bob Miller.

Pierce told Miller, "I just sit here a pickin' and a singin' and a listening to the radio.

"I like them ole sad songs," he tells a visitor to his dreary cell in the Baxley jail, "I like Charlie Pride and Merle Haggard and Marty Robbins. The top song in my book right now is one Charlie Pride has got out — 'I'd Rather Love and Lose You Than Never Know Your Love at All.' I just like the way ole Charlie sings them songs. He puts feelings into 'em, like Hank Williams used to do."

Pierce said he had a girlfriend, but declined to identify her. He said he'd like to marry her, "but I don't think Sheriff Carter will let me out for a while now."

On Monday, May 17, 1971, Sheriff Carroll W. Day, of Lexington County, South Carolina, announced that he was issuing a warrant charging William J. Pierce, Jr., who was still being held in the Baxley, Georgia, jail, with the murder of Kathy Jo Anderson.

This brought the murder warrants against Pierce to seven: he was now awaiting trial for the following:

Helen H. Wilcox, 32	Hazelhurst, Georgia
Vivian Miles, 60	Appling County, Georgia
Mrs. Lacy Thigpen, 51	Treutlen County, Georgia
Joe M. Fletcher, 59	Vidalia, Georgia
Ann Goodwin, 19	North Augusta, South Carolina
Margaret "Peg" Cuttino, 13	Sumter, South Carolina
Kathy Jo Anderson, 17	West Columbia, South Carolina

In an article in The Item on Thursday, May 20, 1971, it was disclosed that Sheriff J.B. "Red" Carter had made some changes at the Baxley jail.

"We took the guitar away and gave him a book to read instead," the sheriff said. "I don't know how much damage you can do with a book."

The sheriff said he had discovered an escape attempt by Pierce after Pierce had shrugged off a newsman's request that he play a song on his guitar. The sheriff previously had told the newsman that Pierce "sings real good — soft and sad."

"You know," Carter said, "I thought about that all night and, after awhile, Little Joe (Chief Deputy Joe Lightsey, the sheriff's son-in-law) and I went up there to search the cell. I knew something was wrong right away when the key didn't work right. We hadn't had that cell open in three or four weeks. We searched the cell and found he'd made a key, using part of the commode as a file and some metal from the light fixture."

The sheriff also said two of the guitar strings had been removed; there was evidence that Pierce had been attempting to saw through a water pipe and that pieces of a small chair - "Which he apparently planned to use as a club" - were found in the cell.

"I don't know what the idea was," Carter said, "unless it was to run water on the floor and get me up there so he could hit me in the head..."

The sheriff, whose living quarters were adjacent to the cell block, said he immediately bought the heavy logging chains and locks and put them on the cell door. "We now have six locks and six logging chains on the cell door," he said.

Pierce would probably not be tried before October, 1971, and must be kept there until then," Carter added.

"My wife and grandbabies are up there," the sheriff said referring to his adjacent living quarters, " — I was pretty angry at the time, but you can't print what I told him. We both had some pretty heavy words."

The Sumter Daily Item, meanwhile, was being bombarded with questions about William J. Pierce and the Cuttino case. *The Item*, feeling a responsibility to it's readers to make some response, printed the following on Friday, May 28, 1971:

COMMENT

REGARDING THE CUTTINO CASE:
Please refrain from asking questions on this matter. Investigating authorities decline to answer these questions and advise such details will be kept confidential until the trial of William J. Pierce, Jr.

On Saturday, June 5, 1971, The Item reported that William Pierce had been charged with two more murders.

At Gastonia, North Carolina, he was charged in the slaying, in July of 1970, of Virginia Carol Mains. Virginia Mains was a 20-year-old, who had been living with an elderly couple as a housekeeper. She disappeared while shopping in Gastonia, and her body was found 11 days later in a rural area of Gaston County.

The other was at Beaufort, South Carolina. He was charged in the slaying, in August of 1970, of James Sires, a Beaufort service station operator.

William "Junior" Pierce now faced trial for nine murders, four in his home state of Georgia, four in the state of South Carolina and one in North Carolina.

Pierce's first trial, for the murder of 60-year-old Mrs. Vivian Miles — the only case where there had been a witness — was scheduled in Baxley, Georgia, for August 16, 1971. He would be represented by court-appointed attorney Randall Parker, of Swainsboro.

Prosecuting District Attorney Glen Thomas, Jr., of Jesup, would not say whether he would seek the death penalty, but said , "We're going after the punishment provided by law. The death penalty goes along with the law."

Sheriff "Red" Carter said that Pierce had been occupying his time writing songs and poems in the Baxley jail. He no longer was playing his guitar, since the escape attempt when it was taken from him.

The Item reported, on Thursday, August 5, that a North Carolina sheriff, Sheriff C.D. Knight, of Orange County, North Carolina, was returning home without accomplishing his mission of questioning Pierce about the strangulation slaying of a young couple near Durham, North Carolina, back in February of 1971.

Sheriff J.B. Carter said he had refused to permit Sheriff Knight and an agent of the North Carolina Bureau of Investigation, Fran G. Satterfield, Jr., to question Pierce because Pierce was scheduled for trial in Baxley soon and "we want to give the man a fair trial."

"I didn't let him (Knight) talk with him," Carter said, "I just said he had had enough publicity right now."

"I think they understood the situation," said Carter, when questioned about the reaction of the North Carolina officers at being told they could not question Pierce. "I did not know they were coming. If I had, I could have saved them a trip."

Carter said Sheriff Knight had contacted him previously by phone and that he expected to be in touch with him further. He said Knight told him by phone "he had two homicides he wanted to question Pierce about."

Presumably, Knight was referring to the slaying of Miss Patricia Ann Mann, 20, a nursing student at Watts Hospital in Durham and Jessie Allen McBane, 19, a student at North Carolina State University in Raleigh.

Bodies of the young couple were found in a wooded area in Orange County, near Durham on February 26, 1971, after they had been missing two weeks. They had been strangled and tied to a tree.

Meanwhile, amid all the confusion, "Junior" Pierce asked for a lie detector test — to prove his innocence in the Cuttino case, but was never given one. He knew that he was not guilty, so he filed for a "quick trial," he said later, and this action insured that he would eventually come to trial for the murder of Peg Cuttino.

CHAPTER THREE

THE PIERCE TRIAL
MARCH 1, 1973

During the November, 1972, term of General Sessions Court in Sumter, presiding Judge Dan F. Laney granted a motion for change of venue after Pierce's attorney argued that the notoriety of the case would prevent Pierce from getting a fair trial in Sumter County. The trial site was moved to Kingstree, in Williamsburg County, and the trial was slated for Thursday, March 1, 1973.

Solicitor R. Kirk McLeod would present the State's case and Attorneys William E.K. Jenkinson, Jr. and James M. Connor, of Kingstree would represent Pierce, along with Joe McElveen, of Sumter.

Pierce's lawyers made two motions for dismissal of the case against him, but Presiding Judge Louis Rosen, of Orangeburg, denied both. They then submitted a list of questions to be asked prospective jurors in the case, and that was accepted.

Thursday, March 1, the jury was selected and the small Williamsburg County courtroom filled with spectators. Some of the 150 or more had to sit in the aisles.

"Junior" Pierce sat impassively throughout the proceedings.

Judge Rosen told the jurors, "I don't know whether this is good news or bad news, but I expect this trial to last at least two days, which means we'll have to eat lunch together and you'll have to spend the night here."

Arrangements were made for housing the jurors, and they were given several minutes to notify their families. Then the trial began.

The charge was read to Pierce, and he pled "Not Guilty," after which the State opened it's case against him by calling Sumter County Sheriff I. Byrd Parnell to the stand.

Item Staff Writer Susan Tiede summarized the testimony presented in an article that appeared Friday, March 2, entitled "Pierce Denies Cuttino Slaying". The following is the content of her summary of the testimony:

> The State's case centered around an alleged statement Pierce made before several South Carolina and Sumter law enforcement officials concerning the death of the Cuttino girl. The alleged statement was made April 29, 1971, while Pierce was being held in jail in Baxley, Georgia, in connection with another case.
>
> Sumter County Sheriff I. Byrd Parnell told the court at about 2:30 p.m, on April 29, 1971, he received a call from the chief of the State Law Enforcement Division (SLED) J.P. Strom. Chief Strom relayed the information that a man being held in Georgia had started to make a statement to Lt. Olin Redd of SLED concerning the death of Miss Cuttino.
>
> The sheriff and several other law enforcement officers then flew down to Georgia to question Pierce.
>
> Sheriff Parnell said after advising Pierce of his rights, he

asked him if he knew anything of the death of Miss Cuttino.

"He (Pierce) said, 'Sumter, Sumter, is that the place where the planes fly close over the highway?' And I said it was," Sheriff Parnell testified.

The sheriff said Pierce told him he had come to Sumter to "rob and steal." The defendant was alleged to have said he was at a drive-in eating place on what was described as Broad Street, on December 18, 1970, when he observed two girls and a young man engaged in an argument, presumably about whether one of the girls, later identified as Miss Cuttino, would go with them.

Pierce reportedly told the officers he listened to the argument "about as long as he could take it" and then told the young man to leave Miss Cuttino alone. The young man allegedly brought a chain out of his car and Pierce reported he brought a gun from his car.

Sheriff Parnell said Pierce told him the young man, upon seeing the gun, "froze in his tracks."

The young man and his female companion reportedly got into the car and drove away. The Cuttino girl then allegedly told Pierce, "I'll ride with you."

The incident at the drive-in, Sheriff Parnell later said, was never verified.

Pierce reportedly told Parnell he drove out 76-378 west to Highway 261, turned left, went through "a little bitty town where the railroad crosses the highway" and turned down a dirt road that led to the landfill area.

"He said he stopped there (in the landfill area)," Sheriff Parnell related, "and the little girl started crying and said she wanted to go home and he said, 'I can't carry you home. The police will be looking for me.' That's when he struck her in the head with the bumper jack," the Sumter County sheriff testified.

The defendant then reportedly related he put the girl's body in the car and drove about one-half mile to a wooded spot. He then was alleged to have said he took the body out and tied a belt she had been wearing around her neck and under her arms and pulled it tight. Pierce was then reported to have said he took the body and covered it with leaves, moss and a few branches.

Reportedly, after he had finished covering the body, Pierce said he saw a man and a boy walking through the woods. The boy, Pierce reportedly told the law enforcement officers, was carrying a rifle.

"He (Pierce) said, 'I stood behind the vehicle I was in...so they couldn't see the license number of the vehicle,'" the sheriff said.

The details concerning the location of the incident, the manner in which the girl died and the way she was dressed all *checked out, Sheriff Parnell said.*

"He went into it pretty detailed," added Chief Strom under testimony, "things you couldn't know unless you were there."

Sumter City Police Chief L.W. Griffin and SLED's Lt. Redd gave essentially the same testimony concerning the alleged statement as the sheriff had.

A 14-year-old Wedgefield youth, Earl Williams, also testified on behalf of the State.

The young man said on December 19, he and his father were in the woods. His father was carrying a saw, and he was carrying a rifle.

"I seen a white Ford station wagon. I thought it was the game warden, but my father said it wasn't, so I started shooting," Williams said.

Williams said a man was standing near the car, standing in front of the license plate. When asked if the man he saw was in the court room, the youth said , "Sure, that's him," and pointed to the defendant.

"I was close enough to see how he had his hair combed and everything," Williams later added.

Pierce, in his alleged statement, said he was driving a maroon Pontiac. He allegedly told law enforcement officials he left the car, containing the bumper jack, at a gas station in Swainsboro, Georgia. The car and the bumper jack were never located.

The other two State witnesses were Dr. Joel Sexton, a forensic pathologist with the South Carolina Medical College at Charleston, who testified as to cause of death, and Sam DuPree, a photographer with SLED. Several photographs DuPree had taken of landmarks along the alleged route Pierce and the Cuttino girl had driven were later submitted as evidence.

Lt. Redd, of SLED, testified that he had gone in search of the maroon Pontiac which Pierce allegedly said that he had left at McGowan's Service Station in Georgia; but that the car wasn't there. That was at the end of April, 1971. He said that he then checked several other service stations in town and, when he was unable to find the car after 40 minutes of looking, gave up the search.

On Friday morning, Pierce took the stand and denied that he had killed Peggy Cuttino, or that he had even been in Sumter on December 18, 1970. He testified that he was at that time employed by Handy House Corporation, which built storage houses in Swainsboro, Georgia, and that he had been on the job there on the day in question. He had received and signed his time card and had received his paycheck at about 4 o'clock and had cashed the check there in Swainsboro. The time card, dated "ending the week 12-18-70" and the paycheck, dated December 18, 1970, were submitted as evidence.

He said that he had done some shopping that afternoon, picked up his date for the evening, Mrs. Nita G. Blackburn, and, along with Mrs. Blackburn's brother and his date, Mrs. Lois Patrick, had attended a party from about 7 until 11 p.m.

Under cross examination by Solicitor R. Kirk McLeod, Pierce was asked about the alleged confession that he had made to the Sumter County Sheriff and other law enforcement officers.

Pierce admitted that he told law enforcement authorities "some of the things they asked me concerning the case about which I had been told," but denied ever having admitted killing Miss Cuttino. "I never said I killed her at any time."

A handwriting analyst, James Durham, of Columbia, South Carolina, took the stand and declared, in his opinion, the signatures on the time card and check were made by the defendant.

Lt. Olin Redd of the State Law Enforcement Division (SLED) testified that he had asked Pierce about going to work on the day of the girl's abduction. "He said he had a friend punch in for him, and I asked him who it was and he said he'd rather not say and I didn't pursue it any further."

Solicitor McLeod asked Pierce if he had made a statement to Lt. Redd and Sumter County Sheriff I. Byrd Parnell, concerning the death of the Cuttino girl.

Pierce replied that he had.

"Everything you told freely and voluntarily (to Sheriff Parnell)?" Solicitor McLeod asked.

Pierce replied affirmatively.

"And what you told him was what he related on the stand yesterday," the solicitor queried.

"Well, except a couple of points," Pierce said.

"Did you tell him you hit her in the head with a blunt instrument?" McLeod asked.

"No," Pierce answered.

"Did you tell him you tied the scarf around her neck and under her arms?" the solicitor asked.

"No," the defendant again replied. "You've got this thing kind of mixed up — I never admitted at any time that I killed Margaret "Peg" Cuttino — I told Sheriff Parnell some of the things which he asked me about which I had been told."

Pierce maintained he knew the details about the girl's death because Appling County (Georgia) Sheriff J.B. "Red" Carter had discussed the case with him and told him if he made a statement he would never stand trial in South Carolina.

Mr. Ray Sconyers, Vice-President of Handy House

Corporation, took the stand and testified that Pierce was indeed at work in Swainsboro on December 18, 1970. Sconyers said he always stood by the clock and watched the men punch in. At 7 a.m., he would take all the cards of the men who had not punched in, out of the slots, so men who were late had to come to him to get their card.

Pierce, he said, was about five minutes late that day and so he personally gave him his card.

Sconyers further testified that he had seen the defendant at lease once an hour, until the noon lunch break. He said that every Friday, after lunch, he went to each man and checked to make certain the hours on his time card were correct and then had the man sign the card in his presence. Pierce, he said, returned to work after lunch and signed his time card. He then saw Pierce at least once an hour between 1 p.m. and 4 p.m., when he handed the defendant his paycheck envelope.

Mrs. Nita G. Blackburn, Pierce's date, testified that she, her brother, her brother's date, Mrs. Lois Patrick, and the defendant had attended a party in Swainsboro on the evening of December 18, 1970.

"Have you ever testified before, when William J. Pierce was being tried?", the defendant's lawyer, Joseph T. McElveen, asked.

Mrs. Blackburn replied that she had testified against Pierce in three other trials. She said she came to testify for him in this trial because, "I want the truth to be known."

Mrs. Lois Patrick then took the stand and verified the story. She had gone to the party with them the evening of December 18, 1970.

The defense then brought hypnotist Robert N. Sauer to the stand.

Robert N. Sauer is a nationally noted instructor and consultant in hypnosis, a certified professional consultant in hypnosis of the International Society for Professional Hypnosis.

He is South Carolina's only certified hypno-technician of the Association to Advance Ethical Hypnosis, an instructor at the South Carolina Criminal Justice Academy, and also has a full time private practice as a certified hypno-technician of a referral basis from over 150 physicians, psychiatrists and dentists.

Sauer had worked closely with law enforcement officers in the past to try to use hypnosis in solving crimes. One suspect, according to Sauer (article in The State newspaper, dated April 7, 1973) in the Cuttino case was released by agents of the State Law Enforcement Division (SLED) after he (Sauer) questioned him under hypnosis.

Unfortunately, the testimony of the persons given while in an hypnotic trance has little, if any, merit in South Carolina courts, *and Sauer was not allowed to testify before the jury.*

The defense rested it's case at about 2:20 p.m., and Solicitor McLeod then recalled Sheriff Parnell, SLED Chief J.B. Strom, Sumter Chief of Police L.W. Griffin and SLED Lt. Olin Redd to the stand.

All men testified they discussed no details of the case with the Georgia Sheriff Carter. Therefore, it was implied, Sheriff Carter could not have given Pierce the information as the defendant claimed.

"What you have been hearing is probably the most important criminal trial that has ever been held in this state," began attorney William E.K. Jenkinson, Jr., in the opening section of the defense's final arguments. "Why? — because this is a murder case that involves a young innocent girl — but, no matter what the verdict is, what difference is it going to make? This man already has three life sentences. So, for all purposes, if you find him guilty, what will you be doing? — The killer of "Peg" Cuttino may be out in the courtroom today, laughing and saying, 'I really made a mockery of justice.'"

Joseph McElveen continued the defense's argument, "—the only thing brought to you today is a statement taken from a man who had been jailed in a five by eight foot cell with four beds, a lavatory and a commode for two months — in this five by eight cell, there were no windows, there was no way to tell night, there was no way to tell day, there was no way to bathe. There was no record ever made of the statement, — no writing, no testimony that Bill Pierce was asked to sign. He was never given a copy of it to admit or deny its accuracy —."

Pierce's other lawyer, James M. Connor, said the evidence offered by the time card, the check and the witnesses constituted an "iron clad proof" that Pierce was not in Sumter December 18, 1970, and therefore, could not have committed the crime.

Solicitor McLeod then gave the State's argument, "I'll tell you what we've got here is a dead little girl and man who admitted killing her and that the facts of the case — Are you going to believe these men (law enforcement officials) or are you going to believe this man and his friends — All I know is that since he's been locked up, I don't know of another little girl who's been killed in South Carolina."

It was about 6 o'clock, Friday night, March 2, 1973, when the jury went into the jury room and began its deliberations.

For six and a half hours, they deliberated — on into the night, until they finally emerged at 11:30 p.m., and the verdict was read.

They had found William "Junior" Pierce Guilty of the slaying of Margaret "Peg" Cuttino, on December 18, 1970.

Pierce quietly approached the bench after the verdict was read, to receive his fourth life sentence.

Judge Rosen asked if there were any reasons why the sentence of the court should not be pronounced.

"I didn't kill Miss Cuttino. I wasn't in Sumter that day, and I didn't kill her," Pierce maintained.

Letter to the Editor

Daily Item - Sumter, South Carolina, Thursday, March 8, 1973

PIERCE DECISION DISPUTED

To the Editor:

William Pierce was found guilty by the petit jury, after six and a half hours of deliberation. I keep wondering why it took six and half hours to find a man guilty of a crime which he could not possibly be guilty of, if the information in the Sumter Daily Item, dated March 3, 1973, was correct.

According to The Item, the only evidence submitted by The State was the testimony given by Sheriff Parnell, SLED Chief J.P. Strom, Sumter Chief of Police L.W. Griffin and SLED Lt. Olin Redd, who testified they discussed no details of the case with Georgia Sheriff Carter. There was no record ever made of a confession made by William Pierce. He (Pierce) maintained he knew the details about Margaret (Peg) Cuttino's death because Appling County (Georgia) Sheriff J. B. Carter had discussed the case with him. NOW! Someone is lying. Why should William Pierce lie? He will spend the rest of his life in prison anyway for other crimes. Why should Ray Sconyers, of Swainsboro, Georgia, lie? He has everything to lose and nothing to gain. Why should Mrs. Blackburn lie? What has she to gain? She testified against Pierce in three other trials. Why should Mrs. Lois Patrick Lie? What has she to gain? If these witnesses are lying, have they been charged with perjury? If not, why?

Apparently someone is trying to cover up some dirty deeds or actions committed by someone. There are still more unanswered questions which the citizens of Sumter County and the state should have the answers presented to them.

What was the murder weapon? Was it offered in evidence by the state? What was the motive of the murder? How could a jury convict a man of murder with no more evidence than that published in The Item on March 3, 1973?

If the South Carolina Law Enforcement Division was looking for a scapegoat for a crime, I would hate to be in their path.

If William Pierce is not guilty, what is going to happen to other young girls? If Peg were my daughter, I could never be satisfied with the verdict of the petit jury of Kingstree.

BILLY R. BROWN
35 Carolina Mobile Court
Sumter, SC

Daily Item - Sumter, SC, Monday, March 12, 1973

WAS PIERCE THE RIGHT MAN?

To the Editor:
*I called Information Please Monday, with the following
questions: I would like the help of Information Please in
understanding the Pierce trial. As I understand, from reading the
accounts of the trial in two leading papers, The Item being one,
Pierce had several witnesses saying he was in Georgia at the time
of Peg Cuttino's murder. I did not read where Solicitor McLeod
proved this wrong. Is it possible the real murderer is still at
large? Was there any information brought out in the trial proving
Pierce guilty, that the public was not informed of?*

*I haven't seen my answer, but I do thank you for printing the
Letter to the Editor from Billy R. Brown.*

*Please take note that I am not saying Pierce is "not guilty."
Since he had previously been convicted of three murders in
Georgia and faces trial in two other cases, I don't see what
difference it makes as far as his life is concerned. But, what
about the rest of our young ladies? If Peg's murderer is still at
large, what does the future hold for these girls? I wonder if the
members of the jury would care to hazard a guess?*

Mrs. Judy Elliott
Rimini, SC

The Daily Item - Sumter, SC, Thursday, March 15, 1973

COMMENT

*Did "Junior" Pierce really kill Peg Cuttino? If so, what
evidence was there that he did? All the evidence reported in The
Sumter Daily Item indicates that he did not. Will the people who
testified that "Junior" Pierce was in Georgia the day of the crime
be charged with perjury? If not, why not? The jury decided he
was in Sumter that day, so these people are obviously guilty of
perjury or else the jury is guilty of a great miscarriage of justice.
This brings to mind another group of questions. Who is the real
murderer? What has the legal clique of Sumter got up it's sleeve?
Let's have some facts, Sumter Daily Item. Let's have some proof*

that the man is really guilty. I think the wrong man has been convicted.

Louis Warmoth, Jr.

In response to the onslaught of inquiries and questions being posed to The Sumter Daily Item since the Pierce trial, Item Staff Writer Alice Potter prepared the following article, which appeared in The Daily Item on Thursday, March 15, 1973:

"IS WILLIAM 'JUNIOR' PIERCE GUILTY?
EIGHT SAY NO - FOUR SAY YES."

Is William "Junior" Pierce guilty of murdering Margaret Cuttino in December, 1970? If The Item's random sample of Sumter area citizens is anywhere near correct, at least half of the people have a nagging suspicion that somewhere the real killer is still at large.

The Item's Inquiring Photographer gathered a jury count, 12 persons, from the streets of downtown Sumter and asked them to rule on the case from the information presented in the media concerning the trial which was held March 1 and 2, in Kingstree. From this "first ballot," no verdict could have been returned. Eight persons emphatically stated there was reasonable doubt of Pierce's guilt from the information they had read, while four stated, just as definitely, he was guilty.

"No, I don't think he's guilty," said PERRY JOHNSON, of 211 West Hampton Street. He based his decision on the testimony of the foreman where Pierce was working, who testified he had seen Pierce three times during the alleged day of the murder.

But, Johnson also said the employer should be investigated to determine if he was telling the truth. "If that man lied about the check (the foreman said he gave Pierce his paycheck that day), then he ought to be tried for perjury," Johnson said.

JETTIE HILL, a social worker in Sumter, who lives at 4311 Catherine Avenue, in Columbia, said she believes Pierce's prior convictions for murder in Georgia were the major factor in the jury's decision. "They didn't prove he was guilty, and I couldn't have voted like that if I had been on the jury. His two prior convictions gave him two strikes against him right there," she said. "He had a hard time because the finger was laid on him. He was convicted before he was tried."

The first guilty vote came from a picture postcard manufacturer and salesman from Winnsboro, who said he is often in Sumter. "From what I read, I would vote guilty," ERNEST FERGUSON said. "Of course, I felt like he was guilty before the trial. I think he's crazy, and I don't think you can trust his testimony or that of those people who backed him up," he explained.

"I think the chief thing is that we're trying a man for something that happened so long ago," Ferguson noted. "Even a sane man's testimony can be wrong when you're dealing with something that happened so far in the past."

E.G. WALKER, of 2361 Mount Vernon Drive, said he could not go with the guilty verdict. "From what I read in the paper, there would be reasonable doubt. Witnesses had seen him in Georgia the day of the murder, and, to my knowledge, they (the prosecution) didn't prove their (defense witnesses') story wrong. My only comment about that confession was it wasn't written down - it seems kind of odd that the statement was not recorded," he said.

ELAINE GRASTY, of 27 Wen Le Court East, said, "I think my decision would have been not guilty. I didn't see much testimony for those who convicted him." She said his time card and the woman who testified she went to a party with him the night of the murder figured in her decision, "and I don't think the employer would have come up here and testified if Pierce hadn't been at work."

CHUCK OSBORNE, of 207 Crescent, concurred with the previous not guilty decisions. "From the evidence that was presented at the trial and shown in the paper, I'd have to say not guilty. His employer had his time card, which he had to have signed," he said. "What I'm getting at is from the evidence they showed here, they apparently wanted a scapegoat. After all, how could he be in South Carolina and Georgia at the same time," he said.

MRS. M.J. JACKSON, of 44 Council Street, would have voted guilty. "If he had never been in trouble before, it might be different, but with him being guilty of other crimes, I think he did this one. I don't think the officers would have lied, and I believe the man is mentally disturbed," she said. "Anyway, I don't see that he would have anything to gain by lying, but I don't think the officers would have either because, if he's not guilty, then the man is still free," she said.

Another guilty verdict was passed by ENOS DeWITT, JR., of 10 North Salem Avenue. "I would say he's guilty if he did those other murders. And then he confessed. Anyway, he looked like the man someone described that picked her up," he said.

"If I based my decision on what I read in The Item, then I would have said not guilty," said PAUL MELVIN, of 1015 Broad Street.

"Everybody testified that he was working in Georgia at the time he supposedly did it, and since he already had two or three life sentences, what good would it do him (to lie)? Melvin *explained.*

BILL TANNER, 8 Woodside Road, said no particular bit of testimony would decide his not guilty verdict. "According to what I read, I don't really think he's the right one. But, no particular thing sticks in my mind," he went on, "It's just my opinion from the overall information I've read that maybe he's not the right man."

MRS. LUCIUS LAWRENCE, of 26 Parker Drive, would have supported a guilty verdict. "It's because of his own testimony," she said. "He knew so much about it and a witness had seen him with the victim and pinpointed him as the murderer."

The comment of THOMAS AYERS, of 1823 Dunbarton, was concise. "If they said he confessed, but didn't have a signed confession, and since he had three witnesses for him, I think that's enough to constitute a reasonable doubt," he said.

A reasonable doubt. That's all that's necessary to uphold a not guilty verdict. Twelve persons in Kingstree are sure. But, in the city where defense lawyers said Pierce could not get a fair trial, there is doubt.

Pictures of the twelve people accompanied the article and in the days after, it seemed that everyone you met wanted to know "How would you have voted?" There was no doubt of one thing — Sumter County citizens were terribly upset over the verdict in the case. They had wanted more than anything to see Peg Cuttino's killer brought to justice, but something just didn't seem right about this affair. The pieces didn't fit in this puzzle.

Feelings ranged from quiet disbelief to vocal, shocked anger, and it was clear that the people did not intend to keep quiet about the way they felt.

Letter to the Editor

The Daily Item - Sumter, SC, Friday, March 16, 1973

STUDENT QUESTIONS VERDICT

To the Editor:

I am a senior at Furman High School, and as I am deeply concerned about the Cuttino case, I have taken the liberty to write this letter.

There has been a murder in Sumter County that has disturbed the inhabitants of Sumter County due to the lack of convincing evidence and the unorthodox tactics of presiding officials (let's wrap this case up before the cow gets out of the barn). Such tactics make one wonder — Is Pierce guilty, as stated by the court, or does his case need further investigation

*even though the testimony which was presented in the trial was
supported strongly by substantiated evidence which was offered
in the defendant's behalf by the vice-president of a Georgia plant,
a Columbia handwriting expert, and several other witnesses who
had no reason to lie. Pierce has already received the maximum
sentence prescribed by law. What then, shall we call justice?
Why then, does this case seem shallow?*

*For further consideration, let's pose a few rhetorical
questions to further evidence the ambiguities surrounding the
investigation. In reply to the vice-president's remarks — Did
Sheriff Parnell, after going to Appling County, Georgia, forget to
make a complete investigation? For instance, discovering that
Pierce was working in Georgia the day of the alleged abduction,
retracing his routine after receiving his paycheck, etc. Why was a
signed confession from Pierce never received? Why did Pierce
confess to other crimes so easily and why was he staunchly
against confessing in the Cuttino case?*

*Did the two hunters or woodcutters who identified Pierce
actually see a white station wagon? If so, where is the white
station wagon?*

*The defendant related a story, which was, according to him,
told to Sheriff Parnell. Parnell denied any knowledge of this
story being related to him. Parnell also said that the defendant
remembers going down a highway where the planes fly low,
passing over — Sumter? Charleston, Macon? Columbia?
Where? When?*

Will the real killer of Peg Cuttino please stand up!

*Denice Ardis
Route 2
Sumter, SC*

Letter to the Editor

The Daily Item - Sumter, SC, Monday, March 19, 1973

WAS PIERCE THE WRONG MAN?
To the Editor:
*I would like to compliment The Item on it's excellent
coverage of the Pierce trial and for publishing the opinions of it's
readers. Too many times bad publicity is the reason for the
wrong verdict. I feel that "Junior" Pierce could have had a fair
trial in Sumter County.*

*I fully agree that it's time people got angry or afraid of our
system of justice, the Pierce case being a small example. If we
remember history, we recall that Barbara Graham was executed
on past reputation and testimony of other criminals who stood to*

gain. *Carryl Chassman was executed after eight years of appeals and no one is yet sure he was guilty. Dr. Sam Shepherd spent years in prison because of public sentiment and the fact that no one cared to discover the truth. Right here in South Carolina we're wondering 50 years later who killed the Bingham family. A man spent his life in prison for those murders, mainly because his reputation was bad.*

Maybe we're all guilty of looking the other way because it can't happen to us. It can and does happen, not only 50 years ago, but today. Maybe we're guilty sometimes of not punishing our criminals but, if we punish the innocent person, in my opinion, it's one too many.

How naive we are if we think that once a verdict is reached it is the truth. Do we really believe that 12 people with no more education than we require for jurors are capable of sorting facts in a matter so important as our lives? Our own government does not use the same system as is imposed on the people. Have we ever heard of a military trial made up of enlisted men? Do we believe that all attorneys are looking for the truth, or are they a little like a ball team with it's recording of wins and losses? Somewhere in our legal machinery we seem to have forgotten that the main object should be to establish the truth.

Someday someone will come up with a better system of justice. Until that time we'll sit placidly by while criminals go free because of technicalities and innocent men go to prison on reputation or lack of funds.

As far as "Junior" Pierce is concerned, he should never have been turned loose in society in the first place. But, did he commit all those murders, or are we, as his mother said, blaming all our unsolved murders on "Junior?"

Peggy Green
Sumter, SC

On Monday, March 19, 1973, most of the citizens of Sumter and Sumter County first learned the fact that Mr. and Mrs. S.G. LeNoir had seen Peggy Cuttino on the day after "Junior" Pierce had supposedly murdered her.

In an article in *The Daily Item,* entitled "WOMAN SAYS GIRL SEEN AFTER DAY OF MURDER," it was revealed that Mrs. S.G. (Carrie) LeNoir had been in Kingstree on Monday morning for the appeal for a new trial for "Junior" Pierce, prepared to go before Judge Rosen, who had heard the case on March 1 and 2, and testify that she had seen the girl in her store in Horatio on December 19, 1970, the day after the alleged murder.

Joe McElveen, Pierce's court appointed attorney, told Judge Rosen that one of Miss Cuttino's classmates had reported seeing her on the day she disappeared, riding with two other persons, sitting in the back of a 1964 white or beige Mercury Comet.

He said that another man, he had recently contacted, said he had seen a brownish or beige car soon after the girl disappeared while he was hunting in the vicinity where the body was found, near Wedgefield.

He told Judge Rosen that, if the jury had heard Mrs. LeNoir's testimony and believed it, that it would have proved that the girl could not have been killed December 18, 1970, as was alleged in the court indictment.

When McElveen was questioned as to why this evidence or testimony was not given in the trial, he told the judge that he was unable to discover the evidence prior to the trial. He said that the LeNoirs had reported the incident to the Sumter County sheriff's department the next day, but that the report was not included in the files he was given by the law enforcement authorities.

McElveen also argued that Judge Rosen should have instructed the jury, in the trial, to disregard certain "inflamatory" remarks made by Solicitor R. Kirk McLeod in his final arguments to the jury. Judge Rosen rejected the defense argument.

Just before Mrs. LeNoir was to testify, Solicitor McLeod asked for a delay because he was ill and that he was not prepared to combat any testimony Mrs. LeNoir might give.

During the arguments, Solicitor McLeod had lambasted the press for "trying the man (Pierce) in the papers. They're (the press) just tearing open the wounds of a family whose little daughter was brutally murdered and the more they do it, the worse it becomes — It just becomes disgusting," he said.

Judge Rosen had said he would be willing to hear the testimony of Mrs. LeNoir, before deciding whether or not to grant Pierce a new trial, but said he would not be inclined to allow the defense testimony of hypnotist Robert N. Sauer, who had placed Pierce under hypnosis and interrogated him about his involvement in the Cuttino slaying.

Since Solicitor McLeod said he was ill, the judge continued the motion for new trial until the spring term of Court of Common Pleas to be held in April in Sumter. Mrs. LeNoir was not allowed to testify.

In response to Solicitor McLeod's attack on the press on Monday, in Kingstree, *The Daily Item* ran the following Editorial, entitled, PUBLIC CONCERNED OVER PIERCE TRIAL, on Tuesday, March 20, 1973.

> *We would like to take this space to correct a misstatement made by Third Judicial Circuit Solicitor R. Kirk McLeod yesterday during a hearing in Kingstree where defense attorneys for William J. Pierce sought a retrial of the case. Pierce was convicted last month of the slaying of Margaret "Peg" Cuttino in December, 1970.*
>
> *McLeod complained during the hearing that the press was 'trying the man (Pierce) in the papers.'*
>
> *Wrong, Mr. McLeod. The only 'trying' that's going on in this paper is legitimate questioning by a concerned public of the performance by law enforcement authorities and the prosecution in the Cuttino murder.*
>
> *Letters and comments which we've published — and it is a newspaper's function to do so — have come from upset citizens*

who are sincerely doubtful about the decision reached in the case, based on the evidence presented.

What worries the people who have written us, and from the feedback we've received from the community is how Pierce could have been convicted for a murder that supposedly occurred on December 18, 1970, when three witnesses testified under oath that Pierce was in Swainsboro, Georgia, on that date.

Now the defense has produced another witness who is convinced she saw the victim on the day AFTER the murder supposedly occurred.

This along with the other contradictory testimony, is, in our opinion, ample reason for public concern over the case.

We have no quarrel with Solicitor McLeod. He is an outstanding public servant who has performed a difficult job admirably for many years, fighting crime in Sumter County to the best of his ability.

Nor do we wish to reopen old wounds for the family of the slain child. They have suffered far too much already.

However, we are genuinely concerned about the peace of mind of this community. When a brutal crime is committed, all law-abiding citizens want and demand that justice be metered out to the complete satisfaction of all.

But, if the conduct of a trial and it's outcome leaves room for doubt, there is a corresponding loss of confidence among the public toward law enforcement authorities and our courts.

This should not be allowed to happen. This community wants, above all, assurance that justice has been served, a murderer brought to justice and the streets made safe again for our children.

So far, judging by the reaction from the public, such assurances have not been given.

Realizing that some response needed to be made to the disturbed public, the Sumter County and City officials drafted a response to the editorial in *The Item* and sent a letter to the editor. *The Item* printed the letter on Thursday, March 22, as follows:

Letter to the Editor

The Daily Item - Sumter, SC, Thursday, March 22, 1973

To the Editor:

We wish to take this means of communicating to the concerned public over the Pierce trial, some information from law enforcement. Many people are asking for an explanation of facts in the Pierce investigation which led to his arrest for the slaying of Margaret "Peg" Cuttino, and subsequently to his trial and conviction. Certainly you, the public, have a right to know certain facts of the case. However, it must also be understood that as long as there is a possibility of a new trial being granted Pierce we cannot, and will not, reveal information of an evidentiary nature which could adversely affect the setting of a new trial, the location of such trial, and even the outcome of the trial. Supreme Court guidelines prohibit the release of information of an evidentiary nature by law enforcement authorities.

There were certain facts related from the witness stand on March 1 and 2, in Kingstree, which may have enabled the public to better understand how the jury reached it's verdict of guilty, but these facts were not given to you, the public, by the news media as they could have been. The entire trial was recorded in detail. Please try to understand that the three law enforcement agencies which handled the investigation, the Sumter County Sheriff's Department, the Sumter City Police Department, and the South Carolina Law Enforcement Division, with help of several other police agencies, are all just as concerned that the right man has been charged as you are. Our responsibility to the victim's family, to you - the public, and to the criminal justice system, was to determine the facts and evidence involved, to the very best of our ability, and to present these facts to the courts. No doubt about it, there was evidence which was never found due to considerable time lapse between the date Miss Cuttino was reported missing on December 18, 1970, and December 30, 1970, when her body was discovered in Manchester Forest.

As to the news releases on March 19 and 20, with reference to Mr. McElveen stating that Mrs. LeNoir saw "Peg" Cuttino on December 19, 1970, Mr. and Mrs. LeNoir were interviewed on December 24, 1970, and they could make no identification at that time.

We are not attempting in any way to hide anything from the public. Several thousand persons were interviewed by police during the investigation and if you were one of those, please accept our thanks for your cooperation and understanding.

Sheriff I. Byrd Parnell
Solicitor R. Kirk McLeod
Chief L.W. Griffin

Mr. and Mrs. LeNoir read the statement made by the three law officials in shock and disbelief.

First of all, they were interviewed by the investigators on Sunday afternoon, December 20 - not December 24 - but that was not so important. It was their statement that the LeNoirs "could make no identification at that time" that disturbed them.

"If we made no identification, why did they come up here at all?" Mrs. LeNoir said, "And why did the police spend all the rest of that day and the next few days scouring the countryside around Horatio, questioning people, checking out old store buildings and farm houses all the way down Highway 261? "Why did they spend so much time and effort on a lead that was not a lead, in a case as important as this one was?"

"Well, we will straighten that out when we testify at the appeal for a new trial," she reported.

Things were quiet for a few days as the citizens of Sumter County patiently waited for the spring session of The Court of Common Pleas, where they were sure the wrong would be righted when Pierce would be granted a new trial.

Court opened on Monday, April 2, 1973, and Judge Louis Rosen was scheduled to hear the motion for new trial at 4 p.m. on Thursday. In the meantime, he would handle some of the other 111 cases and several motions that were on the court docket for this term of court.

That day, Monday, April 2, *The Item* ran a lengthy article by *Item* Staff Writer Susan Tiede, entitled "The Cuttino Case: Is Pierce Really Guilty?"

The article reviewed the case, up to date and presented the unrestful state of mind that existed in the county.

"Questions raised in the trial and never answered are the topic of local discussion. The court-appointed defense attorneys - Joseph McElveen of Sumter, James Connor of Kingstree and William Jenkinson, Jr. of Kingstree - have all received what they term "numerous" calls concerning the case. Those who served on the jury and are involved in any kind of public position say they have been questioned extensively about the trial. *The Item* has received calls, letters to the editor and comments relating to the trial and the case," the article related.

Tiede also listed some of the questions: "How could a jury find someone guilty of a crime when three witnesses testified the convicted man was with them in Georgia on the day of the murder? Why was no recording or written record ever made of the alleged confession? Where is the car containing what may have been the murder weapon, and why was the search for it abandoned after only 40 minutes as was testified? Other suspects were given polygraph tests and released when the tests failed to implicate them, yet such a test was never given Pierce — why? Since the trial, what appears to be two new witnesses have emerged. Mr. and Mrs. S.G. LeNoir of Horatio claim Miss Cuttino came into their store Saturday, December 19, 1970 - the day after Pierce supposedly murdered her. Attorney McElveen said at the first hearing for a new trial he could not find the LeNoirs' report in the copy of the police files he had been given. If a copy of the report was not in the files, then why not?

Yet the most persistently asked question, the one that has created great concern among Sumter residents is, "Did William Pierce, a four-time convicted murderer, kill the young Cuttino girl? Or could it be that the real killer is free, perhaps walking the streets of Sumter?"

If law enforcement officials know the answers to these questions, they are not talking. They say they cannot. Sheriff I. Byrd Parnell, Police Chief L.W. Griffin and Third Judicial Circuit Solicitor R. Kirk McLeod, explain they can't talk about the case at this time because a motion for a new trial is pending.

And so the doubts remain in the minds of many Sumter citizens.

Tiede interviewed Appling County Sheriff J.B. "Red" Carter at the jail in Baxley, Georgia, where Pierce had been held in what amounted to solitary confinement, in a 5 by 8 foot cell for approximately six months.

"It was for his own protection," Sheriff Carter explained as he took the elevator up to the cell, "I'd heard he might try and escape, and so I seldom let him out of his cell... I didn't want to have to kill him."

Carter, contrary to the testimony offered at the trial in Kingstree, claimed he was with the South Carolina law enforcement officials while they questioned Pierce and heard him confess to killing the girl.

"I was there for most of it, but I can't remember what words he used. He admitted it then and he admitted it to me several times later," Carter said.

"I didn't know anything about the case," claimed the sheriff. "I never read anything about it...If any APB's came into this office (concerning her disappearance), I never saw them." Pierce had testified that what details he gave the law enforcement authorities had been told to him by Sheriff Carter.

"You know, he should be killed," Carter concluded, adding after a brief pause, "legally."

Many residents in Pierce's home town of Swainsboro, Georgia, were not convinced Pierce was guilty of all those murders.

"He's just altogether different (from how he's been portrayed)," said Mrs. Lois Patrick, who testified she was with Pierce the evening of December 18, 1970. "He was just as calm, and I never heard him cuss, never heard him raise his temper."

"Now I know he's two people," she said. "It just doesn't make sense to me. I just don't see how he could have done it. If he did do it, then I'd like them to show me how... There's too much that's not unwrapped in this case," she said.

Mrs. Patrick added that the four got together again Saturday night. Pierce, she said, did not join them until about 10 p.m. His car was running hot, and she later heard the Statesboro, Georgia, police had been chasing him in connection with a robbery. The police had no record of such a robbery, however.

Sunday morning, Mrs. Patrick said, he went to church with Mrs. Blackburn and returned to church with them later that evening for a special Christmas service.

"He wasn't crazy," she mused, "but he wasn't right. He must have had — what do you call it — a double personality."

Other than the two women, Pierce apparently had few friends. Those who worked with him shortly before his arrest remembered him as a loner.

"I was only around him during working hours," said Ray Sconyers, Pierce's former foreman at Handy House Manufacturing Company, in Swainsboro, who testified he saw him at work throughout the day on December 18, 1970.

Sconyers insisted that he never made an exception to his habit of having employees sign their time cards between 1 to 2 p.m. on Friday afternoons, nor, he said did he ever give a man's check to someone else.

He added that Pierce returned to work on Monday, December 21, 1970, and also worked, he thought, part of Tuesday, December 22, 1970.

Two men at the company who were working during December of 1970, said they remembered Pierce, but could not definitely say if he was there on any particular day.

An old man, known only as "Ray," a long-time employee at McGowan's, the service station where Pierce allegedly told South Carolina law officers he left his car containing the bumper jack, with which he reportedly struck Miss Cuttino, thought for a moment and then said, "William Pierce's car? Why didn't you say so? Sure, it was here on the lot for a while."

Pierce, he said, had burned out the engine and left it on a side road somewhere in the county. Ray said he went out and helped tow the maroon, 1963 Pontiac back to the station. The car, he said, was rebuilt and later sold at an auction.

An auto dealer, in the nearby town of Reidsville, Georgia, Ernest Collins, purchased the car for $140 and kept it on his lot until about the middle of May, 1971, when it was sold for junk to a man who now lived in Florida.

Lt. Olin Redd, of SLED, who was looking for the car at the end of April, 1971, testified he checked at McGowan's and the car wasn't there. He then, he stated, checked several other service stations in town and when he was unable to find the car after 40 minutes of looking, gave up the search.

Cars had played an important role in other aspects of the case. Earl Williams, the 14-year-old boy from Wedgefield, testified that Pierce was the man he and his father saw on Saturday, December 19, 1970 - the day after the crime - in the area where the body was later found.

The man, he said, was standing, blocking the view of the license plates on a white Ford station wagon.

Under cross examination, the young man said he was a couple of hundred yards away from the man and amended his earlier statement that he was close enough to see how the man's hair was combed too, he was "pretty sure" the man he saw that afternoon was Pierce.

"Mr. McElveen (defense attorney) got me kind of confused there in the courtroom," Williams said a few weeks after the trial. "I wasn't any couple of hundred yards away from him...If my Dad and I hadn't been real sure, we wouldn't have given a description."

The young boy demonstrated how far he was away from the man he identified as Pierce by pointing to a tree about 20 yards away.

The reported identification of Miss Cuttino riding in a dirty white or beige car had become important to the motion pending for a new trial.

Shortly after Miss Cuttino's disappearance, a classmate reported seeing the girl in the back seat of, what was described as being a dirty white or beige car.

An employee at a Shell station in Turbeville, Burnett Plowden, also reported seeing a young lady, he identified as Miss Cuttino. He said she had stopped at the station at about 9 p.m. on December 18, 1970. She and her companions were driving a dirty white car.

Saturday, December 19, 1970, Mrs. LeNoir, of Horatio, said that she had seen Miss Cuttino getting into the back seat of a yellow-brown car. Mr. LeNoir also identified the girl as Miss Cuttino.

Two Sumter County deputies came and spoke with the LeNoirs about the incident, but never asked them to look through pictures or make any attempt to identify the two boys who were with her.

Deputy Hugh Mathis, one of the men who questioned the LeNoirs, explained that this was not done because the couple were unable to positively identify the Cuttino girl at the time. This was the first that the LeNoirs had heard of the claim that they had been unable to identify the girl, and they were astonished to hear it.

The LeNoirs claim they are now, and have always been, certain in their own minds that Miss Cuttino was the girl they saw in their store that day.

A hunter from Columbia reportedly says he saw a dirty white or beige car in the forest area near Wedgefield, sometime around December 19, 1970. Two young boys, he allegedly told defense attorney McElveen, were standing near the car. Neither of them had on hunting clothes, a fact that reportedly struck him as unusual.

A person is presumed to be innocent until proven guilty. It is necessary for the state to prove the accused guilty, beyond a reasonable doubt.

Did the testimony of the defense witnesses constitute a reasonable doubt that Pierce could have been in Sumter on December 18, 1970, and killed Miss Cuttino as he is alleged to have confessed?

Susan Tiede asked some of the jurors who condemned Pierce. And apparently the members of the very jury that condemned him, did not think so.

"I couldn't go along with it (the defense testimony)," explained juror W. Lifton McCutchen, of Route 3, Kingstree. "It was the details that convinced me he was guilty."

"The fact that he didn't deny making the confession and the positive identification by the boy (Williams) - Well, I think that's two leading points," added juror Wofford K. Cocker, of Kingstree.

Juror Larry F. Matthews said, "What makes it look so bad to me, a man's on trial for his life and if he was working with that many people, why couldn't they be there (at the trial)? It looked kind of bad."

Mrs. Eileen Lifrage, of Salters, one of the two women who served on the jury, says she, however, was not completely convinced of Pierce's guilt.

"I might say this," she stated, "I did vote not guilty to begin with, and I am still not thoroughly convinced I did the right thing in changing my vote ... It was a unique experience, however, I don't think I would like to go through that again. It's a lot of weight on your shoulders even though he wouldn't get the death penalty. It kind of bothers you that there was just no straight-forward...no concrete proof one way or the other."

All the jurors, she said, were weary after the long hours of deliberation. "We were all tired, " she said, "and there were just so many who seemed to have so many arguments..."

So Mrs. Lifrage, after perhaps a dozen ballots, changed her vote.

Defense attorney James Connor said, "I might say this...We were not, at least I was not, defending Pierce as a person...but there was a question in my mind about this particular crime...We wanted to try to establish whether or not the right person had been caught."

One thing, Connor said, that made him doubt Pierce, was the type of crime involved. Pierce had been convicted in the past of robbery-connected murders.

"The crimes he was convicted of in Georgia were motivated by robberies," Connor said. "There certainly was no robbery motive in this case."

Connor also implied that under hypnosis, Pierce indicated he was not in Sumter during the week in question.

"The purpose of the interrogation by Mr. (Richard) Sauer (hypnotist) was to account for his whereabouts, not only the day in question, but several days thereafter. The basic results of that interrogation will be put into the trial record at the April hearing," Connor said.

The implication was, of course, that the defense would not submit the evidence if it might be detrimental to their client.

Sheriff Parnell, Chief Griffin and Solicitor McLeod indicated to reporter Susan Tiede that they were assured that the real killer had been brought to justice.

"You've got to be definitely sure (the right man is convicted)," said Mrs. Cuttino, shortly after the conclusion of the trial in Kingstree. "That's why James (her husband) was so satisfied with the jurors chosen...he felt that any decision they would make, he could accept and we have both accepted the outcome according to them. The main thing we are concerned about is that people who commit crimes like this are taken out of society."

A young girl had been brutally murdered. A family had lost a daughter. Had the right man been taken out of society?

That was the question that still bothered the community.

CHAPTER FOUR

APPEAL FOR NEW TRIAL
APRIL 5, 1973

On Thursday afternoon, April 5, 1973, the motion for a new trial came before Judge Rosen.

Pierce's lawyers sought the new trial on the grounds that evidence, not known prior to the March trial, had subsequently been discovered. Specifically, they had two persons, Mr. and Mrs. S.G. LeNoir, of Horatio, testify that they saw the Cuttino girl alive and not in the company of Pierce, the day after the indictment alleged she had been killed.

Law enforcement officials contended that the couple had never been able to positively identify the girl they had seen as the Cuttino girl.

The Judge itemized the five criteria which must be met for something to legally be considered new evidence —

1. Evidence that could not have been discovered with due diligence prior to the trial.
2. Evidence discovered after the trial.
3. Evidence not cumulative in nature.
4. Evidence that would likely change the outcome of the trial.
5. Evidence material to the case.

Prior to placing any witnesses on the stand, defense attorneys argued the five criteria for new evidence had been met.

"The question of due diligence, in my mind, is the only problem," said attorney Joe McElveen.

McElveen said he and another attorney on the case, William Jenkinson, Jr., of Kingstree, looked through the police files for names of persons who might have seen the Cuttino girl and that if the names of the LeNoirs' had been there, he probably would have seen it.

Law enforcement officers responded by stating that the lead sheet, which had been used in the investigation, was in the folder when it was given to the attorneys prior to the March trial, while Pierce's attorneys were preparing for his defense.

The defense placed attorney William Jenkinson, Jr., on the stand. Jenkinson had accompanied attorney Joseph McElveen to the sheriff's office at the beginning of Pierce's defense, in order to obtain the information necessary to defend the man.

Jenkinson testified that the police files were in a state of disorder and that the attorneys had not been able to photostat the lead sheet.

"I believe if it (the LeNoirs' name) were there (in the file) we would have seen it," Jenkinson said.

The lead sheet, and the attached list of the names of persons questioned were offered in evidence, by the state, after Sumter County deputy T.L. McJunken identified it as the same information that he had seen in the hands of the defense attorneys on the day the two attorneys first inspected the files.

Lead number six, McJunken testified, dealt with the LeNoir's report and concluded with the summary that the couple could not offer positive identification of the girl.

Deputies Tommy Mims and Hugh Mathis, who initially questioned the LeNoirs, both testified that the couple was not able to positively identify the girl they had seen the afternoon of December 19, 1970, in the company of two boys as the Cuttino girl.

Furthermore, they testified that Mr. LeNoir, who said in his affidavit that the girl came into the store, told them that the girl remained in the car, and he was only able to see her from the shoulders up.

Mrs. LeNoir, they claimed, contrary to the statement in her affidavit that she had seen the girl get into the car, told them she had never seen the girl. She had seen the two boys who were supposedly in the company of the young girl when they later returned to the store, they testified. Yet the only description of the two boys she could offer, the deputies said, was that they were between 16 - 18 years old and "neat."

Mr. LeNoir, in his affidavit, said he recognized the girl from the picture that appeared in *The Item*, the afternoon of December 19, 1970.

"When I saw her picture in *The Sumter Daily Item* later that afternoon," his affidavit reads, "I immediately said that she was the girl in the store earlier."

Under cross examination, both deputies testified that he never mentioned recognizing the girl in the picture as being Miss Cuttino.

Both deputies also testified that when they later talked with Mrs. LeNoir, she essentially said her husband "didn't know what he was talking about."

Sheriff Parnell also testified that he had talked with the LeNoirs and said that they had not been able to positively identify the girl they had seen in the company of the two young boys as being Miss Cuttino.

James Cuttino, father of the slain girl, took the stand and said he had been out to Horatio several times in the past two years and that the LeNoirs had never mentioned the incident to him.

To further discredit the LeNoirs, Mrs. Portia Myers, sister to Mr. James Cuttino, who was a resident of Hagood, near Horatio, took the stand and testified that the LeNoirs had told her the same story that the law enforcement officers had related. "They could not give positive identification and could not describe the child," Mrs. Myers said.

The defense lawyers put Mrs. LeNoir on the stand and she said that she had told the story contained in her affidavit to "at least 300 people." She had, she claimed, seen the girl get into a car with two boys and saw the boys later return without the girl. She had never, she added, discredited her husband's account of the event.

Under cross examination, Mrs. LeNoir admitted, as was already stated in her affidavit, that she had only seen the girl from the back and had not clearly seen the girl's face.

Mr. LeNoir, on the stand, testified that he told the deputies the same story contained in his affidavit.

"I do hereby certify that I'm positive that Margaret "Peg" Cuttino was in my store on Saturday, December 19, 1970," the affidavit reads.

Mr. LeNoir, when asked if he had heard Sheriff Parnell's testimony from the stand, told them that he had and accused Parnell of telling "a bunch of stories and lies" on the stand.

Jack Floyd, a wholesaler, who supplied the LeNoirs' store, testified that Mr. LeNoir had told him that he thought he had seen the Cuttino girl in the store on the afternoon in question.

The state had put up eight witnesses whose testimonies attacked the credibility of LeNoirs' statements.

A written summary of Pierce's own account, while under hypnosis, of his activities from December 8 through December 23, 1970, was submitted to Judge Rosen.

The testimony, a summation of several sessions Columbia hypno-therapist Robert N. Sauer had with Pierce prior to the March trial indicated that Pierce was not guilty of killing Miss Cuttino.

Little, if any, merit is placed on the testimony of persons under hypnosis in South Carolina courts. The statement submitted contained a series of questions and answers that would have been given at the March trial, if Judge Rosen had allowed the questioning of the hypno-therapist to continue.

According to Sauer's testimony, Pierce was in the sixth, or deepest, state of hypnosis when he, through a technique known as "age regression," was made to "relive" his experiences from December 8 - 23, 1970.

At the March trial, Sauer stated every feeling and event a person has ever experienced, every fact a person has ever learned is stored somewhere in his subconscious. When a person is taken back through hypnosis to a certain time in his past, he not only recalls the events, but actually re-experiences all the emotions he felt at the time.

A person can lie under hypnosis, Sauer said, just as he can while in his conscious state, but the hypno-therapist can insure the subject is telling the truth by putting two of the subject's fingers under the control of his subconscious. When this is done, Sauer continued, regardless of the subject's verbal response, he will twitch his "yes" finger if the true response would be "yes" and his "no" finger if the true response would be "no."

According to Sauer, Pierce's account of his activities, while thus hypnotized, revealed that he committed no criminal acts and was not in Sumter at any time during that period.

The statement by Sauer charged that Lt. Olin Redd, of the State Law Enforcement Division (SLED) and J.B. Carter, sheriff of the county where Pierce was jailed, supplied the facts to Pierce for the confession he later gave for the Cuttino killing.

"It appeared that Mr. Carter was obsessed with a desire to have Pierce confess to this murder and others," Sauer said.

Sauer further contended that Sheriff Carter threatened Pierce's life, and the life of his girl friend (Nita Jean Blackburn) and his mother, and, on at least one occasion, had Pierce injected with some sort of drug.

Sauer's statement concluded with this series of questions and answers:

Q. Did you ask Mr. Pierce if he killed Miss Cuttino?
A. (Sauer) Yes, his reply was "no."
Q. Was his finger response consistent with his verbal response on this particular question?
A. As on all other occasions, his finger response indicated that he was telling the truth.

"Gentlemen," Judge Rosen told the defense lawyers, "I'm not particularly impressed with your motion. A new trial on the grounds of new evidence is not favored in South Carolina, except in rare cases where all of the prerequisites are clearly met..."

Rosen, without elaboration, said he did not think all the requirements had been met.

"Junior" Pierce's appeal for a new trial was denied.

At the conclusion of the hearing on Thursday afternoon, James Cuttino congratulated the attorneys and said, "I, too, wanted to make sure the right man had been convicted. I hope this will mark the end of the trial of this man in the press."

"I'm all for freedom of the press, don't get me wrong," Cuttino continued, "but I also believe in the judicial system and think it's about time we put some confidence in it."

Well, it was over. "Junior" Pierce would stand convicted of Peg's murder forever. Oh, there was still the possibility of an appeal to the South Carolina Supreme Court. Pierce's lawyers now had eight months in which to file transcripts of the proceeding and their briefs to that body, but everyone knew that there was little chance of success there. Judges and courts have a tendency to back each other up, just as law enforcement officers do.

Maybe the people were wrong. Maybe the law enforcement officers had done a good job and Judge Rosen was right in denying a new trial. Maybe Mr. Cuttino was right when he said he believed in the judicial system and thought it was time we put some confidence in it.

After all, Pierce had had a trial, with a jury — and the jury convicted him — not the law officers. He had also had an appeal for a new trial and a highly respected judge had considered the evidence presented and seen fit to deny the new trial. The judicial system had worked. Maybe the people of Sumter and Sumter County should have more faith in the judicial system and it's law enforcement officials.

In any event, it was over — or was it?

The State newspaper, in Columbia, and several other newspapers had followed the Pierce story and carried various reports of the events as they unfolded. However, they reserved their reporting to the basic facts and offered little or no opinion of the affairs that evolved.

The State carried the news of the events of that Thursday afternoon, in the Friday edition, on April 6, and as usual, reported it in a matter-of-fact, straight-forward fashion.

On Saturday, April 7, a quite lengthy article ran in *The State*, written by Greg Smith, of the Pee Dee Bureau, entitled "HYPNOTIC INTERROGATION

INDICATES PIERCE INNOCENCE." The article went into the details of Robert N. Sauer's report that had been submitted to Judge Rosen the previous Thursday and stated that "an interrogation of William Pierce, while he was in a deep hypnotic trance indicates he is innocent of the murder charge for which he has been tried, convicted and sentenced to life imprisonment."

Then, on Sunday, April 8, 1973, the first of a three part report, researched and written by Hugh Munn and Jack Truluck, two of *The State's* staff writers, appeared, entitled "IS PIERCE THE CUTTINO MURDERER?"

It read as follows:

PART ONE OF THREE PARTS

William J. Pierce, Jr., is no backwoods, southern , Good Old Boy, victimized by overbearing lawmen and his own ignorance.

There has been ample evidence to establish that he is a murderer — maybe even a murderer of a dozen or more persons. Juries in Georgia and South Carolina have already convicted him of four capital crimes. He had no compassion for his victims and it's hard to muster compassion for "Junior" Pierce — as he was called around his home town of Swainsboro, Georgia.

Nevertheless, there are compelling reasons to raise doubts that he is the murderer of 13-year-old Margaret "Peg" Cuttino, of Sumter, despite the fact that a jury convicted him of it last month.

The evidence which raises the doubt in the Cuttino case is circumstantial; so was the evidence that convicted him — that and an alleged confession that "Junior" says he didn't make, and that defense attorneys suggest was concocted by the Georgia and South Carolina law enforcement agents, anxious to wipe clean another slate.

It's happened before. Any police reporter can tell you what is almost a standing joke in the station house: find some poor SOB that you can nail with a dozen crimes and you've "solved" two dozen. The man charged — faced with the book anyway — has little to lose and often is a willing party.

Mr. and Mrs. S.G. LeNoir are convinced that "Junior" Pierce did not kill Miss Cuttino. They are convinced they saw the girl in their store with two young boys on the day after law enforcement agents say she was murdered in Manchester State Forest. Mrs. LeNoir is the postmistress of the Horatio community, near Sumter. She has been president of her garden club, has been president of the Grange, and has been a leader in enough other endeavors that won't allow a casual discounting of her credibility.

Many other people in Sumter (not including the parents of the dead child) have doubts, and this is the crux of the story: If "Junior" Pierce is innocent of this murder, then the real murderer (or murderers) is free... perhaps the two young men Mr. and Mrs.

LeNoir say they saw with Miss Cuttino.

Let's take a closer look at the case:

A motion for a new trial for Pierce, on the basis of the LeNoirs' testimony was denied in Sumter Thursday, but instead of putting the matter to rest, the doubts continue.

Pierce was convicted March 2, in Kingstree, of killing Miss Cuttino on December 18, 1970, and leaving the child's body in the woods near Wedgefield.

Motion for the new trial hinged largely on the testimony of the LeNoirs, which defense attorneys said they did not know about at the time of the trial.

Miss Cuttino's father, former state legislator James Cuttino, said after the Thursday hearing, "I hope now we can put this thing behind us. I wanted to know I had the right man. I am satisfied and my wife is satisfied."

But the doubt continues in the minds of others.

Differences in the sworn testimony as to the confession Pierce made to South Carolina officers and the recollections of a Georgia Bureau of Investigation (GBI) lieutenant, who sat in on many of the interrogations, raise doubts as to Pierce's guilt.

Officers said Pierce left the automobile jack with which he struck the girl in the trunk of his red automobile.

GBI Lt. William Parker recalls Pierce confessing that he exchanged the jack in Wrens, Georgia, for $3.25 worth of gasoline at a gas station. Parker could not understand, he said, why South Carolina officers had not checked the stations in Wrens.

South Carolina officers said Pierce was driving a red Pontiac during the time he was in Sumter. Chief Deputy Roy Wheeler, of Emanuel County, said the red car was "broken down, at his mama's" at the time Peg Cuttino was slain, December 18, 1970.

Pierce, Wheeler said, was driving a 1960, light-blue Ford, belonging to his mother, Mrs. Jewel White. Wheeler said the 1960 Ford, which could be described as "a small car," couldn't make it on the extensive travel Pierce is supposed to have made around this part of December, 1970.

A key state witness, 14-year-old Earl Williams, of Sumter County, testified he had seen Pierce on December 19 or 20, in the vicinity of Manchester State Forest, near Sumter, where the body was found. Pierce was standing before a white Ford station wagon, Williams said.

The state contended the slaying took place on December 18 and that Pierce was driving a maroon car.

Pierce was charged with the slaying of a Vidalia, Georgia, salesman and filling station operator, Joe Flecher, on December

20, 1970. He also is charged with killing Kathy Jo Anderson, of West Columbia, on December 22..

If Pierce is the man Earl Williams saw, it means he would have had to drive by the shortest route to Vidalia from Sumter — more than 220 miles — to kill Joe Fletcher. If he left his jack at Wrens, Georgia, as Lt. Parker recalls, the distance would have been much further.

Then he would have had to return to West Columbia to kill Kathy Jo Anderson on December 22..

The testimony of Mr. and Mrs. LeNoir and the reports of others who said they saw Peg Cuttino alive after December 18, casts further doubt on the case.

Pierce's former girl friend, Nita Jean Blackburn, came to Kingstree voluntarily to testify she was with Pierce on the morning and evening of the day he is supposed to have killed the Cuttino child. Mrs. Blackburn previously had testified against Pierce in Georgia.

Georgia officers interviewed and, without exception, told The State newspaper reporters they believe Nita Blackburn's testimony.

Ray Sconyers, Pierce's former foreman at Handy House Manufacturing Company, in Swainsboro, Georgia, testified he saw Pierce at work throughout the day on December 18, 1970.

Lt. Parker, however, said Pierce told him it was easy to leave work without being detected, that no close check was made to keep track of employees.

The doubts linger. Why was not a recorded confession made? Why the difference in dates? How much was "Junior" Pierce capable of traveling? Was he driving a red or maroon car when officers said he was in Sumter? Or a white one as their witness said? Or was it light blue, as the Georgia deputy said?

Another interesting angle in the case is an affidavit from Columbia hypno-therapist Robert N. Sauer, as part of the defense attorneys' efforts to gain a new trial for Pierce.

Under hypnosis, Pierce denies killing Peg Cuttino and denies that he was in Sumter at the time.

In connection with the same case for the Sumter Sheriff's Department and SLED, another suspect was hypnotized by Sauer, taken into "age regression" and proved innocent of the Cuttino slaying. He had, without the hypnosis, been unable to recall his activities on the day Miss Cuttino disappeared.

Under hypnosis, Pierce says he was drugged and forced to confess by Appling County, Georgia, Sheriff J.B. "Red" Carter with facts furnished by SLED Lt. Olin Redd and Carter.

THE STATE - Columbia, SC, Monday, April 9, 1973

GEORGIA POLICE CONSIDER PIERCE A KILLER

"Junior" Pierce is the only man I could ever kill without any remorse whatsoever," a retired Georgia Bureau of Investigation (GBI) lieutenant responded when asked if he thought the four-time convicted killer was capable of murder.

In fact, key Georgia authorities instrumental in initiating murder charges against Pierce in South Carolina and Georgia, see the Swainsboro native as different to allegations in — a 'cold-blooded killer' and in some quarters, Pierce may have received a "bum rap" in South Carolina.

GBI agent William Parker and Sheriffs J.B. "Red" Carter and Herman G. Yeomans told The State in separate interviews last week they are convinced Pierce is guilty of the crimes in Georgia, in which he is charged. They counted that Pierce enjoys playing a "cat and mouse" game in admitting to, and later denying his guilt.

The three men were queried after controversy arose concerning Pierce's conviction last month in Kingstree for the murder of 13-year-old Margaret Ann "Peg" Cuttino, of Sumter, in December, 1970.

However, the three lawmen admit being puzzled over the Cuttino case in at least one respect — they all maintain that two key defense witnesses in that trial are "straight" and probably would not lie on the witness stand.

The witnesses, Pierce's former boss Ray Sconyers and ex-girl friend Nita Jean Blackburn, testified in the Kingstree case that Pierce was in Georgia at the time South Carolina officials say the Cuttino girl was slain.

Parker, a GBI agent for 11 years, told The State that, though he does not doubt the two witnesses' testimony, he had not expected the case to go to trial in South Carolina.

The retired agent was located on his hog farm in Appling County, Georgia. He said that while interviewing Pierce in the Appling County jail, he had been forced to laugh at indescribably bad crimes with Pierce in order to get the man to continue his confessions.

Parker reflected on his discussion with Pierce pertaining to the Cuttino murder and said "Bill" told him the murder weapon used was the extended track portion of an automobile jack, which later was pawned at a gas station in a trade for $3.25 worth of gasoline.

According to testimony in the Cuttino trial, officers testified that Pierce told them he killed the girl with a bumper jack which remained in the trunk of his car. Officers said the car was later sold at an auction in Georgia and has never been located.

Parker, discussing for some three hours his involvement in the Pierce investigation, alluded to the suggestion that Pierce wanted others to think he possessed Extra Sensory Perception (ESP) in knowing about the various murder incidents.

In one instance, the ex-lawman said, Pierce, after lengthy questioning, cupped his hand over his forehead and said he could envision some of the details surrounding a particular slaying.

Parker said, in this case the police department of the city in which the victim had been slain, had sent a representative, who was totally unfamiliar with the case.

While relating things he said he envisioned, Pierce described items on the floor, the way entry was made into the house, detailed description of the room, the manner in which the victim fell, how the victim was dressed, sounds around the neighborhood, a neighborhood description and more.

Parker said, "I asked the officer if these were accurate. He said he didn't know."

He made a call and obtained the information from the other city without revealing his own details, and the information checked out with Pierce's account.

In another case, Parker related, evidence showed that Pierce had come into a store operated in Baxley, Georgia, by Mrs. Vivian Miles.

He said Pierce robbed the woman at gunpoint and then shot her to death before striking the woman's five-year-old grandchild in the head with the butt of his pistol.

"He struck her so hard with his pistol that it bent the handle," Parker said, and added that the child recovered from her wounds.

Parker said he later gave the child a set of 23 photographs and asked her if any of them looked like the man who "hurt grandma." The youngster quickly picked two pictures of Pierce from the stack of photos.

The former agent said that just after the killing, Pierce met a bread delivery man coming into the store.

"Despite the fact that Pierce had considered himself a crack shot with a pistol, he missed twice," said Parker. Parker believes this was because Pierce was backing up while firing.

This was the first real break for Georgia authorities in solving a number of killings and robberies in the area.

The agent said a probation officer had recalled that on the way to Reidsville Prison, where Pierce previously served time,

*"Bill remarked that officials would never again be able to charge
him with anything because there would be no witnesses left."*

The bread truck driver, who was intensely frightened, was
placed under heavy protective guard while making his deliveries
until Pierce's apprehension.

After Pierce was jailed, on March 28, 1971, authorities were
able to put together leads on the slayings. Pierce was arrested by
Baxley, Georgia, police after a service station operator
complained he failed to pay for a gas purchase.

Turning again to the Cuttino case in Sumter, Parker said two
agents from South Carolina had questioned Pierce morning,
afternoon and evening. He said he was in and out of the morning
and afternoon sessions, but did not go in after supper, when
Pierce was being interrogated.

Parker added that the agents were not extracting much
information at first.

*"I talked to Bill and I said, 'You've been peeing on that
lieutenant's leg long enough. You've been peeing on my leg. Now
why don't you tell him something?'*

*"He laughed and said, 'I guess I have been peeing on his leg.
I've wet it all the way up to the knee,'"* Parker said.

The ex-GBI agent said Pierce told officers he had picked the
girl up at a drive-in where she was arguing with two older men.
Pierce said he and the girl left in his car when he saw a woman at
the drive-in pick up a phone and thought she might be calling the
police.

According to testimony at the trial, Sheriff I. Byrd Parnell, of
Sumter County, said Pierce told him Peg Cuttino was arguing
with another girl and a young boy.

Parker continued his account of Pierce's testimony about the
Cuttino killing, stating that Pierce admitted driving down a road
which was *"not a super highway over which planes were flying."*

Pierce said the girl was leaning against the door on the
passenger side of the car and fell out of the auto. He said he
stopped the car at a creek, wet his handkerchief and wiped the
girl's head, according to Parker.

The former agent said Pierce then admitted striking the girl
on the head with the part of an auto jack and later exchanging it
in Wrens, Georgia, for $3.25 worth of gasoline.

Parker wondered why South Carolina agents apparently did
not check this out.

Parker said it would have been easy enough by merely telling
station operators they (agents) were not looking for a stolen
article, but that the jack may have been a murder weapon.

A check inside the Wrens city limits revealed only a dozen
service stations, with an additional four outside the boundaries.

The car in question, which Pierce told officers he was driving apparently was a maroon-colored Pontiac.

In another conversation, Chief Deputy Roy Wheeler, in Swainsboro, told The State that at the time of the Cuttino murder he saw the car broken down in front of the house belonging to Pierce's mother.

He added, however, that she also owned a light blue car, which Pierce "could have been driving."

"Junior" Pierce often was described as "weird" and as a "traveler" by Emanuel County Sheriff Herman G. Yoemans, who believes Pierce killed a lot more people in Georgia than he's been convicted of.

Earlier, both Sheriff "Red" Carter and ex-agent Parker, told The State that Pierce said he would kill both his mother, Mrs. Jewel White, and his former girlfriend, Nita Jean Blackburn.

Sheriff Yoemans related an incident he had heard involving Pierce making keys out of light fixtures in his cell in Baxley.

The story also was echoed by former agent Parker, who said he believes Pierce had succeeded in opening his cell door and had gotten out into the main section of the jail, but had not devised a means of getting past another steel door to freedom when detected.

Pierce apparently was the object of a number of escape rumors and accountings during his period of incarceration in Georgia.

During a reporter's visit to Sheriff Yoemans last week, a dispatch came from Jackson Prison in Georgia, that Pierce had escaped from Central Correctional Institution in Columbia, where he had been held since the Kingstree trial.

Yoemans quickly called CCI where a check was made, and the rumor proved to be unfounded.

Parker told of an incident where Pierce had taken his cigarette lighter and burned around the screws of a stool, loosening the legs. The legs then were hidden beneath his mattress to be used as clubs in an escape attempt.

Parker said Sheriff Carter responded to this escape attempt by placing huge log chains and padlocks on Pierce's cell door.

"We're not talking about an ordinary man," Sheriff Carter responded when asked about Pierce. He said the convicted killer was extraordinarily observant of minute details.

"I'm convinced he's guilty of every one of them," Carter said when asked about the murder charges against Pierce.

Carter, who is attributed by most officers as the man who actually broke most of the cases in Georgia and South Carolina, called Pierce "a peculiar man who has no feelings for anybody."

He added, "He came from everywhere and didn't even know

who they (his victims) were a lot of times."

Carter said that as far as he was concerned, he was convinced Pierce committed the murders.

Carter, who single-handedly disarmed and dispelled an angry lynch-mob outside the jail housing Pierce, lives modestly in quarters over the jail with his wife and three dogs, Candy, Snowball and Precious.

Authorities in South Carolina and Georgia attribute the mystique of "Junior" Pierce to a combination of events and persons, including Pierce's mother, who has exerted a profound influence on her son since childhood.

Pierce was arrested first at the age of 17 for larceny. Since that time, he has been in and out of prison — more often in than out. His prison records list several convictions and sentences of several auto thefts in Augusta, Georgia, in 1954-55.

Pierce was sentenced to six years in prison for three of the thefts, after being convicted in 1955. In 1958, he was given a probationary sentence in Savannah, Georgia, for passing a fraudulent check in that town. In 1960, he was sentenced for burglary and also for probation violation. Pierce received a 10-20 year sentence for burglary and arson in 1963.

That particular charge involved the burglary and burning of a country store near Pierce's home in Swainsboro. His mother spent a year in prison for conspiracy in connection with the incident for which she received a one to three year sentence. In 1957, she also received a 12-month sentence for burglary.

Sheriff Yoemans told The State he felt Pierce's mother often drove the car at the time Pierce was burglarizing stores and residences in crimes for which he has never been charged.

At the time Pierce was being considered for parole in 1970, from Reidsville Prison, a Georgia Department of Corrections psychological report advised to the contrary. Pierce was described by psychologists as "sociopathic and dangerous to himself and others."

The report said Pierce had "little or no feelings for the misfortunes or suffering of others."

Another prison report called Pierce "emotionally unstable" and it said he would probably continue to lead a life of crime.

Once Pierce was released from prison in May, 1970, a string of murders occurred in North and South Carolina and Georgia. The common denominator in all cases, but one, is that there were no witnesses.

After Pierce was jailed, the charges against him began to pile up. First of the cases was for the murder of Ann Goodwin, of North Augusta, an 18-year-old babysitter, who was shot on June 27, 1970. He is awaiting trial next month in Aiken for that *slaying.*

Other warrants soon followed covering a string of brutal murders in the two Carolinas and Georgia, over a period from August, 1970, to mid-January, 1971.

On August 10, 1970, service station operator James L. Sires was killed by a blow from an ax and $970 was taken from his Beaufort, South Carolina, business. Beaufort County Sheriff L.W. Wallace confirmed there apparently were no witnesses to the slaying, but he said Pierce not only confessed to the killing, but also told them details about the incidence which only the killer could know.

The sheriff said Pierce was very observant and knew details about the service station and later told officers the murder weapon was thrown away, somewhere along a stretch of U.S. 21, outside of Beaufort, bounded on either side by marshlands. The ax was never recovered, but Pierce was formally charged with the killing. He still awaits trial.

A short time later, Gaston County, North Carolina, authorities reported the murder of a 20-year-old housekeeper, whose body was found August 21, 1970. Virginia Carol Mains, who had been reported missing from her home, was found buried some 10 days later, near Dallas, North Carolina. Acid had been poured over portions of her body, apparently to speed up the decomposition. Pierce has not confessed to that crime, but he has been charged with the killing.

On December 18, 1970, Sumter County , South Carolina, officers were alerted to the missing-persons status of the 13-year-old daughter of then State Representative James Cuttino. Peg Cuttino's body was discovered 12 days later in a shallow grave some 15 miles from Sumter. She had been strangled and hit on the head with a heavy object.

Early Sunday morning, December 20, 1970, Joe Fletcher, 59, a traveling salesman, was killed at a Vidalia, Georgia, service station where he worked between traveling jobs. Missing from the cash register was $78. Pierce was tried and convicted for the killing and sentenced to life.

Soon after that murder, officers again in South Carolina, reported the December 22, 1970, death of a 17-year-old West Columbia girl, Kathy Jo Anderson. The young restaurant waitress's body was discovered in a shallow grave several miles from her employment. Pierce has been charged but has not been to trial.

Mrs. Lacy Thigpen, 51, who operated a store near Soperton, Georgia, was killed January 12, 1971. She apparently had been shot to death during a robbery attempt. No witnesses were reported.

Pierce was charged, but still awaits court action in that case.
On January 22, 1971, Helen Wilcox, 32 -year-old mother of
four, disappeared from a small grocery store she operated near
Hazelhurst, Georgia. Her body eventually was found in a
wooded area near a swamp. Pierce drew a life sentence for that
slaying.

Another country store operator, 60-year-old Vivian Miles,
was reported by Georgia officials as being shot to death on
January 28, 1971, at her business near Baxley, Georgia, during a
robbery. Her 5-year-old granddaughter was severely beaten with
a gun butt, but she later recovered.

Unlike the earlier killings, however, a witness was left when
bread truck driver Joe Overstreet identified Pierce as the man he
saw running from the scene. He said the man fired at him twice,
but missed.

Similarly, the victim's granddaughter also picked out Pierce's
picture from some 23 photographs as the man who "hurt
Grandma." Pierce also got life for that killing.

Pierce, a Swainsboro, Georgia, native was born November
11, 1931. According to Pierce, he has been married twice and is
the father of a 12-year-old son. He was drafted in 1951 and
spent three months in Army basic training at Ft. Jackson, South
Carolina.

After being declared "mentally incapable," Pierce was
discharged. That verdict of his mental incapability, however, was
not unanimous. One lieutenant termed Pierce "conscientious...a
good worker...and of sterling character."

Pierce also received a medal for rifle marksmanship.

LAST OF THREE PARTS

THE STATE,   Columbia, South Carolina, Tuesday, April 10, 1973

CHARGES EMERGED IN RETRIAL MOTION

Thirteen-year-old Margaret "Peg" Cuttino, daughter of a
former State Representative, disappeared in Sumter on Friday,
December 18, 1970, while on her way from her home to school to
eat lunch with her sister.

Georgia convict William J. Pierce, Jr., was charged in April
of the following year with the killing. Tried in Kingstree,
"Junior" Pierce was sentenced to life imprisonment.

A flurry of charges and counter-charges, reports of new
witnesses and suggestions of obscured evidence emerged in a
hearing for retrial last Thursday in Sumter.

To an outsider, not following the case, a motion for a retrial seems a small matter. A man had been charged and convicted, so what was the minor tempest about?

In Sumter County, it was not a casual matter. Conflicting testimony raises a dire question of credibility.

The Thursday retrial motion was a head-on collision between the word of Sumter and state law enforcement officers and a Sumter County couple, Mr. and Mrs. S.G. LeNoir.

Court-appointed defense attorneys Joe McElveen, William Jenkinson and James Connor also suggested that evidence was not available to them when they checked files of the case for leads suggesting the child was alive after December 18, 1970, the date the state maintained she was abducted and slain.

Mr. and Mrs. S.G. LeNoir, of Horatio, near Sumter, testified they saw Miss Cuttino alive at their store on December 19. Affidavits from a classmate of Miss Cuttino, Noah Artrip, and Turbeville service station employee Burnett Plowden, also stated they believe they had seen Miss Cuttino alive after the date the state contended she was killed.

A key witness for the state, 14-year-old Earl Williams, of Sumter County, said the date he saw a man standing in front of an automobile in the wooded area where Peg Cuttino's body was found was December 19 or 20.

Sumter officers contradicted the LeNoirs' testimony with eight witnesses, including the girl's father, James Cuttino, and her aunt, Mrs. Portia Cuttino Myers, of Hagood, who lived near the LeNoirs.

"Gentlemen, I'm not particularly impressed with your motion," Circuit Judge Louis Rosen, of Orangeburg, told defense attorneys for Pierce.

Rosen said a new trial on grounds of new evidence is not favored in South Carolina "except in rare cases" where five prerequisites are met.

The five criteria for a new trial are:
— *Evidence that could not have been discovered with due diligence prior to the trial.*
— *Evidence discovered after the trial.*
— *Evidence not cumulative in nature.*
— *Evidence that might change the outcome of the trial*
— *Evidence material to the trial.*

The Orangeburg jurist said he did not think all the requirements had been met. Earlier, defense attorneys had contended the five criteria for a new trial had been fulfilled.

At the hearing last week, before Judge Rosen, two prosecution witnesses testified the LeNoirs earlier claimed they really had no opportunity to get a clear look at the girl for a positive identification.

Deputies Tommy Mims and Hugh Mathis told the court that, during their initial interview, Mrs. LeNoir told them she had not seen the girl and could only describe the two boys who came into the store as between 16-18 years old with neat appearances.

In an affidavit submitted to the court by Pierce's attorneys, Mrs. LeNoir said she saw the girl getting into the back of a "brownish-yellow" car and later realized the girl was Peg Cuttino.

Mims and Mathis also testified at the hearing that Mrs. LeNoir's husband told them the day of the interview the girl remained in the car and he only got a glimpse of her from the shoulders up.

The two deputies said when they talked to Mrs. LeNoir about her husband's testimony she implied that her husband "didn't know what he was talking about."

Mrs. LeNoir said later in the hearing she had lived with her husband more than 30 years, and would not have made a statement like that.

The slain child's parents have expressed the feeling that the right man has been convicted. "I hope now we can put this thing behind us," James Cuttino, Peg Cuttino's father, said following the hearing for a retrial last Thursday.

In denying the motion for a new trial, Judge Rosen told defense attorneys he could see where nothing had been concealed. That statement also was maintained by the sheriff and other officers.

Three thousand interviews, about 250 definite leads and other work apparently obscured some of the reports and leads.

This averages out to more than 20 persons a day from the time Miss Cuttino was first missing to the date Pierce was charged.

The enormity of the work is further emphasized by the fact that some of the investigations were out of state.

What was the reason for the Lenoirs' insistence on testifying?

They had reported they saw Miss Cuttino to the sheriff's department. Officers had talked to them. Why not let the matter drop?

Mr. and Mrs. LeNoir feel strongly that the wrong person has been convicted.

Who are the LeNoirs?

She is president of a Sumter garden club, and postmistress at Horatio. She has held the presidency of the Grange and has been honored with offices in almost every civic endeavor in her community.

LeNoirs have been in the Horatio community since 1765. LeNoirs have operated a general store at Horatio for six generations. All six of Mr. and Mrs. S.G. Lenoirs' children have excelled in 4-H club projects and have won awards. She has been Sumter County Mother of the Year.

Mrs. LeNoir said she and her husband first became aware of Peg Cuttino's disappearance about 9:30 a.m., Saturday, December 19, 1970 — the day after the girl was reported missing — when a relative phoned the news.

The Horatio postmistress said little was discussed about the case until later in the afternoon, after she and her husband had determined that the Cuttino girl had been in their small general store earlier that day.

"I took about a five-minute break around 2:30 p.m., went to the house next door to the store, and on my way back I noticed a strange brownish-yellow car," Mrs. LeNoir said.

She told The State that as she approached nearer the store, two boys and a girl came out and entered the car.

She said the boys got onto the front seat and "a girl, wearing a skirt and blouse, with shoulder length hair," got into the back.

Mrs. LeNoir said she intended to ask her husband about the trio, but the pre-Christmas volume of business caused her to forget until later.

She said she finished up her post office work around 4:45 p.m. and was walking back into the store portion of the building when "two boys came in, handed me three dollars and said they had put in three dollars worth of gasoline."

Mrs. LeNoir said the boys "seemed real excited" as they hurried out and she followed them out and watched the two enter the same brownish-yellow car she had seen earlier. She added, however, that there was not a girl in the car at that time.

She said the car left the post office and turned down an adjacent road as it had done earlier.

When the afternoon newspaper was delivered, a short time later, Mrs. LeNoir said her husband noticed a picture of the missing girl and exclaimed, "That girl was in the store today."

A discussion between the two followed, she noted adding, "I started recalling things about the girl I'd seen getting into the car" in comparison with the Cuttino girl she had seen several years earlier.

She said though she had not clearly seen the face of the girl getting into the car, the hair length of the girl she saw on December 19 was not the same as shown in the picture of Peg Cuttino.

Mrs. LeNoir said a phone call the next morning to a cousin of Peg's about the hair length "confirms our belief that she was in our store on December 19."

Recalling being questioned by police later, Mrs. LeNoir said she was at church rehearsal that Sunday afternoon, following the sighting, when two county deputies asked to see her.

"I related to them the events of the previous day concerning Peg Cuttino so far as our involvement reached. We were horrified when her cousin later told us that her murdered body had been found," Mrs. LeNoir said.

Deputies said the LeNoirs could give no positive identification. One said that Mrs. LeNoir had said that she "doubted" her husband knew what he saw.

Sheriff Parnell said he and two other officers talked with Mr. LeNoir and "he said he didn't see anything but the back of her head and the side of her face." Sheriff Parnell was asked if the LeNoirs were not "good fine people, honest, people." The sheriff replied he had "always found them so."

In cross examination of Mr. LeNoir, Solicitor McLeod bore down hard.

He asked if he had heard the sheriff and other officers' testimony. LeNoir said he had heard them testify to "stories and lies."

Asked about Mrs. Myers' testimony, LeNoir said, "she might have told a few, too."

"I'm certain that Peg Cuttino was in my store around 2:00 p.m.," LeNoir testified.

Judge Rosen took issue with defense allegations that investigating officers disregarded evidence. He noted the pressure they were working under and the 3,000 interviews reported. He said he could not imagine "officers of this county disregarding evidence."

And so, Pierce's conviction in the death of Peg Cuttino will stand, at least pending another appeal that defense attorneys have indicated they planned.

Despite the outcome of an appeal, however, Pierce's fate is not in question. Already convicted of four murders and facing charges in several more, "Junior" Pierce will be little affected by the case.

It appears certain that he will spend a lifetime behind bars — regardless of whether his guilt or innocence in the Cuttino case is established conclusively.

But, if he is innocent, it means that the real killer (or killers) is loose. For those who believe this to be so, that is the tragedy.

Sumter and Sumter County boiled with a turbulent mixture of confusion and emotion. It seemed that each segment in this troubling sequence of events opened up new wounds and brought to mind a new set of unanswered questions.

Each attempt to end the uneasiness of the community only resulted in more and greater confusion.

Several of the out-of-town newspapers were following the Pierce case, along with *The Sumter Daily Item,* and as the accounts and articles appeared, written by a host of writers - all working independent of each other, they all reflected the doubt and frustration that the people of the county were experiencing.

The LeNoirs were hurt and disillusioned. They had only done what they believed that any good citizen would have done in their place. They had seen something, that seemed to be important in this case, and had informed the authorities of what they had seen.

"We have always tried to be good citizens," Mrs. Carrie LeNoir said, "and we have always believed that our elected officials were good, honest people. We have never been in a courtroom, in a murder case, but, we thought that we would be allowed to give our statements, as respected citizens...We knew that it would be up to the judge as to whether he believed us or not...but, we were treated as if we were illiterate, ignorant, liars and cheats...trying to pull some kind of hoax on the public. Mr. McLeod talked to my husband and me as if we were no better than cur dogs on the street."

Hurt and disappointment showed in her face and her voice trembled as she remembered the "raving and ranting" of Solicitor Kirk McLeod as he lashed out at her husband, while he was on the witness stand on Thursday afternoon.

Solicitor McLeod had gotten so far out of line, with his harassment of Mr. LeNoir, that the Judge even called him down at one point and told him "This man is not on trial here..."

Solicitor McLeod, panting and huffing from his overzealous attempt to confuse the witness replied, "I wish he was."

"Why would he want to try Mr. LeNoir? And for what? It was clear that the Solicitor was not seeking the truth, but was intent on confusing Mr. LeNoir and making him say something that he did not intend to say, in order to discredit him," Mrs. LeNoir said.

"They called us liars," she said, obviously hurt and upset, "Sheriff Parnell, James Cuttino, Portia Myers, Tommy Mims, Hugh Mathis...and Solicitor McLeod all called us liars...Why?...We've never lied to them, or anybody else, in our lives. They had no reason to call us liars..."

Mr. LeNoir just sat motionless. "You wouldn't want to hear what I have to say," he said.

Many people knew the LeNoirs throughout Sumter County, and the treatment that they had received at the hands of Solicitor Kirk McLeod infuriated a large segment of the public.

The newspaper had only published bits and pieces of the testimony of the LeNoirs, and a lot of people wanted to know just what it was that they had said that made the authorities want to discredit it so badly.

After a number of inquiries, Mrs. LeNoir decided that she would write a letter to the editor of *The Item,* so that people could read their statement in its entirety.

LETTER TO THE EDITOR

The Sumter Daily Item, Tuesday, April 10, 1973

To the Editor:

In view of the cruel treatment we received while trying to testify at a hearing for a motion for a new trial for William "Junior" Pierce, Thursday afternoon, we would like to give our testimony to the public, as we were never allowed to give it during the hearing.

"When, in the course of human events, it becomes necessary for persons to stand up, step out, and take a stand for what they believe in, the task is not always easy. May I say, in the beginning, that in view of the course of events during the past few months, that making this testimony will be one of the hardest and most distasteful tasks I've had to perform during my life. To the family involved, I can offer more genuine sympathy than the average person, as I, too, have a little girl in the grave. Although she was not murdered, but was a victim of cancer, I know the sting of death. Most of the family members have been personal friends of mine for many years. We certainly don't want to open any old wounds, nor do we wish to create new wounds, but we have no choice.

To the law enforcement officers, I pay deepest respect and gratitude. As many of you know, I have cooperated in every possible way to promote law and order; plus having served with you on Mental Health, Cancer Society, United Appeal, Heart Fund and many other worthwhile civic causes. Currently, six boys on probation report to me every Friday afternoon. I receive no compensation whatsoever — only the satisfaction that I'm helping make six good citizens. Judges have released boys in my custody previously.

When some folks became aware that I would be making this testimony, they advised that my life might be endangered, and wondered why I wanted to get involved. I never wanted to get involved, but was a victim of circumstances. I appreciate their concern, but for years my prayer has been, 'God grant me the courage to change the things I can change, the serenity to accept those I cannot change, and the wisdom to know the difference.'

I had a serious conference with God, and He gave me the green light, and although I love life, and live each day to the fullest, I have no fear of death. Finally, although the wheels of justice grind slowly, I believe that they never stop turning completely. With these thoughts, I shall proceed to testify.

On Saturday, December 19, 1970, about 9:30 a.m., a neighbor, Mrs. Walter M. LeNoir, called and asked if I had heard that Peg Cuttino was missing. I told her that I had not heard the news, but, was very sorry to hear it. This being the Saturday before Christmas, we were very busy, both in our store and Post Office, so my husband and I had very little chance to discuss Peg. In fact, we were so busy that we did not take time to go to the house for lunch, but ate sandwiches in the store. I took about a five minute break around 2:30, went to the house, which is next door to the store, and on my way back, as I walked down the back steps, I noticed a strange brownish-yellow car. After being postmaster in Horatio for almost 30 years, and working with my husband in the store even longer, we know all of the local people, and with Horatio being on a farm to market road, we have very few tourists, so we always notice strangers. As I got nearer the store, two boys and a girl came out, the boys getting on the front seat, and a girl, wearing a skirt and blouse, with shoulder length hair, got on the back seat. I intended to ask my husband what the two boys and girl wanted, but as I walked inside, someone was waiting for a money order. As I'm one of the few post offices giving Saturday afternoon service, I was real busy all afternoon, with people getting last minute Christmas mailings off. Not until about 4:45 did I catch up, prepare all mail for dispatch, and walk back in the store to help. As I got almost to the counter, two boys came in, handed me three dollars, and said they had put in three dollars worth of gasoline. I thanked them, and noticed that they seemed real excited. As they hurried out, I followed them, and saw the same brownish-yellow car, but there was no girl in it. Again they made a U turn, and went down the Claremont Road, as they had done the first time. I then got a chance to ask my husband what the girl and two boys had bought earlier, and he told me three small Coca-Colas.

Later that afternoon, The Item delivery man brought the paper in, and the manner in which it was put on the counter showed Peg's picture. My husband immediately exclaimed, 'That girl was in the store today.' 'Are you sure?' I said. 'Certainly, I am sure,' he said. I started recalling things about the girl I'd seen getting into the car, and comparing them with things I remembered about Peg, whom I'd seen several years earlier when she was campaigning for her father's election. For many years, Horatio Grange has sponsored a political campaign speaking affair, and served supper to make money to finance our community service projects. As general chairman for the affairs, I was always the first to arrive, and the last to leave. The candidates always came early and I can vividly recall Peg going around among the guests, passing out cards and saying, 'Please vote for my Daddy.' I had also seen her in the yard of her home later. I had not clearly seen the face of the girl getting in the car, and the hair length I remembered was not exactly as that shown in the picture, so I was not sure at that point.

We finally got through with our day's work about 9:30 that night, went on to the house, and ate supper. We went to bed about 11 o'clock, but slept very little. We tossed and turned all night. My husband said he seemed to see the girl standing in the store, reaching out for the Coke; and I had a picture of her getting in the car throughout the night.

I got up about 8:o'clock, and called the residence of Mr. Cuttino's sister, Mrs. W.C. (Lucy Anne) Eldridge. Her son Jamie answered the phone. I identified myself and told him I called to check the length of Peg's hair. When he said, 'shoulder length,' I said, 'That confirms our belief that she was in our store yesterday.'

I told him of the events, and he said he would notify the police. We went on to church that morning, then on in to town to eat dinner.

We were having our Christmas pageant at the Church of the Ascension, in Hagood, that afternoon. About 4:30, I was sitting at the organ, practicing the carols, while the children were in the Parish House getting on their costumes. John Brabham came in and told me that two men were waiting to see me.

As I walked into the sacristy, there stood two men whom I recognized as Detectives Hugh Mathis and Tommy Mims.

Hugh said, 'Mrs. LeNoir, I've come to tell you that I expect that J. Edgar Hoover will be drafting you 'most any time to serve with the F.B.I.'

We all laughed — the reason for this remark being that I had helped them solve the mystery of who wrecked the train in Horatio the Monday night before this weekend. He then said he had received our message, had come by our house and talked with my husband, who sent them on to talk with me. I related to them the events of the previous day, concerning Peg Cuttino, as far as our involvement reached; and we were horrified when her cousin, Portia Myers, later told us, before we heard by radio or press, that her murdered body had been found.

Carrie Baker (Mrs. Samuel Gaillard) LeNoir

S.G. LENOIR'S STATEMENT

"I do hereby certify that I'm positive that Margaret (Peg) Cuttino was in my store on Saturday, December 19, 1970.

About 2:30 p.m., two strange boys and a girl came in and ordered three small Coca-Colas. The girl reached out for her Coke, and as I looked in her face, she had an expression which impressed me as being sad or unhappy. When I saw her picture in The Sumter Daily Item that afternoon, I immediately said that she was the girl in the store earlier.

As a native of Horatio, and having spent my entire fifty-six years here, except while serving in the Armed Forces during World War II, I know every citizen of this area. I have been in business independently in this same store since 1936, and worked with my father for several years earlier. I have also served as assistant postmaster for almost 30 years, as the Post Office is in a corner of the store.

As we are not on a highway, but instead, a farm to market road, we see very few strangers, and are always aware when strangers come in, and are observant. I will never doubt that Peg was in my store.

After my wife and I had a restless night, during which I seemed to see the girl reaching out for the Coke, my wife called Peg's cousin to discuss the situation. After talking with Jamie Eldridge, my wife also, was convinced that the strange girl she had seen on Saturday was Peg. Jamie said he would notify the police.

Two detectives, Hugh Mathis and Tommy Mims, came out to my house on Sunday, December 20, about 4 o'clock, and I told them everything I knew about the case. I then sent them on to talk to my wife, who was playing the organ for the Christmas Pageant at the Church of the Ascension, Hagood.

Samuel Gaillard LeNoir

AFFIRMATION

We hate to be involved in such controversy as this, and have nothing to gain or lose, but we're trying to do our duty as citizens: also, our honor is at stake, so we have no choice but to defend it.

Carrie B. LeNoir
Samuel G. LeNoir

LETTER TO THE EDITOR

The Sumter Daily Item — Saturday, April 14, 1973

To the Editor:
If there's a Pulitzer booby prize, your paper's got it won.
You could easily answer your own question in the attached copy. (Editor's note: The writer enclosed a clipping of an ITEM

editorial headlined "Where's Everyone?" which bemoaned the lack of attendance at the League of Women Voters' candidates night Monday evening.)

The shameful treatment of the S.G. LeNoirs should prompt someone to report on the political pollution in Sumter County, but your paper is just part of the mess.

Like many transients, my family was transferred to Sumter. Perhaps service families are a little more perceptive, having lived in so many locales. However, an idiot could hardly miss noticing the nepotism in the city and county systems of Sumter. "Everyone and his uncle" is no figure of speech Sumterwise.

I graduated from Edmunds. It was a good school. There are a lot of good people in the Sumter area (e.g. the LeNoirs), and I'm sure they are in the majority. They just don't know how to fight the minority that pollutes Sumter.

The Gamecock City and County are excellent examples of the political proverb, "The national scene is a reflection of the local scene."

My Dad will soon retire, and my parents, like me, will find Sumter a great place to be from.

Observantly yours,
BOBBIE B. JOHANSEN
Zumbrota, Minnesota

On April 15, State staff writers Jack Truluck and Hugh Munn, still following up on the Pierce story, presented another article entitled "Sheriff: Pierce Would Confess to Anything".

Dillon County Sheriff Roy Lee said, when questioned about Pierce's involvement in a double murder at a Latta truckstop in 1970, "Pierce impressed me as a person who, if you gave him enough information about a case, would confess to anything. I'd love to solve that case, but not that way. We felt he didn't do it, so we didn't charge him."

Sheriff "Buck" Knight, of Orange County, North Carolina, also had occasion to question Pierce regarding slayings in that state, but declined to make charges after investigating Pierce's alibi.

A catalyst in tying various slayings to Pierce appeared to be detective story writer Jack Orr, of Columbia, whom Pierce said was present at the investigations in Georgia.

The article said that, "In an interview with The State, Pierce maintained the details of his confessions in the two cases that were furnished him by Orr, Georgia Sheriff J.B. "Red" Carter and SLED Lt. Olin Redd."

Pierce depicted himself as a victim of a tough Appling County, Georgia sheriff who, he said, kept him drugged almost constantly, plotted with a lynchmob leader and finally had him beaten down to such an extent that he confessed to more murders than outside officers would accept.

Pierce said that officers who testified at his March, 1973, trial in the slaying of 13-year-old Margaret "Peg" Cuttino, of Sumter, were giving the court information as he had confessed it to them.

Details such as "a low-flying plane", the manner in which he stood in front of his automobile, branches which covered the child's body and a pistol shot into an old appliance at the murder site all were furnished him by Carter, Redd and Orr, he said.

He confessed to the murders because he had been drugged and beaten and because of implied threats to his former girlfriend, Nita Jean Blackburn, and his mother, Jewel White, Pierce claimed.

When Sheriff Knight arrived from North Carolina, Pierce said, he was prepared to confess to the slaying of two students near Durham, and that Georgia authorities had a "knife" they said was the murder weapon.

Pierce said he received information for the confession through Carter and Orr.

Sheriff Knight said no knife was involved in the slayings. He said he saw no signs of pressure on Pierce from Georgia authorities or anybody else, and that Pierce did not admit to the slayings.

Sheriff Knight was reportedly told by Carter that Pierce was ready to admit the slayings and clear the case.

Pierce said Knight was skeptical, and then Carter told him to either charge Pierce or, "You can go back to North Carolina. You can do like the rest of them from South Carolina or else."

Sheriff Knight said nothing like this happened.

In the interview with Pierce, Pierce said that Jack Orr was in Baxley, Georgia at the time he was being interrogated by outside police officers.

"A lot went on in that jail that people don't know," Pierce said.

When questioned about Pierce's charges, Orr told The State he did not go to Baxley until after Pierce had been charged in three South Carolina cases.

"I wanted to go earlier, but SLED Chief J.P. Strom told me not to go at that time," Orr said. "Strom and other officials were in Baxley on a Tuesday," and he arrived the next day, but did not see Pierce until Friday.

Orr said he was delayed in getting to Baxley because he traveled to four Georgia counties prior to Appling County in order to learn the true facts in Pierce's confessions.

"I did that because I had found out that 'Red' Carter would lie. He took all the credit in the cases," Orr explained.

On Friday, April 20, it was announced in several newspapers that the attorneys for Pierce had filed a notice of intent to appeal with Solicitor R. Kirk McLeod at the Williamsburg County Clerk of Court.

The case was not expected to appear before the Supreme Court before November of 1973, which gave Pierce's attorneys eight months in which to file transcripts of the proceedings and their briefs, but it would be appealed.

This action served to settle the feelings of the people to some degree; however, it was quite obvious that they were still disturbed. The Cuttino case was the topic of discussion everywhere, and the recent events were totally unbelievable.

In the next few days, there was a flurry of letters to The Daily Item posing questions — more and more questions:

The Daily Item - Sumter, SC, Thursday, March 15, 1973

SUMTER SOAPBOX

If the people of Sumter, or our law enforcement officers of Sumter, are sure they have the right man, what are they covering up? We're not sure that the man they have, or have convicted of the Peg Cuttino case is the one. I think — and a lot of other people in the City of Sumter know that the killer is still at large and there is something that is being covered up and we would like to know why.

Mrs. Irene Geddings

The Daily Item — Sumter, SC, Saturday, April 21, 1973

SUMTER SOAPBOX

I would like to know what it is that has got our law enforcement officers covering up about the Peg Cuttino case. I'm sure that the law of Sumter, city and county, are trying to cover up and don't want the people of Sumter to know about it. What is this and just why are they trying to convict a man that is absolutely not guilty? And I'd like to have this question answered.

Hattie Mae Hodge

LETTER TO THE EDITOR

The Daily Item — Sumter, SC, Wednesday, April 25, 1973

QUESTION PUZZLES READER

To the Editor:
First, let me say that I have always looked on Sheriff Parnell as a fine Christian gentleman, doing a wonderful job as a law enforcement officer, as well as witnessing to the people as a servant of God. His Christian leadership will be long remembered, long after he has gone to be with the Lord. This also applies to the Cuttino family, and it is my belief that if Junior Pierce is not the man guilty of Peg Cuttino's death, that the family will surely want the guilty one found.
There are so many rumors that Pierce is not the man responsible, it makes you wonder. If Sheriff Carter, of Appling

County, Georgia, or Sheriff Parnell, or any other person, is guilty of forcing Pierce to confess to something he did not do, then all we can do is pray that God will have mercy on them, for we read in Romans 12:19: "Dearly beloved, avenge not yourselves, but rather give place unto wrath: for it is written, Vengeance is mine; I will repay, saith the Lord."

There is one question that has bothered me since the afternoon of December 18, 1970, when I first heard the report on the radio of the disappearance of Peg Cuttino. Just a few months before this event, I knew of a 15-year-old girl, who lived within three blocks of Peg Cuttino, who left home one morning to go to school, and at ten o'clock, the school called the girl's mother and reported that she was not in school. The mother got busy trying to find her. All of her close friends were contacted, but no one knew her whereabouts.

At seven o'clock that night, the mother called the police. A member of the detective department (I can furnish the name, if it is wanted) came to the home and talked to the mother, and told her that a Missing Persons Bulletin could not be put out under 24 to 48 hours after the girl left home. I was there at the time and I asked "Why?", but until this day, I have not had the answer.

Will someone please tell me how the Cuttinos could get a nationwide bulletin out on their daughter in about an hour's time? Was it because this girl came from a social, political famiy and that other girl from just an ordinary, hard-working family? After all, God loves the poor girl just as much as He does the rich, and the mother of the poor girl loves her daughter just as much as the rich mother loves hers.

Should the law enforcement division make any difference in the two girls, not knowing if either of the two was still alive or not?

Will someone please clear this up for me, for it has been a question that has puzzled me since December 1970?

Mrs. Nettie Geddings

The Daily Item — Sumter, SC, Monday, May 7, 1973

COMMENT

Now that Pierce has been declared guilty, why hasn't Mr. Parnell revealed the mysterious evidence which he claimed was so important during the trial? In my opinion, the so-called trial was a mockery of justice and an insult to the intelligence of Sumter citizens. The inefficiency which characterized the entire case is inexcusable. It is time the egotistical law officers concentrate on finding the real murderer rather than trying to convince intelligent adults that Pierce can be in Georgia and Sumter at the same time.

Cal Green

On May 16, a paid "Wanted" ad appeared in The Daily Item that read as follows:

WANTED: Information leading to the arrest and conviction of persons involved in the Cuttino murder. Write "Box P-16" Care of Sumter Daily Item.

It was apparent that the citizens of Sumter County were not satisfied with the results in this case. They continued to contact certain public officials, which they still had some trust in, and asked that they do something.

Meanwhile, Junior Pierce was tried in Aiken for the murder of North Augusta baby-sitter Ann Goodwin, and was convicted of that crime also.

Pierce's mother, Mrs. Jewel White, was arrested during that trial and charged with trying to smuggle two homemade handcuff keys to her son in an attempt to help him escape.

Pierce was sentenced to a life term on the conviction of murder, to a life term for burglary, and to ten years for larceny, all in connection with the Goodwin murder. The sentences were to be served concurrently.

Sumter County citizens, as well as the entire state's population (all who were interested — and most of them were) watched and followed the events as Pierce was again convicted, claiming all the time that he was "not guilty". Again, there was little or no evidence other than his confession — which was not signed — and, in fact, Pierce had at this time been given an opportunity to sign, but had refused to sign it. Again, the testimony of the officers who had allegedly heard his confession convicted him.

CHAPTER FIVE

THE CONCERNED CITIZENS COMMITTEE
MAY 29, 1973

Then, on Tuesday, May 29, 1973, The Daily Item announced a new development that encouraged the people of Sumter and Sumter County, and set off another baffling and dramatic set of events.

In the article entitled "Coroner Asks for Reopening of Cuttino Case", Sumter County Coroner Howard J. Parnell was reported to have announced on Monday night that he felt that he had enough new information to warrant reopening the investigation into the death of Margaret "Peg" Cuttino.

It had been nearly three months since Pierce had been convicted and the conviction was in the process of being appealed to the South Carolina Supreme Court.

Coroner Parnell had called a meeting of interested citizens in the case to make his plea for a new investigation on Monday night at his funeral home on Church Street. Also present were Capt. Lou Degenhardt, of the Sumter Police Department, and Chief Investigator Tom McJunkin, of the Sumter County Sheriff's Department.

"I feel people in this county are dissatisfied with what has taken place," Parnell said. "They feel like, if Pierce did it, it should have been proven better. They feel it should have been handled better... I'm not here to criticize Sheriff (I. Byrd) Parnell. I'm not here to criticize anybody... but, I do feel that the case needs to be re-investigated," he told the group.

On Tuesday morning, when interviewed by Item staff writer Susan Tiede, Coroner Parnell cited three more reasons why he felt a new investigation was needed:

"I have felt that the Cuttino family was too closely related to the investigation, for one. Secondly, I felt that the separate investigative divisions were so dependent on each other that they overlooked some facts (because of their dependence). And third, I feel that the public's dissatisfaction with the case indicates their (the public's) lack of faith in the court system and in the general system of government."

The coroner reported that City Police Chief L.W. Griffin had offered his cooperation in the case. "The Police Department will work with the Sheriff's Department and SLED to develop any possible new leads in the case," Chief Griffin told The Daily Item.

The Coroner added that Dr. Joel S. Sexton, the forensic pathologist who performed the autopsy on the girl, and SLED Chief J.P. Strom, had indicated their willingness to cooperate with an additional investigation into the death of the girl.

Sumter County Chief Investigator McJunkin said, "The position of the Sheriff's Department has been and always will be to conduct any investigation into new leads that come up."

Coroner Parnell said he was not able at the time to reveal any new facts he may have about the case, but indicated he felt they were sufficient to reopen the investigation into the girl's death.

He added that he planned to hold onto the information he has compiled on the case until it is complete, at which time it would be turned over to Chief Griffin.

"I'm not a professional investigator," the Coroner said, "so my sole purpose is to get everybody back together and work the thing again..."

"I'm the one who's had the pressure put on me," Coroner Parnell continued. "I'm the one who's been harassed... People think of 'coroner' and they think of death and investigations into deaths. They call me up and say 'Why haven't you done something about this?'... For $4,800 a year, I'd resign my job before I put up with another week of this."

The Coroner said he has been investigating the case for nearly a month, and assured those present he had not used any county tax money for that purpose.

"I just think the people would feel better if they knew something was being done. If anyone thinks I've overstepped my boundaries as Coroner, I'll resign," the Coroner concluded.

On Wednesday, May 30, The State newspaper also carried an article by staff writer Jack Truluck. Truluck's article was entitled "Citizen's Group 'Running Scared'".

"A self-appointed citizens committee, which is informally investigating the December, 1970, slaying of 13-year-old Margaret 'Peg' Cuttino, is running scared," the article said.

"On the one hand, they feel if the murderer or murderers of Peg Cuttino are still free and walking around in Sumter County, some of their members, and others, may be in danger...

"The citizens group, which has pledged to continue the investigation, is led by Sumter Coroner Howard Parnell. The group is handicapped by lack of funds and lack of official status.

"Parnell says the committee has received new leads and information regarding the slaying. He says the committee, unlike official police agencies, has no funds to pursue them.

"Some members of the committee have expressed lack of confidence in the law enforcement agencies which investigated the Cuttino slaying.

"At a meeting Monday night, the group's third, representatives of the Sumter Sheriff's Department and the Sumter Police Department were in attendance.

"(Coroner) Parnell said the Georgia murders for which Pierce had been convicted could be put into a pattern. I don't believe this was Pierce's style of murder. 'It could be very possible he did it, it could be very possible he didn't do it, too. The citizens of Sumter County want some answers. They deserve them, too.'

"Coroner Parnell, seeking assurance from Sumter Sheriff I. Byrd Parnell (no relation) that his office would reinvestigate, got no assurance that it would."

The balance of the article was basically the same as the one in The Daily Item on Tuesday, but between the two articles, they had sparked a new hope in the hearts of the people and revealed the existence of the citizens committee, which most of the people were not aware of at the time. Howard Parnell quickly became the people's champion, and everyone was singing his praises for his courageous leadership of the citizens committee. At last, something was going to be done.

A meeting was called of all the departments and agencies of law enforcement, at which Coroner Parnell would present his new-found evidence. The date for the meeting was set for Wednesday morning, June 6, 1973.

But to the disappointment of many, the meeting ended abruptly, after a short time, when Coroner Parnell walked out of the meeting angrily saying, "I'm through!... I'm through!... Do what you want with it!"

The local news media was not invited to the meeting, but Item staff writer Susan Tiede contacted Coroner Parnell later and he further qualified his statement, saying that he was "far from through" with his investigation of the case, but added, "I walked into a hostile group... I'll never meet with them by myself again."

Sheriff I. Byrd Parnell denied that there was any hostility against the Coroner. "There were no hard feelings. I even got up and shook his hand when he came in."

"He had no new leads," Sheriff Parnell said. "And we reassured him if he had anything, we would all cooperate and help him in any way we could... We've answered everything he wanted to know so far. I'm more than willing to do this. I'll meet with him at any time."

Police Chief L.W. Griffin, Solicitor R. Kirk McLeod and SLED Chief J.P. Strom all made similar statements.

The meeting was also attended by Lt. George Fender of SLED and detective magazine freelance writer Jack Orr, who was reportedly to review any facts the Coroner was prepared to present and answer any questions he might have concerning the investigation of the case.

Orr explained that he came with Chief Strom at the request of Sheriff Parnell.

"Sheriff Parnell told him (the Coroner) I had come because of my knowledge of the case," Orr explained further. "The Sheriff said I possibly knew as much about the man (Pierce) as he (the Sheriff) himself knew, possibly more than anyone else."

When asked why other reporters who had interviewed Pierce and Georgia officials were also not invited to "shed light" on the situation, Orr explained he had, to his knowledge, spent more time on the case than any other reporter, and is the only reporter to whom Pierce confessed several murders.

Orr said that, though he was by then employed with the Richland County Treasurer's office, he still did freelance writing. He was not, he said, planning on writing further stories on this case.

The Coroner maintained that he did have what he considered to be new information, new leads and legitimate questions concerning the investigation of the case, but, as the case was at that time under appeal, he was not at liberty to elaborate publicly.

He added that it was "quite possible" that all of his questions about the case would have been answered, had he been included in the investigative meetings and had he been given copies of official reports on the case.

"Let me put it this way," he said, "everyone else was invited to the meetings. I may have been welcomed, but I would have had to go through the door or the window to get in."

Sheriff Parnell maintained that the Coroner was welcome to attend the meetings, and would have had access to the reports, if only he had so requested.

The Coroner further explained that he may not have had what was felt to be "new evidence", and never claimed he did, but he said he did have leads he thought were not followed through on... information he felt was new and pertinent to the case, and legitimate questions he felt were left unanswered.

"The way I understand government, the people who elected me — that's my boss... I've gotten maybe 400-500 telephone calls since Monday night (May 28), people asking me questions that I, as their elected Coroner, can't answer."

He emphasized that he was not out to defend Pierce, but merely to become convinced that everything that could have been done in the case had been done.

If he became so convinced, the Coroner said, he would set a date when the people would be able to know the true story.

"I'm tired now," he said. "I feel like I've been humiliated at this point... I'll just leave it to the public. If they think what I'm doing is correct, I know they'll indicate it to me in some way... If they don't think it's right, I'll resign."

EDITORIAL

The Daily Item, Friday, June 8, 1973

OPINION:
IMPASSE CLOUDING CUTTINO INQUIRY

The controversial Cuttino murder case took on a bizarre note Wednesday with the walkout from a meeting by Coroner Howard Parnell.

Coroner Parnell claimed a "hostile atmosphere" at the meeting convinced him that he was getting nowhere in his efforts to open reinvestigation of the case. The law enforcement authorities maintain that they're willing to cooperate, but must have some facts to justify their consideration of reinvestigating the murder of Margaret "Peg" Cuttino.

Whatever the motives or circumstances surrounding the disagreements between Coroner Parnell and the law enforcement authorities, one thing is clear: a prolonging of this situation without anything substantive coming out of it is unhealthy. It creates suspicion in the public's mind as to the Coroner's motives, and doubt about the authenticity of his so-called new leads and additional information that would warrant reopening the case. At the same time, those who choose to degrade the law enforcement authorities and who harbor the feelings that they're uncooperative conspirators who sent an innocent man up the river also are reinforcing their opinions.

It would seem to us that the burden is on the Coroner. He created this situation by stating at a meeting on May 28 that he felt he had enough new information to warrant reopening the investigation, but that the information could not be revealed at the present time. He explained that he planned to hold onto the information he has compiled on the case until it is complete, at which time it will be turned over to Sumter Police Chief L.W. Griffin.

There seems to be a slight obstacle to this procedure, however. Chief Griffin was present at the Wednesday meeting and a member of the group that Coroner Parnell characterized as "hostile".

If we are to take all this at face value, it means the Coroner is unwilling to communicate with the local authorities in pursuit of satisfying his inquiry because of their alleged hostility.

So what next? Is the apparent impasse between the Coroner and law enforcement officials to go on indefinitely while rumor and suspicion run rampant in this community, to the detriment of both parties?

To repeat: in our judgement, the initiative for resolving this unwholesome situation should come from the Coroner. Some concrete facts, if they exist, have got to be laid on the line sooner or later — preferably sooner.

In that same issue of The Daily Item was the first of a number of Letters to the Editor addressing themselves to the Coroner's recent actions:

LETTER TO THE EDITOR

The Daily Item — Sumter, SC, Friday, June 8, 1973

CORONER PARNELL SUPPORTED

To the Editor:

Congratulations to Sumter County Coroner Howard Parnell for his investigation of the Cuttino case. It is the general feeling of people I have talked with that this investigation should continue. I hope that the different segments of law enforcement can see the necessity of joining the Coroner in this investigation. This is a matter that concerns the whole of Sumter County — there is too much unrest over this case. If, in fact, Junior Pierce did commit the murder, then there is no danger in the outcome of a new investigation.

News media have reported that the Coroner has used no county funds for this purpose. Why? Is he not allowed to use funds on any investigation he deems necessary? If necessary, I think the citizens of Sumter County will support this investigation with donations, but we do pay taxes to this county and in my opinion this should not be necessary.

R.J. Williams

LETTER TO THE EDITOR

The Daily Item — Sumter, SC, Monday, June 11, 1973

PATIENCE IS NEEDED

To the Editor:
On behalf of the Concerned Citizens Committee of Sumter County, I would like to comment on the editorial "Impasse Clouding Cuttino Inquiry".
Your paragraph, "It would seem to us that the burden is on the Coroner. He created this situation by stating at a meeting on May 28 that he felt he had enough new information to warrant reopening the investigation, but that he planned to hold onto the information he has compiled on the case until it is complete, at which time it will be turned over to Sumter Police Chief L.W. Griffin," should answer your question.
The word "COMPLETE" is very important. We acknowledge that our Coroner, Howard Parnell, is a very smart, courageous young man; but we think it is unfair to expect him to do, alone, in a period of a few days, what many men, in fact, teams of them, have been unable to do in many months. We want to assure you, and our concerned citizens, that he is working very diligently, but we must consider legal technicalities and the possibilities that premature releases of facts could prove disastrous.
We therefore solicit your earnest prayers, moral support, patience, and confidence in Coroner Parnell. Our committee has prayed for God's direction in its activities — that we be given wisdom, courage, and strength to do what is right. We acknowledge God's guidance from day to day, as the case progresses, and with His help we shall succeed.

Carrie B. LeNoir

LETTER TO THE EDITOR

The Daily Item — Sumter, SC, Monday, June 11, 1973

CORONER COMMENDED

To the Editor:
I would like to congratulate Coroner Howard Parnell for his stand in the Cuttino Case. It would seem that Mr. Parnell made only one mistake — he should never have entered that door for the meeting (last) Wednesday.
What are the reasons the Coroner cannot sit down peacefully and meet with these men? It seems from the reports that the

meeting was hostile. Can we blame the Coroner for walking out?

I only hope that Coroner Parnell has the stamina to continue his investigation, despite the fact the Sheriff says he has no new leads. Is the Sheriff clairvoyant, since he evidently hasn't seen what the Coroner has on this case?

Mary Mathis

The Daily Item — Sumter, SC, Wednesday, June 13, 1973

*CORONER'S PROBE SUPPORT VOICED
BY CONCERNED CITIZENS*

by Tom Prewett, Item Staff Writer

Mrs. Carrie LeNoir and two other women, Mrs. Nettie Geddings and Mrs. Jean Sieders, representing the Concerned Citizens Committee, appeared before the Sumter County Commission Tuesday to voice support for Sumter County Coroner Howard Parnell's investigation of the slaying of Margaret "Peg" Cuttino.

"I have asked God's help in this matter, and I know that I'm doing what's right," said Mrs. LeNoir, who acted as spokesman for the three-woman delegation.

Mrs. LeNoir, who claims she and her husband saw the Cuttino girl accompanied by two unidentified youths in their country store at Horatio on December 19, 1970, the day after she was allegedly slain by William "Junior" Pierce, said: "We were involved in this and I'm convinced that I have to give my support to the investigation."

According to Mrs. LeNoir, an estimated 265 persons have signed a petition supporting the investigation undertaken by Coroner Parnell after Pierce was convicted of the murder by a Kingstree jury early in March.

She said that since the investigation was begun, individual contributions ranging from a few dollars to $500 have been donated to help finance the expenses incurred by Coroner Parnell.

Speaking of the Coroner, Mrs. LeNoir said, "Howard is keeping a very open mind in connection with the investigation, and is just trying to determine whether Pierce did or did not kill the Cuttino girl.

"We feel that county funds should be contributed for this purpose and that is why we are here today to ask for funds in the amount of $500. We are out of funds," Mrs. LeNoir said.

When asked by Commissioner James P. Nettles what the

funds would be used for, Mrs. LeNoir replied that they would pay for long distance telephone calls, trips and any other expenses connected with the investigation.

She noted that the continuation of the investigation of the Cuttino girl's death by Coroner Parnell is being watched with interest throughout the state. She also said that interest is spreading throughout the nation.

The request for funds was received by the County Commission as information. Action on the request was deferred pending referral of the request to Sumter County Attorney G. Werber Bryan for further consideration.

CHAPTER SIX

SOLICITOR R. KIRK MCLEOD
DEFENDS LAW ENFORCEMENT OFFICERS

MAY 29, 1973

The Daily Item — Sumter, SC, Wednesday, June 13, 1973

SOLICITOR ISSUES STATEMENT ON PIERCE CASE

Third Judicial Circuit Solicitor R. Kirk McLeod, concerned over what he termed "much unfounded talk... about the William J. Pierce murder case", released a statement this morning.

"It has always been my policy not to discuss publicly cases in which I was involved either directly or indirectly — but I am now making an exception because of the injustice being done to the very persons and agencies who are sworn to uphold the law and to protect the people and their property and to bring to trial those who have been accused of crime.

"It is unfortunate that Coroner Parnell has chosen the news media as a forum to air and vent his venomous and foundless accusations and innuendos, and to purposely avoid the proper judicial and investigative channels — so it seems proper, at this time, to at least respond in the news media."

Solicitor McLeod further stated that the facts of the case would not be discussed as they were presented in open court. The trial, McLeod said, was the result of "the most exhaustive and thorough investigation in the annals of South Carolina law enforcement."

The Solicitor highly praised those members of the law enforcement agencies involved in the investigation, the jury and Pierce's court-appointed lawyers.

"Normally, this (the jury's guilty verdict) would have been the end of a case, except for appeal to the Supreme Court, which is pending in this case," the Solicitor continues. "But, what happened in this particular case? Mr. Howard Parnell, duly elected Coroner, has taken it upon himself to second guess the aforementioned law enforcement officers and agencies, the presiding judge, the jury, and even Mr. Pierce's own attorneys, and announces to the news media that he is not satisfied with the handling of the Pierce case, and that he has certain information and leads and is conducting his own personal investigation. He wouldn't divulge any of these to anyone — including the news

media — but called a meeting with the law enforcement agencies for Wednesday, June 7, at 10 a.m. in the Law Enforcement Center.

"Everyone invited was there at 10 a.m. except Coroner Parnell, who called the meeting. After numerous telephone calls by Chief Griffin, Coroner Parnell finally arrived at 11 a.m., swinging on to his brief case, which I assumed contained his 'new evidence'. After searching through his brief case for some time, he produced nothing in the way of facts or new evidence and, to our amazement, not even any new rumors. He was advised that if he had any facts whatsoever, to present them and that they would be thoroughly investigated. He was further advised that if he had any facts or new evidence which was being withheld, then he was obstructing justice. With this he left in a huff, dragging his brief case behind him..."

The Solicitor cited the state law defining the duties of a coroner and continued, "Under the law, a coroner has no authority or duty to conduct an investigation into the death of a person after the inquest and trial... The Coroner has stated that he is not a lawyer, a doctor or an investigator. What, then, are his qualifications...? It would appear... that his only admitted qualifications are that of an embalmer and undertaker, and at this moment it seems that perhaps he used his talents on the alleged facts he has supposedly uncovered and refuses to release and has enbalmed and buried them.

"In closing, let me state that in law enforcement it is not only our duty to investigate, bring to trial and prosecute — but to see that everyone gets a fair trial and to protect the rights of the innocent. This we attempted to do to the best of our ability. I will never attempt to convict a person whom I believe to be innocent — but, by the same token, I will, to the best of my ability, attempt to convict those I believe to be guilty. I did in this case."

The Solicitor concluded by saying any new facts or leads would be thoroughly investigated.

<u>LETTER TO THE EDITOR</u>

The Daily Item — Sumter, SC, Thursday, June 14, 1973

CORONER'S FIGHT BACKED

To the Editor:
Coroner Parnell has stated that he will leave it to the public to indicate whether they think he did what was correct in the Cuttino case.

1. I do not personally know any individual involved.

2. *I have served under Judge Rosen, and watched Solicitor McLeod in his vigorous presentation of a case.*

3. *If evidence was produced in the Kingstree trial during which no media of information was present, then that evidence should be produced now, as it is still inconceivable that the jury could have found for guilty on the basis of what the news reported.*

4. *The fact that only friends and employees came to testify for Pierce does not negate the facts that official time records proved him to be elsewhere.*

5. *The fact that he or relatives may be below normal in intelligence do not prove him guilty.*

6. *The fact that store keepers in a small community felt honor bound to make a statement to the press that was not allowed in court does not lend credence to the official statement that all evidence was pursued.*

7. *Gossip in the community has no part in the allegations, but has left our community wondering what really did go on in the courtroom in Kingstree. Evidence before that jury should have more to do with the verdict than unsubstantiated evidence from a Sheriff in a jail-cell interview.*

We support Coroner Parnell in his fight to get the complete truth before the public, and reflect the desires of many people who do not know to whom they can go to see that justice in our courts is still available.

Mrs. Barbara Ardis

Thursday, June 14, Solicitor McLeod again assailed the Coroner on a local radio broadcast, in which he also accused the news media in general, and The Daily Item in particular, of not publishing certain facts that came to light in the trial at Kingstree, and of not reporting the Pierce trial fairly.

Again, the case began to attract statewide attention. The State newspaper in Columbia carried a lengthy article on Friday, June 15, entitled "Cuttino Case Action Criticized".

Staff writer Jack Truluck told of Solicitor McLeod's criticism of newspapers and Sumter County Coroner Howard Parnell and carried quotes from the Solicitor's statement to the Editor of The Daily Item.

"Coroner Parnell said he had told Chief Griffin the night before that he would not be present at the meeting and he was to have notified Sheriff Parnell," the article said.

He said he felt he was fortunate not to have given them any information at the meeting. Referring to Orr, the detective magazine story writer, "What if I had laid out some real hard facts in front of that man?", Coroner Parnell said.

Solicitor McLeod complained to The Daily Item that his remarks, as contained in his statement on June 13 were taken out of context in the story that The Daily Item had run based on that statement.

Feelings were tense on both sides, and the ball was now in The Daily Item Editor Hubert D. Osteen, Jr.'s court.

What would he do?

First, he decided to run the Solicitor's statement, in its entirety, and then he felt obliged to make a direct response, as Editor, to the Solicitor and his accusations. The articles will be self-explanatory.

LETTER TO THE EDITOR

The Daily Item — Sumter, SC, Friday, June 15, 1973

SOLICITOR RESPONDS TO CORONER'S ACTIONS

(Editor's Note: Because R. Kirk McLeod, Solicitor of the Third Judicial Circuit, has complained to The Item that his remarks as contained in the following statement were taken out of context in a news story which appeared in the Wednesday, June 13, issue of The Item on the front page, we are reprinting it in full. It is this newspaper's contention that the remarks were not taken out of context and that the pertinent and salient points of Mr. McLeod's statement were used in the story in the interest of brevity, clarity and conciseness. However, we will let the reader compare both The Item's story and Mr. McLeod's following statement and judge for himself whether his contention is valid.)

To the Editor:

There has been much unfounded talk, and some reporting of it, about the William J. Pierce murder case, recently tried in Williamsburg County, which tends to discredit and degrade our law enforcement agencies. It has always been my policy not to discuss publicly cases in which I was involved either directly or indirectly — but I am now making an exception because of the injustice being done to the very persons and agencies who are sworn to uphold the law and to protect the people and their property, and to bring to trial those who have been accused of crime. My job brings me in daily contact with these gentlemen of the law — and I know whereof I speak. It is unfortunate that Coroner Parnell has chosen the news media as a forum to air and vent his venomous and foundless accusations and innuendos, and to purposely avoid the proper judicial and investigative channels — so it seems proper at this time to at least respond in the news media. You will note that, at the outset, I referred to the case under discussion as the Pierce case — because William J. Pierce was indicted, tried and convicted — not Representative and Mrs.

James Cuttino, nor their daughter. Of course, it is obvious why the news media refer to the (Cuttino Case) even though they know the heartache and pain they are rekindling.

The facts of the Pierce case will not be here discussed — they were presented in open court by the law enforcement officers and other witnesses, through me as your Solicitor and through the attorneys representing Mr. Pierce. Thousands and thousands of man hours went into the investigation of this case. Hundreds and hundreds of witnesses and suspects were interviewed and every lead checked out minutely. The law enforcement agencies assisting were the Federal Bureau of Investigation, the Sheriff's Department of Sumter County, and the Sumter City Police Department, with able assistance from the United States Air force. Medical experts were called in for their assistance and evaluation. In my humble opinion, I feel that the most exhaustive and thorough investigation in the annals of South Carolina Law Enforcement was conducted, completed and brought to the proper disposition. The gentlemen heading these departments are known and respected nationally for their ability and performance. Chief J.P. "Pete" Strom, of the South Carolina Law Enforcement Division, has held that position for twenty years and has held the presidency of every state and national law enforcement body of which he is a member.

Sheriff I. Byrd Parnell, who has held that position for twenty years, has held the presidency of every state law enforcement agency and is presently First Vice President of the National Sheriff's Association, and this year will be the President of that organization. Chief Leslie W. Griffin, of the Sumter City Police Department, has held that position for some five and one-half years, and is presently heading the South Carolina Police Chief's Association. He is also Vice-President of the South Carolina Police Chief's Association, and has held positions of leadership in the other various law enforcement agencies in the state. All of the officers working under these gentlemen in this case are high caliber and well-trained officers. Incidentally, each of these gentlemen is a graduate of the FBI National Academy and other Law Enforcement Schools. I characterized these gentlemen before the jury in Williamsburg County as "the best law enforcement team that could be assembled anywhere in these United States". Although, there is no question in my mind that Mr. Pierce could have received a fair and impartial trial at the hands of a Sumter County Jury, out of an abundance of precaution, and to avoid any possible prejudice against Mr. Pierce that may have been caused by the news media and other strong feelings in the community, the case was transferred and trial held in Williamsburg County which is also in the Third

Judicial Circuit. There a venire of 75 qualified jurors was called and were thoroughly examined and questioned by the eminent and able presiding judge, The Honorable Louis Rosen, and by Mr. Pierce, through his attorneys, and by the State through me. I am sure that Mr. Pierce's attorneys will agree with me when I state that a more conscientious, intelligent and educated jury could not have been selected anywhere. Mr. Pierce was represented by three very able and experienced attorneys, Mr. Joseph T. McElveen, Jr., of Sumter, Mr James M. Connor and Mr. William E. Jenkinson, III, of Kingstree. These gentlemen were appointed by the court and worked hundreds of hours in preparation and trial of the case — without compensation. They did an outstanding job in defense of Mr. Pierce and brought both credit and distinction, not only to themselves, but to the law profession. They couldn't have done a better job if they had been paid an enormous fee. They examined the State's witnesses thoroughly and very ably put up every possible defense they could in Mr. Pierce's behalf, including alibi witnesses, a handwriting expert and medical testimony. All of the attorneys summed up their thoughts and interpretation of the law and evidence before the jury and judge Rosen instructed and charged the jury the law as it applied to murder. The jury retired and deliberated for some time and returned a unanimous verdict of "Guilty."

Normally, this would have been the end of a case, except for appeal to the Supreme Court, which is pending in this case, but what happened in this particular case? Mr. Howard Parnell, duly elected coroner, has taken it upon himself to second guess the aforementioned law enforcement officers and agencies, the Presiding Judge, the jury, and even Mr. Pierce's own attorneys, and announces to the news media that he is not satisfied with the handling of the Pierce case and that he has certain information and leads and is conducting his own personal investigation. He wouldn't divulge any of these facts to anyone — including the news media — but called a meeting with the law enforcement agencies for Wednesday, June 6, at 10 a.m., in the Law Enforcement Center. Everyone invited was there at 10 a.m. — except Coroner Parnell, who called the meeting. After numerous telephone calls by Chief Griffin, Coroner Parnell finally arrived at 11 a.m., swinging on to his brief case, which I assumed contained his "new evidence". After searching through his brief case for some time, he produced nothing in the way of facts or new evidence, and to our amazement, not even any new rumors. He was advised that if he had any facts or new evidence which was being withheld, then he was obstructing justice. With this, he left in a huff, dragging his brief case behind him, and stating that he was "through with it". However, I have since read where he states that he met with hostile persons and that he was continuing with his so-called "'investigation'.

What are the duties of a coroner? Referring to the Code of Laws for South Carolina, Section 17-91: "Whenever a body is found dead and an investigation or inquest is deemed advisable, the Coroner shall go to the body and examine the witnesses most likely to be able to explain the cause of death, take their testimony in writing and decide for himself whether there ought to be a trial, or whether blame probably attaches to any living person for the death, and if so he shall proceed to summon a jury and hold a formal inquest as required by law.' Under the law a Coroner has no authority or duty to conduct an investigation into the death of a person after the inquest and trial. In the Pierce case under discussion, an inquest was not held for some two years after the death, and then only when one was demanded by the law enforcement officers. The Coroner has stated that he is not a lawyer, a doctor or an investigator. What, then are his qualifications to supersede all of the law enforcement agencies and judicial departments heretofore mentioned to conduct an investigation? He further states that he did not attend the preliminary hearing; he did not appear before the grand jury; he did not attend the trial in Kingstree; and he did not attend the hearing on the motion for a new trial here in Sumter. It would appear then that his only admitted qualifications are that of an embalmer and undertaker, and at this moment it seems that perhaps he used his talents on the alleged facts he has supposedly uncovered and refuses to release and has embalmed and buried them.

In closing, let me state that in law enforcement it is not only our duty to investigate, bring to trial and prosecute — but to see that everyone gets a fair trial and to protect the rights of the innocent. This we attempted to do to the best of our ability. I will never attempt to convict a person whom I believe to be innocent — but by the same token I will, to the best of my ability, attempt to convict those I believe to be guilty. I did in this case.

If anyone has any facts or new evidence which would affect this or any other case in this jurisdiction, it is their duty to present them to the proper authorities and I can assure you that they will be thoroughly investigated, both physically and scientifically.

R. Kirk McLeod
Solicitor
Third Judicial Circuit

CHAPTER SEVEN

ITEM EDITOR, HUBERT D. OSTEEN, JR., DEFENDS NEWS MEDIA

JUNE 15, 1973

The Daily Item — Sumter, SC, Friday, June 15, 1973

ITEM EDITOR REPLIES TO SOLICITOR'S CHARGES

Hubert D. Osteen, Jr., editor of The Sumter Daily Item, issued a statement this morning in response to an interview with Third Judicial Circuit Solicitor R. Kirk McLeod, aired Thursday over a local radio station.

During the interview, Solicitor McLeod accused the news media in general and The Item in particular of not publishing certain facts that came to light in the March trial of William "Junior" Pierce in Kingstree.

Pierce, accused of eight murders across the southeast, was convicted in March of the murder of 13-year-old Margaret "Peg" Cuttino of Sumter.

Osteen's statement follows:

"To borrow a quote from Solicitor R. Kirk McLeod's repertoire, it is unfortunate that he has chosen the news media as a forum to air and vent his venomous and foundless accusations and innuendos.

"Solicitor McLeod went on a local radio station yesterday and conducted a monologue -- or rather a harangue -- that consisted of unsubstantiated charges and opinionated mumbo-jumbo directed against this newspaper and it's coverage of certain news events, specifically the Pierce trial and subsequent related developments.

"The solicitor is using a tactic, which the public should be made aware of, that has been employed by every prosecuting attorney -- and any other public official for that matter -- since time immemorial: when the going gets tough, blame the news media.

"What's happening here is that some people in this community are questioning the handling of the Pierce case by the law enforcement authorities and the solicitor. This is displeasing to the solicitor, who expects the public and the news media to be properly obedient. When public dissatisfaction is aired by The Item, the solicitor immediately indicts The Item, using such familiar phrases as 'I was quoted out of context,' or his statement

was 'altered to fit their (The Item's) own purposes' or 'if the newspaper had reported the facts as brought out in the trial, no one would have had anything to say about it.'

"The last charge is really the nub of the matter. Solicitor McLeod keeps claiming that the reporting of the Pierce trial was inadequate or incomplete. It's interesting to note that the accounts of the trial which appeared in The Charleston News and Courier, The State and The Sumter Daily Item were substantially the same, but were written by different persons and edited by different editors. I suppose what we'll hear next from the solicitor is that the three newspapers' editors all got on the phone and decided on a common version of the trial. Of course this is nonsense, as are the charges made by the solicitor impugning the integrity of our reporter and our newspaper.

"The Item's account of the Pierce trial held in Kingstree in March were accurate, short of running a complete transcript of the court proceedings. If there were pertinent facts left out of our stories on the trial, the solicitor had ample recourse when the trial occurred and still has now; simply write down these missing facts or refer us to them in the court transcript and we'll publish them, verbatim if necessary.

"It's time for the solicitor to put HIS facts where his mouth is. Otherwise, he should refrain from making accusations and insinuations that have no substance.

"The Item is trying to be of service to it's readers, by keeping them informed. We have just as many dedicated people in our news room as the solicitor likes to brag about in the law enforcement field, and they take their work just as seriously. When a public official starts braying about a reporter's performance and insinuates that there is a deliberate attempt to withhold valid news from the public, then such statements should be characterized for what they are: bunko, bull, deceit and obfuscation."

The Daily Item — Sumter, SC, Saturday, June 16, 1973

LETTER TO THE EDITOR

READERS DEFEND CORONER

To the Editor:

We, a few of the members of the younger generation in Sumter, have read many letters supporting and condemning Coroner Parnell's actions concerning the Cuttino case. We feel that our view is important considering that Peg Cuttino was of our generation and a close friend of many. We have watched the *progress of the case, and to us, it is very disheartening. We feel that of a charge such as murder, on such flimsy, contrived evidence. The South has always been pictured as small town with crooked sheriffs, etc. Before this trial we felt this was unfair and cliche. Now, it seems that the law of Sumter is filling it's prepared shoes.*

We read the report from Solicitor McLeod and that really seemed to confirm our beliefs. The whole air of the statement was one of a frightened child trying to hide something. He is putting down the coroner for a well-justified and needed investigation. If Chief Griffin, Solicitor McLeod and the rest of the law present (including Jack Orr) at that meeting would leave Mr. Parnell alone and let him do his work, maybe he could get some new facts, because we are sure there is much more to the case than meets the public's eye.

Also, why should the coroner give all his information to the very same men who did such a great cover-up job before? Perhaps they would like another chance? If we may quote the Honorable Solicitor McLeod, "It is unfortunate that Coroner Parnell has chosen the news media as a forum to air and vent his venomous and foundless accusations, etc." Who is calling who "venomous," Solicitor? Also, where would we be without the press? Also, why was a detective writer asked to be present at the meeting and not the news media? You, sir, would probably be a lot better off as would a few other law officials in Sumter without the press. We feel Coroner Parnell was right in avoiding the proper judicial and investigative channels," considering their previous record on this case.

We want to state that this view is not that of all the young people, but we would like to see other views. We back Coroner Parnell wholeheartedly and we wish that others would too. We are not putting down all of Sumter's law officials, maybe just a chosen few who have been at it too long and acquired too much power. It is time that the people of Sumter wake up and take a look around them. There is a lot to see, the good and the bad. Sure, everybody talks about what should be done, but who does it?

How many of you ever attended a city council meeting or called a law officer and thanked them for saving a life even if it isn't your own? Don't just sit at your supper table and talk. Take a stand, Sumter. If you agree with us, then say it. Look into this case, and take a stand. You may think that it doesn't make any difference. Well, consider this -- the real murderer is still loose, and his next victim could be you or someone near to you. Also, consider you could be the next victim of Sumter's powerhouse.

The Young Citizens Group of Sumter

(Forty names appear on this letter, among them the following: K. Hood, M. Hood, Gail Moore, Randy Bertram, Matty Atkinson, C. Long, Roseann Dennis, Cathy Ross, C. Gregory, C. Brown and S. Topp. Space prevents listing the complete list.)

The Daily Item - Sumter, SC, Monday, June 18, 1973

LETTER TO THE EDITOR

MORE DETAILS DEMANDED

To the Editor:

In Wednesday afternoon's Sumter Daily Item, there were statements made by Mr. McLeod which were totally uncalled for against our coroner, Mr. Howard Parnell, and I think that a lot of other citizens feel the same as we do about these statements. What is Mr. McLeod and the other law enforcement officers trying to hide and who are they covering up for, it surely must be someone from the way they are fighting against the coroner. Why wasn't this trial held in Sumter where the murder took place? We do not personally feel that any trial should be held out of the county in which the crime was committed. We are all for Mrs. Ardis' s article in Thursday's Item about the dishonesty in this city and county.

Mr. McLeod made a statement that the coroner did not have the authority to investigate any death which is not caused from natural causes, and I do believe the Cuttino case was not a natural cause. If our sheriff and law enforcement officers are not covering up some information, why are they trying to stop the coroner's investigation before he begins? He has not been given the chance to prove anything. If the judge thought the witnesses for Pierce were lying, why didn't he charge them for perjury?

We are going to fight against our ring in this city and county and try to break the hands which are tied together. This circle has to be broken some way and the citizens are going to do it by fighting together. We want the truth and we feel we have not been given the truth.

Mr. and Mrs. J. Moore

Meanwhile, "Junior" Pierce was being held in Central Correctional Institution of the South Carolina Department of Corrections, in Columbia. He still faced trial for the murder of Cathy Jo Anderson, of West Columbia, and of filling station operator James L. Sires, of Beaufort, South Carolina.

Coroner Parnell, true to his word, continued his investigation into the case.

On Tuesday, June 19, he traveled to Columbia and met with Pierce for more than three hours.

The following question and answer appeared in the popular and highly used "INFORMATION PLEASE" column of *The Item.* Citizens may call in their questions and *The Item* staff attempt to find and print the answer for them.

The Daily Item — Sumter, SC, Thursday, June 21, 1973

INFORMATION PLEASE

> *Q.* *I, along with many, many more South Carolinians, would like to know if the Cuttino case will be reopened to check out the new leads that Coroner Parnell has?* *(M.N.G.)*
>
> *A.* *The case is on appeal now and will probably not be heard from before the fall by the South Carolina Supreme Court. If new evidence is brought out or discovered, attorneys can move for a new trial at any time, even after an appeal. So far new evidence has not been brought forth.*

In that same day's *Item* appeared another Letter to Editor.

LETTER TO THE EDITOR

> *To the Editor:*
> *I would like to make a reply to a statement by Solicitor Kirk McLeod in an interview on a local radio station concerning the Cuttino case, in which he said: "Nine out of ten persons sign petitions without even reading them and don't know what they are signing."*
> *Let me make it perfectly clear to Mr. McLeod that I got 157 names on one petition and each signee read it and also made comments to the fact that they wanted to see the case cleared up and let the public know what went on in the trial, etc. These people (signees) were of sound minds and knew what they were signing and they are not as dumb as Mr. McLeod implicated in his interview.*
> *Mrs. Nettie Geddings*

Friday, June 22, Coroner Parnell again attempted to visit with Pierce, but, to his surprise, was told that Pierce could not see him. Aggravated and confused, he tried to find out why and got nowhere.

It was not until Monday of the next week, June 25, that Parnell discovered that Pierce had been transferred back to Georgia.

All of a sudden -- on Friday -- the day Coroner Parnell was to meet with Pierce -- to everyone's surprise, including Pierce, they shipped him out of state and back to Georgia, where Coroner Parnell had less authority than the little that his law enforcement companions here in South Carolina claimed that he had.

On Wednesday, June 27, Jack Truluck wrote an article in *The State* headlined "PIERCE RETURNED TO GEORGIA" in which he said that the move caught Pierce by surprise as well as it did Coroner Parnell.

"He (Pierce) has said he 'liked' the South Carolina Correctional Institution, compared to Georgia's, and that he feared for his life in Georgia," Truluck wrote.

Pierce, in a letter dated June 23, said: "On June 22, 1973, the officers from the South Carolina Law Enforcement Division came to the Correctional Institute in Columbia and said they had orders to return me at once to the Jackson, Georgia, Diagnostic and Classification Center.

"I tried to explain that I had two more charges against me in South Carolina to be tried on, but they said all the rest are being dropped. The one in Beaufort, South Carolina (James L. Sires slaying) and the Lexington, South Carolina case (Cathy Jo Anderson slaying) they said, would never be tried. All the charges were dropped," Pierce said. "I was told also to forget about any new trials in connection with either of the convictions (The Cuttino slaying and the Goodwin slaying) in South Carolina."

"When I arrived here at the prison yesterday (at Jackson, Georgia.)," Pierce continued, "I had to move out of 'Big B' house or be killed. They moved me to D 54 because of the setup here I walked into."

SLED Chief J. "Pete" Strom said it is not unusual for an inmate to be moved from one state to another. In this case, Georgia had first call on Pierce and had convicted him in three murder cases.

"He apparently is to be tried in another Georgia case. Two are pending," Truluck surmised.

Coroner Parnell, however, saw the move as an effort to help quiet the discussion over Pierce's conviction that has been going on intermittently in Sumter since the March trial.

Parnell said on hearing of Pierce's transfer to Georgia, "I predict he hasn't got very long to live...his life will be in danger in Georgia."

On occasion, Pierce has expressed the fear that if he were returned to Georgia something would "happen" to him.

Law officers noted that the South Carolina cases had not been "dropped," but that, since Pierce already had five murder convictions against him, the other two would not be pursued, according to Truluck.

That same day, Wednesday, June 27, *The Item* reported that Mrs. Carrie LeNoir, representing the Concerned Citizens Committee, asked what action had been taken on the request made at the last commission meeting for the $500 to be used for the continued investigation of the Cuttino murder case.

She was advised by County Administrator E.M. DuBose that the request had been referred to Sumter County Attorney G. Werber Bryan, who had advised that the request should be directed to the County through the Sumter County Grand Jury, which would determine whether the case merited further investigation.

On Friday, June 29, *The Item* carried a lengthy article which revealed yet another bizarre set of circumstances that has developed and further explained Coroner Parnell's involvement in the case.

The *Item's* News Editor DeVere Williams prepared this article and, although it contains quite a bit of fact and information that has already been covered, it also very dramatically exposed many new facts for the first time. (Note: Although some of this article is repetitious, it is included exactly as written, in its entirety, because of the intermingling of new material with previously covered material which, in some cases, is necessary for the clarity of the new material.)

The Daily Item — Sumter, SC, Friday, June 29, 1973

CORONER TELLS OF PRESSURE OVER HIS PROBE
Surveillance, Threatening Calls

by Devere Williams

The phone rings. An attractive young mother picks it up to hear an anonymous voice declare: "Barbara, you're going to die." Click...that's it until the next time. Or will there be a next time?

Barbara's husband gets into his car for a trip to the grocery store, to visit friends, to go to his office. A car pulls in behind him, keeping track of his whereabouts at all times. He too tells of anonymous, threatening telephone calls.

He believes his home telephone has been and possibly still is tapped. He found what he believes to be a bugging device in his office downtown.

"I've lost about 40 pounds...my nerves are shattered," the husband says, running his hands through his medium length blond hair. The wife describes her husband's plight: 'I worry about him. I see what it has done to him. He can't eat or sleep and he can't sit still.' She adds, proudly: 'I believe in what he is doing; I believe he is right."

Forty pounds was a notable loss for a slender framed 5'5" man. His normal weight, he says, is 160.

"I fear for my family and myself," he says. "I've gotten to the point now where I live for the 24-hour day."

He says he has moved his family and himself out of their regular dwelling several times when the pressure and fear became overbearing. "I've moved over concern, pressure...I can't eat, I stare at the phone, look out the window, can't enjoy TV or anything, can't even eat a meal, have to get away to relax."

Ask these people if they have reported their torment to authorities. They are quick to answer the question with one word: "Who?"

Does this tale reek of a Watergate? Does it conjure up visions of what might happen to a protester in Soviet Russia? Is it a bizarre piece of fiction which would make good reading on a rainy, wind-blown night?

Does it seem a thing which could be happening in quiet, peaceful Sumter?

It IS happening here, according to an elected county official.

Sumter County Coroner Howard J. Parnell and his wife Barbara related these occurrences to this writer earlier this week.

If surveillance and the harassing phone calls are occurring, as Parnell claims, the natural question is, why?

According to Parnell, it all stems from his controversial investigation into the murder of Margaret "Peg" Cuttino, on December 18, 1970; an act for which one William "Junior" Pierce was convicted by a jury of 12, in Kingstree, on March 2 of this year.

The 13-year-old victim, daughter of former State Representative and Mrs. James Cuttino, of Sumter, disappeared one week before Christmas of 1970. Twelve days later, her mutilated body was found in a wooded section of Sumter County, near Wedgefield.

Alarm, anxiety, rumors, a demand for an arrest raged throughout the county. An intensive investigation, probably the most complete in the county's history, was conducted by city and county law enforcement officials, the State Law Enforcement Division (SLED) and the FBI.

About three months after the young girl's body was found, Pierce, who was serving life sentences for several murders in Georgia, was charged with the Sumter crime.

Pierce was later extradited to Sumter. A change of venue was granted. The habitual criminal was taken to Kingstree and convicted last March.

A subsequent motion for a new trial was denied. An appeal to the State Supreme Court is pending. As far as law enforcement officials are concerned, the case is closed unless new evidence is found.

As far as Coroner Parnell and some segments of the public are concerned, the trial left too many unanswered questions as to Pierce's guilt.

Parnell, who didn't attend the trial or the preliminary hearing, decided to investigate. He is assisted by a group of Sumter Countians who call themselves the Concerned Citizens Committee (CCC).

On May 28, Parnell and the CCC scheduled a meeting at Parnell's funeral home, also his private residence, at 248 Church Street, in Sumter. This meeting was attended by representatives of the county sheriff and the city police chief. The coroner told the gathering he thought he had enough new information to warrant the reopening of the case. City and county representatives

representatives indicated they would conduct any investigation into new leads that come up.

Parnell said he was unable, at that time, to reveal any new facts he may have about the case, but indicated he felt they were sufficient to reopen the case.

A later meeting was called on June 7, at the city-county law enforcement center. It was attended by the coroner, County Sheriff I. Byrd Parnell (no relation to the coroner), City Police Chief L.W. Griffin, SLED Chief J.P. Strom, Third Judicial Court Solicitor R. Kirk McLeod, of Sumter, and a free-lance writer Jack Orr, who concentrates his business in detective magazines. The local news media was not invited to this meeting.

A rift developed at this meeting. Coroner Parnell left in a huff, saying, "I'm through! I'm through! Do what you want with it." Sheriff Parnell denies there was any hostility toward the coroner which would have caused him to behave in such a fashion.

The coroner now states he will never again meet alone with this group and that his current problems of surveillance and telephonic threats began after the meeting in his funeral home on May 28. This meeting, as reported by The Item, was the first - general dissimulation to the public that such an investigation was being conducted by the coroner.

Coroner Parnell would not discuss with this writer his "new facts."

He did, this week, relate some of his most recent efforts. They include an interview with Pierce and an interview with Dr. Joel Sexton, a forensic pathologist with the University of South Carolina Medical University at Charleston, who testified into the cause of Miss Cuttino's death at the legal proceedings.

The coroner said the essence of his conclusion from the interview with Pierce was: "A certain amount of wrongs happened when he was incarcerated in Georgia and his confession was not a willful confession, not voluntarily given." Coroner Parnell said he talked to Pierce for about four hours on June 19, at the Central Correctional Institution of the South Carolina Department of Corrections, in Columbia.

Of his talk with Dr. Sexton, the coroner said it was "very fruitful" and added: "The substance of that (the Sexton interview) was that the wording in the autopsy report was somewhat misleading and the wording in the report could lead to different interpretations, depending on who was interpreting.

"The big question was as to time of death and, to be perfectly blunt, it (the autopsy) was not exacting about anything except she had been dead about five or six days. It could not say the definite cause of death. There is a lot more that I don't feel I

should give out."

Pierce was moved recently from the Correctional Institution, in Columbia, to a confinement center in Georgia.

The Coroner said he feels his visit with Pierce, on June 19, has something to do with the convict's move. He said he attempted to see Pierce again Friday, June 22, and was not allowed to do so.

He states that Pierce's life expectancy may be severely shortened, because of the move to Georgia. He explained: "If what Pierce says took place in Georgia, in the very beginning, is the truth, then I would consider his life to be in danger if he is in the same surroundings. I have no reason to believe he is lying about it."

The coroner said Pierce had told him that Sheriff J.B. "Red" Carter, of Appling County, Georgia, had drugged him, beat him, threatened harm to a close female acquaintance, and promised him he would never stand trial in South Carolina if he would confess to the Cuttino murder, when South Carolina law enforcement officers came to interview him.

Coroner Parnell indicated that he had information from an informed source that a publicly undisclosed communique from one of the investigative agencies to another stated that Pierce, "would never again stand trial in South Carolina.." The coroner refused to elaborate on the details of this communique or to tell in what way he received the information about it. Pierce has been charged in other South Carolina cases.

Pierce was recently taken from Columbia to the Jackson County Georgia Diagnostic and Classification Center. This is the same center in which Pierce was confined before he was moved to Sumter. Sheriff Carter has no jurisdiction where Pierce is now confined. It would, therefore, appear that Coroner Parnell's theory over danger to Pierce is invalid, unless "Red" Carter has some kind of incomprehensible influence in all of Georgia.

The boyish looking coroner, who is obviously putting his reputation on the line with the investigation, claims that Orr, the magazine writer, is a key figure in the case. Parnell claims that Orr, through his efforts at gathering material for his detective magazine articles, acquired ample information to assist Sheriff "Red" Carter in helping make Pierce the innocent victim in the Cuttino murder conviction.

The coroner believes Orr and Carter were able through official information, available to Carter, and unofficial details supplied by Orr, to give Pierce all the information necessary to make South Carolina officials believe his confession to the murder of Miss Cuttino.

"If Pierce didn't do it, someone had to give him the

information he had. There were four or five facts he confessed to...planes flying over (Shaw AFB), roads, etc. Orr was over there (in Georgia) to see him on a regular basis. His (magazine) story was printed before Pierce was tried the first time," Parnell says. He adds that approximately 13 magazine articles were written relating to the case. Orr, formerly a police reporter for the Columbia Record, reportedly writes his detective stories under various pseudonyms.

Parnell also claims that Pierce was under the impression that Orr was a SLED agent when he talked to him. The coroner further stated that when he (Parnell) met with law enforcement officials on June 7, that he too assumed that Orr was a SLED agent. He says Orr did most of the questioning during the meeting at the Sumter County Law Enforcement Center and that no one ever identified Orr's connection with the case. Parnell says that, due to the nature of the meeting, it was only natural to assume that he (Orr) was a law enforcement official. Coroner Parnell admits he never asked Orr's identity.

Why did Howard Parnell, whose authority, under the S.C. Code of Laws, to investigate a case at this stage is questionable, become so involved? He answers this way: "The public demand! The public asked me, as coroner, some very logical questions. They asked me questions for which I didn't have the answers. It shook me...I was a public official, supposedly in the know, and I didn't know.

"In this particular case I was never given the reports and all, so I started asking questions, everybody started squirming. And when everybody started squirming, I began to wonder. It seemed that they thought as soon as I started investigating, that they (law officials) thought that I was defending Pierce, which I was not. I just wanted the truth..."

Coroner Parnell says: "Even Mr. Pierce, the animal he is supposed to be, said not to get too involved because he feared for me and my family."

The coroner, a graduate of Hillcrest High School and a mortician institution, indicated he also is being hampered in his official capacity as coroner. He said: "It seems like the pressure, as coroner, in doing my everyday job...there is pressure there...I think some of the officers (city and county) don't want to be seen with me because they think it might make their superiors mad."

As for surveillance, the coroner says, "they know where I am at all times." He said they (the persons who reportedly follow him) "know that I know they are following me."

Asked who "they" are, the coroner says, "it is a combination of them and I don't want to say who. I could name agencies, but not individual names."

The coroner refused to describe the cars which reportedly follow him. Both city and county law enforcement officials say they have no knowledge of Parnell being followed.

What is Coroner Parnell's goal in this matter? He describes it thusly: "I'm going to pursue it. I'm not going to quit, and my goal is to see that justice is carried out; that Pierce, beyond a doubt, did kill 'Peg' Cuttino, or that Pierce, beyond a doubt, did not kill 'Peg' Cuttino."

The Coroner denied rumors that he is seeking publicity which would aid him in gaining higher office. He says: "I want it to be known now that I do not now, or do I plan to seek any further office. All that I want to do is carry out my duty as coroner, as I feel it is right, and do what the people want me to do. Specifically, I do not want to be sheriff or solicitor."

The Coroner indicates he feels confidence in only one law enforcement chief involved in the Cuttino case. That is Chief L.W. Griffin, of the city. The coroner explains his reason for this: "He has talked to me freely about it and has been open minded about it."

As to Sheriff Parnell, recently elected president of the National Sheriff's Association, the coroner has this to say, "The sheriff believes that (the Pierce conviction) is the way it is and no stones were left unturned. That's his right and I respect it. He doesn't respect my right."

What facts Coroner Parnell may have remain a mystery. What he is up against is obvious. He may well, as only the future can foretell, turn out to be a martyr, a wrecked human being, or a thoroughly discredited public official.

There are, without doubt, many questions on the mind of the public in this case -- questions left unanswered or unasked in the trial.

But, there are other questions. How long will the controversy linger?

Will Margaret "Peg" Cuttino ever be allowed to rest in peace?

The Daily Item — Sumter, SC, Monday, July 2, 1973

INFORMATION PLEASE

Q . Where can donations be made to help Coroner Parnell?
(M.N.B.)

A. Make donations to Mrs. S.G. LeNoir, Four Oaks, Horatio, SC 29062
The Daily Item - Sumter, SC, Tuesday, July 3, 1973

INFORMATION PLEASE

Q. *I would like to know why Howard Parnell made an announcement on a radio station saying that he had new evidence on the Pierce case and would give it to the public the following day and hasn't been heard from since. (M.C.C.)*

A. *According to Parnell, the case is now being appealed and he was informed that if he gave out any information, it might be damaging to the case. Parnell says he will furnish the new information he has at the proper time and to the proper authorities.*

The Daily Item — Sumter, SC, Tuesday, July 3, 1973

LETTER TO THE EDITOR

SUPPORT IS SOUGHT

To the Editor:
I have spent many hours in prayer to God concerning the Cuttino-Pierce case, asking God to guide me to the truth of the matter, and I am more convinced that this case should be re-investigated and if Pierce is the guilty man, let questions in the minds of the people of Sumter and surrounding areas be answered, and if Pierce is not guilty, then find the one who is at large before he strikes again.
I think that Coroner Parnell has some very good information and could obtain much more if he had finances to continue with. Coroner Parnell and his family are sacrificing all that they can in order to do what he can in this investigation, and it is up to the interested people to give him a little support. If anyone would like to make a contribution, you may do so by mailing same to Mrs. S.G. LeNoir, c/o Post Office, Horatio, or calling her and someone will be glad to pick it up. These funds are used for tapes, trips, legal documents, etc.
Mrs. Nettie Geddings

The Daily Item, Sumter, SC, Monday, July 9, 1973

INFORMATION PLEASE

Q. *I noticed in a recent edition of The Item where Allison Francis Hill had been missing from her home since June 14. Now that was just about six days before it even got in the paper. When "Peg" Cuttino was missing three or four hours, the police force and Air Force and everybody else were out looking for her. How soon after a person is reported missing does a city-wide search start? Do you have to pay for all the extra help such as Air Force helicopters? (N.N.)*

A. *According to Police Chief L.W. Griffin, "missing persons bulletins are released immediately upon receipt by the police agency except in runaway cases. Other agencies, Air Force, Civil Air Patrol, etc., have participated with law enforcement agencies in searching for lost and missing persons on a number of occasions on a voluntary basis and such services are greatly appreciated."*

CHAPTER EIGHT

THE GRAND JURY INVESTIGATION

JULY 24, 1973

On Wednesday, July 18, *The Item* ran an announcement entitled GRAND JURY MAY HEAR WITNESSES. After Mrs. LeNoir appeared before the County Commission and requested that $500 be given to Coroner Parnell for his investigation, Attorney G. Werber Bryan — attorney for the county, ruled that the County Commission may not appropriate such funds "without prior submission of the matter to the grand jury of the county, followed by an order of the responsible circuit court judge, made in response to a request of the grand jury that funds in a specified amount be made available by the commission to the grand jury so that the grand jury may fulfill its public obligation."

As a result of Mrs. LeNoir's request (she appeared representing the Concerned Citizens Committee) and the ruling of the County Attorney, there seemed to be no other course of action other than a grand jury hearing.

Members of the Sumter County grand jury, which convened at the opening of the summer term of General Sessions Court on Monday, planned to hear 10 witnesses testify in connection with the investigation.

Once again, a ray of hope shone through for the citizens of Sumter city and county. Would the truth, as the citizens saw it, finally come out? Would this lead to a re-trial for "Junior" Pierce?

The State newspaper, in Columbia carried an article by Jack Truluck entitled "CASE MAY BE REOPENED, HEARING SET MONDAY ON CUTTINO SLAYING." Truluck announced the intentions of the grand jury to hear testimony concerning the case and began at the beginning and reminded his readers of all of the events that had led up to this point.

Sometime, just prior to this grand jury hearing, Joseph T. McElveen, Jr. became an associate in the firm of Bryan, Bahnmuller, King & Goldman, Attorneys at Law.

McElveen, having been appointed one of the attorneys to represent William Pierce in the Cuttino murder case, and G. Werber Bryan, senior partner in the firm and Sumter County Attorney, were now associates in the same law firm. This could present some problem in the upcoming hearing. However, as you will see, Judge Laney eliminated any suspicion of conflict of interest in the hearing, by appointing an outside attorney to council the grand jury. Normally the County Attorney would advise and council the County Grand Jury.

On Thursday, July 19, *The Atlanta Constitution* carried the news and several other well-known newspapers also picked up the story.

By Saturday, July 21, *The Item* had learned of some further developments and ran an article entitled "GRAND JURY — 21 SUBPOENAED FOR CUTTINO TESTIMONY."

The Daily Item — Sumter, SC, Saturday, July 21, 1973

GRAND JURY —
21 SUBPOENAED FOR CUTTINO TESTIMONY

A total of 21 South Carolinians have reportedly been subpoenaed by the Sumter County Grand Jury for testimony scheduled to begin Tuesday, in an effort to determine whether or not the investigation into the slaying of Margaret 'Peg' Cuttino should be reopened.

In addition to the 21 South Carolinians, another 10 persons living in other states have been notified of the hearing by registered air mail and requested to appear, since the grand jury's power of subpoena does not apply to out-of-state residents.

Dudley Saleeby, Jr., Assistant State Attorney General, has been assigned by order of Judge Dan F. Laney, Jr., of the Third Judicial Circuit, to assist the grand jury.

According to Laney's order, Saleeby will be required to furnish the grand jury 'such advice, legal help and counsel as they may need, including, but not limited to, the preparation of subpoenas, securing service of same, securing the names of witnesses, insuring their appearance, examination of witnesses and other such services as may be appropriate.'

Judge Laney's order was issued at the request of Thomas M. Parker, Sumter County's grand jury foreman. In the order, Judge Laney stated, "It appears to the court that the relief sought by the petitioner is warranted and appropriate. The court takes judicial notice of the fact that there has been a great deal of controversy involved in the trial of the ...defendant" (William J. Pierce, Jr.).

........(omission of background facts)

Parker said he was not certain when the jury will decide whether the funds should be allocated. "I couldn't tell you whether it will be Monday, Tuesday or Wednesday. It all depends on how many indictments we have to hear."

The grand jury hearing will be the most recent action related to the conviction of Pierce in Kingstree for the slaying of the Cuttino girl.

There are 76 cases continued from the summer term of court held in May. A total of 219 cases are scheduled to be heard during the two-weeks court session.

Judge Laney, of Bishopville, will preside.

It was Tuesday, July 24, when the grand jury finally got to the hearing on the Cuttino investigation. *The Item* reported the events in the following article by *Item*

Staff Writer Alice Potter, entitled "GRAND JURY INVESTIGATES MATTERS IN PIERCE CASE."

The Daily Item — Sumter, SC, Tuesday, July 24, 1973

GRAND JURY INVESTIGATES MATTERS IN PIERCE CASE

by Alice Potter

    The Sumter County Grand Jury began this morning it's investigation into matters surrounding the death of Margaret Cuttino in December of 1970. William "Junior" Pierce has been convicted of her murder.

    Judge Dan F. Laney, Jr., of Bishopville, charged the grand jury with investigation of "what took place before the trial to see if law enforcement officers did a proper job." Judge Laney also told the grand jury they had the right to recommend indictment of law enforcement officials if it was determined they did not investigate the matter properly.

    Judge Laney also instructed the grand jury to determine "if any citizens of this county deliberately withheld evidence."

    Witnesses will be sworn in throughout the day by Dudley Saleeby of the Office of the S.C. Attorney General. Witnesses will present testimony in closed session.

    Saleeby will act as representative of the grand jury under order of Laney, Jr., presiding judge of General Sessions Court. Judge Laney ruled that although the "proper counsel would be the Sumter County Attorney...inasmuch as an associate in the county attorney's office was appointed by this court as one of the counsels for the defendant, the court feels that while it would not be improper to require the county attorney to represent the grand jury and that there would be no conflict of interest involved, the appearance of impropriety would be avoided by having qualified counsel outside the county attorney's office."

    Witnesses who have received subpoenas include:

R. Kirk McLeod, solicitor, Third Judicial Circuit;
L.W. Griffin, Sumter chief of police;
J.P. Strom, chief, SLED;
Tommy Mims, investigator, sheriff's office;
Hugh Mathis, investigator, sheriff's office;
Thomas McJunkin, investigator, sheriff's office;
Earl Williams, testified he saw Pierce near where body was found;
Jack Orr, detective magazine writer;

Mr. S.G. LeNoir, testified he saw Miss Cuttino on December 19, 1970;

Mrs. S.G. LeNoir, testified she saw Miss Cuttino December 19, 1970;

Burnett Plowden, reported seeing Miss Cuttino December 18, 1970

Howard Parnell, Sumter county coroner;

J.B. "Red" Carter, sheriff, Appling county, Georgia;

William Parker, formerly with Georgia Bureau of Investigation;

Robert N. Sauer, hypnotist from Columbia, South Carolina , and

Dr. J.S. Sexton, of Medical University of South Carolina

(Note: This is evidently not a complete list of those subpoenaed.)

The grand jury is composed of 18 members. The first 12 persons drawn by the clerk of court at the beginning of the year for jury duty serve as grand jurors. The remaining six are drawn from the grand jury of the previous year. No persons may serve on a grand jury for more than two consecutive years.

On Thursday, July 26, under a large caption "OPINION" on The Editorial Page of *The Sumter Daily Item* the following article appeared:

The Daily Item — Thursday, July 26, 1973

EDITORIAL

PUTTING CASE TO REST WILL BE TOUGH JOB

Whether or not the rumors, insinuations and innuendoes surrounding the murder of Margaret "Peg" Cuttino are put to rest after a local grand jury completes it's "investigation into the investigation" of the case remains to be seen.

We do agree with the charge made by Third Circuit Judge Dan F. Laney, Jr. to the grand jury on Tuesday that "It is high time and quite proper that you check this off the books of Sumter County." However, whether the grand jury can "check off" this particular case as a result of it's inquiry is going to be a tall order.

While Judge Laney's admonishment that "no case, no judicial matter should be tried on the streets of any county" is a high-sounding phrase with sentiments most people would agree with, it is nevertheless unrealistic to expect human nature to change overnight and a controversial murder case stricken from people's minds like a page ripped from a book. Things just don't happen that way. Regardless of the grand jury's findings, it is unlikely that everyone who has followed the case closely or been directly involved in it will be completely satisfied. Grand juries can't be expected to be miracle workers.

However, they can be expected to make an honest stab at getting toward the truth. If there was negligence on the part of law enforcement authorities in investigating this case, then the jury should say so, in an unequivocal and straightforward manner. Conversely, if the same authorities were diligent in their duties and served the cause of justice properly, then they should be properly commended.

No one wants to lay the Cuttino murder case to rest more than this community, which has been absorbed by the unhealthy controversy surrounding it for nearly three years. Yet it must have substantial reasons why it should put the case to rest. That will be the most difficult task of the grand jury.

The Daily Item — Sumter, SC, Friday, July 27, 1973

"CUTTINO MURDER"
Another Phase In Controversy Reaches An End

By: Alice Potter, Item Staff Writer

Another phase in one of the most prolonged and vocal controversies to engulf Sumter County reached an end in a hushed courtroom Thursday afternoon.
(Omission of background information)
The conviction (of William Pierce) did not hold water with certain segments of the community, particularly Coroner Howard J. Parnell and a group calling itself the Concerned Citizens Committee (CCC).
As a result of Parnell's and the CCC's apparently unofficial post-trial, post-new-trial-motion, denial and pre-appeal action by Pierce's court-appointed attorneys, the grand jury was convened to study the matter.
In essence, the grand jury put it's seal of approval on the pre-trial investigation, announcing that "no substantive evidence has been presented which would support a finding of either incompleteness or impropriety on the part of public officials charged with the investigation of the case."
The grand jury further decided "that there is no basis whatsoever for recommending that indictments be brought against any public official.
That, viewing the evidence in total, it is our opinion that the

law enforcement agencies charged with the investigation of this case have faithfully discharged their duties under the law.

Does this end the controversy? Will the decision allow the Cuttino family peace of no longer finding the issue in newspapers, on radio and TV, and talked on the streets?

Coroner Parnell says that due to the guidelines by which the grand jury conducted it's probe, he was not allowed to introduce any new evidence which he may possess. Parnell is now contending that the grand jury only allowed answers to direct questions, and that he was not asked any which would allow him to produce his material.

The questions "only pertained to the guidelines he (Third Judicial Circuit Judge Dan F. Laney, Jr.) set forth, which was to prove or disprove that the investigators did an adequate job," Parnell said.

When we went there Monday, I thought we were to turn over all we had and really get into the case. But, when I heard him charge the jury...

"I don't blame the jurors, they had very narrow guidelines to go by," Parnell said. "If the jury had come back with any other verdict they would not only have been criticizing law enforcement officials, but the judicial system and Judge Laney."

Parnell indicated he is extremely disturbed by the decision. "As coroner, legally I have to accept this, but as a man, morally, I don't accept it. I don't think I'd be doing justice to the people who are interested or to William Pierce."

However, the coroner still has not turned his information over to anyone in Sumter yet. He says he may. According to Parnell, if the defense's motion for an appeal of the original verdict against Pierce is granted, they will get the material. If the motion is denied, Police Chief L.W. Griffin will get the goods, "to put in their files."

The coroner said this morning that he feels Pierce is not guilty of the crimes.

Joseph T. McElveen, Jr., one of Pierce's attorneys, said he is "sure that the 18 people on the jury did their job," but that beyond that he has no professional opinion on the matter.

McElveen said the appeal to the S.C. Supreme Court will proceed as scheduled, and will not be affected by the results of the hearing. "An appeal to the Supreme Court is based solely on the records of the circuit court," he said.

Satisfaction was expressed by law enforcement officials, Chief Griffin and Sheriff I. Byrd Parnell, concerning the decision, but neither would speculate on public reaction.

"The grand jury has spoken and I just hope they'll (citizens) be satisfied," Sheriff Parnell said.

And in keeping with his role as solicitor, R. Kirk McLeod said he "had no feelings" concerning the decision. McLeod answered charges by Coroner Parnell that, as a citizen of Sumter County and therefore prejudiced, the solicitor should have had a substitute try the case when a change of venue was granted for the trial. "I represent the Third Judicial Circuit of South Carolina, which includes Williamsburg County (location of the trial) and that's (the charge) the most ridiculous thing I ever heard," McLeod said.

Coroner Parnell and the efforts of the CCC are, to a large degree, responsible for the grand jury hearing. During their independent investigation, the coroner managed to run up a list of expenses. The CCC asked the Sumter County Commission to fork over $500 to help cover the investigation.

(Omission of background facts)

Coroner Parnell of the CCC has constantly asserted law enforcement officials did not adequately investigate the matter, a charge he maintains. Now Judge Laney is on his list. "He's just one of the team," Parnell said.

But, it was the grand jury which came up with the decision. It could have issued indictments of any involved officials if they felt the testimony of witnesses warranted it. Instead, they produced the following conclusions, printed in full at the request of Judge Laney:

As a result of the public controversy and turmoil which has prevailed in Sumter County concerning the investigation into the disappearance and death of Margaret "Peg" Cuttino (which led to the arrest, trial and conviction of William J. Pierce, Jr., of Emanuel County, Georgia), the Sumter County Grand Jury, with legal and technical assistance as provided by the Court, has conducted an independent and impartial inquiry into the adequacy and propriety of the efforts made by the public officials and respective law enforcement agencies (Sumter County Sheriff's Department, Sumter Police Department and the State Law Enforcement Division) involved in the investigation of this case.

In keeping with the stated purposes and limitations of this investigation, no effort was made to adjudicate the guilt or innocence of any individual for the murder of 'Peg' Cuttino, in as much as a determination to that effect has previously been made by a jury in a trial conducted in Williamsburg County. Therefore, the Grand Jury wishes to emphasize that this report is not intended to be, nor should it be considered or interpreted as, a comment upon any matters previously litigated in a court of law and now pending an appeal.

The Grand Jury would like to express it's sincerest compliments and gratitude to the many individuals and agencies who assisted it in it's investigation. Those persons in Sumter County who called for this investigation and who subsequently supported it by the submission of evidence have done a considerable public service in enabling this body to deliberate and resolve questions which would otherwise tend to plague the entire community. The public officials and law enforcement agencies who have been tasked during this operation have been most cooperative, to the extent of making available the files accumulated during their investigation. The Grand Jury would also like to go on record as expressing it's hope that the various individuals and agencies who have participated in these proceedings will be as communicative and cooperative with each other in the future as they have been with the Grand Jury in this matter.

In the course of this inquiry the Grand Jury has heard testimony from thirty-one (31) witnesses and considered numerous exhibits introduced by those witnesses. The evidence received has encompassed every aspect of the case from the date and time of the disappearance through the trial and post-trial hearings, up to and including follow-up efforts made after those proceedings. We, as Grand Jurors, collectively and individually, are satisfied that sufficient inquiry has been made in the course of this investigation into these aspects of the law enforcement investigation which have heretofore been the subject of much conjecture and debate in this community. Rather than risk an incomplete listing (which would invite further speculation) these areas will not be specifically enumerated.

Therefore, we the Grand Jury of Sumter County do hereby find:

1. That no substantive evidence has been presented which would support a finding of either incompleteness or impropriety on the part of the public officials charged with the investigation of this case.

2. That there is no basis whatsoever for recommending that indictments be brought against any public officials.

3. That, viewing the evidence in total, it is our opinion that the law enforcement agencies charged with the investigation of this case have faithfully discharged their duties under the law.

4. That, the Grand Jury would like to thank the public officials and law enforcement authorities involved in the investigation and trial of this case for their dedicated and diligent efforts.

Respectfully submitted,
Thomas M. Parker
Foreman

"They think it's over," Mrs. LeNoir said, "they think they have pulled it off...cleared the names and reputations of all individuals in law enforcement and all law enforcement agencies involved."

Visibly disappointed, but not terribly disturbed by the decision, Mrs. LeNoir thoughtfully explained, "Be careful to understand, at this point, that there was no investigation into new facts at all...nor was it to determine whether there was reason to believe that the Kingstree trial produced a wrong verdict...this grand jury investigation was to...at least they hoped that it would, settle the people of this community down and cause them to believe that an investigation has been made, by an impartial grand jury, and that no wrong was done by anyone...that justice has been done."

"All they did was to parade 31 witnesses before the grand jury and prove that there was a detailed, thorough, lengthy and exhaustive investigation done by the law enforcement agencies involved...and nobody, to my knowledge, has ever denied that. You see, the trick to obtaining the desired outcome from the grand jury...clearing everybody involved...was in what the Sumter County Commission asked them (the grand jury) to determine."

"Remember that Judge Laney instructed the jury to 'investigate what took place before the trial (of Pierce) to see if law enforcement officers did a proper job, and to see if any citizen of this county deliberately withheld evidence." They may have thought that I, or Coroner Parnell, or both of us, might get caught in this net, for withholding evidence...but, we have not withheld any evidence. The evidence that we have has been at their fingertips all the time, and the law enforcement authorities, for some reason, choose to simply ignore it."

"Now, for those of you who have never been before a grand jury, let me point out that it is quite different from a regular court appearance. Witnesses come before the grand jury one at a time...and testify...and no witness hears what the other witnesses have to say and you are only allowed to testify to whatever the judge has charged the jury to consider...which in this case was whether a proper investigation had been done and whether anyone withheld any evidence."

"Remember too, that Assistant State Attorney General Dudley Saleeby, Jr., was sitting right there, with the jury members, and Judge Laney had charged the jury to 'recommend indictments' against any law enforcement officer, or agency, that had not done a proper job or any citizen who had withheld evidence."

"No officer, in his right mind, would walk into that court room and admit that he had not done a proper job, nor would he make any accusation against another officer involved. Likewise, no citizen, unless he, or she, had the faith of Daniel in the lion's den, would walk in there and admit that evidence was withheld. Of course, the law enforcement officers, being citizens too, could be indicted for withholding evidence, if they would admit it...but, who would admit that?"

"Coroner Parnell was not allowed to introduce any new evidence, nor was anyone else...that was not what this hearing was all about."

"Judge Laney, in his instructions to the grand jury, said, 'Grand Jury hearings are held in secret. This practice has descended from English common law and offers witnesses protection from intimidation,' according to the article in *The Item* on Wednesday, July 25, entitled 'CORONER LEADS OFF.' The press was not there because of this procedure."

"The Grand Jury did it's job...you mustn't fault them for the outcome...they did what they were supposed to do...there was nothing else they could do, even if they wanted to."

"It seems to me that Judge Dan Laney should have disqualified himself from this case, though...they wanted to be so sure that there was no conflict of interest, and disqualified Sumter County Attorney G. Werber Bryan because Joe McElveen had recently joined that firm, but yet, they let Judge Laney preside in the case when he and James Cuttino served in the South Carolina House of Representatives together. Why didn't that constitute a conflict of interest? Could it have been that they disqualified Mr. Bryan in order to get the Assistant Attorney General into the courtroom...legally? Why was the Assistant Attorney General asked to counsel the grand jury rather than some other competent attorney in Sumter County? I'm sure we have other competent attorneys in this county. However, it doesn't matter, the results would have been the same in any case. It just goes to show how they can maneuver events to suit the powers that be."

"Well, be sure that eventually, justice will prevail," Mrs. LeNoir concluded with a solemn determination that signaled that we had not heard the last of this case yet.

The fight continued in the newspaper under a section called "Sumter Soapbox" in *The Item*, which is yet another service provided by that media enabling the citizens of this county to air their opinions and thoughts.

The Daily Item — Sumter, SC, Thursday, August 2, 1973

SUMTER SOAPBOX

> *"Coroner Parnell has now added Judge Laney to his enemy list."*
> *What right does this public official have when it comes to an independent investigation in an area outside his jurisdiction and what right does he have to intimidate other public officials trying to do their job? From all outward appearances this man has gone off the deep end. As a citizen of this city, I'd like to know if he is still (capable) of holding the job of coroner.*
>
> *Jim Sawyer*

These "Soapbox" opinions usually provoke an answer, and this one was no exception. A few days later, the following appeared:

The Daily Item — Sumter, SC, Wednesday, August 8, 1973

SUMTER SOAPBOX

> *What right does Jim Sawyer have to question (Howard) Parnell's right to do his job? Since the majority of the people in Sumter elected him, they must think he is capable of handling the*

job of coroner. How could Sawyer say that he has gone off the deep end when I think he was only doing his job? Sumter would be a better community if everyone would speak up and say what they feel.

Verda Smith

CHAPTER NINE

CORONER HOWARD PARNELL ARRESTED

AUGUST 9, 1973

On Thursday, August 9, to the dismay of many of Sumter County's citizens, Coroner Parnell was arrested and taken to the Sumter County Jail.

The warrant was signed by the Mayor of the City of Sumter Richard P. Moses and charges Parnell with "breach of trust, with intent to fraud."

Mayor Moses was warden of the cemetery committee of the Sumter Society of Israelites and the warrant read: "Howard Parnell, being entrusted by Ramon Schwartz, Jr., with the care and keeping of the sum of $100, the property of the cemetery committee, Sumter Society of Israelites, did take and appropriate said property to his own use."

The story appeared in Friday, August 10, edition of *The Item*, under large, bold letters entitled **"CORONER ARRESTED, CHARGED THURSDAY."** Parnell was later freed on $500 bond.

"I think it's a form of harassment," the coroner told *The Item* on Friday morning "That's probably connected with my investigation of the Cuttino murder and my questioning their (the local law enforcement authorities') inquiries into the case."

He said he had no intention of resigning as a result of this incident, when asked. "I'm not in jail," he said, "I'm carrying out my duties as coroner and will continue to do so as long as it is humanly possible. It's very apparent that it's a drummed-up charge, and I feel sure there will be more such (drummed-up) charges coming against me."

Ramon Schwartz, Jr., is a partner in the same law firm with Solicitor R. Kirk McLeod and everybody in Sumter knew that, so the public was enraged by this action. Most of them knew no details other than those reported by *The Item*, which you have just read, and they were confused about the whole thing.

On Wednesday, August 15, *The Item* ran the following article on it's editorial page:

The Daily Item — Sumter, SC, Wednesday, August 15, 1973

EDITORIAL

APPEARANCES DECEIVE, YET...

Appearances often deceive, so we'll reserve judgement for awhile on the latest round between Coroner Howard Parnell and local officialdom.

The coroner was arrested last Thursday on a breach of trust charge alleging that he misappropriated $100 in funds belonging *to The Sumter Society of Israelites.*

The immediate reaction by the coroner was that he was being harassed because of his efforts to have the Margaret Cuttino murder case re-investigated. A grand jury inquiry that concluded July 26 and which was limited to determining whether or not there was wrongdoing on the part of the investigating authorities concluded that sufficient investigation had been made of the controversial case.

Perhaps this appearance of harassment is deceiving, and perhaps the charge against the coroner is simply a coincidence and has no connection with him rocking the boat and ruffling some feathers in his criticism of the handling of the Cuttino murder; nevertheless, it leads to ample grounds for conjecture and suspicion.

Let's say for the moment that the timing of the charge has created an impression of harassment, whether it in fact exists or not.

A few days later, however, a few of the citizens felt that they must express their opinions on the subject and the following was printed.

The Daily Item - Sumter, SC, Friday, August 17, 1973

SUMTER SOAPBOX

"Three cheers for Howard Parnell," for I agree this issue was nothing but harassment. Hundreds like myself agree that if there was not enough evidence for a retrial that the coroner might be harmed in some way. As for the grand jury ruling, the public is not interested. We don't care whether or not the public officials did any wrong-doings. It appears that this was the only thing the jury ruled on. New evidence or the possibility of a new trial did not interest them.

Mrs. O.J. Henderson

The Daily Item - Sumter, SC, Saturday, August 18, 1973

SUMTER SOAPBOX

Was there an immediate need for the $100 which went to the Sumter Society of Israelites or was it because everyone knows the coroner has spent everything he has on the Cuttino investigation? I think it very unfair to use this issue as another means of harassing Howard Parnell.

Elaine Gilbert

Meanwhile, down in Georgia, "Junior" Pierce was convicted of the murder of Mrs. J.B. Thigpen. He was now convicted of five of the nine murders with which he had been charged.

But, the people of Sumter County could do little about what was happening to Pierce in Georgia, nor did they feel any responsibility to interfere in the affairs going on down there. They were still upset over Coroner Parnell's ordeal, however, and the following appeared in *The Item.*

The Daily Item - Sumter, SC, Monday, August 20, 1973

LETTER TO THE EDITOR

HARASSMENT CHARGED

To the Editor:

The people of Sumter County applauded as Coroner Parnell stuck his neck out to challenge the system. Are they applauding still? Are we supposed to be stupid enough to believe that the action taken by our good mayor was necessary at this time? It's evident that harassment of the corner must be financial. Contrary to some opinions, the coroner has not had unlimited funds for his investigation. This man has staked his life, reputation and finances on his belief in what he was doing. If necessary, the Concerned Citizens Committee would have replaced this mysterious fund allegedly used by the coroner. From the start it was evident that there weren't enough funds for an investigation. Voice support was strong, but words are much easier to part with than money. If Howard Parnell is going down because of finances, at least he went down fighting which is more than most of us can say.

Since the greatest farce in South Carolina's history was acted-out at Sumter County courthouse, it has been evident that Sumter is a power city. The pitiful part is that the power lies in the wrong place. The pat on the back of law enforcement by the grand jury isn't even worthy of further comment. It's totally inconceivable that any sane person could study the facts of the Cuttino investigation and see no mistakes or cover-ups.

Didn't we expect the coroner to pay in some way for daring to question that "Law Range Legion?" Are we supposed to be shocked by the puny charge brought against him? President Grover Cleveland once felt it necessary to issue an order which read in part, "Elected officials are the agents of the people -- not their masters." Have things changed so much? Are we no longer allowed our constitutional right to petition for a redress of grievances? Maybe it would be a good idea if we studied our constitution. We may be surprised at the rights granted us.

*Maybe we wouldn't be afraid to speak our minds if we knew that
this is part of our heritage.*

*There is a war in the minds of the citizens of Sumter. I want
Howard Parnell to know that my sympathies and support are with
him. It's high time we stopped being mugwumps. Thank God The
Item has not been controlled by our power structure. We still
have a place to make our views known. Stand up, citizens of
Sumter, and be counted. I am reminded of a quotation, "I do not
agree with what you say, but I defend with my life your right to
say it." Are we, as adults, capable of voicing our opinions or are
we going to continue to speak only when spoken to?*

Ray Johnson

"There is war in the minds of the citizens of Sumter" pretty well summed up the
mood of the people in and around Sumter at this time. There was little that they
could do to help their hero, other than talk about the situation on the streets -- and
that they did. By this time there had developed a definite wall between the law
enforcement officials and the people. It seemed that there was no relief for the
situation. There were still those nagging, unanswered questions about the Cuttino
murder that plagued and confused the people -- and that the authorities flatly refused
to answer -- or even to acknowledge.

On Friday evening, September 14, Coroner Parnell's warrant came before
Magistrate O. Lang Hogon and *The Item* reported the following:

The Daily Item - Sumter, SC, Saturday, September 15, 1973

CORONER RULED HELD FOR GRAND JURY ACTION

By Susan Tiede, Item Staff Writer

*Magistrate O. Lang Hogon ruled Friday evening that Sumter
County Coroner Howard J. Parnell be held for grand jury action
in connection with a charge of breach of trust with fraudulent
intent. He is accused of defrauding the Sumter Society of
Israelites of the sum of $100.*

*The ruling of the probable cause was pronounced by Hogon
at the conclusion of a 45-minute preliminary hearing which took
place in the magistrate's court.*

*"I'm not trying the case," Hogon said to Parnell's attorney,
David McInnis, at the conclusion of the hearing, "but I definitely
find probable cause and deny the motion for dismissal."*

*McInnis contended that the matter was, if anything, a civil
issue concerning a debt and that no proof had been presented of
fraudulent intent on the part of Parnell.*

*If charges are not dropped, an indictment will be presented to
the Sumter County Grand Jury when it convenes for the fall term*

of General Sessions Court, on November 5. If a true bill is returned by the grand jury, Parnell's case will be placed on the docket.

A conviction of breach of trust with fraudulent intent in the amount of $50 or over is punishable by a sentence of up to 10 years in prison.

Two men, State Representative Ramon Schwartz (D-Sumter) and Sumter Mayor Richard P. Moses, the prosecuting witness, testified for the state. In the absence of the prosecuting attorney the two were instructed simply to give an account of what they knew about the event.

Schwartz said he had assumed the responsibility for the funeral of his uncle, who died in January. The burial took place at the Sumter Jewish cemetery and arrangements were handled through Parnell-Rutledge-Hurst Funeral Home, managed by Parnell.

He said he received an itemized bill on February 2, from the funeral home which contained a notation of a $100 charge for a burial permit in the cemetery.

Schwartz testified that he made out a check for $595.64 -- the bill minus $500 of his uncle's Social Security and Veterans Administration benefits he instructed to be made out to the funeral home -- and "forgot about the matter."

When informed by members of the society of Israelites that the $100 fee had not been paid, Schwartz said he forwarded copies of the correspondence between him and the funeral home to society officials.

"I want to state," Representative Schwartz concluded, "that I did not request, nor had anything to do with the issuance of the warrant (against Parnell)."

Upon questioning by McInnis, Schwartz stated that he had made out the check to Parnell-Rutledge-Hurst and that it had been endorsed in the name of the funeral home. Schwartz further stated that he did not know if the $500 in government benefits had ever been received by Parnell.

Moses testified that on August 9, on the advice of attorney Lawrence Goldsmith, who represented the society, he swore out a warrant against Parnell, manager, third vice president and secretary-treasurer of the funeral home, whose name was on the burial permit.

Upon questioning by McInnis, Moses said he did not know if Parnell had ever been billed for the $100 and said he had never made an attempt to contact him.

The mayor said he had not made any inquiries into Parnell's status with the funeral home and would not deny that the president of the home was someone other than Parnell.

"At what period of time would you say that Mr. Parnell had intent to defraud the Sumter Society of Israelites?" questioned McInnis.

"I have no idea," replied Moses.

"If he'd paid the day before you signed the warrant, would it have been issued?" McInnis asked.

The mayor indicated he thought the warrant would not have then been issued.

"In other words, the mayor swore out a warrant charging Parnell with intent to fraud, but he 'had no idea' when the 'intent to defraud' occurred. Parnell may have never been billed for the $100 and no one ever even contacted him about the oversight -- they just swore out a warrant for this popular public servant that could possibly have cost him 10 years of his freedom, or could have permanently ended his investigation into the Cuttino case.

"You -- be the judge," Mrs. LeNoir commented later.

Well, as usual, things got hot in Sumter County after these facts were revealed.

Perhaps the following Letter to the Editor amply sums up the feelings of the people about this incident.

The Daily Item - Sumter, SC, Wednesday, September 26, 1973

<u>LETTER TO THE EDITOR</u>

HARASSMENT OF CORONER CHARGED

To the Editor:

Many concerned citizens of Sumter are troubled about the article in The Item of September 15, concerning the arrest of Coroner Parnell. If Mayor Moses did not know, as he stated to Mr. McInnis, if the coroner had even been billed for the $100 or not, nor that he had ever tried to contact Mr. Parnell, then why did he, a man elected by the people of Sumter to serve the citizens of Sumter, issue a warrant and embarrass Mr. Parnell, by having him arrested in a public establishment without first digging into the matter and giving him a chance to come forward? It could have been another "typographical error." I can't see why a man should be harassed to the breaking point just because he is a little man who is trying to please the people. GOD FORBID!

There are quite a number of people who have expressed the desire to pay the Society of Israelites the $100, if the people who are trying so hard to prosecute him, will leave him alone. What is the problem? Do they want to give the job of coroner to someone else?

Another thing? If they are going to issue warrants against all who owe $100, they had better forget about a Downtown Mall *and start building more jails, my cell included.*

Have we forgotten the incident in John 8, where the charge was given, "He that is without sin among you, let him cast the first stone?" How many stones were cast? None! The accusers disappeared. We are living in a time when our nation, our state, and even our county seems to have forgotten that God is still on the throne, and that one day we will all stand before the judgement seat, and "Oh! What weeping and wailing there will be."

Mrs. Nettie Geddings

It may be that the citizens had nothing to do with it, but on Tuesday, November 6, the following appeared in The Item:

The Daily Item — Sumter, SC, Tuesday, November 6, 1973

General Sessions Court, Case Not Prosecuted...

In other court action Monday, Judge Hayes granted a motion by Third Judicial Solicitor R. Kirk McLeod to nol-pros (not prosecute) a case against Sumter County Coroner Howard J. Parnell. Parnell had been charged with breach of trust with intent to fraud.

Solicitor McLeod announced that the motion was made at the request of the prosecuting witness in the case, the Sumter Society of Israelites. Representatives of the society reportedly told the Solicitor that Parnell had paid the money he allegedly owed them.

Junior Pierce had insisted for a year now that he had an alibi which proved that he could not have killed Peg Cuttino. But the problem was... that his alibi was embodied in the testimony he gave while under deep hypnosis, and the courts would rarely accept such evidence.

Pierce's appeal to the Supreme Court of South Carolina was due to be heard on February 13, 1974, and his attorneys intended to maintain that the refusal to admit Columbia hypnotist Robert N. Sauer's testimony (of what Pierce had said while in deep hypnosis) constituted a denial of Pierce's right to be heard in his own defense.

The attorneys planned to insist that the information that Sauer could give about Pierce's testimony while under hypnosis would corroborate the alibi that Pierce was not in the Sumter area when the murder occurred.

Pierce's appeal also maintained that the hypnotic testimony would prove another point: that a confession used as the main evidence in the Cuttino murder trial was not voluntary, and thus was illegal.

The appeal also asserted that other important factors should have resulted in a new trial.

It took exception with a statement attributed to Third Circuit Solicitor R. Kirk

McLeod in arguments to the jury: "All I know is that no little girls have been killed around here since this man has been in jail."

Pierce's attorneys argued that the statement was highly prejudicial and that Judge Rosen should have admonished the jury to disreguard the statement.

More important than these, though, the appeal contended that a new trial should have been granted based on the fact that after-discovered evidence produced enough information to prove the victim may have been alive after the date authorities said she was killed.

On Wednesday, February 13, 1974, Pierce's attorneys, Joseph T. McElveen, James M. Conner and William E. Jenkinson, III, plead the various points of the appeal with conviction and detailed diligence before the South Carolina Supreme Court.

They argued that the five rules of "new evidence" had been met in this case; therefore, the testimony of the LeNoirs and of Jerry Artrip was valid evidence.

They argued that the testimony of Earl Williams had placed Pierce at the scene of the murder on December 19, 1970, the day after Miss Cuttino was allegedly murdered, not December 18... the day Pierce allegedly murdered her. Solicitor McLeod said that the testimony of Williams was valid because it placed Pierce at the scene at about the time the crime was committed. The Solicitor said that he had no idea why Pierce was there.

Pierce's lawyers argued that the Solicitor is a representative of all of the people, even the accused, and that he is the protector of the accused: to see that the accused had a fair and impartial trial. They said there was no evidentiary basis for the Solicitor's alleged remark (referred to earlier) and if the remark was made and if it was prejudicial enough, then a new trial or a mistrial should be granted to the accused.

McLeod said of the remark that no objection was made by defense counsel and that no record was made of it by the court. He said that he neither confirmed nor denied that he might have made the remark. Solicitor McLeod said that if such a statement were made that he did not think that it would be prejudicial to the jury.

When all arguments had been made, the court reserved opinion on the appeal and gave no indication when an opinion might be issued by the justices.

The Daily Item carried the complete story on Thursday, February 14, in an article entitled "PIERCE'S LAWYERS TELL OF NEW WITNESSES — PIERCE CASE APPEALED".

The citizens of the city and county settled back and quietly awaited the decision of the court.

And they waited...

And they waited...

And they waited.

Finally, on Thursday, August 8, 1974 — seven months later — by a unanimous 5-0 vote, the South Carolina Supreme Court upheld the conviction of Pierce.

In an article by Item News Editor DeVere Williams on that date, entitled "NO NEW TRIAL — PIERCE APPEAL DENIED", it was reported that the decision said, "We are not convinced that there is any showing of an abuse of discretion, amounting to a manifest error of law, in denying the motion for a new trial on the grounds of after-discovered evidence. We deem all exceptions of the appellant to be without merit and the judgement is accordingly."

"The decision marks another landmark phase in what has come to be regarded as the most infamous crime in Sumter County history, one which has seen vicious rumors engulf the community and cause rifts between elected officials," Williams wrote..

Well, it was over at last... There was nowhere else to go... The people of Sumter and Sumter County would just have to accept the outcome.

"Of course, we're disappointed," Joe McElveen said. "We felt the appeal was meritorious from a legal standpoint, or we wouldn't have instituted it."

"I would have to see the decision and the reasons behind the decision before making a statement," McElveen said, when asked what the defense might do next.

Another defense attorney, William E. Jenkinson, III, said, "I have not read the opinion. We will have to read it and evaluate what other steps can be taken. At this stage, a petition for re-hearing to the (Supreme) Court would look to be the next step."

Jenkinson, however, pointed out that this would be difficult. "If the Court is split, you have one of two justices ruling in your favor, you might get a re-hearing, but when the whole court rules against you, that's pretty overpowering. A re-hearing is a pretty rare animal. This (court decision) could be it. I don't think that we have constitutional grounds to go to the U.S. Supreme Court."

Sheriff I. Byrd Parnell said he was "glad it's over and I felt we were right about it the whole time and I'm glad it's over with."

City Police Chief L.W. Griffin said he thought the Supreme Court "had good reason to take the action that they did." He refused to go into detail, saying, "I really see no point to elaborate. I think that everything was handled properly."

Solicitor R. Kirk McLeod, the prosecutor in the case, was on vacation and was unavailable for comment. Coroner Parnell said he "would have to consider" the decision before commenting. He said that he still had relevant material, which he had never disclosed.

Mrs. LeNoir said she had evidence which has never been brought to light. She alluded to a "cover-up" in the case, but had never publicly explained that charge.

She said that she was "very disappointed" in the decision and reiterated that she does have new evidence. She said she had no plans to offer the evidence "at this time." She said her citizen's committee would have another meeting soon.

Well...maybe...just maybe... it wasn't over.

CHAPTER TEN

CORONER HOWARD PARNELL RESIGNS

JULY 15, 1975

On Tuesday, July 15, 1975, The Item announced that Sumter County Coroner Howard J. Parnell was expected to resign his post as Coroner.

"We have not received formal notice, but understand that he intends to resign," said Bob Liming, communications director for then-Governor of South Carolina, James B. Edwards.

The Item was unable to contact Parnell to confirm this action until Thursday, July 17, when he did confirm his resignation.

It had been long and hard for him... these past few years. He had first been elected in 1968, at the age of 24... the youngest Coroner in the history of Sumter County. At the time he was re-elected, in 1972, he was a funeral home operator. In 1974, he made his unsuccessful bid for the Democratic nomination for Congress from the Fifth Congressional District, and from October of 1974 to April of 1975 had worked as a salesman for a local automobile dealer in Sumter.

The pressure from the people and the threats against his wife and family... and threats against his own life, in addition to the difficulties with law enforcement officials in Sumter County were finally more than he could stand.

Howard Parnell left Sumter County... in fact, he left the state of South Carolina... about the middle of June, 1975, and accepted a position as funeral director for Patterson Oglethorpe Hill Mortuary in Atlanta, Georgia.

Charles Skey and Verna Moore had served as Deputy Coroners for the past few years, working for Parnell and being paid by him out of the $5,200 that the Coroner was paid at that time. They had inherited the duties of the office totally, since Parnell was out-of-state.

The S.C. Code of Laws provides that in the event of a vacancy in the office of Coroner, the Governor may fill the office by appointment and, if it is an elected office, the interim position will be filled by the appointee until the next election.

Sumter County elected its Coroner. Therefore, the Governor would be impelled by law to appoint someone to serve until the next election. Victor C. Jones, who was then Sumter County Civil Defense director, had been Parnell's Republican opposition in 1972, but was not interested in the position any longer.

Governor Edwards appointed Bennie Raffield to fill the balance of the term that Parnell had vacated. The next election would be in 1976.

The Daily Item — Sumter, SC, Thursday, September 25, 1975

LETTER TO THE EDITOR

JUSTICE NEEDED IN SYSTEM

To the Editor:
I have been impressed with the requests from officials recently in asking for more citizen involvement (The Item, Sept. 18, "Chief Deputy T.L. McJunkin made an appeal to the public for any information which might aid investigators in solving the murder of Mrs. Hattie Ahrembeck, etc.", then Sept. 20, from Sheriff Parnell. "We are hoping for more citizen involvement, etc.")

Earlier, Judge Julian Ness had made a similar appeal. I agree that if a person knows anything which might help solve a murder, he is morally and legally obligated, as a good citizen, to speak out, because law enforcement officials are only human, and do not possess supernatural powers, but need help.

However, I fear that citizen involvement will continue to dwindle, if our experience a few months ago was typical of the judicial system proceedings.

After a hearing in which my husband and I testified, I heard quite a few of the spectators say, "If I saw someone kill my next door neighbor, and knew who did it, I will not get involved, if I'm going to be treated like a criminal," or similar statements.

Unfortunately, if one's testimony is in conflict with what the Sheriff and Solicitor wish, it's a sad state of affairs for the witness. If, in spite of threats, a witness musters the courage to appear, everything possible, short of physical attack is done to make the witness change his story.

This should not be allowed, and unless justice can be restored to the judicial system, the courthouse would serve a better purpose for the citizens as a recreation building.
Carrie B. LeNoir

On the surface, things were quiet for the next few months, but behind the scenes, the Concerned Citizens Committee was still at work on the Cuttino case.

Charging "obstruction of justice" and that "officials committed perjury" in the 1973 conviction of William J. Pierce for the murder of Margaret "Peg" Cuttino, Mrs. Carrie B. LeNoir asked for a new trial for Pierce.

She filed the application in the Williamsburg County Court of Common Pleas on Wednesday, November 19, 1975, and thus began a new chapter in the already notorious murder case that refused to die.

The application asked for relief from the March 12, 1973, conviction of Pierce, which sentenced him to life imprisonment on four grounds, alleging:

1. Victim not killed on day of murder conviction.
2. Obstruction of justice by officials at inquest.
3. Information withheld from defense attorneys.
4. Officials committed perjury at trial and hearing.

Accordingly, the application asked for "a new trial on newly discovered evidence and witnesses."

To back up the allegations, Mrs. LeNoir presented four pages of conclusions based on testimony and other data. The application also contained an affidavit from Mrs. LeNoir, sworn before Fifth District Magistrate W.M. LeNoir, dated November 5, 1975, in which she claimed Sumter County Sheriff I. Byrd Parnell and Deputy Sheriffs T.R. Mims and Hugh A. Mathis, Jr., lied about certain aspects of the Cuttino investigation, perjured themselves and offered testimony that was "inconsistent and contradictory."

In the affidavit, Mrs. LeNoir quoted from Mims testimony, in which he stated under examination by Third Circuit Solicitor R. Kirk McLeod that she had said she had seen no girl at all. "I charge that he was deliberately lying, or else suffering from a bad memory, as I positively told him and all others who interviewed me that I was between the house and the store when the girl and the two boys came out."

Mims had also testified that Mrs. LeNoir said her husband probably could not remember what he saw, if he saw the girl. "I charge that that statement also is a lie!" she said.

"I also certify that Deputy Hugh Mathis committed perjury in his testimony," Mrs. LeNoir charged in rebuttal to Mathis' testimony that she said she was in the house and did not see the girl and that he (Mathis) also heard from Mrs. LeNoir that her husband "didn't know what he was talking about."

"That's a LIE!" Mrs. LeNoir emphasized in the affidavit.

On the charge of inconsistent testimony, Mrs. LeNoir pointed to the testimony of the officers which said that after talking to the LeNoirs, they spent the remainder of the afternoon interviewing people in Horatio and checked a clubhouse known to be frequented by young people, as well as abandoned farmhouses.

"Why would they have spent that whole afternoon, which by their own testimony, they did... checking out that community, if my husband and I had told them that we had not seen Peg Cuttino?" asked Mrs. LeNoir. "There would have been no reason to check any further, if we had denied seeing the child, but we did see her... and we both told them that we did."

Sheriff I. Byrd Parnell was also accused of committing perjury when he stated that Mrs. LeNoir never had said that she had seen the girl.

The application was also based on the allegation that the body of a young woman could not have lain in the Manchester State Forest for 12 days, considering the condition of the body and "considering high temperatures, dogs, wild animals and vultures."

She charged that the inquest into the death "was railroaded through by the Solicitor (R. Kirk McLeod), and the Coroner (then Howard J. Parnell) backed him."

On the charge that information was withheld from defense attorneys, the application said that two potential witnesses for the defense, Noah Jerry Artrip and Burnett O. Plowden, were withheld by law enforcement officials.

Bob Craft, a staff writer for The Item, prepared a detailed article, which ran in The Item on Thursday afternoon, November 20, entitled "NEW TRIAL ASKED IN PIERCE CASE".

The papers filed by Mrs. LeNoir was an application for "post conviction relief" and were signed by William J. Pierce. Williamsburg County Clerk of Court said that she had never had an application like this one, and it seemed that she did not know what to do with it.

She indicated she would meet with Solicitor R. Kirk McLeod and Judge David W. Harwell on Monday, December 1, to ask their advice, but the meeting never came to pass. She gave the papers to Judge Harwell... who said that he would look them over and advise her at a later time.

And so, Mrs. LeNoir waited... and she waited... and she waited.

The Daily Item — Sumter, SC, Tuesday, January 18, 1977

LETTER TO THE EDITOR

JUSTICE MUST PREVAIL

To the Editor:

May I use your paper to respond to the Sumter County legislators who invited their constituents to express views on the very important subject of capital punishment, in a story "Local Lawmakers Review Legislature's Issues" in a recent issue of The Sumter Daily Item. First, I'd like to congratulate Bob Craft for his excellent reporting, then thank those members of the delegation who realize that they are representing the citizens of Sumter County, and will listen, and consider their wishes. Of course we know that they can't please everyone, but I'd like to briefly analyze some of the aspects of capital punishment.

Needless to say, I believe that the majority of the citizens might favor capital punishment, if we can be sure, above and beyond a reasonable doubt, that an accused person is guilty: but cases dating back in our generation to the Charles Lindbergh, Jr., kidnapping in 1932, for which Bruno Hauptmann was electrocuted, the John F. Kennedy assassination, on through more recent local murder cases, leave many doubts in our minds as to the efficiency of the judicial system in always securing justice.

We realize that the judicial system is a vast and complex organization, depending upon many factors working together, but with avenues open for obstruction and miscarriage of justice, whether accidental or intentional. A jury may be honestly convinced with the case as presented that a just decision has been rendered, only to discover later that vital information has been withheld, which would have reversed the decision.

We would urge our legislators to give long, prayerful

consideration to this very important matter, hopefully that they may be able to pass legislation which would protect the citizens, but at the same time avoid having innocent victims lose their lives, as science has not yet discovered a way to restore life.

Carrie B. LeNoir

CHAPTER ELEVEN

APPEAL TO SOUTH CAROLINA STATE
ATTORNEY GENERAL DANIEL R. MCLEOD

FEBRUARY 15, 1977

Feeling that something more needed to be done, Mrs. LeNoir packed up her materials on the Cuttino affair and traveled to Columbia on Tuesday afternoon, February 15, 1977.

With luggage in hand, she marched into Attorney General Daniel R. McLeod's office and asked for a new trial for William Pierce.

The suitcase, traincase and briefcase she carried contained several thick notebooks filled with materials, newspaper articles, affidavits and other papers accumulated since she became involved in the notorious murder case.

Mrs. LeNoir informed Mr. McLeod that she was there "to try to get justice for Junior."

Mr. McLeod said that he could not comment on the case because it was currently before the courts. "Pierce has recently filed proceedings in Williamsburg and Aiken Counties, and it would not be proper for me to make any comments on the case because of ethical considerations."

"I don't know what's legally right, but I do know what's morally right," Mrs. LeNoir said.

"I want to see justice done. An innocent man has been made to serve as a scapegoat. The murderer or murderers are still loose. I don't know who they are, but I've had mothers tell me that they worry that the murderer might be dating their daughters," she told him.

"If officials can railroad a man through the courts in the name of justice, then nobody has any security," she declared.

"I'm not saying he never killed anyone," Mrs. LeNoir continued. "Just because someone killed 40 doesn't mean he should be convicted of the 41st."

Speaking to the State's Attorney General as a mother would to her son, and occasionally pointing an accusing finger in his direction, Mrs. LeNoir told Mr. McLeod, "Your hands are going to be as bloody as the next one if you don't give Junior Pierce a new trial."

Courteous, but unmoved, McLeod said Pierce's case would be handled as any other request for post-conviction relief, and he gently advised Mrs. LeNoir, "You supervise morals and I'll supervise the legal aspects."

The visit produced very little, if anything, in the way of help for a new trial for Junior Pierce, but the newspapers carried lengthy articles and pictures of the event and Mrs. LeNoir was hailed as "Pierce's Guardian Angel" in large, bold headlines — a title that would follow her for many years to come.

She told the reporters, "If my endeavors fail here in South Carolina, I will contact the United States Justice Department. If I have to spend the rest of my life

— if it's only a few minutes, a few days, a few weeks — I'm going to work to put justice back in the judicial system."

A group of Clarendon County citizens gathered in the home of Mr. and Mrs. Ralph Graham on Monday night, February 21, to meet with and listen to Mrs. LeNoir. They had heard and read about this new evidence that was supposed to exist concerning the Cuttino murder and Pierce trial and about her involvement in the case. They wanted to see and hear — from her — just what it was. Mrs. LeNoir met with them and showed them the various documents that she had.

On March 3, 1977, The State newspaper published a letter from a man who responded to that paper's article on February 16.

"Sir," the letter began, "I congratulate Ms. Holly Gatling for her article 'Pierce's Guardian Angel Has Her Say With McLeod', and Mrs. S.G. LeNoir for having the perseverance and courage to stick with the 'Cuttino-Pierce' case. It appears that very important information was indeed withheld during the trial, and each court to which the case has been appealed has denied a new trial.

"Let's pray that the officials who have the power to grant a new trial for Mr. William J. Pierce will do so before Mrs. LeNoir does have to contact the U.S. Justice Department. If she does have to take that drastic measure, we should all hang our heads in shame that we have elected, and allowed to remain in office, such officials who are responsible for this catastrophe."

The letter was signed: Theodore Tedder, Rt. #1, Mayesville, SC.

CHAPTER TWELVE

APPEAL TO THE
UNITED STATES JUSTICE DEPARTMENT

APRIL 3, 1977

In an article in The Daily Item by Item staff writer Jerry Adams, Monday, April 4, 1977, entitled "MRS. LENOIR GOES TO WASHINGTON", another aspect of the baffling Cuttino case was first introduced to the public — the coat.

"... Mrs. LeNoir has a raincoat which she believes belonged to Peg Cuttino. The dark blue coat with "PEG" embroidered on the lapel was found in the Horatio community center after the girl's death.

"The coat was first noticed shortly after Miss Cuttino disappeared. It was found by maids cleaning the center, but they left the coat, thinking that its owner would return to reclaim it, Mrs. LeNoir said.

"That coat was inadvertently pushed aside until two years later, when it was found in a corner of the center," she explained.

Mrs. LeNoir believes the coat was left in the center several days after authorities say Miss Cuttino was killed.

Having had no success with South Carolina State Attorney General Daniel McLeod, on Sunday morning, April 3, 1977, Mrs. LeNoir boarded a plane for Washington, D.C.

Her plans were simple. Go to the First Baptist Church for a Palm Sunday worship service, where President Jimmy Carter and his family would be attending church, and then to the White House in hopes of talking with the President.

Since President Carter was himself from Georgia, Junior Pierce's home state, she was sure that he would be interested in seeing that justice was done. "I'm going to tell him (Carter) that we have exhausted all the courts in South Carolina in trying to get justice in the case that we believe in and that we have no alternative now but to go outside the state and appeal for help in getting justice," she determined.

She arrived in Washington on Sunday morning, found a motel room and went to the church too late to get into Carter's Sunday School class. But she was in time to get a seat in the church — right behind the First Family.

She did not get in to meet with President Carter; however, she went to the Justice Department, where she talked with a special assistant to the Attorney General, and to attorneys in the Public Integrity and Civil Rights sections.

"The civil rights angle is our best bet, " she said. "I don't want to get anybody in trouble, but justice is our aim. If we let them get away with this, there's no telling what will happen next."

At the Civil Rights section, she talked with David B. Adler, a trial attorney in the criminal section, who promised to check into a civil rights complaint filed by convicted murderer William J. Pierce, Jr., and to investigate possible rights violations.

Item staff reporter Jerry Adams wrote an article entitled "PIERCE CASE TAKEN TO JUSTICE DEPARTMENT", which appeared in the Friday, April 8, 1977, edition of The Daily Item, in which he reported, "Adler said this morning that he 'would not order a federal investigation of the case, based on what she (Mrs. LeNoir) told me. I told her that I would take a look at the file again and I ordered a copy of the Pierce file from the Federal Records section. But I haven't gotten that file yet," Adler said.

Adler also said he had gotten copies of parts of the extensive file that Mrs. LeNoir has on the Cuttino case and that he promised to get back in touch with her after his investigation. "But, based on what she told me, I saw no basis for a federal civil rights violation. There were no federal violations indicated and I tried not to give her encouragement that there would be a federal investigation into the Pierce-Cuttino case."

Mrs. LeNoir had returned to Sumter on Thursday night, buoyed by her reception in the nation's capitol and confident that she had made progress in her "fight for truth and justice".

"Now that we have a born-again Christian in the White House and an Attorney General pledged to absolute integrity, I'm sure we'll get justice in the Cuttino murder case," she said. "I'll give them a few weeks and if I don't get results, I've got enough money for a few more plane tickets to Washington. They're going to have trouble keeping me down on the farm now."

CHAPTER THIRTEEN

"PEE WEE" GASKINS CONFESSES

APRIL 25, 1977

Donald Henry "Pee Wee" Gaskins — already convicted of one murder and facing trial for the murder of a Florence County farmer named Silas Barnwell Yates, was scheduled to go on trial in Newberry on Monday, April 18, 1977. His attorneys had secured a trial in the nearby county in order to assure a fair trial.

Police had said that Gaskins was the "ring leader" of a murder-theft gang under their investigation for what was widely thought to be the worst mass murder case in South Carolina history.

Eleven bodies — four men, three women, two teenage girls, a teenage boy and a two-year-old girl had been found so far — to which Pee Wee Gaskins had been linked. The first eight bodies were found in December, 1975, buried in shallow graves near Prospect, South Carolina, a small Florence County farm community. The last three bodies were found in late 1976 in Sumter and Williamsburg counties. Silas Yates was the last of these bodies found.

Gaskins was only one of four people charged in the Yates murder. However, he had become the focal point of attention all of a sudden, because of rumors that persisted that he, a native of the Prospect area, was a killer-for-hire. This had never been proved, but there was talk that one of the first victims found, Johnny E. Sellers, may have been a "contract" target. And police now said that Yates was killed for $1,500.

Another persistent rumor was that Gaskins and some of his associates were members of a major theft ring based in the South Carolina lowcountry. There had been no charges in that connection, however, even though Gaskins had testified at a recent court hearing about burglaries in Georgetown and Williamsburg counties.

Silas Yates' body had been found in Williamsburg County, which was in the Third Judicial Circuit; so the prosecutor in the case would be Third Judicial Circuit Solicitor R. Kirk McLeod, of Sumter.

The Yates trial promised to be a gangbuster already. To make matters more tense, Pee Wee told some of his fiends and reporters that, when he got on the stand to testify in the Yates trial, he intended to "drop a bomb" that would be "highly explosive" and "potentially embarrassing to a lot of people".

The only access to the old Newberry Courthouse was through the front door when the trial began, and spectators were searched before being allowed to enter. News people had been assigned to the balcony and the courtroom was packed with curious onlookers expecting this to be a very exciting case.

Gaskins would be the last of the four charged to be tried and the news media reported the proceedings with little interest, except for the comments made by Gaskins, as the trial wore on.

"I will promise you I am going to shock a lot of people at this trial," Gaskins said. "I don't know if the people of South Carolina will ever know what really happened, as the law won't let the true story out, and I have been cut off from letting the people know what really went on.

"The state might try to stop me," Gaskins said, "but as you know, I am hard to stop once I get started."

He said his scheduled appearance on the stand that week may be "my last chance" to "let it all hang out".

On Monday, April 25, 1977, against the advice of his attorneys, Pee Wee Gaskins took the witness stand. Speaking in a rapid-fire, sometimes scratchy voice to the standing-room-only crowd, he dropped the bomb that he had promised. He testified that he was ordered by an un-named lawman to kill 13-year-old Margaret "Peg" Cuttino. He termed the murder an "assassination".

He said he was forced by lawmen to commit two assassinations in Sumter County, one involving Peg Cuttino, and one involving an approximately twenty-year-old black girl named "Clyde".

Gaskins refused to give the name of the lawman who ordered the murders until after Clyde's body was dug up. He said if he did so, he feared lawmen would move the body and hide it.

The black woman, Gaskins said, was killed with poison concealed in a soft drink, and that he showed Sumter County lawmen and State Law Enforcement agents where the body was more than five months before this trial, but no efforts had been made to dig it up.

He also said he was responsible for the February 4, 1975, shotgun slaying of two men in Horry County, for which another man had been sentenced to die. Claiming to be a professional contract killer, he promised to tell about even more bodies and crimes in the future. (See The State, April 17, 1977, article "PEE WEE GASKINS DUE TO DROP 'BOMB", by Duncan Hite"PEE WEE GASKINS EXPLODES 'BOMBS' IN COURT"; The State, April 23, 1977, article"'I AM HARD TO STOP ONCE I GET STARTED' — GASKINS", by Duncan Hite; and The State, April 26, 1977, article "GASKINS EXPLODES 'BOMBS' IN COURT", by Duncan Hite.)

Sumter County Sheriff I. Byrd Parnell, when asked about Gaskins comments, said he did not plan to begin digging for the body of Clyde until after the trial was over. He said the area was not searched when Gaskins pointed out the spot in November, 1976, because of "high water" in the ditch where the body was said to be located, but said he would begin looking for the body "as soon as the weather clears".

The Daily Item carried a lengthy article on Tuesday, April 26, entitled "AUTHORITIES DOUBT CLAIM GASKINS KILLED CUTTINO", by Item staff writer Jerry Adams.

"The man who killed Peg Cuttino is in jail in Georgia and I can go to sleep on that," said Sheriff Parnell.

Assistant Third Circuit Solicitor Kenneth R. Young, Jr., who was prosecuting Gaskins for the Yates murder, also discounted Gaskins' testimony and said he didn't think a new investigation on the Cuttino murder would be held.

"I don't believe there will be much more investigation of it (the Cuttino case). I don't believe he did it. He's just trying to take credit for it," Young said that morning.

"As far as I'm concerned, Gaskins' statement does not change anything in the Cuttino case at this time," Sumter Police Chief L.W. Griffin said.

However, during Jerry Adams' interviews with officials for this article, some new information was brought out that the public had not previously known.

Adams wrote, "Sumter Police Chief L.W. Griffin, who was in charge of the (Cuttino) investigation, said this morning that Gaskins had been investigated in 1970, when the girl disappeared, and again later in 1975, soon after several bodies were discovered in Florence County. Gaskins was charged with those (Florence County) murders."

Chief Deputy T.L. McJunkin, who had returned on Monday night from a five-day criminal justice seminar in Tennessee and did not know the details of Gaskins' testimony, told Adams that Gaskins had been working as a roofer for the Fort Roofing and Sheet Metal Co. on the day that Peg Cuttino disappeared, and that a check with his foreman, Roy Harrington, accounted for Gaskins' whereabouts on that day.

"Our information at that time was that he was working at Fort Roofing and his activities were accounted for at that time," McJunkin said. He said that he and SLED agent J. Leon Dollard, who assisted him in the investigation of Gaskins at the time of the Cuttino girl's disappearance, had not questioned Gaskins at that time because it was not thought to have been necessary.

"We were trying to develop leads, anything that might be unusual, out of the ordinary, that might warrant a more intensive investigation," McJunkin said.

The records show that the Cuttino investigation led to Gaskins because of reports from a woman that Gaskins had tried to sexually assault her at the Thunderbird Motel on U.S. 15 South. That report later proved to be unfounded, McJunkin said, according to reporter Jerry Adams.

Gaskins had also admitted in his testimony on Monday that he had showed Sheriff Parnell where to find the body of 17-year-old Patricia Ann Alsbrook, but he denied killing the girl.

Patty Alsbrook had left her parents' home on the night of November 10, 1970, to go riding with some girlfriends. Authorities believe she may have been with Janice Kirby, Gaskins' 15-year-old niece, when she disappeared. The two girls were seen on the Edmunds High School campus in Sumter the morning after Patty Alsbrook left home. The Kirby girl is still missing and is believed to be one of Gaskins' victims. Patty Alsbrook's decomposed body was found six years later in a septic tank near where Gaskins had once lived, after Gaskins told Sheriff Parnell where it was.

Autopsy reports failed to determine either the cause or time of Patty Alsbrook's death.

Another of the bodies found and linked to Gaskins was that of Jesse Ruth Judy, the wife of James K. Judy.

James Judy pled guilty to being an accessory after the fact in the death of another of Gaskins victims, Johnny Sellers. Sellers was found buried with a woman, not positively identified, but believed by police to be Jesse Ruth Judy. She was 22 years old when she disappeared, but was just a teenage girl, along with Patty Alsbrook and Janice Kirby in the 1970's.

Mrs. LeNoir wondered if there might have been some connection between these girls and Peg Cuttino, prior to Peg's disappearance in 1970.

Assistant Solicitor Kenneth Young, Jr., had accused Gaskins of "trying to claim credit for everything in the last 20 years" to promote a book that he was supposed to be writing, but — Mrs. Lenoir thought — something didn't add up right.

The Item's editor summed up Mrs. Lenoir's thoughts... and a lot of other people's feelings on the subject:

The Daily Item — Sumter, SC, Wednesday, April 27, 1977

OPINION

Donald Henry 'Pee Wee' Gaskins," the editorial read, *"dropped one of his promised bombshells Monday during his trial in Newberry for the murder of Silas Barnwell Yates of Lake City. It was a bombshell whose shock waves reached all the way to Sumter County.*

What the convicted murderer, who used to work in Sumter, said in open court was that he killed Margaret "Peg" Cuttino in December 1970. He also claimed he was paid to kill her by an unidentified "law enforcement man".

Local law enforcement authorities were quick to repudiate Gaskins' revelation, claiming that he could not have committed the murder for which William "Junior" Pierce was convicted in 1973.

Of course, Gaskins could not have committed the murder — if one accepts the conviction of Pierce. Unfortunately, local law enforcement and the criminal justice system have a credibility problem that stems from an undercurrent of suspicion among a substantial number of people in this community that the real murderer of Peg Cuttino has never been brought to justice.

If local authorities are going to dismiss Gaskins as a liar and publicity seeker, they will add to their credibility problem. Those who have kept up with the strange story of Pee Wee Gaskins know that he claims he pinpointed the location of a grave containing the body of Patricia Alsbrook of Sumter, although he denies killing her. He also says he has shown authorities the site of another grave that contains the body of a girl he allegedly murdered in 1971. If this body is found, Gaskins will have been 100 percent correct so far in his grisly disclosures.

So, rather than dismissing out of hand Gaskins' open court confession, local authorities should be substantiating their disbelief with facts as to why Gaskins is not telling the truth. He should be questioned and his answers made public.

The public has every right to know what Gaskins knows or claims to know, and to make up its own mind as to his credibility.

Sheriff Parnell had not attended any of the Gaskins trial in Newberry, but in the wake of the charges made by Gaskins on Monday, he showed up in court on Tuesday morning.

Pee Dee Bureau reporter Duncan Hite asked Parnell about the comments made by Gaskins.

"Preposterous," said the Sheriff, "I'm not surprised. He's a very vindictive man and he's wanting publicity."

When asked about the alleged body of the black girl named "Clyde", which Gaskins said he had told the Sheriff about some five months ago, Sheriff Parnell confirmed that Gaskins showed lawmen where the body was allegedly disposed of the previous November — six months before — but said he had been unable to organize a search since then. He said he would have searched just prior to the start of the Yates trial on April 18, but feared he might "prejudice the jury". Parnell said that he would organize a search for the body — said to be in a water-filled ditch in the Concord section of Sumter County — "as quick as we can" after the trial.

Hite, in his article entitled "PARNELL TERMS GASKINS' ALLEGATIONS PREPOSTEROUS", which ran in the Wednesday edition of The State, said, "The State has learned that the black girl may have been pregnant when she was killed, probably in the fall of 1971."

The Gaskins testimony on Monday opened up a whole new can of worms back home in Sumter County. The citizens wanted to know who "Clyde" was, and all about it.

Item staff writer Jerry Adams was assigned to do a story following up on the testimony. He interviewed Sheriff Parnell and published his questions and the Sheriff's answers in a lengthy article headed by the question "Who is 'Clyde'?" and entitled "SEARCH FOR BODY PLANNED MONDAY".

Things got hot in Sumter County again. The county and city were buzzing about this latest development.

Parnell had said that they had planned to search for the girl's body, but that those plans had been hampered by high water in the ditch, heavy rains, frozen ground, an inability to get several investigative teams together for the search, conflicts with General Sessions court, and conflicts with the Yates murder trial. Many of Sumter County's citizens, alot of them black, were hopping mad about the Sheriff's inability to — or disinterest in — search for the black girl's remains. Some believed that he was not telling the truth about the obstacles that had prevented the search, since heavy machinery would still have to be brought in to drain the ditch so that the body could be searched for. They could have done that six months ago, if they had really been interested, some said.

The papers were filled with coverage on the developments in Gaskins' trial and most of it was rehashing the whole story from the beginning, but once in a while a small tidbit of information would creep out that had not been reported before. In an article in The Daily Item, Wednesday, April 25, 1977, entitled "CUTTINO'S KILLER?", Jerry Adams related that during Gaskins' investigation back in 1970, when Peg Cuttino disappeared, "The supervisor, Roy Harrington, told authorities that Gaskins had been working at a job on Willow Drive (the new Sumter YMCA building) that day with another man, sheet metal mechanic Thomas E. Christmas. Christmas told police at the time — and told The Item Tuesday — that he had been with Gaskins from 7:30 a.m. until 5:30 p.m. on the day Peg Cuttino disappeared, and that "if he took that girl, it had to have been after 5:30."

Pee Wee Gaskins was found guilty of the murder of Silas Yates and sentenced to life in prison, but the comments he made on the witness stand would be remembered for many years to come.

On Friday, April 29, the search for the remains of the black girl known only as "Clyde" began.

"Friday's search started off with all the excitement of a carnival. Members of the press were led to the dig site in a seven-car caravan by Sheriff Parnell. Reporters and investigators joked about how to best divvy up the proceeds from the coke, candy, sandwich, and popcorn concessions which might develop at the scene," Item reporters Kathy Edwards and Jerry Adams wrote.

"Chief Deputy Tom McJunkin ordered deputies to block off each end of the dirt road leading to the site to keep the curiosity seekers away, and wondered jokingly where he could arrange for bleachers on such short notice. But, as he said, it was serious business and investigators were prepared to spend the day, or possibly the weekend, draining, digging out, and examining every inch of the 150-yard-long ditch where Pee Wee claimed to have thrown the girl's body," they said.

It seemed apparent that some of the law enforcement people did not take Gaskins' testimony seriously, but when the ditch yielded ten or twelve human bones, probably those of a black female beyond her teen years, according to forensic pathologist Dr. Joel Sexton of the Medical University of South Carolina in Charleston, things got serious.

The skull and two bones of the skeleton were found at 10:50 a.m. by Sheriff Parnell's son, Ira Byrd Parnell, Jr., a SLED agent, who was involved in the search. A gold wedding band was also found at the site, which was later reported to be a silver ring.

Item Editor Hubert Osteen, Jr., reflected on the situation in an editorial:

The Daily Item — Sumter, SC, Monday, May 2, 1977

OPINION

SOCIETY WAS VICTIM

In last week's trial of Donald Henry "Pee Wee" Gaskins, the confessed murderer of at least five people was described by Solicitor R. Kirk McLeod and Assistant Solicitor Kenneth R. Young, Jr., as "a man without a soul" and a person with a "demented, warped mind" who "should be locked up and for-gotten".

After his recent conviction in the Silas Barnwell Yates

murder, Gaskins probably will be locked up for the rest of his natural life, but unfortunately, he won't be forgotten. Judging by his past criminal record, he should have been locked up for good many, many years ago. That he has been allowed to move about as a free man for so many years is a severe indictment of the court system and judges that failed to keep such an animal off the streets.

Gaskins' criminal career began 25 years ago, when he was convicted in Florence of assault and battery of a high and aggravated nature and sentenced to five years.

Exactly five years later, in 1957, he was again convicted in Florence, this time for accessory after the fact of murder. He got three years for this.

Two years later, he was convicted in Atlanta of transporting a stolen car across state lines and sentenced to three years. (One must assume the previous sentence was shortened for good behavior.)

In 1964, he was back in Florence, where he was tried, convicted and sentenced to six years for having carnal knowledge of a child.

He escaped from the Central Correctional Institution in Columbia, but was caught and convicted in 1968, receiving a two-year sentence.

In 1973, again in Columbia, he was convicted of illegally possessing dynamite, for which he was sentenced to two years suspended, and probation for three years.

Last year, the first conviction in Florence, for murder, was returned by a jury in the Prospect killing case. After the Newberry trial, his record reads: convicted of two murders, charged with nine. There may be even more, if one is to believe his startling confessions in court last week.

So, there you have it. The prosecutors did not exaggerate. Somehow this mad dog was allowed to roam the countryside, thanks to a criminal justice system severely distorted by misdirected concern for the defendant rather than the victim. In this case, society became the victim because Gaskins got set free once too often.

In the days and weeks that followed, the authorities continued to unearth fragments of the black girl's skeleton in and around the drainage ditch. The newspapers were filled with the daily accounts of the slow, tedious search.

The bones were believed to be those of a young black woman known on the streets of Sumter as "Clyde", whose real name was Martha Ann Dicks. Miss Dicks was last seen by her family on March 29, 1972, when she left her home to go to a Manning Avenue bar. Reports were that she left the bar that night with a white man. She was 19.

After Ann had not been heard from for several days, her mother notified police. But the police and Sheriff's department said there is no record of a missing person's report being filed.

When the family got no help from law enforcement officials in 1972, they began searching for her on their own, but with no results, according to her mother.

The public was furious. The breach between the citizens and the law enforcement officials seemed to widen daily now and a group of citizens, many of them from the old Concerned Citizens Committee, organized a new group, calling themselves the Sumter County Citizens for Justice.

Item Editor Hubert Osteen, Jr., presented an editorial by the Editor of the Florence, South Carolina, newspaper:

The Daily Item — Sumter, SC, Saturday, May 7, 1977

OTHER EDITOR'S OPINION

GASKINS' GRISLY STORY

Circuit Judge Dan Laney, whose unenviable duty it was to preside over the trial of Donald "Pee Wee" Gaskins and three others charged in the 1975 murder of Florence County farmer Barnwell Yates, says it's time to close the books on the Prospect slayings.

While Gaskins has confessed to nine murders, Laney observed, "I see no reason for him to be tried in all the rest of the cases."

In some respects, Judge Laney makes perfect sense. Gaskins is now under two consecutive life sentences. Barring some unforeseeable twist of fate, he will spend the rest of his life in jail, shut off from society.

Additional trials, moreover, would be costly to the taxpayers and traumatic for the families of the victims. And all the while, Gaskins would be reaping additional publicity for the book he says he plans to write.

There are, however, compelling reasons for continuing to prosecute Gaskins for as long as he's willing to go on making confessions and pointing out gravesites.

Gaskins has been prosecuted, successfully, for two murders. Each time, others were convicted along with him. And each time, he's led authorities to more bodies.

Granted, he has nothing to lose and everything to gain by making the rest of his saga as grisly and sensational as possible — even if that requires twisting the truth into a pretzel. But several questions persist about the remaining bodies.

If Gaskins killed them, did he have help? Are there accomplices who will remain free unless the state draws more information out of him? And if he didn't kill the others, if he's simply spicing up his story, then who did?

If Gaskins was indeed a professional "hit man", who paid him to make the hits? And what's to be done about the un-named "law enforcement man" Gaskins said ordered the killing of Margaret "Peg" Cuttino and others? Indeed, how many "others" are there who were shot or stabbed and hidden away where only he can find them — if he's prompted to do so? Perhaps none, but who will ever know if the probe ends now?

Of more immediate concern, of course, is the fact that two men are now serving life sentences for crimes Gaskins says he committed — the Cuttino murder and a double slaying in Horry County. Gaskins' "confession" casts a reasonable doubt, if only temporarily, on their guilt. The state should take the initiative in removing that doubt once and for all.

Last Friday, officers found a body in a Sumter ditch — right where Gaskins had told them, five months earlier, that they'd find one if they bothered to look. He says the body is that of an unidentified black woman he killed years ago, on orders from that nameless — and perhaps mythical — lawman.

Suppose Judge Laney's logic had been accepted after Gaskins drew his first life sentence, for murdering Dennis Bellamy. The body — along with the disturbing questions about who put it there, and why — might have remained buried forever.

One doubts that the public would be satisfied with a criminal justice system which so easily wrote off the taking of human life.

FLORENCE MORNING NEWS

CHAPTER FOURTEEN

THE CITIZENS FOR JUSTICE

MAY 9, 1977

Amid the confusion of events being covered by the news media, the citizens of Sumter County became very concerned about the quality of law enforcement being provided by their public officials.

The Sumter County Citizens for Justice drafted a letter to South Carolina Governor James B. Edwards, U.S. Justice Department Civil Rights investigator David Adler and Sumter County Council, requesting an investigation of the whole thing.

In an interview with Item staff writers Jerry Adams and Kathy Edwards on Monday, May 9, 1977, spokeswoman for the group, Mrs. Peggy Burleson, outlined the reasons for the request.

"We are requesting of our county commissioners that they request, through Governor Edwards' office, an investigation into the events which are now going on in Sumter County.

"We are requesting an outside investigation, either by the FBI or the U.S. Justice Department."

Allegations in the letter stemmed from Pee Wee Gaskins' confession that he killed the black girl named "Clyde" and Peg Cuttino. The citizens raised questions about the investigations into the disappearance of those two and that of Patricia Ann Alsbrook.

Less than three hours after the disappearance of Peg Cuttino, there had been a massive search by city, county and state law enforcement agents, while no formal search parties had ever been organized at all for the other two missing girls.

Missing persons reports on Miss Dicks ("Clyde") and Miss Alsbrook were reportedly turned in to the city police department, but city officials now said that they had no record of the reports being filed.

Chief Deputy Tom McJunkin told the Item reporters that those records may have been lost when law enforcement departments moved to the new law enforcement center, which had recently been occupied by city and county agencies. He said that investigators would begin talking with Miss Dicks' family and friends to find out whether they could shed any new light on her mysterious disappearance — six years before. Pee Wee Gaskins told them where her body was.

Miss Alsbrook's badly decomposed body, you will recall, was found November 5, 1977, in a septic tank in the Concord section of Sumter County — almost six years after she disappeared, and Pee Wee Gaskins told them where it was.

There had been virtually no investigation in the latter two cases and the citizens wanted to know why.

On Tuesday, May 10, at a County Council meeting, Mrs. Burleson read the letter to County Council. Sheriff Parnell countered with a five-page statement, which he read to the Council, in which he recounted events leading to the arrest of Gaskins in 1975 and he countered allegations that his department may have improperly handled the three Sumter missing persons reports.

Council Chairman Lauren P. Booth said that Council would meet with County Attorney Werber Bryan and, as a result of Attorney Bryan's advice, said that the matter would be referred to the Grand Jury — the only organization that has the powers to investigate a constitutional office, such as the Sheriff's office.

In her letter, Mrs. Burleson also alleged that a man, under indictment for drug distribution, was hired as dispatcher at the law enforcement center. She said that after he left that job, all charges against him were nol-prossed (not prosecuted) by Solicitor R. Kirk McLeod.

"I have nothing to do with hiring in communications," was Sheriff Parnell's only reply to this charge.

But perhaps the most important testimony at this Council meeting was that of F. Parker Haley.

Mr. Haley said that he had been at a trash dump in the Manchester State Forest on December 20, 1970, just two days after Peg Cuttino disappeared from her home, and that he had seen a man standing behind a white Ford Station wagon. The man appeared to be holding something down in the back of his car. He described the man as having "a ruddy complexion, about 200 pounds, with black hair".

He said he called Sheriff Parnell's house and talked with Mrs. Parnell, who said she would tell the Sheriff about the call. He had made that call because of a request for any information about suspicious activities that might be connected to Miss Cuttino's disappearance. But, Mr. Haley said, Parnell never came to check out what he had seen.

Parker Haley had opposed Sheriff Parnell for the office of Sheriff a few years before this incident, but had been handily defeated by the old law veteran. Some wondered if that may have had some bearing on the fact that Parnell never responded to the information.

Parnell said Mr. Haley's statement to Council was the first time he had heard of the call.

After 90 minutes, the meeting, which had been witnessed by more than 25 spectators packed into the small County Council chambers at the county courthouse in anticipation of fireworks from a confrontation between members of the Sumter County Citizens for Justice and Sheriff Parnell, left in sullen disappointment. There were no raised voices, no stormy exchanges between partisans, and no lengthy debates or arguments. But they had some new testimony to think about.

Following is a transcript of a statement prepared by James Cuttino and read by his attorney, George James, at that meeting. For Mr. Cuttino, it was a rare public statement on the investigation.

> *Mr. Chairman and Members of Council:*
> *Six-and-one-half years ago, our little 13-year-old daughter, Margaret, left her home just before noon to walk several blocks to Willow Drive School to have lunch with her little sister Pam.*
> *As you all are aware, she was abducted and brutally*

murdered and, 12 days later, her body was found in Manchester State Forest. Two years later, her murderer was brought to trial and convicted.

He was convicted by a jury of his peers after having been given a change of venue, and I do not question that verdict. This matter was thoroughly investigated and I believe justice was done.

Following this trial, I understand that Mr. (William J.) Pierce was granted and had full avenues of appeal. And I further understand that on at least one occasion, the Sumter County Grand Jury has again investigated this matter.

From reading the newspaper, I gathered that additional investigations of this is being requested by a committee whose membership is not known to me, which identifies itself as being Sumter County Committee for Justice.

I am personally aware that Sheriff (I. Byrd) Parnell, Chief (L.W.) Griffin, Chief (J.P.) Strom of SLED and their officers diligently, conscientiously and tirelessly did everything they could to investigate this matter and apprehend the criminal. And I can assure you that they have my complete confidence.

Mr. Chairman and gentlemen, for six-and-one-half years, this group, with the full and complete cooperation of the news media, has succeeded, without one shred of new evidence known to me, in creating doubt in the minds of the public and with disrupting and interfering with the work of our law enforcement officials.

This has caused my family great distress and already has had a detrimental effect on the lives of my remaining children.

I earnestly request that this matter be ended and laid to rest, and that it not be allowed to continue on the sort of evidence and accusations reported.

Mrs. LeNoir, wanting to answer a statement made by James D. Riel, a member of the Grand Jury in 1973, in a letter to the Editor that appeared in the Tuesday, May 10, edition of The Item, made a request of Circuit Judge Earnest A. Finney, Jr., for a copy of a portion of the sealed Grand Jury transcript containing information about the Peg Cuttino murder investigation.

"James Riel said in his letter, 'All witnesses were given ample time to present to the Grand Jury any and all evidence which they might have concerning this case," Mrs. LeNoir said. "...of course, he was speaking of the Cuttino case... but I wanted to get the transcript and answer his statement... showing the treatment that I and my husband received at that hearing.

"I wanted to find a statement by Assistant Attorney General Douglas Saleeby to the effect that he thanked me for coming to the Grand Jury meeting and that I may be called to testify at a later time. I was never recalled. I was subpoenaed to appear there... I still have the subpoena," she said.

"Three times, they have forbidden me to testify," Mrs. LeNoir told Judge Finney. "If citizens who are willing to come forward are to be treated like criminals, the persons responsible are destroying our judicial system."

The three occasions referred to by Mrs. LeNoir were: in Kingstree, March 19, 1973; in Sumter, April 5, 1973; and again before the Grand Jury in July of 1973.

After a search of South Carolina law, however, Judge Finney found that he could not grant her request, and denied it.

Mrs. LeNoir was disappointed, but not surprised by Judge Finney's decision.

CHAPTER FIFTEEN

THE SECOND GRAND JURY HEARING

MAY 23, 1977

Chairman Booth, at the request of County Council, sent a letter to Grand Jury Foreman Hugh Betchman requesting the Jury's review of information on police investigations received at Tuesday's Council meeting.

For the second time in four years, the Sumter County Grand Jury would be investigating investigations.

The Sumter County Grand Jury, under state law, has the power to fully investigate matters of public concern. The Jury can hand down indictments for criminal activity — indictments not initiated by law enforcement or the Solicitor's office. Such an investigation is unusual for a Grand Jury.

Usually, the Grand Jury studies indictments on major charges to decide whether law enforcement officers have produced enough evidence to send an accused person to trial. It is a probable-cause hearing.

However, Grand Juries are also charged with investigating "everything that may occasion danger, disturbances or dismay to citizens."

"Grand Juries are watchmen stationed by the law to survey the conduct of their fellow citizens, and inquire where and by whom public authority has been violated, or our constitutional and laws infringed," according to a 1932 court decision.

Grand Juries have wide investigative powers, including the power to subpoena witnesses through the prosecutor and take heresay evidence which cannot be presented in regular court sessions.

In past years, Grand Juries have been criticized for becoming "rubber stamps" for law enforcement, that the Juries are no longer the investigative bodies they are charged to be.

Sumter County's Grand Jury has 18 members, six of whom are holdovers from last year. Twelve are new members, drawn from qualified voter lists, as required by law.

The Circuit Solicitor usually acts as "legal counsel" for the Grand Jury. The Solicitor subpoenas witnesses, assists in questioning witnesses and helps interpret the law. But the Solicitor cannot be present during the Grand Jury's deliberations.

Grand Jury deliberations are always closed to the public to protect anyone who may be unjustly accused of a crime.

Kathy Edwards, Item staff writer, provided the aforementioned facts in order to reacquaint the public with Grand Jury procedures, prior to the upcoming session.

On Wednesday, May 18, 1977, the Grand Jury foreman, Hugh Betchman, called a special meeting of the Sumter County Grand Jury, but refused to say what the panel would discuss.

"We have no way of releasing any information to be discussed at the meeting," he said. Neither a judge nor a Solicitor would be present.

The resident judge is empowered to charge the Grand Jury and explain its powers, but Judge Ernest A. Finney, Jr., this session's presiding judge would not be present at Wednesday's special session.

"This is a called meeting, not a charged one," Betchman told Item staff writer Jerry Adams.

The public felt uneasy about this meeting. They had come to distrust their public officials and any unusual procedure became suspect to the disillusioned citizens.

However, their fears subsided when Chairman Betchman emerged from the special meeting after more than an hour of deliberation with the following statement: "Those who wish to present information of grievances are to meet with the Sumter County Grand Jury on Monday at 10:00 a.m., May 23, 1977. Register with Clerk of Court."

Mrs. LeNoir, who up until now had never been able to present her evidence in court, said, "I definitely plan to go. This restores our faith in the human race."

Mrs. Burleson said, "I'm going to present to the Grand Jury the documents to back up charges I made in the Council meeting."

Travis Timmons, who also spoke out at the May 10 County Council meeting, planned to go before the Grand Jury, too. Timmons contended that Pee Wee Gaskins' witness-stand confession to the murders of Miss Cuttino and the black girl known as "Clyde" should be investigated.

Sheriff Parnell had said that he would prosecute Gaskins for his judicial confession to the murder of "Clyde", but he was convinced Gaskins was not involved in the Cuttino murder.

"If he (Parnell) was going to charge him (Gaskins) for one murder, why not charge him for both?" Timmons had asked at the Council meeting.

B.L. Shirah, another speaker at the May 10 Council meeting said he had an out of town commitment, but would do his best to be there. He said he wanted to express his views on the Cuttino-Pierce-Gaskins situation.

At the Council meeting, Shirah said, "If a man confesses to a crime, especially murder, and the one that is serving time denies the murder, in my mind, I believe that this deserves an investigation.."

City Police Chief L.W. Griffin said he would be there. "The Police Department will cooperate 100 percent with the Grand Jury," he said.

But Sheriff Parnell said, "If they ask me to go, I'll go." Otherwise, he said, he had no plans to attend.

Item Editor Hubert Osteen, Jr., made a statement to the people that was clearly designed to settle down the very explosive situation which existed in Sumter County at that time:

The Daily Item — Sumter, SC, Thursday, May 19, 1977

OPINION

LET THE PEOPLE KNOW

The community, as well as local law enforcement authorities, should be pleased that the Sumter County Grand Jury has decided to conduct hearings into citizens' grievances, presumably about the performance of the authorities in various investigations, notably the Gaskins and Pierce cases.

This will be an opportunity for the Grand Jury to, as Police Chief L.W. Griffin recently put it, "clear the air" over the controversy surrounding local law enforcement and the judicial system.

As we have commented before, the climate of distrust and suspicion enveloping certain elected officials is unhealthy for our community. An impartial inquiry into the entire situation, which the Grand Jury is capable of doing, would go a long way toward purifying the atmosphere.

If there is fault to be found, or wrongdoing, or dereliction of duty on the part of anyone, or if there are facts to the contrary, let it be noted by the Grand Jury when its deliberations are completed. The people need to know. And they should know.

Through their surrogates on this most important Grand Jury, we hope they will know.

Members of the Grand Jury would be:

Hugh B. Betchman, Foreman, insurance agent
James H. DuBose, employee with B.L. Montague Co.
Howard W. Adams, Assistant cashier, South Carolina National Bank
John R. Baxter, owner of Baxter's Book Store
Nola C. Salisbury, owner of Newman Realty Co.
Ray G. Ardis, assistant vice president of the Peoples National Bank
Pearl S. Bradford
Gloria J. Boykin
Raymond S. Fowler, Jr., service station owner
Jack L. Galloway, manager, Palmetto Baking Co.
Glenn C. Goodson, manager, Time Finance Co.
Aubrey Hatfield, president, HAPCO, Inc.
George R. Elmore, assistant vice president and manager of the
    Palmetto Plaza branch of the National Bank of South Carolina
Joseph McMillan, Jr.
Grady B. Mullis, counselor, State Vocational Rehabilitation Center
George E. Parker, Communications Officer, Shaw Air Force Base
Herbert W. Pearson

Page 149

Alternates:

Rometta A. McCoy, teacher
Shirley H. Patterson, teacher
Charlie Robinson, employee, Burgess-Brogdon Co.

On Thursday, May 12, 1977, Sheriff's Department investigators launched a full-scale, three-front attack to "dig up every rumor in Sumter County" connected with Pee Wee Gaskins' possible murder victims.

Investigators, with the assistance of a county-operated back-hoe, began excavating at three well sites near the septic tank where the body of Patricia Ann Alsbrook had been found the previous November. Gaskins had at one time lived in a house next to one of the three wells.

Gaskins, who worked as a roofer while he lived in Sumter, from 1968 to 1972, also worked as a well digger. One of the places being searched, in a trash dump, was a slightly overgrown area between two large oak trees. The ground was covered with roofing materials.

County crews arrived at daybreak and began digging the first well shortly after 9:00 a.m. That well was only about 30 feet from the septic tank where the Alsbrook girl's body was found.

Nothing was found there, and workers began to dig into a second well, one which served the house where Gaskins lived. Authorities had heard reports that Gaskins had poured acid into the wells. But they found nothing in any of the wells.

County crews also began scaling the sides of the ditch near where the skull and bones of Martha Dicks had been found.

It was obvious that the Sheriff and other law enforcement officials were irritated by the Sumter County Citizens for Justice request for investigation into law enforcement activities that the public felt should have been investigated long ago.

The Sumter Daily Item was filled with accounts of the searches, accompanied by large pictures of the equipment and men at work. The State newspaper in Columbia, The Florence Morning News, and a number of other newspapers carried news of the sudden all-out search for bodies in Sumter County, seemingly in nervous anticipation of the upcoming Grand Jury investigation.

On Monday, May 16, The Item announced that the Sumter County law enforcement officials had ended their search, but that investigations into the three murders and the missing person case (all of which may be linked to Gaskins) continued.

Sheriff Parnell and Police Chief Griffin sent a letter to Gaskins' attorney, O. Grady Query, asking for an interview with Gaskins "at the earliest possible time". They said in the letter that they wanted to interview him in connection with his April 25 witness-stand confession to the murder of Margaret "Peg" Cuttino and the black girl he called "Clyde".

They also said in the letter that they wanted to question him in connection with the disappearance of his niece, Janice Kirby, who was last seen with the Alsbrook girl.

Not everyone was against the law enforcement officers in Sumter County, however; and a few of their supporters began to write letters to the Editor of The Item.

The Daily Item — Sumter, SC, Monday, May 16, 1977

LETTERS TO THE EDITOR

COOPERATION OUTSTANDING

To the Editor:
"Having been on the inside looking out" as County Coroner from July 1975 to January 1977, I would like to express my views of the Sumter County Sheriff's Department.

When I was first appointed, all of the news media (radio and newspapers) wanted to know how I was going to handle all of the problems ex-Coroner Parnell had with the law enforcement people. I said that I did not anticipate any. I was only looking for cooperation and assistance, and this I found in great abundance. All I had to do was ask and it was cooperation and assistance one hundred percent.

The Sheriff did not try to run the Coroner's office and vice-versa. The Sheriff only gave me one piece of advice as how to run the Coroner's office, and I quote verbatim: "Keep it open, don't hide anything from anybody."

During my term of office as Coroner, there wasn't anything swept under any carpets or hidden in any closets by the Sheriff or any man of the Sumter County Sheriff's Department.

I will always be grateful for their interest, cooperation and assistance and I sincerely appreciate your letting me express my views.

Ben Raffield

OFFICERS ARE ONLY HUMAN

To the Editor:
This is concerning the article of May 11 entitled "Police Chief Confirms Hiring Former Felon". In this article, Mrs. Burleson criticizes Chief Griffin for his role in the rehabilitation of a former drug dealer. The Sumter County Citizens for Justice may have reason to probe into the law enforcement agencies, but why should they dig into the past of a young man who has now been rehabilitated? Where is the justice in tearing down the life of one who is doing his best to live a respectable and productive life?

Mrs. Burleson's comments indicate a bitterness toward the Police Department because of their lack of help when she discovered that her own son was involved with drugs. Granted, the law enforcement officers should investigate reports of drug usage, but they sometimes fail in their efforts, as they are only human. If a mother can only "watch" and "fink" on her son, what kind of miracle does she expect the law enforcement officers to perform?

There is a need for the Sumter County Citizens for Justice, but this organization should not be used as a means for carrying out personal vendettas. It seems that Mrs. Burleson's "finking, finking, finking" accomplished nothing, so, hopefully, she will start "thinking, thinking, thinking" before she aids in damaging a young man's life beyond repair.

Citizens for "True Justice"
Mary L. Meadows
Carolyn A. James

The Daily Item — Sumter, SC, Wednesday, May 18, 1977

LETTER TO THE EDITOR

STAND TALL FOR LAWMEN

To the Editor:
The show of blood increases the frenzy of the spectators and stirred the lions into a faster kill action... the eating of the Christians in the Coliseum of Rome, Emperor Vespasian or Titus could be the cheerleaders to stir the frenzy into a faster tempo for the kill. As the kills increase, the blood flows faster... the lions become more savage... the passion of the spectators demands more... more... more.

This letter does not start off to indicate that I am writing a personal endorsement for our Sheriff, Byrd Parnell... a Christian... dedicated... and educated... experienced and hard-working Sheriff. I am, though. I believe in him.

The few drops of ink in our news media pertaining to the expressions of Pee Wee Gaskins... a psycho... a pathological liar... a murderer many times over... and, as our fine young assistant solicitor, Mr. Kenneth Young, stated of Gaskins, "he is a small man... real brave... he gets his kicks out of murdering the young and the weak. He should be put away and forgotten."

The few drops of ink in our media are helping to cause improper thoughts and statements of a few loud mouths pertaining to the fiber of our local law enforcement chief and his equally qualified and hard-working staff. Do not be one of the spectators in the Coliseum of Rome... with the thumb down for the kill. Be a citizen of Sumter... proud to be here... standing tall in

the saddle for our police force. Support them and pray that they
may always be on your side, or I should say... you on their side.
For they operate under the laws of our state and land... our
Constitution and our Bible. I pray that it will always be this way.
Sic 'em, Sheriff. We believe in you.

Fred F. Dean

Some of the citizens just couldn't stand all this praise for the law enforcement officers and rebutted with their answers to these letters

The Daily Item — Sumter, SC, Friday, May 20, 1977

LETTER TO THE EDITOR

'A LETTER TO FRED'

To the Editor:
Fred, your fifth letter to the editor was published last night
(Wednesday). With some regret I must answer this letter. Fred, I
have known you for 14 years. You have been (and hope still are)
my best friend.
I supported you in your campaign against the free loaders in
the welfare and food stamp programs. I went with you to the
courthouse and sat with the ladies of the anti-ERA movement. I
endorsed your letter to the editor berating John Miles on his
stand for ERA.
Your letter of personal endorsement for Byrd Parnell was
wrong and not in line with your usual sense of reasoning. You
have let your better judgement be blinded.
Yes, Sheriff Parnell is a fine gentleman, member of Boyle
Bible Class, a Christian, dedicated and most certainly hard-
working. However, in any governmental agency, be it federal,
state, county or city, a certain laxness can creep in over the years.
The taxpayers have every right to demand full explanations of
any inconsistency in the Sheriff's Department.
Yes, Fred, remember Richard Nixon was also a back-slapper,
good guy, Christian, dedicated and educated. Where is he today?
We won't throw Sheriff Parnell to the lions, but we certainly
deserve the chance to look closely at his work and give him the
thumbs up or down as we see fit.

Alan D. Salisbury

By Saturday, May 21, eighteen persons had registered to testify before the Grand Jury, according to Clerk of Court O.V. Player.

After being re-instructed by Judge Ernest A. Finney, Jr., on its duties and responsibilities on Monday morning, May 23, the Grand Jury began its work.

Judge Finney, acting on a request by Grand Jury Foreman Hugh Betchman, "re-instructed" the Grand Jury in open court on "a portion of the appropriate laws" governing the conduct of the Grand Jury. The Grand Jury had also been instructed in January at the beginning of the 1977 session.

In a 10-minute statement, Judge Finney told the Jury's 18 members that the law permitted them to hold a "secret proceeding". He said, "... it is entirely within your province or discretion to decide if an investigation should be made and the extent of the investigation. No one can tell you what to investigate or what to recommend."

Mrs. Peg Burleson, spokeswoman for the Sumter County Citizens for Justice, was the first witness to testify. She began her testimony at 10:30 a.m. by reading her letter to the Sumter County Council dated May 6.

And one-by-one, citizens and law enforcement officers paraded before the court, unleashing charges against each other and defending themselves against their accusers.

Mrs. Ann Cason, a witness scheduled to testify about a plane that flew low over a pond near her home and (she said) dropped dope into the pond, complained that a man had walked into her office at Shaw Air Force Base, where she worked, and told her that she had been put on "the extinct list". Another office employee verified the conversation, and she considered this a threat on her life.

But threats were nothing new to Ann Cason. She said she had been living with the idea of someone taking her life for many years now. She had reported this dope activity to the Sheriff's Department and that nothing had been done.

She then said that she had also had difficulties getting her name on the witness list to testify before the Grand Jury. However, shortly before the Grand Jury convened on Monday morning, she had signed a list being circulated by a bailiff. She then found that her name was not on the "official" list of witnesses in the Clerk of Court's office. So, she went back to the courthouse to make sure she was registered to testify. It is not hard to understand why Mrs. Cason came to believe that someone did not want her to testify.

Hugh Munn, a former newspaper reporter for The State newspaper in Columbia (who was at the time of this Grand Jury investigation Public Information Officer for the South Carolina Law Enforcement Division) was there to witness. Kathy Edwards and Jerry Adams, reporters for The Item, asked Munn what he would testify about.

Munn said Sheriff Parnell had asked him to come and testify in connection with his (Munn's) reporting on the Cuttino murder. He had been involved in a sequence of events concerning a blue raincoat with the initials "PEG" monogrammed on the collar. The coat, as you will recall from reading Munn's article earlier in this work, was found at the Horatio Community Center and came into the possession of Mrs. Carrie LeNoir. She gave the coat to Hugh Munn and Jack Truluck, who were both State reporters at that time, and they turned the coat over to the South Carolina Law Enforcement Division. The coat was shown to Mr. and Mrs. James Cuttino, and they said that the coat *did not* belong to their slain daughter, Peg.

The Item apparently tried to find out some facts, in the interest of keeping the public informed, but began to find that there were some things going on that were secret and, though there seemed to be no reason for the secrecy, they could get no answers. So they reported exactly what they found.

For one thing, Dr. Joel Sexton, forensic pathologist, who you will remember came up on the day Miss Cuttino's body was found and then performed the autopsy on her body at the Medical University in Charleston, was asked who had asked him to come and testify before the Grand Jury — remember now, that all of this testimony was strictly voluntary — Dr. Sexton declined to name the person who asked him to testify. Why?

Then, there was a woman who sat in the courtroom apparently taking notes on the entire proceedings. When asked who she was, the Grand Jury declined to identify the woman. They did later confirm that she was present for the hearings, but would not give her name nor her official position.

The Item said that she *presumably* had been taking notes for special prosecutor Joe Barker of the South Carolina Attorney General's office. They asked questions under that assumption, but could not find out who, if anyone, had asked Barker to assist the Grand Jury, or why his services were retained.

This seemed strange to the citizens of Sumter and added to their mistrust of the whole proceedings. Judge Finney ordered an FBI-Air Force investigation on Tuesday afternoon, after he had read news reports of the alleged threat against Mrs. Ann Cason. He called representatives of the FBI, the OSI (Air Force Office of Special Investigation), the South Carolina Law Enforcement Division, the Sumter Police and Sheriff's Departments, and Grand Jury Foreman Hugh Betchman into court and ordered that they investigate the threat.

Since the incident was alleged to have happened on Shaw Air Force Base, the OSI interviewed Mrs. Cason and determined "no offense took place on Shaw Air Force Base which would require federal jurisdiction."

The FBI in Columbia said the FBI had no jurisdiction in the case. And that was the end of that.

However, when Item reporter Jerry Adams contacted Mrs. Cason to obtain her reaction to the refusal of law enforcement agencies to further investigate the incident, she would not talk to him. Her only comment to any of his questions was "no comment".

On Thursday, after a recess, Judge Finney introduced Joseph R. Barker in open court.

Barker, who said that he was from the state Attorney General's office, said he and Kay Crowe (the woman who had been mysteriously attending the court's sessions) were providing legal advice to the Grand Jury and swearing in all witnesses. But, Barker said, he nor Miss Crowe, who was also from the Attorney General's office, had any effect on the Grand Jury's deliberations.

"Well, why couldn't they have told everybody that the first day of court?" Mrs. Carrie LeNoir mused.

The testimony continued through Friday and they adjourned until Tuesday, May 31, of the next week.

Bernard L. Shirah, the first witness that day, made a definite request of the Grand Jury. He told The Item, after his 45-minute testimony that he requested that Gaskins be subpoenaed in order to clear up remarks he made at the Barnwell-Yates murder trial in Newberry.

Shirah, a member of the Sumter County Citizens for Justice, along with many of its other members found it hard to understand why the local law enforcement officials had not followed up on this and wanted the Grand Jury to direct that it be done.

"Time is of the essence," Shirah said. "Do we in fact have all of Gaskins' cohorts in jail? If a man confesses to a crime — especially murder — and the one that is serving the time denies the murder, in my mind, I believe this deserves an investigation. In my opinion, William "Junior" Pierce was tried and convicted of a crime he did not commit. The oral testimony of Sheriff I. Byrd Parnell was largely responsible for Pierce's conviction. No murder weapon, no means of transportation, no signed confession, no time of death were ever established; and in my opinion, no motive was ever established."

Mrs. Carrie LeNoir finally got to present her evidence before a court on Thursday, May 26, 1977. She had prepared, at her own expense, 18 packets of "evidence", one packet for each Grand Jury member. The packets contained the picture of Peg Cuttino taken during the autopsy report prepared at that time, a temperature chart for the 12 days Miss Cuttino was missing before her body was found and other information that she believed would prove to anyone that Peg Cuttino could not have been dead for the full 12 days.

But she walked into a room full of jurors who apparently had a preconceived dislike for her and what she was trying to do. "I felt like a Christian walking into a den of lions," she said later.

"I appreciated the interest and questions, and tried to answer to the best of my ability, but at times was made to feel that I was a criminal being tried for a big crime, and that I should feel guilty for being involved in the Cuttino-Pierce affair," she said. "I certainly resent the harsh treatment I received from several men while trying to testify."

"If I have done anything wrong or illegal, I'm sorry; but I know of no way I'd do differently if I had to start all over again. I assume full responsibility for all actions I've taken and am ready for any consequences which might result," she concluded.

At the request of the Jury, Mrs. LeNoir listed the names of the few persons to whom she had given a picture of the body of Peg Cuttino.

She told the Grand Jury that she had seen Peg Cuttino on December 19, 1970, the day after "Junior" Pierce was supposed to have killed her.

After testifying for more than three hours, longer than anyone else before this Grand Jury, Mrs. LeNoir left the courtroom after being instructed by the Grand Jury not to talk with reporters.

F. Parker Haley then testified of his knowledge, which he believed was pertinent to the Cuttino murder case. He also told the Jury that the prosecution did not prove a time of death, place of death or murder weapon at the Pierce trial.

When it was all over, 33 people had testified before this Grand Jury. According to an article in The Item on Monday, May 30, 1977, by Kathy Edwards and Jerry Adams entitled "GRAND JURY'S NEXT MOVE COULD BE SUBPOENAS", of the 33 who appeared, eight were law enforcement officials; at least three citizens spoke out in favor of law enforcement; and several others testified about the investigation into the abduction and murder of Peg Cuttino.

Many of the witnesses voiced concerns about the "drug problem" in Sumter County. Those witnesses contended that no major drug dealers or distributors had been arrested in the county.

The Grand Jury had completed its hearing of voluntary witnesses and now began to issue subpoenas in order to bring before the Jury persons who might be able to shed some light on issues raised by the voluntary witnesses.

Pee Wee Gaskins, in a move that surprised law enforcement officials and citizens alike, arrived at the Sumter County courthouse at about 9:30 a.m. on Thursday, June 2, in answer to a subpoena which Clerk of Court O.V. Player said he had mailed to the Central Correctional Institute in Columbia.

In fact, apparently, the Sumter County Sheriff's Department was so sure that Gaskins would not show up that they made no arrangements for security if he did arrive.

About five minutes before Gaskins appeared at the courthouse, Sheriff's investigator Sgt. Hugh Mathis told Clerk of Court Player that the Sheriff's Department did not know anything about Gaskins' arrival, according to Item reporters Jerry Adams and Kathy Edwards.

It should have come as no surprise to law enforcement officials when Gaskins turned up at the courthouse because he had been subpoenaed and was in the custody of the law.

On the other hand, why should he come? A contempt of court sentence would mean very little to a man who was already serving two life sentences.

He arrived heavily guarded by SLED agents. Security was tight around him at all times when Gaskins made a "public" appearance, because he had previously escaped from courthouses and prisons.

Several SLED agents ushered him through the back door of the courthouse, into the elevator and up to the third-floor holding room where he would wait until he was called to testify.

"It looks like the President has arrived," SLED Public Information Officer Hugh Munn said, as Gaskins was brought into the courthouse.

Then, shortly before 11:00 a.m., he was before the Grand Jury, where he testified for two hours. Local authorities and SLED agents lined the corridor leading into the Grand Jury room as Gaskins and his two attorneys, J.K. Grisso and O. Grady Query, were led into the room.

It is not known what Gaskins said before the Grand Jury, nor if he identified the law enforcement official that he claimed had him "assassinate" Peg Cuttino and the girl he called "Clyde".

Others subpoenaed before the Grand Jury were:

Walter LeNoir, magistrate in the Horatio community, who gave an affidavit about the coat found in the Horatio community center;

Cabel Rowland;

David L. Timmons, a member of the Sumter County Citizens for Justice Group;

Howard Parnell, the Coroner of Sumter County at the time Miss Cuttino disappeared;

Thomas E. Christmas, who worked with Gaskins at Fort Roofing and Sheet Metal Company and had said he was with Gaskins the day of Miss Cuttino's disappearance;

Jack Floyd, who was in the LeNoir store in Horatio after Mr. and Mrs. LeNoir saw Peg Cuttino and heard them discussing their seeing the girl;

Samuel Frierson;

John Brabham, who owned a real estate agency in Sumter. This agency handled the trailer at Wedgefield belonging to Mrs. Martha Pauline Casey (then Mrs. Edward Graber). The mobile home was discovered on the day Peg Cuttino's body was found and is believed by many Sumter residents to be the place of Miss Cuttino's murder;

Charlie Singleton, who was juvenile officer in Sumter at the time of Miss Cuttino's disappearance. He was working in Clarendon County at the time of this hearing;

Samuel T. Dees, an employee of Unclaimed Freight in Sumter, who delivered mattresses to the mobile home at Wedgefield shortly after Miss Cuttino's body was found, and who saw people burning other mattresses in the back yard.

With the exception of Howard Parnell, all testified before the Grand Jury. He declined to appear. Because he was not a current resident of South Carolina (Parnell was at this time a resident of Atlanta, Georgia), the Grand Jury's subpoena was not binding.

On Saturday, June 4, The Item headlined a new development in an article entitled "ATTORNEYS CONSIDER FILING FOR NEW TRIAL FOR PIERCE".

Joseph T. McElveen, Jr., William E.. Jenkinson, III, and James M. Conor, Pierce's former court-appointed attorneys, were again appointed by Judge Ernest A. Finney, Jr., to defend him.

McElveen denied that a new trial was definitely being sought at this time, but... he had read a petition in open court on Friday before Judge Finney that said, "...Gaskins' confession would be material to the charges against Defendant (Pierce)... and could change the results of the jury verdict convicting the Defendant."

"We feel it is our duty to investigate this matter fully and take such steps before the Court as may be necessary in accordance with the desires of our client and the ends of justice," McElveen said.

But, almost before they got started, barriers began to appear in their path toward justice for Junior Pierce.

In that same courtroom on Friday, Joe McElveen asked that they (Pierce's attorneys) be permitted to order, at the State's expense, transcriptions of Gaskins' testimony at his trial for the murder of Silas Yates. Finney agreed to that motion.

But Judge Finney refused a motion to allow the attorneys to review or to photocopy law enforcement files on the Cuttino disappearance and murder or on the disappearances, deaths and discoveries of Martha Dicks and Patricia Alsbrook.

He then refused the attorneys' request to review any evidence which "connects Donald Henry Gaskins to any of the above individuals or cases."

Judge Finney said he refused those motions because he felt it would not be "appropriate at this time".

A motion that Pierce's attorneys be allowed to visit Gaskins at the Central Correctional Institute in Columbia at "reasonable times" was also denied.

So it seemed that Pierce's attorneys would have to fight the same odds in trying to obtain a new trial that they faced in defending him in the original trial. They would be denied access to the very facts and evidence that could clear Pierce of the crime that it was obvious (to everyone but the law enforcement people, the judges, the Cuttino family and a few citizens) that he did not commit.

The Grand Jury was not finished with its investigation yet, and Sumter County patiently waited and watched to see what they would decide.

Meanwhile, Sumter County law enforcement officials made several attempts to see Pee Wee Gaskins in connection with his confessions, but Gaskins had not allowed his attorneys to grant authorities an interview.

One question, to which no one seemed to have the answer, surfaced. Since the actions of the law enforcement officials were being investigated, who would investigate if the Grand Jury found fault with them or the judicial system?

By June 10, more than 40 witnesses had testified and been recalled (some of them) to testify before the Grand Jury, and still it was not satisfied. Jury foreman Hugh Betchman, Jr., said that when the Grand Jury convened on Monday, June 12, 1977, to begin its fourth week of this investigation, "some people may be called in to bring some records."

Foreman Betchman said he didn't know how many witnesses might be recalled the following week, but he said he doubted that Pee Wee Gaskins would be back to testify.

On Monday, six witnesses answered subpoenas that had been issued on request of the Jury. Some were from out-of-state. Those were here as a courtesy to the court, rather than by force of their subpoena.

Georgia's Police Chief Baxley, J.B. "Red" Carter (the former Sheriff of Appling County, Georgia, who first introduced Junior Pierce into the Cuttino case) appeared and testified for about 20 minutes.

Red Carter was the man to whom Pierce allegedly first confessed that he murdered Peg Cuttino. Carter had then wired Sheriff I. Byrd Parnell of Sumter County. Parnell, SLED Chief J.P. Strom, and Police Chief L.W. Griffin went to Georgia and took Pierce's oral confession to the murder.

Carter, Chief J.P. Strom, SLED Lieutenants Olin Redd and Ted Owens, and two Central Correctional Institute officers testified before the Jury.

On Monday, June 20, 1977, the Sumter County Grand Jury presented the following report to Judge Dan F. Laney, Jr., in the morning session of the Sumter County Court of Common Pleas:

> June 20, 1977
> The Honorable Dan F. Laney, Jr.
> Presiding Judge
> Third Judicial Circuit
>
> This Grand Jury has met during the weeks of May 23 through June 13, 1977, for the purpose of investigating certain allegations against law enforcement and other public officials in Sumter County.
> During this term, this body has listened to the testimony of approximately 40 witnesses, examined exhibits presented by those

witnesses, and considered in-depth every allegation presented to it. We appreciate the concern of and information presented to it by all those who testified.

No effort will be made to list the various allegations; however, it can accurately be stated that they fall into three general categories. The first category of allegations concern the murder of Margaret "Peg" Cuttino in 1970. The second category concerns the drug traffic in Sumter County. The third category would best be described as "miscellaneous", since the allegations falling within this category have little if any relationship either to those falling within the first two categories or to each other.

In reference to those allegations arising from the Cuttino murder, this body has reviewed evidence which has encompassed every aspect of the case from the date and time of disappearance, through investigation, arrest, trial, and post-trial proceedings. We as Grand Jurors, collectively and individually, are satisfied that sufficient inquiry has been made in the course of this investigation into the conduct of law enforcement at every phase of the Cuttino case.

Therefore, we the Grand Jury of Sumter County do hereby find:

1. That no substantive evidence has been presented which would support a finding of either incompleteness or impropriety on the part of the public officials charged with investigation of this case.
2. That there is absolutely no basis for recommending that indictments be brought against any public officials.
3. That, viewing the evidence in toto, it is our opinion that the law enforcement agencies charged with the investigation of the Cuttino case have faithfully discharged their duties under the law.
4. No new substantive evidence has been brought to our attention that would justify our recommending a new trial for William J. Pierce, Jr.
5. That the Grand Jury would like to thank the law enforcement and other public officials involved in the Cuttino case for their dedicated and diligent efforts and for their unstinting cooperation in this investigation.

In reference to those allegations concerning the drug traffic in Sumter County, it is the finding of this body:

1. That no substantive evidence was presented before this body that would indicate any wrongdoing or other failure on the part of any law enforcement or other public

officials to perform their duties with reference to the apprehension and prosecution of drug offenders.

2. That those law enforcement officers charged with enforcement of the drug laws in Sumter County have performed their duties faithfully and diligently and to the limit of their resources.

3. That there is absolutely no basis for recommending that indictments be brought against law enforcement or other public officials.

4. We recommend that the law enforcement divisions of the city and county be immediately staffed with four narcotics officers and combined into a "Metro" type unit. The staffing of this unit should not necessarily be based on receipt of Federal funds, but by reallocation of existing funds because we consider this an immediate need. Toward this end, we request a status report be given to this Grand Jury from the City and County Councils when we convene at the next term of court.

In reference to the other allegations made before this Grand Jury, it is the finding of this body:

1. That no substantive evidence was presented which would indicate either wrongdoing on the part of law enforcement and other public officials in this county, or which would indicate that said officials either negligently failed or refused to perform their duties with respect to those allegations.

2. That there is absolutely no basis for recommending that indictments be brought against law enforcement or other public officials in reference to those allegations.

Hugh B. Betchman, Jr.
Foreman

About 20 citizens sat in the back of the courtroom when the jury filed in at about 10:30 to give its report.

As Clerk of Court O.V. Player, Jr., read the Grand Jury findings, the citizens sat quietly, stared and then began whispering among themselves. Grand Jury members breathed a sigh of relief and were smiling as they filed out of the courtroom some ten minutes after the report was read.

Well, now it was over. Finally, it was over. The Cuttino murder could be laid to rest now and forgotten... or could it?

The citizens had asked for an "independent" investigation on law enforcement and the judicial system in Sumter County. But since the Sumter County Council had no power to order an investigation, it had forwarded the material to the Grand Jury, who did have the power to ask for an "independent" investigation... and now they had reported that they found no reason to do anything about anything.

Bernard L. Shirah, who had asked the Grand Jury to reopen the Cuttino case said, "This is not the end of it, by any means. I think they (the Jury) avoided their responsibility."

Attorney William B. James, who had complained about law enforcement in general in Sumter County, called the Grand Jury's findings a whitewash.

"At first glance, it (the report) was a whitewash from a bourgeois Grand Jury," he said. "They didn't find anything because they didn't look for anything. How could they find anything without investigators?"

Mrs. LeNoir said, "I'm disappointed at their report... but not at all surprised that they found nothing wrong. This is just another step in our war for justice. We've lost another battle... but we haven't lost the war. We have presented facts which should not have been overlooked. Under no circumstances will we drop it until we see justice done.

Mrs. Peg Burleson, spokeswoman for the Sumter County Citizens for Justice, whose allegations prompted the Grand Jury investigation in the beginning, told Item reporters Jerry Adams and Kathy Edwards that she wasn't really surprised by the Grand Jury report. But she questioned the report because, she said, she had presented documents which showed that the Solicitor's office had nol-prossed an indictment and charged the defendant a fine. "They're trying to tell me that's legal?" she asked.

The Reverend Ralph Canty said he gave no specific details when he testified before the Grand Jury. He said he told the Grand Jury that "a full-scale investigation would clear the air of doubt and suspicion."

"I'm disappointed (with the Grand Jury findings)," he said. "I feel the citizens were due more than that sort of response. I am shocked and appalled."

Foreman of the Grand Jury, Hugh Betchman, would not go into specific charges raised to the Grand Jury, but said, "You've got to realize the fact that either something is criminal or negligent. Now, if it's negligence, we can't point the finger and say, 'okay, we're going to slap your hand.'"

But, he added, the Grand Jury found no negligent acts committed by law enforcement authorities. He said he was satisfied with the Grand Jury's unanimous vote to give law enforcement a clean bill of health.

"I've got to look at myself in the mirror every morning. We had all the evidence at our disposal, and the evidence is clear. And I wish everybody could see all the evidence. It's that plain," he said.

Sumter County Sheriff I. Byrd Parnell was in San Diego, California, at that time at a National Sheriff's Association Convention, and was not available for comment.

Judge Dan Laney, who received the report, said Sumter County had the best Solicitor and law enforcement officers in the state.

"If you don't believe it, compare it to somebody else," Judge Laney said.

Police Chief L.W. Griffin was pleased with the Grand Jury's report. "It was very thorough — and I feel that law enforcement in Sumter and Sumter County and the court system — will benefit from it in the long run," he said.

Lt. Ray Isgett, METRO Crime Prevention Unit officer, who had testified at one point before the Grand Jury, said the report "restored faith in law enforcement".

"After a while, you (as a police officer) begin to wonder — could any of this (the allegations) be true?" Isgett said. But he added the investigation cleared his mind of any doubt. "Let's forget it and get on with our jobs."

It was clear that Sumter County was not settled and satisfied with law enforcement, nor did they derive any comfort from the Grand Jury's probe. The general feeling seemed to be that they didn't expect anything, and they didn't get anything from it. It was a Sumter County investigation into Sumter County affairs, and no one ever expected the county to purge itself... not as long as those very powerful officials were in power. The people on the streets and in offices and in homes of the area felt completely defeated by this latest failure to change things.

Letters to the Editor came in to The Item's office and were printed almost daily. They criticized the judge, the jury foreman, called for an investigation of the Grand Jury, and one said "the gap keeps growing", referring to the gap between law enforcement officials and the citizens.

Peg Burleson wrote, "From reading the report of the joint City and County Councils meeting on the Grand Jury's request for a Metro Squad, it sounds as though the Sheriff is now taking County Council down the same 'garden path' as he did the Grand Jury and the citizens of this community. The people of Sumter County in its entirety would do well to heed the words of the father of one of those little Girl Scouts in Oklahoma (whose daughter was murdered): 'It was always someone else's world, but now it's mine.'

"I really thought since the events which were happening had gone out across the state that the citizens of the Grand Jury would give much more thought about what they were told and would really investigate each situation thoroughly," Burleson continued. "They heard, but obviously didn't listen. They only talked to people involved in the Cuttino case and checked law enforcement's investigation in the case. Since they have given them a clean bill of health, if they were given positive proof that (William) Pierce killed Miss Cuttino, I wish they would share their findings with the rest of the community. The court transcript shows there was none offered during the trial.

"Their decision only confirms, in my mind, that we need a Federal investigation in Sumter County... Attorney General Dan McLeod told Mrs. (Carrie) LeNoir and me that being related to Solicitor R. Kirk McLeod didn't matter. Not only have they had control for many years of the judicial system in Sumter County and the state of South Carolina, my information is they are first cousins," Mrs. Burleson concluded.

There was one letter that made a vicious attack on Sheriff Parnell, accusing him of unethical, immoral practices while holding public office. Many others spoke in general terms of the situation, which they considered intolerable in Sumter County.

However, the Grand Jury had spoken, and it seemed very unlikely that there would be any further investigation into the Cuttino murder or other complaints brought before them.

"The Grand Jury has made a report to the people — now the people want a report on the Grand Jury," Theodore Tedder wrote in a letter to the Editor of The Item.

In confusion and disillusionment, the citizens could only express themselves through the newspaper. They didn't know what else to do. And it may have ended here... but you never know what to expect in Sumter County.

CHAPTER SIXTEEN

MRS. LENOIR GOES TO JAIL

AUGUST 29, 1977

On August 8, at the request of James Cuttino, father of the slain girl, Third Circuit Judge Dan F. Laney, Jr., issued an order that "all unauthorized individuals, including Mrs. Carrie LeNoir, Mr. Parker Haley and any others who have in their possession any official documents, or copies thereof, pertaining to the investigation into the murder of Margaret 'Peg' Cuttino..." to deliver the documents immediately to the Sumter County Sheriff's office or the State Law Enforcement Division (SLED) for delivery to the Clerk of Court of Sumter County.

In the order, Laney said that Mr. Cuttino "is suffering irreparable harm for which he has no adequate remedy at law."

But, then the order instructed SLED agents who delivered the order to Mrs. LeNoir to collect the documents from her.

It also said that anyone "aggrieved" by this order should appear before him (Judge Laney) at 11 a.m., on August 29, in Bishopville.

Friday afternoon, August 12, two SLED agents brought the order to Horatio and delivered it to Mrs. LeNoir, demanding that the documents and materials that she had in her possession be handed over to them at once.

Mrs. LeNoir refused to give them the documents, assuring them that she planned to fight Judge Laney's order in the courts.

But, to everyone's surprise, on August 16, Judge Laney signed another order...ordering Mrs. LeNoir to appear before him in his chambers at 11 a.m., August 29, to show cause why he should not hold her in contempt.

"I'm going to be my own lawyer," Mrs. LeNoir told Jerry Adams, of *The Sumter Daily Item,* "I'm going to fix up an affidavit with plain, simple facts to present to the judge. But, I won't turn the pictures over. These are our only tools to see that justice is done."

"I will say this, however," Mrs. LeNoir continued, "The autopsy photographs and reports will be turned over to the attorneys for William J. Pierce, Jr., when Pierce is given a written guarantee of a new trial for Miss Cuttino's murder."

Realizing the pain and agony that the Cuttino family must be experiencing from the continued re-hashing of the events surrounding "Peg's" unfortunate, fatal experience...and with genuine feelings of her own...Mrs. LeNoir wrote the following letter to James Cuttino and his family:

Mr. James Cuttino, Jr.
c/o Mr. George C. James
Sumter, SC 29150

Dear Mr. Cuttino,
    In reply to your petition of July 21, which I received August 12, concerning certain documents connected with Peg Cuttino's death, I wish to say that we are very sympathetic with the Cuttino family, and realize that you are suffering irreparable harm, but I wish you would realize that we, also, are suffering irreparable harm, and we did not choose to get involved in this horrible ordeal. We are victims of circumstances. We are certain that Peg was in our store the day after Junior Pierce was supposed to have killed her, and we have to defend our honor; but more important is the fact that we want to see that justice will eventually prevail, and that is our only motive. We realize that Peg cannot be brought back, and that Junior Pierce will be in jail the rest of his life, but if Pee Wee Gaskins did not kill her, then we feel that the murderer or murderers are still at large, and this is a very disturbing factor. No, we have absolutely no malicious motives whatsoever -- only the desire to restore justice to the judicial system.
    Please let me remind you of the horrible suffering to which we were subjected when, at the hearing for a new trial on April 5, 1973, Deputy Sheriff Tommie Mims, upon being examined by Solicitor Kirk McLeod -- "Yes, sir, she did. She stated that -- something to the effect, I'm not, this is not word for word, that she doubted that he could remember what he saw, if he saw the girl." Then later Solicitor McLeod asked Deputy Sheriff Hugh Mathis, "What did she say, if anything, about the, about Mr. LeNoir's statement?" Hugh's answer -- "She said she didn't think he knew what he was talking about. He had seen this thing in the paper." They both committed perjury, which is bad for anyone to do, but those statements, plus the fact that they testified that I told them I did not see the girl at all, are very contradictory to Tommie's earlier testimony -- Q. "As a result of talking to them (the LeNoirs), did y'all pursue any further investigation in the neighborhood?" A. "We did. The remainder of the afternoon we interviewed other people in the Horatio area, and checked all known clubhouses that the young people usually congregated at, as well as abandoned farmhouses."
    Yes, Mr. Cuttino, your family and my family are suffering irreparable harm, and so are the citizens of South Carolina, and especially those in Sumter County who have lost confidence in certain categories of the judicial system. We believe that 95% of our Law Enforcement personnel are good, brave, honest people,

and we appreciate them very much, but the other 5% are our chief concern. Apparently, there are some facts that have been withheld from you, which you should know, and which should cause you to join us in our fight for justice. "The finding of mature, whole sperm in the rectum and vagina are considered conclusive proof that sexual intercourse occurred in both these body orifices." "It is the opinion of these prosecutors with the information found in this protocol that the deceased had been dead at least five days prior to the discovery of her body."; "I was called to pick up the body of Peg Cuttino on December 30, 1970 -- there was no odor to the body" ; "I went to pick up the body of Peg Cuttino on December 31 -- there was no odor to the body." Had Peg's body lain in the woods for the twelve days she was missing, with temperatures up to 80 degrees (according to Columbia weather station, and our area is always within 2 or 3 degrees of Columbia), we feel that it would have been completely decomposed. Mr. Cuttino, we're very sorry to have to bring up these facts, but we feel that they are so important in our efforts to restore justice to the judicial system. You see, any one of us, or a loved one, could be a victim, and we'd hate to have this type performance by the Sheriff, Police, FBI and SLED -- it is unacceptable.

The investigation into Peg's death has been a political football from the beginning, and we have to keep the game going for awhile longer. The fact that we have two officials who are in position to help, and will have to run for re-election, is to our advantage because they must take a stand for justice, or reject it, before the voters go to the polls. I will contact Attorney General Daniel McLeod, and if he refuses to help, we will contact Senator Strom Thurmond, who can have a federal investigation made. And well it might take a federal investigation, due to the kinships, friendships, social, business and political ties which exist in South Carolina.

I will be very happy to turn over the documents to attorneys for Junior Pierce, if and when we are guaranteed, in writing, that he will get a new trial, and that these documents will be presented in open court, as they should have been in the original trial.

Agreed, this has been very hard on all of us, and I have been threatened and warned of the dangers I face, but God has given me courage to fight thus far for justice, and I have faith that He will continue His support. James Russell Lowell must have faced a situation similar to ours, when, in 1845, he wrote -- "Once to ev'ry man and nation comes the moment to decide, in the strife of truth with falsehood, for the good or evil side; --Then it is the brave man chooses, while the coward stands aside--", and finally, "And, behind the dim unknown, standeth God within the shadow keeping watch above his own." What comfort as we continue to *fight for "Liberty and Justice for all."*

Sincerely yours,
Carrie B. LeNoir

cc: Attorney General McLeod
Senator Thurmond

Monday, August 29, 1977, shortly after 11 a.m., in a small legal library in the Lee County Courthouse, in Bishopville, South Carolina, where Judge Dan F. Laney, Jr., had ordered her to appear, Mrs. Carrie LeNoir sat alone...acting as her own attorney...and heard the judge read his "show cause" order.

A few of the members of the Sumter County Citizens for Justice, James Cuttino and his attorneys, George James and Henry B. Richardson, Jr., SLED agents Ernie Ellis and Tom Henderson, Chief Deputy Sheriff from Sumter County, Thomas McJunkin, and a few others patiently looked on.

Mrs. LeNoir had brought a small overnight case along with her which she kept close to her at all times and onlookers were sure...even though no one asked her...that the case contained the photographs and documents which she had been ordered to surrender.

Judge Laney told Mrs. LeNoir, "You have refused to obey the order, tell me why."

The judge nervously twiddled his thumbs while awaiting her answer. He told her, "You don't need those pictures."

Mrs. LeNoir stated her position that she would only turn the papers over to Pierce's lawyers if he was guaranteed a new trial.

When he was sure that her answer was a refusal to turn over the documents, Judge Laney found her in contempt of the order and sentenced her to 90 days in jail. The sentence was to be served in the Sumter County Correctional Center.

Judge Laney then said he would give her another 24 hours to turn over the autopsy pictures and reports and said he would purge the sentence if she would comply.

At this point, most of the onlookers in the room were stunned by the realization of what was actually happening, but somewhat relieved when Judge Laney extended the offer of 24 hours.

"I will have to take the sentence," Mrs. LeNoir calmly replied.

Judge Laney told her she would still have to give up the documents. But, Mrs. LeNoir restated her position that she would give them only to the attorneys of William J. Pierce, and then only when he was guaranteed, in writing, a new trial.

"You'll turn them over," Judge Laney said obviously aggravated, "You'll stay in jail until you do."

Mrs. LeNoir had delivered and read in open court a letter in answer to Judge Laney's order as follows:

Judge Dan F. Laney, Jr.
Third Judicial Circuit
Bishopville, SC

Dear Judge Laney,
In answering your Orders of August 8, 1977, and August 16, 1977, I wish to show cause why I did not comply, and why I should not be held in contempt of Court. First of all, I would like to say that I have tried to live the life of a Christian and good citizen, but when I am faced with challenges which require a decision such as I have faced recently, I have to weigh the issues very carefully. I certainly hate to be involved in controversial issues, but feel that I must not forsake principles in which I believe, and my only motive in this case is to help the cause of justice. I would like to incorporate my letter to Mr. James Cuttino with my answer to you. Please read attached letter to Mr. Cuttino.

Now, I would like to say that hundreds of persons have contacted me during the past several years relative to various decisions and actions of the courts, and especially, concerning the handling of the Peg Cuttino murder case. There are many unanswered questions, and questionable actions taken by officials; the latest, of course, being your Court Orders. First of all, even if legal, we consider it unethical that you be involved in a Court Order of a personal friend who is the Petitioner.

Secondly, your Order of August 16, states: "It is reported in said Affidavit and in the Proof of Service that the Defendant LeNoir has refused to comply with this Order and has refused to deliver the documents described in the Order of August 8, 1977, as required, although said Order of August 8, 1977, clearly states in part -- " --this Order shall be complied with immediately--" "-- But, thank God, we have a higher Court, and a recent ruling by the State Supreme Court states: "{It is fundamental doctrine of law that a party whose personal rights are to be affected by a personal judgement must have a day in court, or opportunity to be heard; without due notice and opportunity to be heard the court has no jurisdiction to adjudicate such personal rights. A personal judgement by a court without jurisdiction of both the parties and the subject matter is a nullity and must be so treated by the courts whenever and for whatever purpose it is presented and relied on."

Therefore, we believe that this ruling renders your Orders null and void, and request that they be dismissed, so that the Concerned Citizens for Justice can continue working.

Sincerely yours,
Carrie B. LeNoir

It is interesting to note Mrs. LeNoir's reference to the fact that Judge Laney and James Cuttino were personal friends. Dan Laney and James Cuttino served in the South Carolina Legislature together.

Nearly everything pertaining to the Cuttino-Pierce case over the past several years has been sent to Judge Dan Laney, who had also illegally denied Pierce a new trial three times since his conviction, without the proper hearing.

Mrs. LeNoir picked up the little overnight case, which did not contain the documents and photographs, as everyone thought...It held her toothbrush, toothpaste, hairbrush, clothes and other articles of personal need, and said, "I'm ready to go."

She had come prepared to pay the price for what she believed was morally right.

"Awe, come on, Mrs. Carrie," one of the law officers pleaded, "you don't have to go to jail...He has given you another 24 hours..."

"He sentenced me...and justice must be carried out," she said. "I'm not going to turn the papers over now, nor 24 hours from now, and you must carry out his order...I'm going to jail."

Chief Deputy Tom McJunkin, carried her overnight bag and they left the courthouse and traveled back to Sumter where she was put in the Sumter County Correctional Institution.

Mrs. LeNoir used her phone call to call her husband and tell him not to worry about her. Of course he was upset and found it unbelievable that Judge Laney had put her in prison.

"She told me not to worry," he said later. "I told her I wouldn't worry, I've placed it in the hands of the Lord. We are both steadfast in our decision not to turn over the documents and I will keep the home fires burning until she returns."

Sumter County Citizens could not believe what they read and heard. A 57-year-old grandmother, jailed in Sumter County, for her belief in justice. Without even a public hearing on the subject.

During the 20-minute "hearing" in which she was sentenced, the SLED agents, who went to her home to collect the documents on Friday, August 12, testified that when they arrived at Mrs. LeNoir's home that day, she showed them stacks and binders of papers and told them they could "go through these documents and take what we wanted."

But, then, Mrs. LeNoir asked to make a phone call, asked to speak with a woman named Verna, and asked her advice on how to respond to the Court Order.

"I could not hear Verna's reply, but Mrs. LeNoir then told Verna, 'You say I should not give it to them.'" Tom Henderson wrote in his affidavit. The woman was believed to be Sumter County Deputy Coroner Verna Moore, an employee of *The Sumter Daily Item.*

After this phone call, Mrs. LeNoir refused to let them have any of the papers, photographs or documents.

Verna Moore denied advising Mrs. LeNoir against returning the documents, "Mrs. LeNoir did call me at *The Item* office and, out of courtesy to her, I listened and informed her to return the documents as they are no longer useful to her. I would never refuse an Order of the Court."

would never refuse an Order of the Court."

Mrs. LeNoir has said that she did make the statement to Verna during the conversation, when she misunderstood something that was said, but that the advice that she received from Verna Moore in that telephone conversation was not what made her decide not to let the documents go. "It is understandable, just hearing my end of that conversation, how someone would get that impression," Mrs. LeNoir said.

So, Mrs. Carrie LeNoir sat in jail. She said that she would appeal the decision of Judge Laney; and Joe McElveen, Jr., who you will recall was Junior Pierce's court-appointed lawyer, began work preparing that notice of appeal.

Parker Haley said that he did not have any of the photographs and autopsy reports and no action was taken against him.

Item Editor Hubert Osteen, Jr., surmised the current situation.

EDITORIAL

The Daily Item, Tuesday, August 30, 1977

OPINION:
THE POINT HAS BEEN MADE

Another dramatic and unfortunate turn was taken Monday in the William J. Pierce-Peg Cuttino murder case with the imprisonment of Mrs. S.G. LeNoir for contempt of court.

Third Circuit Judge Dan F. Laney, Jr., sentenced Mrs. LeNoir to 90 days in jail after she refused to turn over documents relating to the case. The documents, which included a picture of the dead girl and autopsy reports, has been used by Mrs. LeNoir in her efforts to arouse support for a new trial for Pierce, convicted in 1973, for the murder of Miss Cuttino. The father of the dead girl, James Cuttino, had requested that the court order Mrs. LeNoir to relinquish the documents because of mental anguish caused the family by Mrs. LeNoir's use of them.

Mrs. LeNoir has gained a lot of support in this community through her campaign on behalf of Pierce and no doubt those who back her cause will interpret her imprisonment as evidence of the "system" trying to "get" her.

However, it should be noted that Cuttino did not seek to have the documents in question destroyed, but merely turned over to the Sumter County Clerk of Court. If and when a new trial is ever secured for Pierce, the documents would be available for possible use in his defense after proper legal procedures are followed. We cannot conceive of anything happening to these documents while under the control of the Clerk of Court.

We admire Mrs. LeNoir's determination against great odds to pursue her cause, but we are also sympathetic toward the Cuttino

*family, which has been subjected to far more stress and strain
than they deserve.*

*Mrs. LeNoir has made her point. She is willing to go to jail
for her cause. Now she should relinquish the documents because
no constructive purpose is being served by the withholding of
them. While her doubts about the judicial system may be well-
founded, most citizens still have enough confidence in local
authorities to believe that the controversial documents will be in
safe hands in the Sumter County courthouse.*

Meanwhile, under the leadership of Mrs. Peg Burleson, the Sumter County
Citizens for Justice were busily setting up a defense fund for Mrs. LeNoir. They put
jars in country stores and ran a large ad in *The Daily Item*, telling citizens where to
send donations for "MRS. CARRIE LeNOIR'S DEFENSE."

By Thursday, Joe McElveen had filed a notice of appeal with the South
Carolina Supreme Court, and Chief Justice Woodrow Lewis had agreed to hear the
appeal at 10 a.m., Friday, in Darlington, South Carolina. Justice Lewis waived the
usual minimum four-day requirement between the filing of the appeal and the
hearing, before a Justice.

Normally, an inmate would be transferred to the Woman's Correctional Center
of the South Carolina Department of Corrections in Columbia, to serve a sentence
such as Mrs. LeNoir's, but Len B. Mathis, Sumter County Correctional Center
Director, didn't know exactly what to do with her.

"I haven't made a firm decision on it (the transfer)," he said in an interview with
The Item, "we'll hold onto her to see what (Justice) Lewis' decision is on her appeal.
Monday is a state holiday. I wouldn't do anything until Tuesday."

On that same day, a Letter to the Editor from, Mrs. Portia Myers, gave the
public some insight into the feelings of the Cuttino family at this time.

The Daily Item - Sumter, SC, Monday, May 16, 1977

Letters to the Editor

PUBLICITY HURTS FAMILY

To the Editor:

*As a member of the Cuttino family, I think the general public
needs to know how very much all the recent unnecessary publicity
about the Peg Cuttino case has needlessly hurt and concerned my
brother's family.*

*If my brother were not completely convinced that (William J.)
Pierce killed his daughter, he would not cease to have the earth
combed to find her killer.*

*It has been seven long, heart-breaking years since Peg
Cuttino was brutally murdered. A fair and just trial was held and*

My family has been deeply hurt by the excess publicity and sensationalism caused by so many newspaper articles. We are all sincerely convinced that the judicial system has been fair and honest in all it's dealings in this situation and that justice has prevailed.

It is now time for The Sumter Daily Item to get on with other news articles. We feel that the general public is tired of reading over and over again the same thing. It is time that the James Cuttino family be able to pick up The Item without seeing in headlines a continuous repetition of the whole horrible ordeal. If people would just stop to consider the feelings of the Cuttinos, how very, very much they have suffered needlessly, then I am sure that these articles would cease.

This has been a terrible, heartless ordeal for the entire Cuttino family. IT IS TRULY like thrusting a knife into a broken heart, and then turning it.

Portia Cuttino Myers

Another Letter to the Editor that same day also expressed the fact that not everyone supported Mrs. LeNoir.

GROUP CALLED 'MISGUIDED'

To the Editor:

For the past several months, periodically Mrs. S. G. LeNoir has made the news in The Sumter Item along with a bunch of followers called the "Citizens for Justice." Well, I for one think that this entire group of misguided individuals think justice is their own personal desire and refuse to abide by the decisions of the judicial system, which is used throughout this entire state and country, because it does not agree with them in their unfounded allegations, and for no other reason.

I, for one, don't agree with Mrs. LeNoir and I'm sure I'm not the only citizen in Sumter County with this feeling. I personally think she got what she deserves, 90 days for contempt of court, just like any other citizen would under similar circumstances.

I hope to see this in The Item just to show that not all of the people in Sumter County are as ridiculous as the "pack" who go under the misnomer of "Citizens for Justice."

Liston Ducom

Chief Justice Woodrow Lewis met with Joe McElveen, representing Mrs. LeNoir and George James, Mr. Cuttino's attorney, in Darlington on Friday morning and ordered Mrs. LeNoir released pending her appeal to the South Carolina Supreme Court of Judge Laney's contempt of court charge.

Mrs. LeNoir agreed to turn the documents and photographs over to Justice Lewis and that they be sealed and kept in the custody of the South Carolina Supreme Court until the outcome of her appeal was known.

Joe McElveen argued before Justice Lewis that, "What Judge Laney has done - is decide that Mr. Cuttino's right to privacy is more important than Mrs. LeNoir's right to free speech. We may not like what she has done, but the First Amendment protects it."

George James, however, argued that, "It's an effort on his (Cuttino) part to protect the memory of his child. There is nothing in the order to restrain Mrs. LeNoir from saying anything she wants to say. We just want to get the photographs off the streets."

McElveen also argued that Mrs. LeNoir's right to property had been violated because she had been charged with contempt of court and sentenced without having a hearing on her right to possess the documents.

James disagreed. "I do not see that Mrs. LeNoir has any property rights," he said, "She admitted that she got them (the documents) from former Coroner Howard Parnell. They are not her property. They belong to the state of South Carolina."

Mrs. LeNoir was not present for this hearing, but Justice Lewis signed an order releasing her from custody immediately. Her son, Samuel I. LeNoir, brought the documents to the Darlington courthouse where they were sealed.

This action achieved the objective of both sides. Mrs. LeNoir felt that the materials were in hands of law enforcement officials that would protect and preserve them. She was not at all sure that would have been the case had they been turned over to the Sumter County officials. Records and materials have been known to disappear, or get lost, in Sumter County officials' care. (Referring to the missing persons report on Martha Ann Dicks)

George James said Justice Lewis' order "achieves the result of having the documents sealed." So, this took them out of circulation, which satisfied Mr. Cuttino for the time being.

"I had to make some kind of deal to get out of jail," Mrs. LeNoir said with a devilish little smile. "I have to play the organ at church every Sunday...so, I had to be out by then."

"I'm delighted to be out of jail," she said with a more serious tone, "I needed to get home. I figure that compromising was the wisest thing to do. It would accomplish everything I wanted at that time...to protect and preserve the materials and get me out of jail. Had I not done this, I would still be there. My freedom is precious to me, but I would give my very life for this cause, if I had to."

So, Mrs. LeNoir was free...at least for now. She had spent four days of her life in prison...with murderers, arsonists, rapists and every kind of criminal you can imagine, on (what she believed to be)an illegal order from a judge, who (she believed) should have disqualified himself in the beginning, because of his personal involvement with Mr. Cuttino.

At the Correctional Center, many of the inmates appeared to rally around the efforts of Mrs. LeNoir. She acquired a page of a calendar...the months of August...and inmates and some security personnel signed it, much in the fashion of a college yearbook.

college yearbook.

One woman, who had killed a man, wrote, "Good luck and God bless you."

Another woman inmate, an arsonist, wrote, "I am proud of you."

Still another, who Mrs. LeNoir said, "was playing with a knife, and the knife killed a man" wrote, "I'll be forever loving you."

"It was quite an experience, but I wouldn't want to go back, though," Mrs. LeNoir recalled. "I always knew I was in some sort of Paradise (outside), but I didn't realize it was so good until I heard the perils and problems some of them have to face."

"I don't want to go back, though," she said, "but I will, if I have to."

Needless to say, the citizens of Sumter and Sumter County were confused about the recent events.

Generally, citizens respect the judicial system and part of them wanted to believe that the courts had administered justice where Mrs. LeNoir was concerned, but they were aware of the doubts cast on our public officials and judicial system over the past few years. Another part of them felt deeply that she had been wronged.

Most of the general public still did not know what information or documents, or whatever it was, that Mrs. LeNoir had that the officials wanted to get away from her. They were bewildered.

On that same day, September 1, 1977, another letter was printed under "Letters to the Editor."

THEIR "FINEST HOUR?"

To the Editor:

In his speech of June 18, 1940, Sir Winston Churchill said as he addressed the people of Britain, that the battle of France was over, and that the battle of Britain was about to begin. He went on to say that the leader of the opposing force knew that he would have split his forces into the islands and lose the war. In closing this well-remembered address, Mr. Churchill said, "Let us therefore brace ourselves to our duties, and so bear ourselves that if the British empire, and it's Commonwealth last for a thousand years, men will still say that this was their finest hour."

If the Concerned Citizens of Sumter devote their all, as has Mrs. S.G. (Carrie) LeNoir, to achieve victory in the cause for which they stand, they can truthfully say when their goal of obtaining a new trial for William J. Pierce, Jr., convicted of murder in the now legendary "Cuttino case" of Sumter County, that this was indeed a job well done.

However, if the Concerned Citizens of Sumter do not do everything in their power to secure this new trial, the aura of doubt, suspicion, and fear towards our supposed law enforcement officials, the very same people that we pay and trust to protect us, will always exist. I most sincerely hope and pray that this not happen, though it very easily could if the Concerned Citizens of Sumter flinch one muscle in their quest to see justice prevail.

I close now by paraphrasing Mr. Churchill in saying that the battle to abolish deceit, corruption, and dishonesty where certain law enforcement officials are concerned is almost over, and that the crusade to, not only restore truth, honor, and dignity to our judicial system, where who knows for how long, this high degree of moral turpitude has been prevalent, but more importantly, the battle to keep it there is about to begin.

If our glorious United States of America, the American flag, which "so proudly we hailed," and our beautiful Palmetto State of South Carolina are still in existence, a thousand years from now, people everywhere can look back in retrospect, and in all sincerity say: "This was the Concerned Citizens of Sumter's finest hour."

Fred J. Wilcox, Jr.

Newspapers and other media were full of this new development and the Cuttino case was again headlined across the state of South Carolina and surrounding states.

During all the publicity, in *The Sumter Daily Item*, under the "Sumter Soapbox" heading, the following appeared:

I would like to conduct a survey of opinion on Carrie LeNoir's involvement in the Cuttino murder case by asking the following questions:

Do you think William Pierce is guilty of Miss Cuttino's murder?

Do you think he should be given a new trial?

Should Mrs. LeNoir be allowed to keep her materials, reports, etc. to help her get Pierce a new trial?

Do you think Mrs. LeNoir was unjustly imprisoned?

Please send responses to Fred Wilcox, Jr., P.O. Box 541, Summerton, SC, 29148, or call 775-6733, if replying before Tuesday. Call 485-4432, if replying after Tuesday. Names and respondents are not necessary.

Fred Wilcox had been concerned about the activities surrounding this case for some time, and had met and supported Mrs. LeNoir's cause. He was ill and was a patient at Tuomey Hospital in Sumter at the time of this article, thus the instructions on the phone number. He hoped to return to his home on Tuesday.

Responses to the inquiry poured in...some in support of Mrs. LeNoir and some against her position. Some expressed great admiration for her and what she was doing and these were a great encouragement to her in the days ahead and the trials that, though she didn't know at the time, she still faces. There were those, who opposed her, who were quite nasty to her in their responses, but the support greatly out-weighed the opposition, and Mrs. LeNoir would never forget Fred Wilcox and would always be grateful to him for soliciting this information.

Fred Wilcox, Jr., passed away on August 1, 1978. He was only 33.

A hearing was set, to hear a motion to dismiss the appeals of Mrs. LeNoir because of alleged late filing, to be heard by Third Circuit Judge E. Harry Agnew, but Agnew died several days before hearing that motion. The matter came before Third Circuit Judge Ernest A. Finney, Jr., but he declined to rule on the motion on December 28, saying, "This court should not be asked to render a decision on a Notice of Intention to Appeal in a vacuum, without the benefit of being able to review the facts which led up to the order purportedly being appealed from; The court is of the opinion that...Laney (Third Circuit Judge Dan F. Laney, Jr.) would be the only Circuit Judge with the authority to rule upon the motion..."

"this court is of the opinion that it is without jurisdiction to entertain the motion (to dismiss the appeals). This opinion is based on the view that one circuit judge does not have the authority to review the order of another circuit judge," Judge Finney said.

In an article, printed in *The Daily Item* on January 4, 1978, entitled "JUDGE FINNEY WON'T HEAR LeNOIR APPEALS," it was also learned that Mr. Cuttino had a new attorney, who had been representing him, along with Sumter Attorney George James, "for about a month or so."

Ronald Motley, of the Barnwell, South Carolina, firm of which then South Carolina House Speaker Emeritus Solomon Blatt was a partner, had joined with George James in representing Mr. Cuttino against Mrs. LeNoir.

CHAPTER SEVENTEEN

THE OSCEOLA INVESTIGATION AND REPORTS

SEPTEMBER 9, 1977

Osceola — September 9, 1977

WHAT THE CUTTINO AUTOPSY REPORTS SHOW
by Elton Manzione

On December 18, 1970, Margaret "Peg" Cuttino was reported missing by her parents, State Rep. & Mrs. James Cuttino of Sumter. Twelve days later the girl's body was found in a wooded area of the Manchester Forest near Sumter. On March 3, 1973, William "Junior" Pierce, a Georgia drifter and sometime gas station attendant was convicted of the slaying. But that was not the end of the matter.

Almost before the ink dried on the guilty verdict, several Sumter area residents began to question whether Pierce was indeed the killer of the Cuttino girl. Carrie LeNoir, retired postmistress of Horatio, a small community near Sumter, was one of the first. Pierce had been charged with killing the girl on December 18, the day she disappeared. LeNoir maintained she saw the Cuttino girl in the company of two boys the following day. It was the beginning of a seven year crusade by LeNoir — a crusade which was to find the 56 year old grandmother sitting in a jail cell seven years later.

Last Monday, August 29, Carrie LeNoir was sentenced to 90 days in jail for refusing to turn over certain documents to Circuit Judge Dan Laney. She was later freed pending appeal. Laney, who served in the state legislature with James Cuttino, based his order on a petition submitted by the former state representative. The petition stated that LeNoir's possession of the documents constituted a trespass on the memory of the dead girl and represented a great deal of distress to the girl's family. The documents are an autopsy report and a photo of the dead girl's body.

Osceola has obtained copies of both documents and on the face of it, they seem to represent not a trespass on a dead girl's memory, but evidence that casts doubts on the state's contention that William "Junior" Pierce was the slayer.

Pierce was convicted on the basis of an alleged "confession" which he made to SLED Lieutenant Olin C. Redd, Chief J.P.

"Pete" Strom and Sumter County Sheriff I. Byrd Parnell. The officers alleged Pierce told them he saw the Cuttino girl arguing at a restaurant with a boy and a girl who were attempting to get her into a car. "I took it about as long as I could," Pierce reportedly said and intervened in the argument. The boy threatened Pierce with a chain and Pierce, in turn drew a pistol. The incident was apparently being watched by a woman inside the restaurant who, according to Pierce's "confession", dialed the telephone.

Then officers said Pierce told them the Cuttino girl voluntarily got into his car and they drove off thinking the woman inside had called the police. Upon reaching the wooded area where her body was found, Pierce is said to have struck her in the head with a tire iron and strangled her with her own scarf so she could not identify him to police. All this occurred, according to the confession and police testimony, on December 18.

Police never located the pair that Cuttino had allegedly been arguing with, the woman in the restaurant or any witnesses to the incident with the gun despite the fact the incident supposedly occurred in downtown Sumter at lunch hour. The confession was never reduced to writing for Pierce's signature or recorded in any fashion. The entire state case hinged on the "confession" that the murder was committed on December 18 within a half hour of leaving the restaurant. The pathology report, however, casts some serious doubts on this version of the murder.

"Mature spermatozoa with tails were numerous in smears from the vagina. They were present in smaller numbers in smears from the rectum," a portion of the pathology report reads. It is a statement which casts strong doubts on December 18 as the date of the girl's death.

Osceola has contacted a respected forensic pathologist for interpretation of the autopsy report. He explained mature sperm usually lose their tails within three to seven days under any circumstances.

The pathologist also viewed a picture of the dead girl's body and a histological protocol, a study to determine the amount of decomposition present in a dead body with the intent of determining the time of death. Temperatures during the 12 days the Cuttino girl was missing reached a maximum of 80 degrees and averaged about 50 degrees throughout the period.

"If the temperature had remained below 50 degrees night and day it would slow the decomposition somewhat," the pathologist told Osceola. "There is very little decomposition present in the histological data or the photo. With the reported temperatures that high during the period she was missing, I don't think she could have been dead for the full 12 days she was missing."

The pathologist was asked to place an estimate on how long the girl had been dead based on the information contained in the report which had been ordered surrendered and sealed by Laney.

"If I had to go with a set date, in court, based on the best of my knowledge, I would have to say the girl was dead about five to seven days; closer to five days," he said.

The pathologist also told Osceola several aspects of the pathology indicate the girl may have been held and tortured before being killed. The report noted the presence of bruises and cigarette burns on the girl's thighs, legs and back. When told it was LeNoir's theory that the girl had been held and tortured for several days prior to her death, he replied that the theory was a good one: "a real good one".

In addition to the pathology report, support for the five to seven day estimate came from an unexpected quarter. On December 24, 1970, six days after her disappearance, one day before the pathologist's estimate of the date of death, and six days before her body was found, three men were hunting in the area of the Manchester State Forest where the girl's body was later discovered. In sworn affidavits, the three stated they did not see the body, even though they had been over the area thoroughly while looking for game. Temporary hunting permits issued to the three on December 24 support their story that they were in the area on that date.

Another piece of interesting evidence presented by the pathology report came in the form of some pubic hairs which had been removed from the dead girl's body during the autopsy.

Whenever two people engage in intercourse, forced or voluntary, pubic hairs on one person become entangled with those of the other and are often pulled off to remain on the other person's pubic region. Modern forensic science can identify these hairs with a great deal of accuracy.

According to the report "several dark, curly, loose hairs" were removed from the girl's inner thighs, pubic and rectal areas. These were placed in an envelope and never mentioned again even though they could go a long way toward eliminating or confirming Pierce as a suspect in the case. But it was a pattern of the state in the case to ignore evidence that might contradict Pierce's "confession".

When pathologist Dr. Joel Sexton, chief pathologist at the Medical University of South Carolina and the person who performed the original autopsy testified at Pierce's original trial he was not asked to testify about the time of death, only the cause of death. Sexton was not asked, nor did he testify, regarding the evidence of sexual assault or torture which the pathology report uncovered. The report was a thorough, scientific investigation which was nearly totally ignored by the state.

William "Junior" Pierce may indeed have "confessed" to the murder; he confessed to another murder according to state law enforcement officials but that "confession" didn't hold up too well.

According to authorities, Pierce confessed to the December 22, 1977 slaying of Lexington waitress Kathy Jo Anderson. Unfortunately for authorities Pierce had been 500 miles away in Macon, Georgia all that day, that night and part of the following day and had a motel bill to prove it. Pierce was never brought to trial on that charge, even though one officer claimed, in a published account, Pierce had "talked so much about that case it made us sick".

Despite the fact the autopsy report strongly suggests Peg Cuttino could not have been dead on the date Pierce is charged with murdering her and despite the fact that evidence exists which might clear Pierce, Pierce has twice been denied a new trial. Both times the requests have been turned down by the same Judge Laney who issued the order to collect and seal this evidence.

According to one area attorney, the fact that Cuttino could have been alive on the date Pierce is charged with killing her could, itself, present the basis for a new trial — something Carrie LeNoir has been trying to get for Pierce for the past four years.

All this is merely the tip of the iceberg according to LeNoir. As with any major case, this one presents a web of unanswered questions, blatant contradictions and leads which have never been followed. Next week Osceola will attempt to follow some of those leads and answer some of those questions.

Osceola — September 16, 1977

THE CUTTINO MURDER: "IT'S LIKE A SPIDER'S WEB"
by Elton Manzione

Margaret "Peg" Cuttino is dead and William "Junior" Pierce is doing life for her murder; that's a fact, one of the few associated with the Cuttino case which has not been distorted, twisted or outrightly contradicted over the intervening years since the girl's body was found in a wooded area a few miles from Sumter in the winter of 1970.

Poking around Sumter asking questions about the Cuttino murder gives you a very uneasy feeling. The half-answered and totally unanswered questions you pose have to be sifted, weighed and analyzed before some sort of sense can be made of them. Some people talk willingly, some not at all and others reluctantly. Eventually some sort of order begins to take shape — one thing flows into another and a picture begins to form and it's a peculiar one.

"It's like a spider's web," one Sumter resident said, "You have a center and a series of lines radiating from it to other points and each of those points becomes the center of another web with more radiating lines." It's not a totally inappropriate simile.

The web/picture/story goes back to December 18, 1970 — it's an important date in the overall picture. On that date Margaret "Peg" Cuttino left her home in Sumter to walk a few blocks to her sister's school where the two of them would have lunch. Peg never kept the lunch date.

Within two hours a massive search had been organized with officers from the city, county and the S.C. Law Enforcement Division (SLED) taking part. Two days later the FBI was brought into the case. Hundreds of leads and suspects were checked and filed; all to no avail. Twelve days after her disappearance two Shaw Air Force Base personnel, riding motorcycles in the Manchester State Forest, came upon the girl's body close to a dump pile in the woods. She had been beaten and strangled.

The police work did not stop there however — a killer was still loose. Again hundreds of leads were checked and possible suspects interviewed; finally a glimmer of a clue arose. A boy and his father, hunting in the woods near the area where the body was found, remembered seeing a man standing near a white car and acting strangely. From a description of the man given by the two a composite drawing was made and distributed throughout the area and the country. A long wait ensued as the information on men who looked like the drawing came in and was processed. And once again the results were frustrating; no new leads were developed and no suspects apprehended. For nearly four months state, local and federal authorities worked on the case to no avail. Then, in April of 1971, a break in the case came.

On April 21, 1971 SLED Lieutenant Olin C. Redd travelled to rural Baxley, Georgia in connection with another murder case in North Augusta. He interviewed one William "Junior" Pierce regarding the crime and, almost as an aside, asked him if he had killed the Cuttino girl. Pierce, already charged in four murders, said that he had not — he had been working on December 18. Eight days later, on April 29, Pierce allegedly changed his story.

"Sumter... Sumter... Is that the place where the planes fly real low over the highway?", Pierce reportedly asked. Redd, at this time, called SLED chief J.P. Strom, Sumter police chief Les Griffin and Sumter County Sheriff I. Byrd Parnell and the men listened to Pierce relate his confession.

According to police testimony Pierce had driven his maroon Pontiac to Sumter to "rob and steal" and was parked around noon Friday, December 18, at an eating place on what he had described as Broad Street in Sumter.

At the eating place, according to police version of Pierce's confession, he saw two girls and a boy arguing. It appeared to him that one girl and the boy were trying to get the other girl, described as Peg Cuttino, into the car and she refused. "I sat there about as long as I could," Pierce reportedly said, then got out of the car and told the boy to leave her alone. The boy left and Pierce looked inside the restaurant where he saw a woman on the phone. He assumed she had seen the gun and was calling the police. He got into his car to leave and Peg allegedly said "I guess I'll ride with you."

Leaving Sumter, Pierce said they drove a few miles out of town and he thought it would be best for him to leave the main highway because he knew the police would be looking for him. He took a left turn and drove through a little town he allegedly described as Wedgefield. A few miles later he turned off the paved road and onto a dirt road leading into the Manchester Forest until he came to a dump.

At this point Peg started crying and told him she wanted to go back home to Sumter; and he told her he wasn't about to take her back because the police would be looking for him. According to police versions of his testimony, Pierce said at this point he knew he had to kill Peg. He hit her twice in the head with a tire iron, once on the right front forehead and once again on the back of the head. He drove a little further into the woods and tied the girl's polka dot scarf around her neck, around her shoulders and under her armpits and pulled it.

He said that after this he was standing behind his car and saw a man and a boy; the boy had a rifle. He said he stood in front of his license plate so it couldn't be seen. He said he stood like that for four hours or so until it got dark.

He then drove back into Sumter, got gas and asked a service attendant how to get to Savannah and drove out of Sumter on the Savannah highway.

That was Pierce's "confession" as related by Sumter police chief Les Griffin at Pierce's 1973 murder trial. Pierce, at his 1973 trial, said he had indeed given the statement to police, but he claimed he had been beaten and coerced into giving it by Appling County Georgia Sheriff J.B. "Red" Carter. Carter, Pierce said, provided him with the details of the crime and promised him he could see his girlfriend and mother if he confessed to the South Carolina authorities; if not, Pierce said, he was told he would be tortured with a cattle prod.

According to a statement given by Pierce to the U.S. Justice Department, Carter assured SLED Lieutenant Olin C. Redd that "Pierce will never go to South Carolina to question your word in *a court of law." According to Pierce, Parnell, Griffin and Strom were unaware of this "deal" when they questioned him.*

The confession was never recorded or reduced to writing for Pierce's signature. Although Pierce was indicted for the crime in April of 1971 he was not brought to trial for nearly two years and then only on his motion for a speedy trial.

Columbia hypnotist R.N. Sauer spent six hours interviewing Pierce in the presence of his attorney Joseph McElveen and the prison psychiatrist at the S.C. Central Correctional Institute. Sauer, who is a SLED constable and has worked with the agency on several cases, including the clearing of one suspect in the Cuttino case, said Pierce's testimony under hypnosis substantiated his claim that he had been coerced into giving the confession. Sauer said at one point he asked Pierce about a drug he allegedly had been injected with by Carter.

"His body writhed with resistance as he described being injected with a drug which made his skin burn," Sauer said.

Sauer also said he was prepared to testify that Pierce, under hypnosis, had accounted for his whereabouts and actions from December 18th through 25th. Sauer said Pierce was testifying in a state known as "age regression" where a subject is actually taken back to the day in question.

"Briefly, these regressions revealed no criminal activity and that Pierce was not in Sumter at any time during this period," Sauer said in an interview shortly after the trial. In a recent interview with Osceola, Sauer said it is possible for a person to lie under hypnosis and, as a control, he put two fingers of Pierce's left hand under the control of Pierce's subconscious mind to insure he was telling the truth. "Regardless of his verbal response, if the true answer were 'yes' his 'yes' finger would twitch or vice versa if the answer were 'no'," Sauer said.

In a synopsis of Sauer's testimony attached to Pierce' trial transcript, McElveen asked if Sauer had questioned Pierce regarding the killing. "Yes. His reply was 'no," Sauer said. McElveen then asked if his finger response was consistent with his verbal response on this question. "As on all other occasions, his finger response indicated that he was telling the truth," Sauer replied.

Although testimony regarding statements made under hypnosis has been allowed in courts in Florida, California and Michigan, it has never been allowed in a court in South Carolina and was ruled inadmissible at the Pierce trial.

It was Pierce's "confession", along with identification by Earl Williams, the boy with the rifle, that convicted Pierce, and it is this "confession" and identification which literally fall apart under close scrutiny. It is this confession and identification which contradict one another and the hard evidence in the case.

For example; although the argument which Pierce describes in the beginning of his confession took place on a busy street at noon on Friday, no witnesses to the incident have ever come forth. The woman on the phone, the boy and girl in the car or anyone in the restaurant at the time have never been located. Indeed the whole incident has never been substantiated.

According to the "confession" all the actions took place on December 18, 1970, a Friday; but all the hard, physical evidence contradicts this. For one thing Pierce was at work that day and had a time card to prove it. His statement under hypnosis also supports this.

Pierce's time card shows he arrived at his place of work in Statesboro, Georgia at 7:03 a.m. and left at 4 p.m. At 1:20 p.m. Pierce signed for his paycheck as required by Georgia law. Pierce's supervisor, James Sconyers, testified at the trial that he saw Pierce several times during the day and that he was on the job all day except for lunch. His testimony was substantiated by the owner of the company and the bookkeeper who gave Pierce his check. Sconyers drove over 400 miles from Alabama, where he was then living, to testify at the trial.

SLED chief J.P. Strom said he believed Pierce was lying in regard to his being at work on that day, but one Georgia officer disagreed with him. William Parker, an agent for the Georgia Bureau of Investigation, said he did not doubt the testimony of Pierce's supervisor in the case.

Parker also pointed out an inconsistency in the Pierce confession. In the confession Pierce said he was driving a maroon Pontiac on the day Peg was killed, but Chief Deputy Roy Wheeler of Swainsboro told Parker the maroon car was broken down in front of Pierce's house on the day of the murder. On that day Pierce could have been driving a light blue Ford which belonged to his mother. But some authorities have stated the blue Ford was in too poor shape to make the trip to Sumter. Also, according to Parker who was present when Pierce made his confession, Pierce said originally the Cuttino girl had been arguing with "two older men."

In addition to the contradictions raised by Parker and Wheeler, the state's chief witness, Earl Williams, contradicted Pierce's confession on two important points during his trial testimony.

Williams testified he and his father had been hunting in the area when they came across a man standing in front of a "dirty white" car. The man, Williams said, combed his hair like Pierce and he identified the man as Pierce. But there were a couple of weak points in the boy's testimony. For one thing the boy said he *was approximately 300 feet from the man, a distance which would make a positive identification difficult indeed. For another, Williams said the man was standing by a white car and not a maroon car, which Pierce said he had been driving. But most important, the boy said he witnessed the incident on December 19 or 20 and not on December 18. He said it had to be Saturday or Sunday as he was in school Friday. Both the white car and the date raise some of the most serious questions in the case.*

Mr. and Mrs. S.G. LeNoir, of Horatio, S.C., a little town near Sumter, claim they saw the Cuttino girl alive the day after she disappeared. The girl, they said, was with two boys in a "dirty white or beige" car when the three stopped at LeNoir's general store on Saturday. In addition to the LeNoirs, two other employees of the store saw the Cuttino girl on that day.

Edward Carolina, one of the employees, was later hypnotized by Sauer. Carolina described the girl perfectly even down to how her skirt was buttoned and on which side.

"We were attempting to get the license number of the car," Sauer said, "but due to the boy's position we didn't have much luck." Sauer said the boy did not come forth with the information until Pierce had petitioned for a new trial in 1974. "The boy had gone to his grandmother with the information but she had told him to stay out of it. Reportedly she said 'You know what happens to colored people who get in white folks' business,'" Sauer said.

Sauer said the boy described the car as "muddy white" on one occasion and as "rusty white" while under hypnosis. Carolina said the car was a Comet or Falcon.

A classmate of Peg's, Jerry Artrip, also said he saw the girl the day she disappeared, riding in a car with a man and a woman. He described the car as "a beige or dirty white Comet or Falcon." Artrip said this occurred about 1:30 on December 18. Officers questioned both Artrip and the LeNoirs, even taking Artrip to Barnwell to identify an automobile. None of the three were called to testify at the trial. Pierce's attorney Joseph McElveen explained why.

"When we took over the case, the sheriff's file was a mess. All the leads were written on small slips of paper and we just never came across the names of the LeNoirs or Artrip," McElveen said.

A lead sheet, or a list of possible suspects and persons who may have information on the case, dated March 22, 1971, lists the LeNoirs as a possible lead. A notation near their names reads, "Mr. LeNoir could not say that the girl was the Cuttino girl" — something he and his wife both deny. The list does not contain Jerry Artrip's name despite the fact he was questioned by city, county and state officers.

Carrie LeNoir has what she believes is proof that the Cuttino girl was in Horatio that Saturday. Shortly after the girl's disappearance a blue coat was found in the Horatio Community Center, next to the LeNoir's store. On the collar of the coat is the monogram "PEG". LeNoir believes the coat belonged to the Cuttino girl. Authorities claimed the girl did not have a coat when she disappeared, although morning temperatures were in the low 40's. The coat has been described as Peg's by at least one of her classmates and a shopkeeper who knew the family.

One curious fact still remains regarding the coat. "Today, almost seven years later, that coat is still unclaimed and still in my possession in spite of the fact I ran an ad on it and everything. I just believe if the girl who owned that coat were alive, it would have been claimed," LeNoir said.

William Pierce confessed to committing murder on December 18... The state charged Pierce with committing murder on December 18, a contention it is supposed to prove beyond a reasonable doubt. It is a contention that is refuted by the LeNoirs and by the state's own witness, Earl Williams, but this contention is most strongly refuted by the autopsy which was performed on the dead girl.

In the autopsy report it is noted that "mature spermatozoa with tails" were found in the girl's rectum and vagina. Several pathologists agree the spermatozoa would lose their tails within five to seven days of the girl's death. It is possible then that the girl was alive for at least five days after she disappeared, a possibility which would give credence to LeNoir's contention and damage the state's case against Pierce.

It was vital that the state prove beyond a reasonable doubt that Pierce did indeed kill the Cuttino girl on December 18 as charged. Even Circuit Judge Julius Rosen agreed to that during Pierce's 1973 hearing for a new trial.

At that hearing McElveen quoted a state law which required the state to prove the time and place of death.

"So the burden of proof was, therefore, on the state to prove beyond a reasonable doubt that the offense was committed on December 18, 1970," McElveen told the court.

"No argument, no argument about that," Judge Rosen replied.

Just this past spring the Cuttino case took another interesting turn. While testifying at one of his murder trials, Donald "Pee Wee" Gaskins claimed he killed Peg, a claim which was immediately dismissed by authorities. But is the claim so outlandish?

According to the police leads sheet, Gaskins was interviewed early in the Cuttino investigation based on the allegation that he *had sexually assaulted a woman at a motel near Sumter. Gaskins was dismissed as a suspect when the woman could not prove the allegation and when Gaskins produced an alibi. The alibi was no stronger than Pierce's — he had been at work that day — in Sumter.*

But the Gaskins connection did not end with the questioning early in the case. Osceola has obtained information from an affidavit that Jesse Ruth Logan Judy, one of Gaskins' victims and the wife of his cohort James Judy, was visited on several occasions by the Cuttino girl. In addition it is claimed Gaskins told Jesse Judy as early as 1973 that he had killed the Cuttino girl on a contract hit set up by a law enforcement officer.

Any attempt to pursue the Cuttino case can be frustrating; rumors abound, some residents want the matter to drop, others are afraid for their jobs, some fear the real killer is still loose, others are intimidated by the possible law enforcement involvement. All this leads to a peculiar reluctance to talk, and when talking to produce some peculiar embellishments to the story. But the fact remains that even a surface investigation produces some interesting questions and contradictions.

For example, why did Pierce drive 299 miles to commit a burglary? Why did he go to a strange town where he was not familiar with the movements of residents or police to commit a daylight break-in? Why did he get involved in the argument at the restaurant? Why pull a gun in broad daylight on a busy street? And why take the girl with him? Peg Cuttino's mother and maid both do not believe the girl would have gotten into a car with a stranger; indeed the girl's mother doesn't believe she was ever on Broad Street, and why wait in the woods four hours? Finally, why kill a girl just because she saw you had a gun? If you take Pierce's "confession", it just doesn't make sense.

The contradictions, too, are numerous. What about Pierce's statement in Georgia that the girl had been arguing with a boy and a girl? It was the state's contention, and Pierce's confession, that the girl had been killed on the day she disappeared, but evidence suggests this was just not the case. What about the contradictions in the color of the car Pierce was supposedly driving?

Despite the questions and contradictions, Pierce has twice been refused a request for a new trial. The court argued that Pierce had presented no new evidence which would substantially affect the outcome of the original trial.

In 1974 and again this spring the Sumter County grand jury looked into the Pierce case. On both occasions the grand jury found there was no new evidence in the case and nothing amiss in the police investigation of the murder.

"The (1974) hearing was nothing but a whitewash. They asked specific questions about statements in the transcript and would not allow anyone to elaborate or explain. The jury did not even have a copy of the transcript and I don't see how they could even know what was being discussed," one witness in the 1974 hearing said.

The hearing this spring was apparently not much better. LeNoir said she gave the grand jury the names of several persons she felt could shed light on the case and was assured they would be subpoenaed. "Most of them were never subpoenaed," she says.

One Sumter resident described the hearing this year as "unusual" and said at least one juror told him he had doubts that Pierce committed the crime.

"Many of us know something is wrong, but we just can't get involved because of our families or our businesses," one man said.

The Cuttino case is an enigma; each fact or bit of information gathered produces more questions than it answers. If Peg Cuttino was not killed the day she disappeared, what happened in the interim? Why were the authorities called in and a massive manhunt undertaken within two hours of her disappearance? Who raped the girl? Accounts of Pierce's confession never mention the sexual assault. Pathological evidence indicates she was tortured — cigarette burns were found on her legs and back — but this evidence does not correspond with Pierce's "confession" and was not brought out at his trial.

And finally, and most importantly, if Pierce did not kill Peg Cuttino, who did?

(Over the next several weeks, Elton Manzione will continue his research into the Cuttino murder.)

Osceola — October 14, 1977

WHO KILLED PEG CUTTINO?
by Elton Manzione

Who killed Peg Cuttino? That seems to be the major question in Sumter County these days. It's a question which should have been answered, and according to authorities was answered four long years ago. For some the answer is William "Junior" Pierce, who was convicted of the murder in 1973. But somehow there are still too many contradictions for that answer to fit comfortably in the minds of many Sumter County residents.

For example, Pierce, in his confession, said he was driving a maroon Pontiac on the day he supposedly came to Sumter, but

Earl Williams, a state's witness who identified Pierce as the person he saw at the scene of the crime, says he was in a white car.

Pierce's confession says he encountered Peg after a lunch hour incident in a local drive-in restaurant. Pierce is supposed to have waved a gun at Peg's companions. The incident, if it actually occurred, must have been witnessed by dozens of persons, yet it was never substantiated.

According to the confession, Peg asked Pierce if she could ride with him; something which her mother, friends and the family maid say she never would have done. And there was the little matter of the non-coinciding dates.

Williams, the state's chief witness against Pierce, testified he saw a man whom he said was Pierce in the area where Peg's body was later found, on Saturday, December 19, 1970. Pierce's confession said he killed the girl on Friday, December 18.

Pierce came to trial in what might be understated as "an emotionally charged atmosphere". The case had been in the headlines ever since the girl's disappearance. In the interim between the girl's death and the trial then state representative James Cuttino, the girl's father, introduced a bill to have all school aged children fingerprinted; a move which he said was prompted by his daughter's death.

During the time between the Cuttino girl's murder and Pierce's trial in Kingstree, former Columbia Record police reporter and detective magazine writer, Jack Orr, was busily writing stories on Pierce under various pen names. The stories, titled imaginatively "The Corpse Littered Trial of the Cold-Hearted Killer" and "He's Fresh Out of Stir, He's Mean, He'll Kill", were highly inflammatory in some instances and took great liberties with the facts in others. For example, in one story Orr eliminated the conflict in car colors by changing Earl Williams' statement to say Williams had seen a maroon car at the scene. In another story Orr had Peg's "badly decomposed body" being identified by "scraps of clothing". The girl's body was remarkably intact and easily identified when it was found.

It was not hard, under the circumstances to get an indictment and conviction against Pierce in the case. According to one member of the Grand Jury which returned the murder indictment, it was a cut and dried procedure.

"Sheriff Parnell (I. Byrd Parnell, Sumter County sheriff) came before the Grand Jury with a sheaf of papers in his hand. 'I have a signed confession here from William Pierce. He has given us details which only the killer could have known.' He asked if we wanted to read the confession but the foreman told him we would take his word for it," the former Grand Juror said.

Whatever Parnell may have had in his hand at the time, it was not a signed confession from Pierce. Pierce's "confession" was never reduced to writing and never signed.

Pierce's story of how the "confession" in the Cuttino murder was obtained from him is intriguing at best and frightening in any case. According to Pierce the confession was far from voluntary.

Pierce was arrested in Appling County, Georgia, on March 8, 1971 in connection with a murder and robbery and was confined by Appling County sheriff J.B. Carter in the county jail at Baxley.

On April 21 SLED agent Olin C. Redd arrived in Baxley to question Pierce regarding the murder of Ann Austell Goodwin, a North Augusta babysitter.

According to Pierce, Carter then requested that Redd go to lunch and give him a chance to talk to Pierce in private. Pierce then said Carter told him, "Bill, why don't you help him with his case." Whereupon Pierce refused. Pierce said the exchange then turned into an argument during which he and Carter cursed at each other and Carter finally left, returning with a deputy and the keys to Pierce's cell.

"I was then handcuffed to the cell bars and was again asked to cooperate; that it was going to put a bad light on Carter's office if I didn't help the officer," Pierce said in a letter to Osceola. Pierce said he again refused and this time Carter burned him several times on the arm with a cigarette.

Shortly after this, according to Pierce, Georgia Bureau of Investigation (GBI) agent William B. Parker came into the cellblock and told Carter it was wrong to scar up a prisoner before he came to trial.

"Parker then told Carter he had a unit which would not leave any tell-tale marks and would make a hog jump over a six foot fence," Pierce said.

Pierce said the unit resembled an aluminum tube with an electric cord on one end. The unit, Pierce said, was plugged into a socket in the cell block and touched to his chest.

"In reflex I kicked out in an effort to get away from the unit and kicked Carter in the stomach. I was struck in the face and Carter ordered the deputy to secure my feet to the cell bars," Pierce said in his letter.

Pierce's feet were then secured to the cell bars and he was again worked over with the electric unit, according to his account. Finally, he says, he agreed to confess to the Goodwin murder and was given a list of details to memorize regarding the crime. Pierce says he related these details to North Augusta Police on the following day.

According to Pierce, Carter then told Redd that he could go ahead and charge Pierce with any crime, and he would see to it that Pierce never got to South Carolina to question his word in a court of law.

Pierce says he was later provided the details of the Cuttino murder and on April 29, 1971 he confessed to the Cuttino murder to Sumter County Sheriff I. Byrd Parnell, SLED chief J.P. Strom and two other SLED agents. Sumter police chief Les Griffin was also present during this time. Pierce contends that none of the men present at this questioning, with the exception of Strom and Redd (who remained in Baxley) were aware of his having been primed with details of the murder.

Pierce's confession omitted some important details of the crime. For one there was evidence the Cuttino girl had been sexually assaulted, something which Pierce never made reference to in his confession. The omission was explained in a note to a police report prepared by Griffin on June 30, 1971.

"Pierce was not questioned concerning the sexual assaults on the body of Peg Cuttino because Lt. Parker of the GBI and Lt. Redd of SLED advised prior to the questioning of Pierce that he had some sort of mental block against talking about sex offenses, and that he would refuse to talk at all when sex was mentioned by officers questioning him," the note said.

Another detail left out of Pierce's confession was the color of the scarf the Cuttino girl had been wearing and with which she had been strangled. The scarf had been described in newspaper accounts and missing persons reports only as "polka dot". Pierce, in his confession, described the scarf only as "polka dot". At one point, while being questioned under hypnosis, Pierce was asked what color the scarf was; "I don't know. They didn't tell me," Pierce replied.

The police report also indicated it was Redd himself who first focused attention on Pierce as suspect in the Cuttino murder. The report noted that Redd informed Strom on April 29 that he had "determined Pierce was possibly responsible for the death of Peg Cuttino." In addition the report noted Pierce was questioned after Carter and Parker had been briefed on the details of the crime.

Sheriff Carter was described by one Georgia newsman as "a guy not averse to publicity." Another Georgia law enforcement officer described him as "taking all the credit" in the 18 or so murders Pierce supposedly "confessed to".

Pierce himself was described by one Georgia sheriff as the "confessing kind". "Pierce impressed me as a person who, if you gave him the details, would confess to anything. I don't like to solve my cases that way," Dillon County sheriff Roy Lee said.

And Pierce may indeed have been the "confessing kind". At least one case to which he allegedly confessed has never been *prosecuted; that of the Kathy Jo Anderson murder. On the date the Lexington teenager was killed Pierce was in Macon, Georgia and had spent the night there.*

Regarding Carter's statement that Pierce would never reach trial in South Carolina, Parker, in a 1973 interview, said he was surprised Pierce came to trial on the Cuttino murder. Indeed the fact that Pierce came to trial at all on the case seems to be largely a result of his own filing of a motion for a speedy trial.

South Carolina authorities made a notably poor attempt to bolster Pierce's alleged confession with hard physical evidence. For example Pierce claimed he left his maroon Pontiac at McGowan Motors in Swainsboro, Georgia. Redd said he stayed in Swainsboro for "30 or 40 minutes" attempting to find the car but was unsuccessful.

"He told us he left there; it wasn't there, hadn't been there," Redd said in Pierce's appeal hearing in March of 1973. It was a contention disputed by personnel at McGowan's.

"The car was here from about the end of December to the middle of February," an employee at McGowan's said. The car, he said, was then sold at auction to a used car dealer in Reidsville, Georgia who kept it on his lot until the middle of May when he sold it to a man named J.C. Cressman. All this the SLED agents failed to unearth.

Pierce also allegedly told officers he had exchanged the bumper jack used to strike the girl for $3.25 worth of gas at a Wrens, Georgia gas station.

"I always wondered why the South Carolina agents apparently did not check this out," Parker said. Parker said it would have been easy since Wrens only has a dozen or so service stations.

Even some South Carolina officers were bothered by the confession Pierce allegedly made.

"There was a conference held afterward in which it was decided to throw some parts of it out and keep other parts. They eliminated the parts which didn't fit and kept everything else. I was bothered by it because there were too many holes and there wasn't much done to support the verbal confession. It was pretty poor police work," one Sumter County officer who declined to be identified told Osceola.

Pierce was also refused a lie detector test by authorities even though some 36 suspects in the Cuttino case had been given polygraph exams. Pierce, however, did undergo a polygraph exam independently administered at the request of his defense attorneys. The results were inconclusive.

The inconclusive results, according to a source close to the case, were due to Pierce's extremely unemotional response to the questioning. The flat response, the source said, could have come from Pierce's ability to lie well or his having been told to confess and provided with details of the crime while in a state such as drugged, hypnotized or under extreme emotional distress. One textbook cites, as one of several reasons for inconclusive polygraph results, "letting the suspect learn too much about the offense before the test." The text book Modern Criminal Investigation explained if a subject was questioned thoroughly regarding the details of a crime before the test, it would be difficult for an examiner to later evoke the strong emotional response which usually accompanies a first intrusion on certain knowledge.

During his trial this spring on charges of murdering Silas Barnwell Yates, convicted murderer Pee Wee Gaskins surprised the packed courtroom by saying he had killed the Cuttino girl and a black girl named Clyde on orders of a law enforcement officer.

Gaskins' admissions were immediately dismissed by law enforcement officers connected with the Cuttino investigation.

"The man who killed Peg Cuttino is in jail in Georgia and I can go to sleep on that," Sheriff Parnell told newsmen the day after the courtroom statement. Most officials thought Gaskins was seeking publicity and discounted the possibility that he could have committed the crime. But is it so far-fetched as to be impossible? The facts indicate otherwise.

Early in the Cuttino investigation Gaskins himself became a suspect but was eliminated because he had been working that day. According to police, Gaskins' supervisor, Roy Harrington, accounted for Gaskins' whereabouts on the day Peg disappeared.

Harrington, however, indicated to Osceola that Gaskins' alibi was not so airtight as police indicated.

"I told them he punched in on time and punched out on time. What he did in between I have no idea," Harrington said. Harrington was unaware of Gaskins' actions because Gaskins had been sent on an outside roofing job on the day Peg disappeared.

That job, according to records, was on the roof of the Sumter YMCA which was then under construction and directly across the street from Willow Drive School, Peg's destination on the day she disappeared. It was also where Peg's trail ended as far as the authorities were concerned.

Police have discounted statements by Carrie LeNoir, Burnett Plowden, Jerry Artrip and Edward Carolina that they all saw the Cuttino girl on either the evening of the 18th or the afternoon of the 19th. The last sighting of the girl accepted by police were reports from men working on the YMCA building who saw her walking. The sightings by LeNoir, Plowden, Carolina and the

Artrip boy, who was a classmate of Peg's, do have an interesting thread in common however.

The four all claim they saw the girl at different times, places and with different people in what they have alternately described as a "white", "dirty white", "beige or tan" "Comet or Falcon". According to Sumter County personal property tax records, Gaskins owned a 1960 white Mercury Comet at the time the Cuttino girl disappeared.

And there are other intriguing facts which make it difficult to entirely dismiss Gaskins' story.

For one thing, Gaskins apparently had an attraction for young girls. Two of Gaskins' alleged victims, Patty Alsbrooks and Janice Kirby, were both 17 at the time of their disappearance. The two disappeared just one month before the Cuttino girl was murdered. Another 13 year old, Kim Ghelkins, was allegedly killed by Gaskins in the same manner as the Cuttino girl. In 1964 Gaskins was charged with statutory rape and in 1966 was sentenced for unlawful carnal knowledge of a child. At least three of his female victims were under 18.

One link between Gaskins and the Cuttino girl was forged by one of his own victims, Jesse Ruth Logan Judy, who was an acquaintance of both Peg and Gaskins.

According to the Judy woman's mother, Mrs. Maddie Logan, Peg Cuttino visited the Judy girl several times while the family lived in Sumter.

"I remember one time she came to the house to see my daughter, who was in the bathroom at the time. She went in and spoke to her through the door and then left," Logan said. Logan was sure that the girl was Peg Cuttino. At the time of Peg's death the Judy girl would have been 16. Peg was known for being a mature girl so it is possible the story is not entirely without credibility.

Mrs. Logan also said the subject of Gaskins' participation in the Cuttino murder came up several years before the Yates trial.

"One night Jesse Ruth told me Gaskins was outside our trailer waiting to kill her. I told her, Jesse Ruth, don't be silly, he's not going to kill anyone. And she said, Momma, you don't know that man. He's killed before. He killed that Alsbrooks girl, the Kirby girl and the Cuttino girl. I asked her how she knew that, and she said Gaskins had told her," Logan said. In addition, several other persons close to Gaskins say he admitted to the Cuttino killing prior to taking the stand in Newberry.

"He couldn't possibly have been seeking publicity then, could he?" one source said.

Gaskins' contention was that he had been forced into killing the Cuttino girl and Martha Ann (Clyde) Dicks because of a criminal charge which was hanging over his head at the time. Osceola has been unable to locate any official charges outstanding against Gaskins at the time.

One year later, however, on October 28, 1971, Gaskins was arrested on charges of grand theft of an auto and possession of dynamite. Gaskins was indicted on both charges the following week and reportedly the cases were ready to go to trial when they were mysteriously dropped.

According to Parnell, the car theft charges were dropped because the officials could not prove Gaskins had stolen the vehicle, even though the warrant charges he was in the process of stripping it when apprehended. The dynamite charge was found in a house which Gaskins had rented at one time but had since moved out of.

Osceola has learned that the dynamite was found in the same house where Gaskins was stripping the auto. It was found, according to one source close to the investigation, as police searched the premises after arresting Gaskins on the auto theft charge. The place of the offense on both warrants is listed as Route 1, Sumter. Both warrants were signed the same day — October 28, 1971.

Osceola has obtained additional information that during an off-the-stand discussion of the Cuttino killing, Gaskins related details of the crime which were generally not known. Details which Pierce himself had not related.

"I believe Gaskins did know what color the girl's scarf was, and he related other details which were not in the newspaper accounts," one source close to the investigation said.

Currently there is a tight lid clamped on interviews with death row prisoners. Osceola tried unsuccessfully to obtain an interview with Gaskins in an attempt to clear up some of the questions regarding his admissions. Without talking to Gaskins many of the questions still remain; especially the main question: "Who killed Peg Cuttino?"

Whether that question will ever be answered to the satisfaction of all concerned is, itself, an open question. As one investigator put it, "After seven years it's a frustrating and cold, cold trail."

Mrs. LeNoir had had little or no involvement, up to this point, with convicted murderer Donald "Pee Wee" Gaskins. Everyone interested in the Cuttino case had watched and waited anxiously since Gaskins' confession in Newberry that he had slain the Cuttino girl, but he had received only life sentences for his crimes and there was no apparent danger of his being executed because there was no death penalty in South Carolina at the time.

However, in January of 1978, State Attorney General Daniel R. McLeod announced that he would ask the South Carolina Supreme Court to send six men who were at that time sitting on Death Row to the electric chair during arguments on January 9. Pee Wee Gaskins was one of those men.

The six inmates were condemned under the state's old capital punishment law, which was declared unconstitutional by the South Carolina Supreme Court in June of 1976.

A new law had been passed a year later, but several of the 20-odd men on Death Row at the time already had had their sentences commuted to life imprisonment. Twelve had hot, but McLeod only intended to argue for execution of six of them at that time.

Mrs. LeNoir was naturally upset. If Gaskins died, we would never know if he had really committed the Cuttino murder. She had never endeavored to try to prove who did the crime — only to prove that Junior Pierce did not commit it. She knew that, as long as Gaskins was alive, there was a possibility that he may provide proof to the authorities that he had committed that crime, which would, in itself, prove that Junior Pierce did not commit it.

Knowing nothing else that would help, she wrote another letter:

The Daily Item — Sumter, South Carolina, Friday, January 6, 1978

LETTER TO THE EDITOR

MORE FACTS ARE NEEDED

To the Editor:
Please allow me to use your paper to urge the citizens of South Carolina to seriously consider an appeal from the Attorney General's Office to the Supreme Court, which will be heard Monday, January 9, seeking the death penalty for several Department of Corrections inmates.

We are especially concerned about Donald Henry (Pee Wee) Gaskins, and earnestly pray that he will not be killed until he can, or will, talk to lawyers and/or reporters, as we feel that he has much valuable information which may answer many questions. His claim that he was hired to kill Peg Cuttino should certainly be investigated, and not suppressed, as some officials have insisted upon.

Also, we Sumter County citizens who testified at the Grand Jury hearing in May, 1977, find it very disturbing that Assistant Attorney General Joe Barker, who sat in and heard the entire testimony, instigated this action! If the judicial system of South Carolina insists upon the death penalty for Pee Wee Gaskins before a complete and impartial investigation in to his criminal activities is made, we fear that it will drive a deeper wedge of suspicion between citizens and law enforcement officials.

Carrie B. LeNoir

Gaskins made his confession on the witness stand in Newberry, but had not made further statement since that time. He refused to talk about it with anyone. Naturally, one wonders why.

It could be that he was planning to use that information to bargain with the authorities (the authorities claimed that Gaskins would not talk to them about it) — or could it be that he had been told by those authorities, in whose custody he was held, not to talk about it. The public wondered. One could see the embarrassment to the law enforcement and judicial officials after the extreme lengths to which they had gone to uphold their conviction of Junior Pierce, if Pee Wee Gaskins now provided positive proof that he had, in fact, slain the Cuttino girl — and especially if it had been on the instruction of a Sumter County police officer — as Gaskins had claimed. Some official may have to go to prison, and it would cast an unfavorable reflection on the others. The only one who could possibly benefit from a conviction of Gaskins for the Cuttino murder would be Junior Pierce, but a lot of people would be in hot water.

In late March of 1978, Mrs. LeNoir's attorney, Joseph McElveen, Jr., filed a brief with the South Carolina State Supreme Court outlining why it should overturn the August 8, 1977, court order of Judge Dan F. Laney, Jr., which ordered the documents in her possession surrendered and sealed by the Sumter County Clerk of Court and the contempt of court conviction which sent her to jail for four days.

McElveen said in his brief that, "Mrs. LeNoir was ordered by Judge Laney to turn over to the court certain items. She was given no notice that the court was going to act. She was given no opportunity to appear and state her position on the matter. The (August 8) Order that decided the merits of the case, in effect, was a nullity.

"Clearly the lower court knew that there was an adverse interest in the matter," the brief stated. "...Mrs. LeNoir had long been an advocate of certain ideas and opinions..."

The brief contended that "...the lower court (Judge Laney) had no right to seize the materials... A Circuit Judge, at chambers, may grant a temporary injunction if the facts, in his discretion, justify same. On the other hand, the court may merely grant a temporary restraining order until the Defendant has an opportunity to appear and present his side of the case."

McElveen said that Mr. Cuttino did not qualify for "injunctive relief". To qualify, the requesting party could have no other remedy at law, or that the party must immediately be threatened with or be suffering irreparable harm.

Mr. Cuttino could have used the courts to sue Mrs. LeNoir for "infliction of mental anguish", or other charges.

"Ultimately, before a temporary injunction should be granted, there must be some showing of immediacy," McElveen said. "...But there was no such situation, as evidenced by the fact that the original complaint against Mrs. LeNoir was dated July 21... and Judge Laney's order was not issued until August 8, and the papers were not served on Mrs. LeNoir until August 21... There was no such immediacy in this case."

Finally, the brief alleged that Mrs. LeNoir should not have been jailed for contempt. "Mrs. LeNoir takes the position that the order of Judge Laney, incarcerating her for three months, was a coercive measure which amounted to civil contempt.

"The law of this state clearly indicates that one may not be convicted of contempt for violating a court order which failed to tell him in definite terms what he must do," the brief said. Mrs. LeNoir had been confused by unclear wording in the August 8 order and by the August 29 hearing.

"The wrong which this appeal seeks to correct is one which affects every citizen of our state. This case could serve aptly as a textbook example of how our legal system would work without the safeguards of the United States and South Carolina Constitutions. For in this case, the lower court disregarded the principles which distinguish our legal system from those of other countries — 'due process of law', or 'fundamental fairness'."

Item staff writer Kathy Edwards, in preparing an article which appeared Friday, March 31, 1978, contacted Mr. Cuttino's attorney, George James, for comment,, and found that he was no longer involved in the proceedings. Ronald L. Motley, of the Solomon Blatt law firm in Barnwell, South Carolina, could not be reached for comment.

On Saturday, April 1, a "Notice" appeared in The Daily Item, which appealed for contributions for legal fees for the Supreme Court appeal in behalf of Mrs. Carrie B. LeNoir.

In the days and months following, there was little to do but wait for the South Carolina Supreme Court to meet in June. However, the media was filled with startling events involving prominent law enforcement officials and about Pee Wee Gaskins.

SLED Chief J.P. Strom found himself in a rather embarrassing situation in mid-April, when a special unit from the United States Justice Department began to reveal what was going on inside the SLED organization.

There had been many rumors and accusations against members of SLED in the past few years centering on narcotics activities. Chief Strom had taken a "no comment" position about the matter until April 12, four days after a U.S. District Court jury found former SLED agent Albert A. Lawrence guilty of racketeering and conspiracy charges. Four other ex-agents faced similar federal charges, but had pleaded guilty to lesser offenses.

Chief Strom said that SLED had begun its own investigation into these activities when federal authorities stepped in.

"We stopped our inquiry when the federal task force declined to let us participate," Chief Strom added.

Chief Strom said that his first knowledge of problems in the narcotics division had come in October 1974 — four years before — but no action had ever been taken by that agency against its own people.

There was much publicity about these activities and SLED's already tainted image faded into complete distrust by the people it was formed to defend and protect.

SLED was once an agency in South Carolina which answered to the Governor of the state, but in 1974, for its own political reasons, the General Assembly enacted legislation removing SLED from the control of the Governor.

SLED was made an independent agency, set adrift to form its own policies, manage its own budget, and do pretty much as it pleased, without having to answer to anyone.

Chief Strom had repeatedly insisted that SLED could take care of its own internal problems and didn't want or need any help from outside.

It became very apparent to South Carolina citizens that the General Assembly needed to look very hard at the inherent dangers of the present SLED set-up. The agency should again be placed under the administrative arm of the Governor's office, so that it would be answerable to someone who is answerable to the electorate.

The Assembly also needed to weigh the wisdom of allowing unlimited tenure to the person who headed SLED. It was a powerful position — one that rivaled, and in many cases surpassed, the power and influence of those in top elective offices.

Police power, without built-in checks and balances, leaves too much opportunity for excesses and abuse.

At the same time, SLED was having these internal problems, Pee Wee Gaskins was in the custody of Florence County Sheriff William C. Barnes, and was talking his head off trying to make a deal with law enforcement officers in order to obtain immunity from the death sentence he knew he surely faced in this state.

For days and weeks, Gaskins talked and admitted to crimes. He implicated others who had been involved in these crimes with him, enabling law enforcement officials to clear up many of their unsolved cases, and even some that they didn't know had been committed.

They even went so far as to place Gaskins under truth serum. He was taken to a Florence hospital, and there, under the supervision of a psychiatrist and in the presence of his attorney, O. Grady Query, he was interrogated by Twelfth Circuit Solicitor T. Kenneth Summerford, Florence County Sheriff William C. Barnes, and SLED agent Tom Henderson.

It was reported to the press, and carried in an article by Sylvia Wise in The Daily Item on Thursday, June 8, that Gaskins was also asked about his confession to the murder of Peg Cuttino.

"Ain't nothing to that," he reportedly said. "There was a little pressure being put on me at different angles right there, Mr. Summerford."

Gaskins reportedly said the pressure was coming from "different people... Like I said, there was a lot of pressure put on me and I figured by going out and saying a lot of that would get a lot of pressure off of me and everything."

Gaskins supposedly said at one point that he wanted to direct attention away from Junior Pierce, with whom he was corresponding at the time.

As a result of this interrogation, and in return for his assurance of life sentences, Gaskins pled guilty to seven more murders. He was sentenced to life for each, as promised.

But some Sumter County citizens knew right away that there was something wrong. Peg Burleson and Carrie LeNoir had been corresponding with Junior Pierce and Pee Wee Gaskins. They compared notes and letters sent to the two men and received from them. The pieces of the puzzle didn't fit.

Peg Burleson, spokesperson for Citizens for Justice, fired a letter to The Item:

The Daily Item — Sumter, South Carolina, Wednesday, June 14, 1978

LETTER TO THE EDITOR

'SERUM' STORY DOUBTED

To the Editor:

Somehow, when I read the article about Gaskins' "truth
serum" confessions, I get the idea he had been corresponding
with William "Junior" Pierce prior to his "bombshell" at
Newberry. I doubt seriously if Pierce had ever heard of Gaskins
until that time, at least he never mentioned him in all his letters to
Mrs. S.G. (Carrie) LeNoir.

In February of this year, I sent the name and address of
Donald Henry Gaskins to Junior Pierce. I received a letter back,
dated February 2, 1978, from Junior in which he said, "I've wrote
(sic) to Mr. Gaskins and THANK YOU for sending me his address
in Columbia, S.C. I know he will welcome any letters, as I do,
and maybe through the grace of God, he will come out."

On March 16, 1978, I received another letter from Pierce, in
which he states, "Two weeks ago, I wrote to Mr. Donald H.
Gaskins, 1515 Gist Street, Columbia, S.C., and he answered my
letter in regards to the 'Cuttino' case in Sumter. I'm sure proud
that Mr. Gaskins wrote me, and I pray for him for his life."

If Pierce and Gaskins had been corresponding for over a
year, WHY wait until February of this year to discuss the case?
Why is it that the state is willing to take Gaskins' word for all
things except about the Cuttino murder and the fact he was hired
to kill Peg and 'Clyde'?

Since our officials accepted the use of the truth serum to
refute Gaskins' confession of the murder and the fact he was hired
to do so, why don't they use the same truth serum on Junior
Pierce? I know he is willing to do so. They wouldn't use the
hypnotist's report in court to clear Junior. Again, I say there is no
justice in Sumter's judicial system and this is just more proof.
Junior denied on the witness stand killing the girl, and his
witnesses said he wasn't even here.

I have never thanked the past Grand Jury for their help in
events which are unfolding in Sumter County, but would like to
take this opportunity to do so. Thank you — had you found a
little something wrong, the majority of the population might have
bought your decision, but the term "absolutely no wrong-doing"
was just too big a bite for the average citizen to swallow. You did
more to help the Citizens for Justice than you realize. Again, we

thank you.

Peg Burleson

It should be pointed out that, at this point, Mrs. Carrie LeNoir had never met Junior Pierce, nor Pee Wee Gaskins. She corresponded with them both and sent them religious tracts and assured them that God loved them and that she and others here in Sumter County prayed for them regularly.

You will notice in Mrs. Burleson's reference to Junior Pierce's letters that he spoke of God and his prayers for Pee Wee Gaskins. Some time before, Pierce claimed that he had accepted Christ as his personal Saviour, and that he was saved. He said that he regretted all of the bad things that he has done in his life, but denies that he had anything to do with the Cuttino girl's murder. He was, however, very concerned that the real killer be brought to justice. He expressed concern for the people of Sumter County, because if he didn't kill her (which he said he was sure of), and if Pee Wee Gaskins didn't kill her (which the law enforcement officials said they are sure of), then the real killer could have been still walking the streets of Sumter and could possibly have killed again.

The Sumter County Grand Jury went into session on Monday, June 19, 1978, for the spring session of court. This was the week that the South Carolina Supreme Court was to hear Mrs. LeNoir's appeal also, and she went about her daily affairs calmly and prayerfully, but with full faith that God's will would be done in the matter. She realized that it was possible, if she lost, that she would have to return to prison to finish serving the 90-day sentence of Judge Dan Laney for contempt of court.

Nevertheless, as was her usual manner, she went about doing for others, instead of worrying about her own affairs. Tuesday morning, she appeared before the Grand Jury at the Sumter County Courthouse and made a request that Donald H. Gaskins and William Pierce be brought together and jointly questioned under the influence of "truth serum" in order to find out which one, if in fact either of them, killed Peg Cuttino.

In a letter to Grand Jury foreman Aubrey Hatfield, she proposed that the Grand Jury bring the two convicted murderers together in Sumter, give them the truth serum (sodium pentothal) and question them in front of the Grand Jury.

Mrs. LeNoir said she felt "hopeful" after she met with them, but foreman Hatfield had declined to speculate when the jury might respond. All grand jury proceedings are secret, as you will recall.

In her letter, she said, "I apologize that I had to get to this stage, but only death or disability will stop me in my attempts to get justice in this case."

On Wednesday of that week, June 21, 1978, the Supreme Court heard the LeNoir appeal. Both sides presented their arguments, and they left it in the hands of the judges.

Using what Mrs. LeNoir later referred to as "character assassination", Mr. Cuttino's attorney, Ronald Motley, stated in his brief, "A more debased and depraved effort cannot be imagined by this writer. The cruel exhibition of the photographs of the deceased to passersby, seven years after the conviction of her murderer is shocking and outrageous conduct which should be condemned by all in a civilized society."

These words hurt, but she knew that they were not true, and she knew that the Cuttino family knew that they were not true.

That same day, she received word that the Sumter County Grand Jury would not conduct the investigation which she had requested on Tuesday.

She had had a bad day. Ronald Motley had told the court that Mrs. LeNoir's actions were "grisly" and said, "I have never seen or heard of viler conduct on the part of a citizen... Mr. Cuttino's family had endured the publicity of this case for eight years... They hoped Mrs. LeNoir would stop this grisly campaign of showing the pictures to passersby."

Motley, speaking for Mr. Cuttino, made it appear that she had stood on the street showing the picture to anyone and everyone passing by, and that was a lie. She had been very reluctant to show the picture, but had taken it to some prominent people in an effort to get citizen support for her belief that Junior Pierce did not commit the crime. She was the first to admit the unfortunate circumstance of the photograph's importance in proving her beliefs. Anyone seeing the photograph could readily see that the body had not lain in the woods in warm temperatures for a period of twelve days, as the law enforcement officials claimed.

Of course, Mrs. LeNoir had expected all of these things to be said, but it still hurt.

Then began the long wait for a decision from the Supreme Court. She did not know it then, but it would be October before a decision would be rendered.

Meanwhile, life went on and the Citizens for Justice continued its struggle to restore some degree of justice to the process in Sumter County.

In his letters to Carrie LeNoir and to Peg Burleson, Pee Wee Gaskins indicated that he had been threatened by certain officials and warned not to talk about Sumter County and the events there.

Fearing for Gaskins' life, Mrs. LeNoir and Mrs. Burleson traveled to Columbia and met with Central Correctional Institution Warden J.R. Martin and Assistant Warden C.R. Claypool.

For 45 minutes, they pleaded with these men to protect Gaskins and presented them with a letter requesting the same.

"We realize that he is probably your most notorious prisoner," the letter said," ... and we certainly don't condone his behavior, but it is imperative that he live to help obtain facts which are needed to establish justice in some cases."

Warden Martin assured them that Gaskins was being protected and, when asked if he thought Gaskins' life was in danger from enforcement officials, Martin said bluntly, "Certainly not."

Sylvia Wise, Item staff writer, prepared an article entitled "LENOIR APPEALS TO WARDEN FOR GASKINS' PROTECTION", which ran on Saturday, July 8, in which she quoted Warden Martin as saying Gaskins had a "high security risk status" and had been segregated from other inmates.

Mrs. LeNoir said after the visit, "I was impressed with the sincerity of the two officials. I certainly feel they understand the situation much better." She emphasized that she had no complaints about any CCI officials.

After the Saturday paper hit the newsstands and was delivered to the homes in

Sumter County, Mrs. LeNoir began to get telephone calls from interested citizens, and on Monday she sent the letter that had been delivered to the warden at CCI to The Daily Item. The newspaper printed it in its entirety under Letters to the Editor.

No one knows what went on at CCI after Mrs. LeNoir's visit, but something must have happened, because The Item received a letter from Pee Wee Gaskins:

The Daily Item — Sumter, SC, Thursday, July 13, 1978
LETTER TO THE EDITOR

GASKINS: "NO FEAR" IN PRISON

To the Editor:
I am writing you about the item that was in this paper on July 8, stating that I was afraid for my life here in the prison. I have "NO FEAR" whatsoever here in prison.

I feel that no convict will bother me in any way. They seem to want to help me in any way they can. My only fear comes from certain law officers. I have no fear from anyone from Sumter or Williamsburg Counties.

I feel that Mrs. S.G. LeNoir was wrong in coming up here last week and going to the warden about what she did. I am going to write her and tell her so. As I have said, I don't think there is a man in this prison who is a inmate who will try to harm me in any way. I have not even had any hard words with anyone here, except some guards who are prejudiced against me to start with. I am treated very bad by some prison officers here.

I am now in the process of bringing law suits against Commissioner Leeke, Warden Martin and Deputy Warden Joyner for the way I am being treated here now. I am supposed to see my attorney this week on this matter.

But I want to make it clear, I cannot say anything whatsoever against Sumter County law enforcement.

Donald H. Gaskins
Central Correctional Institute
1515 Gist St.
Columbia

"Wonder why he wrote that letter?" Mrs. LeNoir asked.

On Tuesday, July 18, 1978, William Pierce filed petitions with the clerks of court in Sumter and Williamsburg Counties asking that he be questioned about the Cuttino crime while under the influence of sodium pentothal.

In the petition, Pierce claimed he never signed a confession saying he killed Miss Cuttino and that Sheriff Parnell perjured himself by telling the Grand Jury the document was signed.

Parnell told The Daily Item, "I have never in my life stated that Pierce signed a confession." He denied referring to a signed confession in front of the Sumter Grand

Jury. A study of the transcript of Pierce's trial, he said, would show he had never claimed to have a signed confession.

The petition also said that the Grand Jury violated his rights by accepting the confession as the basis for indicting him for murder.

Pierce's petition listed 14 instances in which he thought his rights had been violated.

Of course, the petition came before Third Circuit Judge Dan F. Laney, Jr., who again denied the appeal on August 4, saying that there was no constitutional basis for returning Pierce to South Carolina to be questioned while under the influence of "truth serum". Pierce had contended in his petition that he had a right to such questioning similar to that administered to convicted killer Pee Wee Gaskins.

"The applicant (Petitioner) has no right," the order stated, "under the Equal Protection Clause — or under any other constitutional guarantee — to be questioned under the influence of "truth serum".

Pierce had also filed the petition in Williamsburg County, where his trial had been held after it was changed from Sumter County. Williamsburg County Clerk of Court Winnie P. Jones also received a copy of Judge Laney's order that was identical to the one sent to the Sumter County Clerk of Court.

Williamsburg County and Sumter County come under Judge Dan F. Laney's jurisdiction. So that was the end of that. Of course, Pierce could appeal the decision, but he had about as much chance as the proverbial "snowball in hades".

On Tuesday afternoon, October 3, 1978, Mrs. LeNoir's attorney, Joseph T. McElveen, received a telephone call from a court spokesman at the South Carolina Supreme Court in Columbia informing him that, by a 3-2 decision, the court had reversed the lower court order finding Mrs. LeNoir in contempt of court for refusing to surrender documents concerning the Cuttino slaying.

The majority decision said Judge Dan F. Laney, Jr.'s order to turn over the documents "amounted to an ex parte (on one side only) personal judgement against appellant and was, therefore, a nullity."

The decision said the provisions of the August 8 order issued by Judge Laney to appear"... did not grant the right of a hearing to determine whether the direction to 'immediately deliver' the documents was proper."

She had won. Mrs LeNoir was relieved and elated with the decision.

"I feel this is a victory for the people," she said. "It shows... that we still have some justice in the judicial system."

"I would welcome a hearing on the documents," Mrs. LeNoir said. "These documents were never even presented in court and anyone who saw them would know that there is no way that body laid in the woods for 12 days. It would prove that Junior Pierce did not kill her (Peg Cuttino)."

She was graceful, poised and brave as she assured the news media of her determination to continue the fight for justice and as she received the compliments of her many friends who called or came to wish her well and tell her of their delight in the Court's decision, but when she was at last alone — she and her husband — cried and praised God for his grace and mercy.

"It felt like a great burden had been lifted from my shoulders," she said. "I thank God for his help and guidance through this ordeal, and I thank God that it is finally over... it has been so long and drawn out... the tension was almost unbearable... waiting for the court's decision... knowing that I could be sent back to prison... you can't begin to understand the feeling... unless you have been there... but it's over now... and I am so relieved."

Yes, it was finally over. What more could happen in this bizarre, seemingly unending affair?

CHAPTER EIGHTEEN

THE THREE MILLION DOLLAR LAWSUIT

OCTOBER 26, 1978

On Thursday, October 26, 1978, attorneys for Representative James Cuttino served complaints on Mrs. Carrie LeNoir; Sumter Daily Item Editor Hubert D. Osteen; and Sumter County Deputy Coroner Verna Moore (an Item employee).

They were notified that libel suits in the amount of three million dollars each would be filed in the Lee County Court of Common Pleas within ten days.

Mrs. LeNoir was accused in the complaint of an "outrageous and offensive" public campaign to gain a new trial for William "Junior" Pierce, and with obtaining and publicly displaying photos of the Cuttino girl's body and autopsy and pathology reports.

Item Editor Hubert D. Osteen was accused of encouraging and promoting Mrs. LeNoir's efforts and causing the Cuttino family "severe mental anguish and renewed grief" through articles, editorials and advertisements concerning the case.

Verna Moore was accused of counseling Mrs. LeNoir. She said, "I don't know why they picked me out as an individual."

Mr. Osteen's only comment was, "The case has no merit." Mrs. LeNoir made no public comment at all, but inwardly she could not believe that this was happening.

Mrs. LeNoir, The Sumter Daily Item and Verna Moore were residents of Sumter County. Mrs. LeNoir wondered why Mr. Cuttino had filed his suits in Lee County, which was the county adjoining Sumter County... and also the county in which Judge Dan F. Laney, Jr., resided. She was sure that Judge Laney was not happy with her for taking his August 8 ruling to South Carolina Supreme Court, where it was reversed by that court, but surely that had nothing to do with this. Or did it?

Soon her hurt and dismay faded into resolve and determination to weather whatever storm might come, and she busied herself with thoughts of what would be best to do at this point.

Having determined her best avenue, with the help of attorney Herbert E. Buhl., III, of the American Civil Liberties Union in Columbia, on Thursday, November 30, 1978, in response to Mr. Cuttino's suit, Mrs. LeNoir counter-sued for one million dollars.

In her answer, she denied all the allegations in Mr. Cuttino's suit, except the fact that she had possession of the autopsy and pathology reports and photographs of the dead child, and she charged that she had been "injured, intimidated, harassed and harmed" by his actions. She charged that if any damage was done, it was due to Mr. Cuttino's "own actions and conduct" and that she "sought only that justice be done".

She accused Mr. Cuttino of "abusing the process of laws and courts of this state" and further maintained that her actions in the matter "are fully protected by the First Amendment to the Constitution of the United States", which guarantees freedom of speech.

Mr. Hubert D. Osteen, Jr., said that Columbia attorney William L. Pope was retained to prepare a response for The Sumter Daily Item.

Verna Moore said that she had retained an attorney in Manning, South Carolina, but had not yet responded to Mr. Cuttino's complaint.

The waiting game began again for Mrs. LeNoir and her family. They wondered where it would all end... or if, in fact, it would ever end.

"How did it all begin?" Mrs. LeNoir reasoned. It was hard to remember now just how this all got started. But as her thoughts rambled back over the events of the past several years, she realized that it all started when Peg Cuttino walked into the LeNoir store in Horatio on December 19, 1970.

As good citizens of this great country of ours, as she and her husband believed themselves to be, they had simply offered that testimony to the authorities who, they thought, were trying to solve the vile and cruel murder case, which some claimed had happened the day before they saw the child. They had been ignored, badgered, called liars, harassed, thrown in jail, and now sued as a result of the events stemming from that day.

Where would it all end? She placed it all in the hands of God and proceeded to live her life as normally as could be done under the circumstances — still with a calm, deep and determined resolve to continue the fight for justice.

Until now, Mrs. Carrie LeNoir and the Sumter County Citizens for Justice had fought the fight alone. Then, on Friday, December 21, 1978, The State newspaper in Columbia carried a story headlined "LAWYER SAYS HIS EVIDENCE PROVES INNOCENCE OF CONVICTED KILLER", by UPI writer Richard Beene.

The story read:

> *Atlanta attorney Charles King said Wednesday he could prove the innocence of a man convicted of killing a 13-year-old South Carolina girl and accused police of deliberately suppressing evidence that could lead to a real killer.*
>
> *King, president of the Atlanta-based Urban Crisis Center, said he would turn over the results of a five-month investigation to the U.S. Justice Department in hopes it could clear William J. "Junior" Pierce of killing Margaret "Peg" Cuttino of Sumter...*
>
> *King charged authorities had obtained confessions from Pierce "by torture and the evidence of physical maltreatment may be secured from existing medical records."*
>
> *King refused to release his evidence to reporters. He said he would do so to Federal officials, but not to South Carolina law enforcement officers, whom King said could not be trusted.*
>
> *King said his investigation, prompted by a letter from Pierce, had proven that two of Pierce's confessions could not be true because records showed he was in prison at the time of the crimes.*
>
> *With overwhelming documentation supported by four witnesses, our investigation reveals that William "Junior" Pierce*

could not have killed "Peg" Cuttino...
Pierce was legitimately employed on that day, and the
owner-supervisor and foreman of the firm that employed him
verified that...

King charged Donald H. "Pee Wee" Gaskins was the real killer, but South Carolina authorities refused to believe him. He said Gaskins had confessed to the murder of the Cuttino girl and a black woman, but authorities did not consider his statements credible.

The next day, The Sumter Daily Item picked up the story and ran it, entitled "CENTER PRESIDENT: PIERCE INNOCENT", giving even more detail:

> *The president of the Atlanta Urban Crisis Center says a*
> *South Carolina inmate who has confessed to four slayings should*
> *be moved to a federal prison for his own safety...*
> *Charles King said Wednesday at a news conference that*
> *officials in Sumter County have kept Donald H. "Pee Wee"*
> *Gaskins from coming to trial because they are concerned others*
> *would be implicated in the cases.*
> *King said Gaskins 'fears for his safety and should be moved*
> *as quickly as possible to federal custody...*
> *King, a prison critic and prisoner advocate, said he had*
> *evidence showing Pierce was working when Miss Cuttino was*
> *killed...*
> *He said the Cuttino case and others were "a horrendous*
> *portrait of the plan of victims, their families and communities that*
> *have been victimized by botched investigations, suppression of*
> *evidence by law enforcement officers and instantly manufactured*
> *confessions to clear up crimes."*

Essentially the same story was carried in The Atlanta Constitution and other Southeastern newspapers on Friday, December 22.

Sumter County Citizens for Justice were delighted to have Dr. King involved in the case. Maybe now someone would listen.

As 1978 came to a close, the new year looked promising to those involved in the struggle for a new trial for Pierce.

Meanwhile, on Saturday, January 6, 1979, The Sumter Daily Item ran an article entitled "ITEM ASKS DISMISSAL OF SUIT BY CUTTINO":

> *An answer has been filed by attorneys for The Sumter Daily*
> *Item asking that a $3 million lawsuit brought against the*
> *newspaper by James Cuttino be dismissed.*
> *The answer was filed in Lee County Court of Common Pleas*
> *in Bishopville, along with a motion for change of venue of the*
> *trial, should it be held, to Sumter County. This motion is*
> *expected to be argued before 3rd Circuit Judge Ernest A. Finney,*
> *Jr., at a date to be announced later.*

...The Item, in denying these allegations, contends in its answer that the Cuttino murder and the controversy surrounding it was "a matter of grave public concern in the Sumter community and throughout the state of South Carolina, and consequently, the police investigation, the arrest and trial of the accused, and subsequent legal proceedings, were all matters of intense public interest and... received publicity in The Sumter Daily Item, as well as in other newspapers serving South Carolina.

The answer also states that published stories on the controversy were privileged as an exercise of the right of free speech and freedom of the press protected by the Constitution and laws of the United States and of the state of South Carolina.

In addition, The Item contends that individuals referred to in the stories were public figures and public officials, and reference to them is also privileged as an exercise of the right of free speech, as protected by the U.S. and state constitutions and federal and state laws.

Finally, The Item denies any malice in publication of stories about the case, claiming that its coverage was "an attempt to fulfill its public responsibility" and that any grief caused the Cuttino family was not the newspaper's fault.

In its motion for a change of venue, The Item argues that its only office and place of business is in Sumter County, and that it does not maintain a place of business or own property and conduct business in Lee County. Also, the newspaper contends that the convenience of witnesses and the "ends of justice" would be promoted by a change of venue.

The article disclosed that The Sumter Daily Item would be represented by William L. Pope of the Columbia law firm of Robinson, McFadden, Moore & Pope.

Monday, January 8, in The Atlanta Constitution, in an article entitled"Dr. King Asks Justice Department To Reopen Reidsville Case", it was announced that Dr. Charles King had called on the United States Justice Department to investigate new evidence surrounding the Cuttino murder case.

The article read:

Witnesses further alleged that Sheriff Carter (Sheriff J.B. "Red" Carter of Appling County, Georgia) did conspire with another man to have Pierce lynched. However, the lynch plot was discovered and Carter arrested as co-conspirator. For that act, Carter was commended by then-Governor Jimmy Carter.

Dr. King is turning over the entire record of his investigation to three sources:

1. The Justice Department, with a plea for intervention in behalf of Pierce and protective custody for Gaskins.

2. To proven investigative reporters who can, if they will, certify that the predominance of information is compelling enough to discount all of Pierce's confessions and to mandate trials for Pee Wee Gaskins.

    3. To the Federal Court in the form of a habeas corpus. If these efforts are successful, I am convinced that the ultimate outcome will result in indictments against:

    1. Sheriff I. Byrd Parnell, Sumter, South Carolina.

    2. Former Sheriff J.B. "Red" Carter, Baxley, Georgia.

    3. Deputy Sheriff Joe Lightsey, Baxley, Georgia.

    4. Lt. Olin Redd, S.C. Law Enforcement Agency.

    5. Mr. William P. Parker, retired G.B.I. officer.

    6. Tom Henderson, S.L.E.D., Sumter County, South Carolina.

"Time will tell," said Mrs. LeNoir. She was pleased to have someone else leading the fight for awhile and pleased to know that someone else, looking at the same evidence that she knew existed, saw things the same way she and the Citizens for Justice in Sumter County saw them.

Meanwhile, every effort to protect Pee Wee Gaskins was being made at the South Carolina Department of Corrections in Columbia, where he was being held.

SCDC officials required him to remain locked in his cell at all times, unless he was accompanied by a guard. His hands were cuffed and his legs were chained whenever he was removed from his cell.

Gaskins began a hunger strike on January 1, 1979, to protest his full-time confinement in the small death row cell where he was being kept. In a letter, he told The State newspaper that he believed he was entitled to be released into the population of the Central Correctional Institution because he was not under a death sentence.

However, Corrections Commissioner William D. Leeke said Gaskins was being restricted for his own protection because he could be killed by other inmates if he were allowed out of his cell without supervision.

Gaskins said that reason was factless.

On Friday, January 12, 1979, The State ran an article by staff writer Holly Gatling entitled "Gaskins Claims Hunger Strike", in which the current circumstances were revealed.

Gaskins, a short, thin man in his mid-40's, claimed that he had begun his hunger strike on January 1, but SCDC spokesman Sam McCuen claimed that candy bars and raisins had been found in Gaskins' cell since that date.

Just to be sure, however, Commissioner Leeke said Gaskins was being checked twice a day by a physician and that the department was prepared to obtain a court order to force feed Gaskins if the fast appeared to threaten his life.

About the same time the story hit the news media, Gaskins gave up his hunger strike and resumed his regular meals, even though there was no change in his confinement.

Meanwhile, the Citizens for Justice worked on, and although Pee Wee Gaskins claimed to have no fear for his life, almost everyone else did.

CCI Warden Joe Martin said, "We're worried about his safety." Mrs. LeNoir said, "I look to hear that he (Gaskins) has been killed at any time."

Just about this time, some new evidence came to Mrs. LeNoir concerning the case, and she found out that a lot of people were scared for their lives.

A man... a member of the Citizens for Justice Committee, talked to two other men, both of whom had worked with Pee Wee Gaskins... and they told him that Pee Wee Gaskins had admitted killing Miss Cuttino, and that he had mutilated her body with acid.

They found evidence that linked each of these men to Pee Wee Gaskins, and Mrs. LeNoir took the information directly to Solicitor Kirk McLeod, who had prosecuted Pierce in the Cuttino murder trial.

On Monday morning, January 15, she presented a bail bond certificate which Gaskins himself had posted for one of the men in 1972, before he was arrested and charged with any of the murders, which linked him with that man. The other man was linked to Gaskins by a time card which proved that the two of them worked together. She would not identify either of the two potential witnesses publicly at that time.

Solicitor McLeod refused to take the material and referred her to Pierce's defense attorney, Joe McElveen.

On Tuesday, January 16, The State newspaper ran the story of the new evidence in an article entitled "Carrie LeNoir Claims Evidence Proves Pierce Is Innocent", by Jerry Dyer of the Pee Dee Bureau.

In that article, Mrs. LeNoir said, "I have not talked to either of the two men who say Gaskins confessed the Cuttino murder, but a member of our Citizens for Justice Committee has. Even he is running scared at having this information. I think this new evidence will conclusively prove that Gaskins, not Pierce, killed Peg Cuttino."

When asked what she thought Gaskins' motive for killing Peg Cuttino would have been, Mrs. LeNoir responded, "I can't say anything about what I think Gaskins' motive might have been for killing Peg Cuttino. I'm already facing one lawsuit, as it is."

Of course, Mrs. LeNoir followed Solicitor McLeod's advice to take the new evidence to Pierce's defense attorney, Joe McElveen, whereupon Mr. McElveen said he would check into the information and see if it warranted re-opening the case. He said he was not sure that he was still Pierce's attorney, but added that he was "professionally obligated" to follow any new leads in the case. He also said, however, that he would need "iron-clad" evidence before he would make a motion for a new trial.

It had been eight years since the murder and the Cuttino case was still a hot item in Sumter County. Apparently, Mr. McElveen did not think that the evidence provided was "iron-clad", because no appeal was made for Pierce.

Time moved on slowly. Two witnesses who Gaskins had confessed to, yet nobody was interested, other than the Citizens for Justice in Sumter County.

February dragged by... and nothing was done by the authorities, nor by Pierce's attorney.

By Thursday, March 15, Mrs. LeNoir's and the Citizens for Justice's patience had run out. She called a press conference and asked Sheriff I. Byrd Parnell and

Sumter Police Chief L.W. Griffin to be there, too.

The conference was held at the Law Enforcement Center, and the atmosphere in the room became noticeably tense when James Cuttino, the slain girl's father, walked in with Sheriff Parnell, according to Item staff writer Sylvia Wise, who covered the conference for The Sumter Daily Item.

Chief Griffin was delayed. Mrs. LeNoir began by reading a six-page statement chronicling the case, beginning with the disappearance of Miss Cuttino in December of 1970. She then offered the evidence to Sheriff Parnell.

"I would suggest that you take everything you have and put it in a sealed packet and give it to the Solicitor," Parnell said, and he refused to take it.

"I get the run-around everywhere I go," Mrs. LeNoir said, "Nobody wants it."

She told Sheriff Parnell that she had tried to give the evidence to Solicitor McLeod in January, but he refused to accept it, saying that she should give it to Pierce's attorney, Joe McElveen.

Of course, she had given it to Mr. McElveen, and nothing had been done. Now, the Sheriff refused it.

Mrs. LeNoir told them that she was offering the materials first to local officials because, "I always believe, if possible, we should handle this locally. We are very sympathetic with Peg's family and certainly don't want to hurt them any further, but it is imperative to the people of South Carolina that justice be restored to the judicial system. We think this information surely is sufficient to either warrant a new trial for Pierce, or to bring Gaskins to trial and, if convicted, to exonerate Pierce of the conviction.

"If the evidence isn't acted on," Mrs. LeNoir said, "I will turn the documents over to federal officials... if local officials fail to make a positive commitment to act on the evidence within ten days."

She told them that she had been contacted on Thursday by a "federal investigator" in Georgia, but she couldn't name what agency the investigator was with.

Mr. Cuttino said little throughout the conference, except to ask a Columbia television cameraman not to take his picture, reported Sylvia Wise. He said nothing to Mrs. LeNoir.

Dr. Charles King turned over the results of his investigation to the F.B.I. in Atlanta, and The Sumter Daily Item contacted that agency to see what they intended to do with the materials.

A special agent at the Atlanta bureau said the information would be turned over to the Columbia, South Carolina, bureau.

The Item contacted the Columbia F.B.I., and there, special agent George Ross said the bureau could not make any decisions about how to proceed until it had received the material in the mail. This contact was made on Wednesday, April 11, 1979.

On Monday, May 8, The Item contacted the Columbia F.B.I. again, and asked what had been done. The agents said that they did not receive the materials until a week ago, and that they would refer any new information to the Justice Department, since the case involved a possible violation of Pierce's civil rights.

On June 9, JUJU Publishing Co., publishers of The Black News in Columbia, the Black Voice in Orangeburg, Black Times in Charleston, Black Sun in Florence, Black Post in Sumter, Black Star in Greenville, and Rock Hill News & Views, carried the first in a series of articles by Dr. King telling of his investigation:

GUILTY OR NOT? PART I
by Charles H. King
President, Urban Crisis Center

The following is a personal account by Charles H. King, president of the Urban Crisis Center, of his efforts to assist William "Junior" Pierce, a convicted murderer, in proving his innocence. King is a race relations consultant, who has assisted prisoners for the last 25 years. He got interested in the Pierce case when Pierce contacted him.

Since August of last year, I have been attempting to prove that William "Junior" Pierce is innocent of the murder of Margaret "Peg" Cuttino, who he was convicted of killing December 18, 1970. That search for justice for Pierce has taken me into two states, South Carolina and Georgia.

As a result of that search, I have compiled a voluminous file of letters, transcripts, documents, and now, ten hours of tape recorded information that now not only certifies Pierce's innocence, but indicts the judicial and law enforcement systems and officials in both states.

All of the information and documents that I have, have charges and allegations of law enforcement misconduct and corruption that I uncovered in the six months working on this case. I have been assisted by volunteer citizens, ex-convicts, attorneys for William Pierce, and by the leadership of Citizens for Justice, Sumter, South Carolina. All funds expended during this time have been my personal ones, and all volunteers have given of their time and energy without compensation. I have spent over six (6) hours with a special agent of the FBI, interpreting the complex picture and names of persons who are too numerous to name, nor do I wish to compromise the FBI investigation that is already underway. I have informed the FBI of this conference, and have been assured the right to say what I please as a free citizen, but my main concern was whether or not what I say now would interfere with their work.

I was informed it would not. I have taken the Pierce case to editors and reporters in both states. With two exceptions, none of them would offer to invest either time or their investigative skills into either my findings or the leads that I could not personally check out. This fact highly illustrates one of my findings, and that is if you are poor white, or black, the system is rarely challenged, and it is out of the context and philosophy, that spurred me into continuous activity to point out and expose the corruption of the system and the political maneuverings it undergoes to protect both itself and the officials who run it.

February 13, 1975, Donald "Pee Wee" Gaskins killed Silas Barnwell Yates, a prosperous farmer near Lake City, South Carolina. Those who assisted him in that murder were: Dianne Neeley, Johnny Owens and Howard Evans, Gaskins informed me. Gaskins claims prior to his trial, S.L.E.D. agent Tom Henderson and Solicitor Kenneth Summerford promised him conjugal visits with his wife, if he would name a man named John Powell, an ex-convict, as the murderer and Susanne Owens as planner of the murder. Gaskins obliged, and made such a statement. The conjugal visits were not allowed.

An angry Gaskins then stated to Henderson that the deal was off, and that he would testify to the truth. The arrangement had been that if Gaskins would testify against Susanne Owens and John Powell, he would be given a life sentence, and not be tried for death.

Faced with Gaskins' change of testimony, Solicitor Summerford, by letter, informed Gaskins that if he went through with his plan to deny the statement he had given, that he would do all he could to insure Gaskins received the death penalty. (That letter is now in the hands of the FBI.)

A frightened Susanne Owens was told by her attorney in the middle of Gaskins' trial that Gaskins' statement implicating her in the murder was impossible for her to beat in court. He insisted that she change her plea from not guilty to guilty; if not, she was told, she could face a death penalty with Gaskins. A helpless and confused Susanne Owens pleaded Guilty, and is now serving a life sentence at the Women's Correctional Institute, Columbia, South Carolina, in spite of the fact that in court at the time were five witnesses who could substantiate her alibi, and the fact that she did not know nor had ever met Gaskins at the time of the murder of Yates. This fact is substantiated by reading over 200 letter exchanges between Susanne and Pee Wee, during the past two years of confinement.

Because the law had reneged on its promise, when Gaskins took the stand, he decided to tell the whole story, the true story, that it was he who killed Yates, not John Powell, that it was Dianne Neeley who had assisted him, not Susanne, and that it was John Owens who had planned and paid him to make the "hit". It was at this trial that Gaskins revealed that it was he who had killed Margaret "Peg" Cuttino in Sumter, South Carolina, on December 19, 1970, and that he had also killed a black girl named Clyde in 1971.

Gaskins further revealed that he had assassinated a man, whom he did not know, shot him with a .45, while lawmen watched and allowed him to go free.

Gaskins also confessed that he had shot-gunned and killed two men, dealers in drugs, in Horry County.

At that trial, Gaskins refused to name the lawmen, but hoped to do so if he could be brought to trial on either the Cuttino or "Clyde" killings.

It was in the middle of a recess in the Yates trial that an angry Sheriff I. Byrd Parnell stormed into the counsel room, interfering with a discussion between Gaskins and his attorneys, in a futile attempt to get Gaskins to "stop his lies" about lawmen.

On April 27, 1977, Gaskins was convicted and given a life sentence for the murder of Barnwell Yates.

On April 29, 1977, Sheriff I. Byrd Parnell led a search for the body of "Clyde", later identified as Martha Ann Dicks. Her skeleton bones were found exactly at the spot Gaskins had pointed out to the Sheriff six months prior to Gaskins' open court confession. Gaskins had also pointed out that spot to the law enforcement officers of another county, but before they could go searching, they were warned by Sheriff Parnell to stay out of Sumter County.

Tom Henderson, S.L.E.D., prior to the trial, was told by Gaskins' attorney that Gaskins wanted to reveal to him the location of a black woman that he killed. Henderson refused to look, sending back information to Gaskins that he was "not interested in digging up a nigger girl".

A total of eight bodies were dug up in Prospect (in Florence County). Gaskins had revealed the locations. Prior to going to trial on one of the murders, Gaskins was once again approached with a deal by Tom Henderson and Solicitor Summerford. He was to plead guilty to all murders which they told him to plead guilty to, and to deny killing the Cuttino girl, the two men whom he had shot-gunned down in Horry County, and the Clyde killing, should it be mentioned again.

If Gaskins would do that, they would give him consecutive life sentences, and not seek the death penalty.

Once again, Gaskins agreed to that bargain, even though he, by his own admission, had killed four persons out of the total of 13 which he was asked to confess to.

To certify that bargain, Gaskins, with his lawyers and about 25 persons looking on, was given truth serum. Under that serum, he denied killing those he was ordered to deny, and confessed to those which he was ordered to confess.

Solicitor Summerford then held a press conference to announce that, under the serum, Gaskins said that he did not kill

Peg Cuttino.

Yet, *the truth of the matter, according to Gaskins, is that they did not give him the serum, and that they dared him to say anything other than as told to say. As he had been coached, he acted as if he was under the drug.*

A partial transcript of that "truth serum session" is in my possession and the possession of the FBI, where Summerford insists that William Pierce wrote to Gaskins asking him to confess to the Cuttino killing. Gaskins' reply was "yes".

The story was continued in the June 16, 1979, issues of those publications by JUJU Publishing:

But, I have copies of letters from Pierce to Gaskins and Gaskins to Pierce that clearly indicate that Pierce contacted Gaskins after his confession, and not before.

The Solicitor was clearly attempting to establish a motive for the Cuttino confession that would keep Pierce in prison for that crime, and to protect either the lawmen involved or to (prevent) protect public knowledge of the abortion of justice.

The following named officials have been charged by William Pierce as either accepting or forcing confessions with the knowledge that his "confessions" were not true:

STATE OF GEORGIA
Sheriffs: Howard McCook, Swainsboro, Georgia; Marcus Hall, Hazelhurst, Georgia; Red Carter, Baxley, Georgia.
G.B.I. Agents: Brooks Moses; William Parker; retired Deputy Sheriff Joe Lightsey, Baxley, Georgia.

STATE OF SOUTH CAROLINA
Sheriffs: I. Byrd Parnell, Sumter, South Carolina; Day, Lexington, South Carolina.
S.L..E.D. Chief: J.P. Strom, Columbia, South Carolina.
Agent: Olin C. Redd, Columbia, South Carolina.
Circuit Solicitor: Donald V. Myers.

The following named officials have been charged by Donald "Pee Wee" Gaskins as knowingly obstructing justice in the Peg Cuttino, "Clyde", and other murders:

STATE OF SOUTH CAROLINA
S.L.E.D. Agent: Tom Henderson, Columbia, South Carolina.
Solicitor: Kenneth Summerford, Florence, South Carolina.

Sheriff: I. Byrd Parnell, Sumter, South Carolina.
Deputies: Thomas L. McJunkin and Johnny Nesbitt,
Sumter, South Carolina.

As a result of a press conference held on December 22, 1978, indicating my belief in the innocence of William "Junior" Pierce, the foundation of that belief has been substantiated by an open court confession of Donald "Pee Wee" Gaskins that he, not Pierce, committed that murder.

On January 8, 1979, I received a letter from Mr. Gaskins, confirming the fact that he did kill Margaret "Peg" Cuttino.

He described the manner, motive, details and a 20-minute conversation that he had with the murdered 13 year-old victim before her death.

The details of that conversation give insights into the reasons why the Cuttino family and law enforcement officers have consistently thwarted every effort to bring Mr. Gaskins to trial, which would possibly result in Pierce's freedom.

The Cuttino murder, according to Mr. Gaskins, was accomplished under the orders, direction, and assistance of two officers, both of whom are currently members of the Sumter County Sheriff's Department, and an ex-convict, who was assigned the task of hiding the girl until 8:30 p.m., December 19, 1970.

It was at that hour that Gaskins, assisted by a law enforcement officer, transported the girl in the back seat of a police vehicle to a place in the woods where the body was discarded.

Gaskins asserts that he, Janice Kirby (his niece) and other young girls were participants in the making of pornographic movies, under the direction of... an attorney in Sumter, who died "mysteriously" (according to Gaskins) the morning after the Cuttino girl was declared missing.

As a consequence of receiving the letters from Gaskins, answering pin-pointed questions and offering back-up proof of his allegations, he wrote that he desired to talk to me personally.

Through the cooperation of his lawyer, Mr. John Grisso, Columbia, South Carolina, who did not object, and the Warden of C.C.I., I was able to visit Gaskins three times for a total of six hours.

I tape recorded each session, with Gaskins' permission. As a consequence of those interviews, I have asked the F.B.I. to conduct a thorough investigation into the conduct of the Sumter County Sheriff's Department, the Sumter Police Department, the South Carolina Law Enforcement Department (S.L.E.D.), and the Florence County Solicitor's office.

Separate and apart from the Peg Cuttino murder, a series of bizarre murders occurred in Prospect, S.C., called the "Prospect 8" murders, that Gaskins acknowledged he either accomplished, directed, or has knowledge of the real killers, most of whom are still free.

Gaskins was forced to confess to all of them by S.L.E.D. agent Tom Henderson and Solicitor Summerford. Throughout the checkerboard array of crimes, ranging from theft and drug traffic to murder, an intricate web of law enforcement participation in, or acceptance of, and falsifications persist.

Not only has justice been obstructed by some officials, but twisted and changed to meet their public relations and political needs, by utilizing condemned and helpless convicts as their conducts and agents. The usage of such persons to commit acts, as described, has been documented by my office, separate and apart, but supportive of Gaskins' experiences with the law, especially in Sumter, S.C.

Tapes have been made by my investigators of acknowledged "wheelers and dealers" in drugs, who will cooperate with any official investigation that will expose the officials who now have them taped by "set up" crimes that could send them back to prison.

Gaskins' description of how he was initially "set up" by corrupt officials began in 1969. He was commissioned by a woman, whom he knew only as "Irene" to kill her husband for the amount of $5,000.

Gaskins, by his own admission, told her of, and showed her the spot where he would make the hit. He shot the man at that spot with a .45 automatic. Immediately, four law enforcement officials, hiding in the weeds, approached him, took his weapon, unloaded it, handed it back, and left the scene of the crime. From that date on, Gaskins was forced and ordered to commit crimes, not daring to resist.

The body? With persistent searching and digging, it should not be hard to find. Since the officials named by Gaskins already know the location, the named area should be immediately searched before knowing parties remove whatever remains there might be.

The credibility of Gaskins is heightened by the fact that he is now serving three consecutive life sentences. A confession to other murders involving law enforcement officers could result in a death penalty for Gaskins.

The story was concluded in the publications on June 29, 1979:

Secondly, he names living witnesses to these crimes, which when questioned by the FBI, should produce verification of the detailed Gaskins account.

Thirdly, Gaskins has repeatedly attempted to come to trial for these murders, but has been prevented from doing so by officials involved and cooperating Solicitors in Sumter and Florence, S.C.

Gaskins was warned by Solicitor Summerford of Florence that if he would discount the murders after a "deal" had been made to confess to them, he (Summerford) would try Gaskins for the death penalty instead of life sentence. That letter has been turned over to the FBI.

Gaskins was told to deny the fact that he killed Peg Cuttino and the two drug pushers that he killed with a shotgun. The pressure for him to deny those twin murders in Horry County was applied because... John McDougal had been convicted for those murders and was sentenced to die for the same, and William "Junior" Pierce had already been convicted for the Cuttino murder.

Although he constantly denied it, Gaskins was forced to confess to the murder of his niece, Janice Kirby, who is now married and living in New York. Gaskins named seven persons who have knowledge that the Kirby girl is alive and well. The body dug up by officials which they claim was Kirby, was a young lady named Jackie Freeman, from Wisconsin, who had lived with Gaskins and O.D.'d on drugs, and was buried by Gaskins. Janice Kirby's father can testify to the fact that that body, which he (Gaskins) identified, was not his daughter's.

Janice Kirby, when found, can support the rationale and motive for Peg Cuttino's death (they were friends) and also the allegations that Martha Ann Dicks (Clyde) was a drug pusher for Sumter officials.

Janice Kirby, when found, can also testify to the existence of a pornographic movie set, owned by a prominent Sumter citizen, now deceased, and from whom she, Gaskins and others received $100 per day for their participation in the making of the movies.

All of the young girls who were participants in the pornographic movies are now, systematically, either dead, murdered, or missing. The names of these persons have also been turned over to the FBI for tracing.

Gaskins was also forced to confess to the murder of Jesse Logan Judy, even though law enforcement officers know who the real murderer of Jesse Judy was, but he was not arrested because he has been utilized for years as a law enforcement "set up" man. This fact can be certified by Mr. Logan, Jesse Judy's father, who also is an inmate at C.C.I.

Tom Henderson and Solicitor Summerford together conspired to have Gaskins falsely accuse Susanne Owens and

John Powell of assisting him in murdering Barnwell Yates.

At the time of the murder, Gaskins had never met and did not know Susanne. That fact is verified by my personal interview with Ms. Owens, who is now serving a life sentence at the Women's Correctional Institute, Columbia, S.C., and through documentation that conclusively supports Ms. Owens' innocence.

Furthermore, Solicitor Summerford and Tom Henderson, SLED agent, knew who assisted Gaskins in that murder, namely Dianne Neeley, Howard Evans, and John Owens, Susanne's husband. For his testimony implicating his wife, Owens received a ten-year sentence (accessory after the fact), and Evans remains free to this date.

Ex-convicts who have lived or who now live in Sumter County are utilized as "set up" men to occasion the arrest of known offenders or suspects. Evidence is planted on the ex-cons, who with police assistance, plan crimes that would involve persons that law enforcement officials desire to have imprisoned. A list of those persons and specific "crimes" and the officers involved, have been submitted to the FBI.

The murder of Martha Ann Dicks (Clyde) was accomplished for the following reason. "Clyde" was a pusher of drugs for two law enforcement officers. She received her drugs from the "evidence" soon after it had been confiscated in a bust; she sold it on the street and split the take with the officers who had given her the drugs. On one occasion, the night before she was murdered, Clyde recklessly spoke of her tie with the Sheriff's Department. She also revealed that she was pregnant by one of them. The next day, a "set up" man contacted Pee Wee Gaskins; Clyde was given cyanide in a soft drink, and Pee Wee was ordered to dispose of her body outside of Sumter County, in Clarendon County. The man in whose house the murder was committed, still lives in Sumter. His name has been given to the FBI.

The supporting evidence of Clyde's activities and connections with the law have been obtained through investigation and questioning of Clyde's close associates and members of her family. These interviews were tape recorded, and have been turned over to the FBI.

To establish a rationale for Pee Wee's confession of that murder, Sandy Gaskins, Pee Wee's wife, was forced to state that she, Clyde, and Pee Wee were in a love triangle. The fact is, Sandy Gaskins never knew or ever met Clyde, and will now so testify.

Clyde's immediate family, when searching for further information about her death, were visited by law enforcement officers, threatened and had a rock thrown through the window with a note warning them to "lay off". The intimidation and fear *were so great that the family had to move to a new location. They are now ready to testify.*

The innocent people are now imprisoned for life for murders which they did not commit, Susanne Owens, John McDougal and William "Junior" Pierce. I will not be satisfied with only an FBI investigation to bring these officials into the very courts of justice that they have mutilated and maligned, but to begin a campaign to have the Governors of the States of Georgia and South Carolina establish a Citizen's Review Board, with adequate funding, to investigate a prisoner's claim of a denial of justice, possible innocence, and forced confessions.

The practice of forcing confessions to "clean up" unsolved crimes must be halted, and officials who so conduct themselves, depending upon the loss of credibility of a man once behind bars, tears at the fabric of decency and fair play.

I have learned in the past six months that the credibility of a prisoner should never be questioned until proven wrong. I have come to that conclusion as a consequence of my Reidsville report on drugs and weapons, and I shall continue to fight to free all men and women who now know that I will always be in a continuous search for justice for poor whites and blacks who are brutalized by the courts, stigmatized by their pasts, and ignored once confined.

Doubts began to arise in Columbia about the Kathy Jo Anderson murder, for which Junior Pierce had been charged. A group of citizens there began to ask questions and dig up evidence contrary to what the law enforcement officers had determined.

Kathy Jo had disappeared from her car on Platt Springs Road in West Columbia on December 22, 1970, four days after the disappearance of Peg Cuttino.

Lexington County Sheriff Caroll Day, sheriff at that time, had obtained one of Pierce's oral confessions, according to him, and had closed the case, charging Pierce with the murder. Pierce was never tried for the crime. In the presence of several other officers, Sheriff Day had told Pierce that if he confessed, he would not be prosecuted for the slaying.

Since that murder, Lexington County had elected a new sheriff, Sheriff James Metts, and ex-sheriff Carroll Day had passed away.

On December 18, 1979, Sheriff Metts called a news conference and announced that even though the murder may now never be solved, he would file the necessary papers to dismiss the charge against Junior Pierce. His investigation into the matter had shown him that there was absolutely no way that Pierce could have committed the murder.

This event gave hope to the Citizens of Sumter County that had found and made public statement of the fact that Pierce had been working in Georgia when the slaying occurred and that he had been "drugged and tortured" while in jail in Georgia, where he made the confession to the crime.

In an article entitled "Sheriff Says Pierce Drugged, Tortured", which ran in The Daily Item on Wednesday, December 19, 1979, SLED spokesman Hugh Munn was quoted as saying that SLED Chief J.P. Strom was in the Georgia jail cell when Pierce allegedly made the oral confession to Sheriff Day and that Chief Strom heard Sheriff Day promise Pierce what amounted to immunity, if he would confess to the Anderson girl's murder.

The SLED chief was quoted as saying that after Pierce was promised that no notes or other record would be taken, he made a confession. Chief Strom tried to get Pierce to repeat the confession "without the promise of immunity, but it was no deal," Munn said.

Sheriff Metts was reluctant to accuse his predecessor, the late Sheriff Caroll Day of "covering up" anything, but he said he believed that there was "a lot of pressure on the former administration to clear up the crime".

"It looks like it was one of those convenient situations where there was a convenient confessor to the case," Sheriff Metts said.

Now, with all of this information coming to light, and with SLED's own public confession that SLED Chief Strom had been a party to these irregular and unorthadox procedures, it seemed to the citizens of Sumter County that it was just a matter of time and filing the proper paperwork in the Cuttino case — and justice would finally be done in Sumter County.

Nothing happened.

The citizens of Sumter County wanted to know why nothing was being done, and Item staff writer Marcia Milligan began to investigate the current situation for a follow-up article.

As far as the U.S. Justice Department was concerned, time had run out for William "Junior" Pierce.

Despite recent events that tended to lend some credibility to Pierce's contention that confessions to several South Carolina murders were forced from him in Baxley, Georgia, in 1971, Pierce had no recourse in federal court because civil rights claims are subject to a five-year statute of limitations.

A spokesman for the Justice Department said the statute of limitations had also run out for action against alleged corruption or cover-ups on the part of law enforcement officials in Georgia and South Carolina, who were involved with Pierce while he was in the Baxley jail.

The Justice Department had received the results of Dr. Charles King's six-month investigation and his request for a Justice department investigation into the matter, but the spokesman said that they (the Justice Department) had no further jurisdiction in the cases because the Pierce confessions were to "local murders".

Marcia Milligan contacted Pierce's former attorney, Joe McElveen, Jr., who said he did not believe Metts' action would be sufficient reason to ask for a re-trial for Pierce.

"The decision Metts made was based on the same type of evidence we introduced in court in 1973," McElveen said. "There is no new evidence (from the Lexington investigation) that can be related over to the Cuttino case in a legal sense."

From a practical standpoint, McElveen said, he believed Metts' action was significant, but "from a legal standpoint, it would not be admissible evidence."

"Before a new trial can be applied for," McElveen said, "new evidence must be available that was not available through 'due diligence' at the original trial, the evidence must be material to the issues, it cannot be cumulative to other evidence and the trial judge must determine that it would most likely change the outcome of the trial.

McElveen said he had not heard from Pierce and did not anticipate any action on his behalf as a result of the dismissal of the Lexington County murder charge.

"If Pierce has no basis on which to apply for a new trial, and the statute of limitations has run out on civil rights actions," McElveen said, "Pierce's only recourse would be a decision by local law enforcement agencies to re-open the case."

Mrs. LeNoir and the Citizens for Justice were disappointed and disheartened. There was no chance that the local law enforcement officers would change their minds and re-open the case. I. Byrd Parnell was still Sheriff, R. Kirk McLeod was still Solicitor, Judge Dan F. Laney was still Judge, and they were a combination that represented a power that seemed unbeatable. And now all other sources had abandoned the quest for justice and thrown the matter back into the very hands that had perpetrated the injustice in the beginning.

Sheriff James Metts had also said that his office's investigation showed that a number of other law enforcement officers were called to Baxley, Georgia and were told "that there is a man down there who was confessing to crimes and if you want to clear up your cases, bring them down here and we'll talk with him about them."

"We've been able to document that with others in the state who were heads of law enforcement agencies," Metts said, "and we know in several instances that he (Pierce) confessed to crimes that did not, in fact, take place."

Sheriff Metts said he had received no requests from the Justice Department for information or evidence collected during the course of his department's investigation.

Why would the United States Justice Department refuse to touch anything that concerned the Cuttino murder case in Sumter County?

Mrs. LeNoir had carried Junior Pierce's appeal to the Justice Department in April of 1977, and an official appeal was filed at that time. The five-year statute of limitations had not run out when it was filed. Why, then, would they not investigate?

Could it have anything to do with the fact that one Jimmy Carter, former Governor of the State of Georgia, was elected President of the United States in 1976, and was now serving in that high office in Washington, D.C.? Sheriff J.B. "Red" Carter was the instigator of the Pierce confessions. Could it be that the two Georgia men were related and the Justice Department didn't want to dig up any dirt in the President's home state — especially dirt that soiled a "Carter" from Georgia?

Junior Pierce seemed to be caught between a very powerful Sumter County trio and a very powerful Washington situation that denied him the justice to which every citizen of this country is entitled.

But there was an election coming up in Sumter County in 1980, and Sheriff I. Byrd Parnell would have to step down from the office or run for re-election. Either way, there was a possibility of change in that office. The Citizens for Justice turned their attention to that possibility and Sumter County got hot again.

CHAPTER NINETEEN

SHERIFF PARNELL DEFEATED

JUNE 10, 1980

On December 17, 1979, in an article by Item staff writer Peter O'Boyle entitled "S.C. PATROLMAN PONDERS RACE AGAINST SHERIFF", it was announced that Hazel F. Reeves, a 26-year Highway Patrol veteran, would possibly oppose Sheriff I. Byrd Parnell in the upcoming June primary.

Reeves, 49, was married to the former Edith L. Johnson of Manning, South Carolina, and had three children. He lived in Sumter and was a member of St. Johns United Methodist Church. He served in the Air Force during the Korean War, and had been a Sumter County Highway Patrolman since 1954.

Hazel Reeves was not well known in Sumter County, because he had never been in the limelight in his career, but he was a quiet, yet determined and forceful man, who commanded one's respect by his sincere and polite determination to the ideals that he sought for Sumter County law enforcement.

On January 3, 1980, in another of Peter O'Boyle's articles, entitled "POTENTIAL SHERIFF'S CANDIDATE RESIGNS FROM PATROL", it was revealed that Patrolman Reeves had resigned after being accused of campaigning while in uniform and in a state-owned vehicle, which is in violation of state rules.

The only accusation in the article came from an anonymous source who wished "not to be named". Whatever the situation, Hazel Reeves resigned from the South Carolina Highway Patrol and became a fulltime candidate for Sheriff of Sumter County.

Many of the citizens thought that it was unfair for Reeves to have to resign his only means of livelihood while he campaigned against a man who could and would remain on Sumter County payroll and continue to transport himself in a county vehicle.

Letters began to come in to the Editor of The Sumter Daily Item:

The Daily Item — Sumter, SC, January 7, 1980

LETTERS TO THE EDITOR

RESIGNATION QUESTIONED

To the Editor:
Please explain to the people of Sumter County why Sgt. Hazel Reeves, a veteran of the South Carolina Highway Patrol for 26 years, was fired or had to resign from his position. Sgt. Reeves had not announced his candidacy and he had not been soliciting votes for Sheriff of Sumter County.

Sheriff I. Byrd Parnell announced his candidacy in June 1979, and has been soliciting votes ever since. If it was supposed to have been illegal for Sgt. Reeves, why wouldn't it be illegal for Sheriff Parnell?

Why isn't Sheriff Parnell fired or made to resign, if this is an illegal situation?

M.C. McGee

The Daily Item — Sumter, SC, January 9, 1980

SITUATION IS UNJUST

To the Editor:
Thanks for keeping the public informed as to what is happening in law enforcement in Sumter County.

I have read two articles by Item staff writer Peter O'Boyle in the December 27 and January 3 issues of The Item with much interest.

The articles being referred to are entitled "S.C. PATROLMAN PONDERS RACE AGAINST SHERIFF" and "POTENTIAL SHERIFF'S CANDIDATE RESIGNS FROM PATROL". All within a week's time. What transpired in these few days? The only accusation in the article of any campaigning or solicitation on the part of the officer came from an anonymous source who wished "not to be named". Why?

Now I have a question. Why can the present Sheriff be allowed to campaign or politic while in office in county-owned, taxpayer vehicles any more than the state officer in a state uniform and state vehicle? I'm not quite sure where the discrepancy lies — on the state level or the county — but it seems there is a gross error somewhere.

Another point of interest — how can the Sheriff concentrate on his job while politicking any more than the patrol officer?

It seems once a Sheriff is elected it is virtually impossible to unseat him. He either retires or resigns because a truly qualified opponent is not allowed to campaign under equal circumstances. Who is better qualified to offer for this office than a veteran officer (26 years, in this instance) unless Sheriff Metts from Lexington County offers. He is the only Sheriff in the National Sheriffs Association with a doctorate from a university.

In my opinion, this situation is unjust and I would like to see some change made.
Susan M. Hamilton

The Citizens for Justice were also upset over this situation and Peg Burleson, their spokesperson, prepared a letter to the Editor which expressed their feelings on the matter:

The Daily Item — Sumter, SC, January 10, 1980

LETTER TO THE EDITOR

NOW'S THE TIME TO STAND UP

To the Editor:
When Sgt. Hazel Reeves is forced to resign from the Highway Patrol for attending a social function and using his First Amendment right to freedom of speech, then he too has lost his civil rights. It is time for the God-fearing citizens of this community to stand up for everyone's rights.

William J. Pierce is not the only victim of the elected officials who have forgotten they were elected to be servants of the people. We are in bondage to a very few powerful people only because the good citizens of this community keep electing these officials regardless of what they might do.

Monday, I sat through a federal hearing in Florence and watched County Council spend our tax dollars on a law professor from the law school to defend their actions in the matter of how we people elect our Council. I am asking the Council publicly to tell the good citizens of this community how much they spent on lawyers' fees so far just to stop us from electing new Council members.

When new Council members, a Sheriff and a Solicitor are elected in Sumter County, I wonder what Pandora's Box will offer the citizens? Will Sumter ever recover from the shock wave that will hit this community? I wonder.

The most common phrase I've heard in public is, "I'd like to help, BUT I'm afraid," or, "My family has a business here and I'm afraid for the business."

That proves to me the distrust the majority has for the people in authority. It is time to stand up and say, "I'm afraid, but I'm going to stand up publicly and be counted," all the way from the people who run the churches and their members to those who never hit a church door, everyone young and old.

I have spent a lot of time with many of the young people of this community in the past several months. I know of their pasts and the attitudes they have of the present and the outlook for their future in this community. If the older, responsible citizens of this community don't stand up for the rights of all people, it will only get worse. Silence of the majority has allowed a cloud of shame and disgrace to cloak Sumter from which it will take years to recover statewide. It has nothing to do with honesty and justice, but politics.

In order for the Pierce issue to be covered up all these years, it has to be from someone in Washington, D.C. William J. Pierce, Jr., filed an appeal with the Justice Department prior to April, 1977, which means it was filed before the five-year statute of limitations ran out.

Seems asinine to say a man's civil rights expire in five years anyway, and that is a law which most definitely should be changed. Also, in order for law enforcement and the judicial system to deliberately arrest and prosecute the wrong man for a crime and then have time expire for the prosecution of these men is also asinine. This type of crime is inexcusable.

The timing of the Justice Department's decision coincides with (Lexington County) Sheriff James Metts' decision that Pierce was drugged and tortured. Who in Washington, D.C., has the power to squash an investigation?

They could not have investigated or they would have found the things Mr. (Charles) King (Atlanta civil rights leader) gave them to be true, and they would not have reached the decision they did.

Was Sheriff Parnell chauffeur for one of these power men when he was with the Highway Patrol?

Is the Solicitor of Sumter County and prosecutor of Pierce related to one of the most powerful men in the judicial system in South Carolina?

Was Chief J.P. Strom taught everything he knows by one of our oldest SLED agents, who is a resident of Sumter County?

Did the state's only witness against Pierce receive $5,000 through the law enforcement center for something to do with the Pierce case?

Is Sheriff J.B. "Red" Carter of Georgia related to the President of the United States?

If the answer to these questions is yes, then it explains why Pierce's rights never existed, or at least why he's never had any rights in any of our courts.

There is nothing we can do about the past, but plenty we can do about the present to drastically change the future. Every parent and grandparent owes it to the young generation that is learning from us. In plain English, it's time to put action where our mouths have been for the last decade.

Peg Burleson

Sheriff Parnell was on the South Carolina Highway Patrol when he ran for and was elected Sheriff of Sumter County in 1952, and the reference made to his being a chauffeur for "one of the power men" related to that period of his employment. Highway patrolmen are, or were, called upon at times to transport certain politicians.

The reference to the relationship of the Solicitor of Sumter County to "one of the most powerful men in the judicial system" was relative to Sumter County Solicitor R. Kirk McLeod's kinship to South Carolina State Attorney General Daniel McLeod.

The SLED agent referred to, "who is a resident of Sumter County", is veteran law officer Leon Dollard.

Of course, the $5,000 was paid to state witness Earl Williams, who testified that he saw William Pierce at or near the spot where Peg Cuttino's body was found.

The President of the United States referred to was Jimmy Carter of Georgia.

The race was on. Sheriff Parnell, now a veteran of 28 years as Sheriff of Sumter County, said he would stand on his record and stressed only two issues — his law enforcement experience and his education — the selling points he wanted the voters to remember at the polls on June 10.

Parnell was a graduate of the University of South Carolina, the FBI National Academy, and the Institute of Applied Sciences. He was a former president of the South Carolina and National Sheriff's Associations, and was once voted state "Sheriff of the Year". At the time of this election, he expected to be installed as president of the FBI National Association (in July).

However, Hazel Reeves contended that Sheriff Parnell had none of those credentials when he assumed office in 1952, and charged that Parnell's numerous posts and affiliations were taking him away from his duties in Sumter. If elected, Reeves said, he would remain in Sumter County and "be the fulltime Sheriff there, not traveling all over the nation."

Meanwhile, Junior Pierce wrote a ten-page letter to South Carolina Governor Dick Riley, outlining the cases and asking that the Sumter County case, and other South Carolina cases be investigated further.

A copy of the letter was sent to the respective Solicitors involved, and on February 5, Russ McKinney, the Governor's press secretary, told Item staff writer Sylvia Wise that no replies to the letters had been received by the Governor's office.

"And we probably won't, to be honest with you," McKinney added. "It's something the Solicitors would probably investigate on their own, if they felt the case should be reopened."

Third Circuit Assistant Solicitor Wade Kolb said that Solicitor McLeod had received the letter from the Governor's office, but no new evidence had been found that would warrant reopening the case.

However, on Saturday, March 22, The Item carried an article entitled "SECOND CHARGE AGAINST JUNIOR PIERCE DROPPED".

Beaufort County authorities had dropped a murder charge against Pierce in the 1971 slaying of James L. Sires. No reason was given other than they had no plans to prosecute the case.

Junior Pierce was angry that the case was just dropped and not brought to trial. "I was charged with this crime in 1971, and the dismissal leaves me holding the bag for a murder that I never committed, and rewarded the real killer with his freedom to kill again," Pierce said in a letter to The State newspaper in Columbia. "I would like for the James L. Sires case to be reopened, and my classified records of evidence checked in an effort to catch the real killer. Mr. Sires had rights; he was a citizen and a taxpayer and for the state to simply dismiss or reward his killer with freedom

is a disgrace."
Pierce signed his letter "The scapegoat".
On April 28, attorneys for The Item, Verna Moore and Mrs. Carrie LeNoir (who acted as her own attorney) argued before Fifth Circuit Family Court Judge Robert H. Burnside to move the trial site in the suit pending against them by Mr. James Cuttino, Jr., to Sumter County. Mr. Cuttino had filed the suit in Lee County and they felt that a move to Sumter County (where they all, including Mr. Cuttino, lived) was appropriate.
Mr. Cuttino's attorneys argued that it would be difficult to draw an impartial jury in Sumter because of the "sensational, protracted" news coverage by The Item. The attorneys contended most Sumter County residents had already formed opinions and preconceived notions about the case from the newspaper and could not render a fair verdict in the civil suit, and the trial should, therefore, be moved to Lee County.
On Wednesday, May 28, The Item announced that Judge Burnside had ordered the case be moved from Lee County to Sumter County.
Reeves continued to bombard the veteran Sheriff with charges as he moved about the county gathering materials and listening to the people of the county.

Among those charges were:
Deputies pay scale "a shame and disgrace".
Too many unsolved murders.
Drug abuse in the county.
Favoritism and preferential treatment to prominent people.
Not enough manpower to cover the county at night.
The 65 year-old Parnell was too old for his duties.
Afraid that Pee Wee Gaskins may get on the stand in Sumter.

Reeves said he had purposely shied away from making any issue of the Cuttino murder case, but the people of Sumter County plagued Parnell with it every time he appeared during the campaign.
They had not been able to get Parnell to talk about the case up to this point, but now, every time he appeared, he was open for direct questions from the public. And they, sometimes angrily, attacked him at every opportunity.
The two candidates appeared on Sumter radio station WFIG on May 23, and telephone lines were open to the public.
A caller asked (of Sheriff Parnell) why Pee Wee Gaskins had not yet stood trial in Sumter County for the 1970 murder of Patricia Ann Alsbrook.
Parnell answered that he was not responsible for calling cases to trial and added that he was told by Solicitor R. Kirk McLeod that trying Gaskins would be superfluous, since Gaskins was currently serving eight life sentences. *Parnell said that because Gaskins confessed to that murder, he felt the case was solved.*
"I personally don't consider a case solved until a person has come to trial for it," Reeves told Parnell.
"Even when you have a confession from the man?" Parnell asked.
"I know a lot of people would like to hear what he (Gaskins) has to say on the stand. Maybe we can clear up some of these other unsolved murders in Sumter

County," Reeves responded.

Reeves drew heated response when he wondered aloud during that debate "if my opponent is afraid that Pee Wee may get on the stand in Sumter and get to talking like he did in Newberry."

"I'm not afraid of anything Pee Wee's got to say," Parnell replied.

On Thursday night, June 5, the League of Women Voters sponsored a political forum at the courthouse in Sumter and it got hot.

Reeves, among many other charges, criticized Parnell's affiliations with several state and national organizations, saying "anytime you have a county as fouled up as Sumter County is, the Sheriff has no business traveling all over the country."

The overflow crowd in the courtroom that night got their ears full of the two candidates. As always, the debate finally got around to the Cuttino case.

"I'm one of 95 percent of the people in the county that believe Pierce did not kill Cuttino," Reeves said.

In conclusion, Parnell said he had carried out the promises he had made in 1952 and solicited the audience's support, asking them to "cast a ballot for a man with experience and education... who knows what to do and when to do it."

On June 10, 1980, the citizens of Sumter County turned out in record numbers and quietly cast their votes. The people finally were heard.

More than 15,000 citizens voted, and the long Parnell dynasty went down in disgrace. Reeves collected 11,357 votes to Parnell's 3,812 — a 3-to-1 landslide. This was an "outstanding" turnout for an election in Sumter County and clearly indicated that the people had something to say, and they said it.

Sheriff Parnell had joined the traditional crowd at the courthouse for the counting of the ballots early that night and found Reeves leading him with only a few precincts in. "It's not over yet," he said.

But later, with 60 percent of the vote counted, showing Reeves with an overwhelming lead, Parnell was reticent, but gracious, saying only, "It looks like he (Reeves) got there firstest with the mostest."

Parnell awaited final results and Reeves' appearance until late that night, but when Reeves did not come, Parnell left saying, "I just wanted him (Reeves) to know that he ran a good race and I congratulate him."

The entire County was amazed at the landslide. Many were delighted, as the vote would indicate, but most people had expected a close race.

People who had voted against the popular Sheriff were seen to weep openly, and many of those who had helped to oust him expressed their regrets that it must be done. They still loved the man, but felt that there had to be a change. They had lost trust in him.

"I didn't expect this," said Jim Ross, Reeves' campaign manager. "Sheriff Parnell was an awful fine Sheriff in Sumter County, and he's done a fine job. I just think most of the citizens thought it was time for a change."

The Citizens for Justice chalked up one change and immediately began to concentrate on the next step. They, like many voters, had cast their votes with mixed emotions — hopeful of victory, but aware of the power of this man. Many of them, whether founded or unfounded, actually feared the man, and had hastily cast their vote against him, half afraid that somehow he would know that they had opposed him and would try to "get them".

Most of the people, however, knew Mr. Parnell as a quiet, gracious, Christian gentleman, who had served the county long and well, but had gotten to the point that he no longer listened to, nor cared, what the people who had elected him wanted and needed.

They had wanted answers on the Cuttino case; but Sheriff Parnell would not, or could not, give them the right answers.

Whatever the case, and though most of the leading citizens and officials said that the Cuttino incident had little effect on the election results, the citizens of Sumter County knew that it had a lot to do with it.

Candidate Reeves had said that he, "like 95 percent of the citizens did not believe that Pierce killed Peg Cuttino," and had promised to look into the Cuttino case, if elected. And the people now looked to him as a new source of hope for justice.

On Tuesday, July 29, 1980, in an article by Item staff writer Mike Smith, entitled "PIERCE WANTS NEW TRIAL", it was announced that Junior Pierce, acting as his own attorney, had filed a petition asking for a new trial on the Cuttino slaying. Pierce said that he had discovered two witnesses "who saw him at work at the Handy House Manufacturing Co., in Georgia, on December 18, 1970."

He also claimed new evidence that was turned up during the investigation by the Lexington County Sheriff's Department by Sheriff James Metts. This was to include his time card, a three-month work record and a record of wages paid him in December, 1970.

Pierce also cited publicity and the fact that the confession that he made in the Georgia jail was coerced by force and promised torture if he refused to cooperate, then attested by Sheriff I. Byrd Parnell.

This petition was filed with the Williamsburg County Clerk of Court's office in Kingstree and a copy was sent to South Carolina State Attorney General Daniel R. McLeod, who was named as respondent.

On August 16, Judge Dan F. Laney denied and dismissed the appeal, saying that the petition was representative "of a seemingly endless flurry of groundless petitions submitted by petitioner Pierce. The present petition vividly illustrates the justification for the rule against successive petitions."

The Judge also said Pierce's latest petition for a new trial makes "absolutely no showing that he could not have presented the current allegations in his original petition for post-conviction relief."

On August 22, The Daily Item reported that an attorney for James Cuttino, Jr., had subpoenaed Sumter County Clerk of Court O.V. Player in an effort to obtain records relating to 1977 Grand Jury proceedings.

The 1977 Grand Jury hearing investigated whether new developments warranted reopening the case, and determined that no further action was necessary.

In a letter of subpoena to Player, Joseph F. Rice, of the Barnwell law firm of Blatt and Fales, which represented James Cuttino, asked Player to "testify under oath by deposition, and to produce any and all records, documents and transcripts of record that refer, reflect, relate to the 1977 Grand Jury proceedings in regard to William Pierce, Jr."

O.V. Player, however, said that since Grand Jury proceedings are secret, he would not turn them over to Rice without a Judge's order.

A hearing was set for motions and demurrers in the suits by Cuttino against The Item, Mrs. Verna Moore and Mrs. Carrie LeNoir for Friday, August 15, 1980, but the hearing was moved a day ahead and nobody notified Mrs. LeNoir.

Mrs. LeNoir said, "I was told by several attorneys associated with the case that they had agreed that Joseph F. Rice, Mr. Cuttino's attorney, would notify me of the change. But I was not contacted, and I just happened to go by the courthouse on Thursday morning and heard of the change. The hearing was before Seventh Circuit Judge Paul Moore."

Item staff writer Barry T. Berlin wrote in an article entitled "GRAND JURY RECORDS SOUGHT" on Friday, August 22, that, "According to Mark Dillard, a spokesman for the South Carolina Attorney General's office, there is no state law that specifically charges a lawyer or court official with the responsibility of notifying a litigant of a hearing schedule change."

"It was a tricky move, designed to have the hearings without me being there," Mrs. LeNoir said, "But the Lord looks out for me, I guess, and I learned about it and was there."

"Common courtesy would have dictated that someone notify me," Mrs. LeNoir added, "however, I have learned that I cannot rely on common courtesy nor professional courtesy in matters that concern the Cuttino-Pierce affair."

On September 19, it was learned that Seventh Circuit Judge Paul Moore, ruling on the August 14 hearings for motions and demurrers in the three-million dollar James Cuttino, Jr., vs. The Sumter Daily Item, Verna Moore and Carrie LeNoir lawsuit, had thrown out the one-million dollar countersuit by Mrs. LeNoir.

Judge Moore of Spartanburg had sustained Cuttino's demurrer, ruling that his suit did not "amount to an abuse of process", nor was it brought to "harass and intimidate the defendant", as Mrs. LeNoir had charged in her countersuit.

Verna Moore had filed a demurrer to be removed as a defendant in the case, but Judge Moore denied the demurrer and ruled that Mrs. Moore must remain as a defendant.

Mrs. Moore would now have 20 days to appeal the decision.

In addition, Cuttino's attorney, Joseph Rice, had filed a motion to have the trial moved from Sumter County to Richland County. This would be considered later.

The trial was originally scheduled for the Common Pleas Court term beginning September 29, but was put off until November because several depositions necessary for the case had not been taken.

So, Mrs. LeNoir was now facing a three-million dollar lawsuit and her countersuit was thrown out. She was disappointed, but not defeated. She had learned to be a real fighter in the past ten years. She had been forced to learn.

After pondering the situation for a few days, she filed a suit of her own against James Cuttino, Jr. — this time, she sued for *two-million dollars.*

The suit alleged that, as a result of a petition filed by Cuttino in July, 1977, that she was found in contempt of court by Third Circuit Judge Dan F. Laney, Jr., of Bishopville for refusing to turn over documents regarding the Cuttino slaying, and that, as a result of that order, she had spent four days in jail.

The suit further asserted that the South Carolina Supreme Court overturned Judge Laney's contempt ruling in October of 1978, and that, during her "four days of illegal incarceration", she was locked in with and at the mercy of convicted murderers, thieves, and arsonists, and additionally exposed at times to rapists.

The suit continued: although all records of the plaintiff's (Mrs. LeNoir's) illegal incarceration are supposed to have been destroyed, the wounds which she and her family had suffered will never heal. They have been exposed to embarrassing front-page newspaper, radio and television publicity, which has created permanent damage.

As a result of the defendant's (Cuttino's) actions, the plaintiff... as well as her family, has been injured, suffering enormous mental and emotional distress, as well as financial stress, and is entitled to both actual and punitive damages in the amount of two-million dollars, the complaint said.

She had decided to fight fire with fire. "I was not interested in Mr. Cuttino's money," Mrs. LeNoir said later, "but I couldn't just sit by and do nothing."

A hearing was held on the last day of September on the motion by Cuttino's lawyers to move the trial to Richland County. On Friday, October 17, Judge Moore issued an order denying the move.

As you will recall, Mrs. LeNoir had surrendered the documents in her possession, concerning the Cuttino case, to the Supreme Court, and they were still in the Supreme Court's possession.

Mrs. LeNoir needed those documents now for her defense against Mr. Cuttino's lawsuit. On Monday, November 10, she went before that court to ask for the return of the documents.

Mr. Cuttino's attorneys, of course, opposed the return of the documents. On November 24, it was announced that the Supreme Court had decided to return the controversial documents, sealed, to Sumter County Clerk of Court O.V. Player, Jr., to be held there until the three-million dollar Cuttino suit was tried.

The suit was not tried in 1980, but was set for trial on January 19, 1981. Twelvth Circuit Judge John H. Waller, Jr., would be the presiding judge over the first week of the two-week Common Pleas term.

Third Circuit Judge James M. Morris, of Manning, had been scheduled to preside over both weeks of court, but he had at one time represented Mrs. Verna Moore, and therefore would not try the Cuttino suit. He was, however, expected to preside over the second week of court.

In anticipation of a heavy case load, Judge Ernest Finney asked Clerk of Court O.V. Player, Jr., to call 50 extra jurors, in addition to the 60 normally called for a week of court.

The stage was set and all Sumter County waited breathlessly to see what would be the final outcome.

But the suit, originally brought in 1978, and scheduled to be tried on January 19, 1981, finally was continued by Judge Waller so that he could study and rule on motions made by the defendants.

On Tuesday, January 20, it was announced that Judge Waller had granted a motion for a summary judgement to The Sumter Daily Item, which, in effect, dismissed the suit against The Item.

Judge Waller called publicity of the case to which the Cuttino family was subjected "regrettable", but added, "The publicized events were matters of public interest."

"The publication by a newspaper of matters of public interest and newsworthy events is not such conduct as would impose liability for such publication," the Judge continued.

"As to the cause of action for invasion of privacy," he said, "the (newspaper) articles complained of involved facts in the public domain, and not strictly private facts."

Judge Waller also negated the conspiracy claim. "There is no evidence that The Daily Item participated in a conspiracy to inflict injury on the plaintiff (Cuttino)," he said.

"Although the defendant, Verna Moore, was in its employ, there is no evidence that she was acting in her capacity as such employee in any of the matters alleged as to her and the defendant, Carrie LeNoir," he continued.

"After careful consideration," Judge Waller concluded, "I find there is no genuine issue of any material fact, and that on the undisputed facts, The Sumter Daily Item is entitled to a judgement as a matter of law."

Item Editor Hubert D. Osteen, Jr., said of the Judge's decision, "I said at the time the suit was brought against The Item that it was without merit and now the court has agreed with this contention. The Item defended itself vigorously against what we felt was an attack on freedom of the press, as provided for in the First Amendment of the United States Constitution. Our defense of this basic right has been sustained by the court, and what we felt was responsible, objective coverage of major news events has been vindicated. We're pleased with Judge Waller's decision. We feel this ruling will be a beneficial and reassuring one, not only for The Item, but also for the free press in South Carolina."

In the Judge's chambers a few weeks later, Mr. Cuttino's attorneys had produced a document and asked Mrs. LeNoir to sign it, in order to end the dispute and lawsuit — a consent order.

The order mandated that Mrs. LeNoir turn over to Sumter County Clerk of Court O.V. Player, Jr.:

Notebooks in her possession dealing with the Margaret "Peg" Cuttino case (numbering approximately six or seven);

Boxes of materials pertaining to the case, including any duplicates;

Any pictures and copies relating to the case;

All reports from law enforcement officials or medical officials relating to the death of Peg Cuttino, including autopsy reports;

Any affidavits from any person or persons which had any bearing on the case.

All correspondence relating to the case, whether personal or that of the group "Citizens for Justice", including letters from William "Junior" Pierce and Donald "Pee Wee" Gaskins;

All newspaper clippings and copies which contain any notes made by Mrs. LeNoir for the purpose of investigation.

Any other notes made during the course of the investigation pertaining to the investigation in any way;

All materials in any form which had any bearing on the case which were in the possession of Mrs. LeNoir.

The order also placed restrictions on any future investigation by Mrs. LeNoir. "It is further ordered that the defendant Carrie LeNoir, be... restrained from pursuing any independent investigation into the death of Margaret "Peg" Cuttino and/or trial of William J. Pierce, Jr., and is hereby restrained from any public speaking on the above subjects," the order said.

"She is further restrained from collaborating, assisting or aiding," the order continues, "any person in the investigation of the above case other than proper law enforcement officials, nor is the defendant to collaborate, assist or aid with any written document to be written or published by anyone as it relates to the circumstances surrounding the death of Margaret "Peg" Cuttino, or the trial and conviction of William J. Pierce, Jr."

Mrs. LeNoir said that Judge Waller told her, "If you do not sign the agreement, the case will be put back on the docket and will go to trial."

"What a threat," Mrs. LeNoir said in unbelief, "I have been through too much to sign that thing."

She told them that she would not sign the order and issued the following statement for public quote regarding the agreement:

> *I regret that, thus far, we have not been able to settle this suit out of court; but I feel that the order and restraining order is not only unconstitutional, but actually illegal, and I cannot consent.*
>
> *I was told that if I refuse to sign it, we will go to trial. If we go to trial, I have no choice but to defend my actions. Mr. Cuttino, in his deposition on October 27, 1980, under questioning by The Item's attorney, in answer to a question, "are you saying the amount of publicity?" answered, "Yes, and the perpetrated fraud that this woman has tried to put over on Sumter County." I plan to subpoena many witnesses, who will testify and prove that what I've been telling the people of Sumter County is true. This trial will prove that William J. Pierce, Jr., is serving as a scapegoat for Peg Cuttino's murder and that there has, indeed, been obstruction and miscarriage of justice in the judicial system."*

When Item staff writer Barry T. Berlin printed the article entitled "Cuttino Lawsuit Against LeNoir May Still Be Tried" on Friday, January 23, he wrote:

> *(Judge) Waller would not say yesterday whether the case will go to trial if Mrs. LeNoir refuses to sign the order. He said he would wait until she officially notifies him that she will not sign before he makes any decision regarding the case. "I prefer not to say anything about the case because of its delicate nature," Waller said. "I really am not in a position to comment."*

"In other words, the Judge may throw Mr. Cuttino's case out entirely," Mrs. LeNoir said, "and his attorneys know it. They don't want this case to go to court in Sumter County, because if it does, the cat will be 'out of the bag'."

Meanwhile, Mr. Cuttino's attorneys appealed the Judge's decision involving The Sumter Daily Item, to the South Carolina Supreme Court.

On Monday, March 23, Judge Waller granted Mrs. Verna Moore's motion for a summary judgement, eliminating that part of Cuttino's suit.

Now, it was down to a three-million dollar suit against Mrs. Carrie LeNoir, and a two-million dollar suit against James Cuttino by Mrs. LeNoir. And it seemed that the only difference in the two was that Mrs. LeNoir was eager to get her case into a courtroom, but, apparently, Mr. Cuttino was not sure he wanted to go into court.

Mrs. LeNoir did not sign the consent order. But at the last moment before trial, she agreed to drop her suit against him, and he agreed to drop his suit against her, with no strings attached.

Mr. Cuttino's attorneys also dropped the appeal to the Supreme Court in the matter of The Sumter Daily Item.

Another round in the long and unbelievable chain of events had come to a close. The people of Sumter County sighed a sigh of relief. None really wanted to see Mr. Cuttino and Mrs. LeNoir go at it in an open courtroom. They knew that it would be a nasty and trying experience for both of them, and they knew that these two respected and responsible citizens really had no cause to fight each other. The chain of events had simply (almost) gotten out of hand.

Mrs. LeNoir kept her documents, and everybody was back where they started.

The Citizens for Justice were still dedicated to seeing that justice was done in the Junior Pierce case; Mrs. LeNoir was still dedicated to that same purpose; and Junior Pierce still sat in prison in Georgia, convicted of the murder of Peg Cuttino.

CHAPTER TWENTY

OTHER OFFICIALS FALL

Just as Sheriff Byrd Parnell was defeated in his bid for re-election, so was Appling County, Georgia, Sheriff J.B. "Red" Carter. In 1976, his ex-son-in-law, Joe V. Lightsey, won the election, but that was a minor problem, considering what was to follow. The October 30, 1981, edition of The Savannah Morning News (Georgia) carried a big headline "18 CHARGED IN APPLING PROBE".

The Savannah Morning News — Savannah, Ga., October 30, 1981

18 CHARGED IN APPLING PROBE

Two former Appling County sheriffs and other state and county law enforcement officials were among eighteen persons charged Thursday in a federal bust of an alleged racketeering operation which involved drug smuggling, arson and bribery in Appling. The eighteen, among them former Appling sheriffs James Bazel "Red" Carter and Joe Veston Lightsey, were charged in a ten-count federal grand jury indictment handed down Wednesday in Savannah and unsealed Thursday.
Carter was Appling's sheriff from 1960 to 1976, and is also a former chief of Baxley's police department.

The Daily Item — Sumter, SC, December 17, 1981

EX-GA. SHERIFF CONVICTED
ON DRUG RELATED CHARGES

Former Appling County Sheriff James B. "Red" Carter and the co-owners of a large dairy farm were among 11 defendants convicted Tuesday night on racketeering and drug charges in connection with a smuggling ring operating in Appling County.
The 57 year old Carter first came to prominence in 1971 for his role in the apprehension of William "Junior" Pierce, who was subsequently charged with the December 1970 murder of Margaret "Peg" Cuttino of Sumter. Pierce was being held in the Appling County jail in Baxley, Georgia, on other murder charges when he was charged with the murder of Miss Cuttino. Carter was instrumental in securing a confession from Pierce, which Pierce later denied during his trial in Kingstree in 1973. Pierce was convicted of the Cuttino murder, but has maintained ever since that he was innocent and was coerced by Carter into

making a confession. Controversy about the verdict and the case has continued over the years.

Savannah Evening Press — Savannah, Ga., January 22, 1982

APPLING CASE SENTENCES STIFF

... 11th U.S. Circuit Court of Appeals Judge Gerald Tjoflat revoked bonds for all but two women involved. Tjoflat said, "Not a kind word I can say about you," as he sentenced former Appling Sheriff J.B. "Red" Carter of Baxley, to 35 years in prison and a $150,000 fine on racketeering and drug conviction.

At about that same time, the news media was watching one of the Supreme Court Justices rather closely.

The State — Columbia, SC, December 30, 1982

<u>EDITORIAL</u>

NESS'S APPEARANCE FOR SCHAFER UNWISE

S.C. Associate Justice Julius B. "Bubba" Ness, a former state senator, is a product of the "Good Ol' Boy" school of politics in this state, and one of the things one learns in this school is loyalty to one's friends and allies. So, Justice Ness said, he was only trying to help a friend, and was not using his influence as a state judge when he arranged for and appeared before a meeting of the state's congressional delegation to make a plea for special treatment of his old college roommate, Dillon County businessman and Democratic kingpin Alan H. Schafer...

Mr. Schafer, along with others, had been convicted in the Dillon County vote fraud case, and the lengthy article included the paragraph:

Justice Ness should have gotten someone else to appear for his old friend. To the public, at least, his personal involvement appeared unseemly or worse, if not unethical.

This brought to mind the October 3, 1978, S.C. Supreme Court Opinion No. 20773, James Cuttino, Jr., Respondent V. Mrs. Carrie LeNoir, Appellant, in which Chief Justice Woodrow Lewis wrote: "The ex parte order of August 8 (by Circuit Judge Dan Laney) was a nullity and the findings of contempt for its violation must be set aside." Associate Judge J.B. Ness dissented, but, thank God, he was in the minority.

Addison wrote, "Justice discards party, friendship and kindred, and is therefore represented as blind," but it seems that friendship blinds some of our justices when their friends are involved. We'll hear more about Judge Ness in a later chapter.

Meanwhile, just as Sheriff's Parnell and Carter were experiencing bad times, Solicitor Kirk McLeod's time had come:

The Daily Item — Sumter, SC, May 15, 1982

LETTER TO THE EDITOR

BREAK UP THE OLD GROUP

To the Editor:

Solicitor McLeod making such an issue over Wade Kolb running against him is absurd. The solicitor's office has been in the McLeod family for over 60 years; regardless, it is still an elected office, not privately owned. Since the people of the 3rd Judicial Circuit have never had the privilege of choosing between candidates, no one knows if Kirk McLeod is the best person for the job or not. At least Wade Kolb will be chosen by the voters and not ride in on his dad's coat tail like our present solicitor did. It is time the local good ole boy group is broken up so our elected officials can get back to serving the people who put them in office.

Anyone who has been concerned about the drug problem and watched the arrests and sentences received by individuals probably feels as discouraged as I do when most of the dealers receive suspended sentences, fines and probation. I'm not sure WHY, whether it's plea bargaining or lack of vigorous prosecution. The majority have pleaded guilty. The only advantage in plea bargaining is a quick conviction or for invaluable information has been forthcoming. At least there's not been many drug suppliers arrested. I realize arrests are made by law enforcement, but plea bargaining is done in the solicitor's office.

Judge Dan Laney's comment in Williamsburg County about Solicitor McLeod being the best in the state is the same old tired comment he made when he read the verdict in the 1977 grand jury hearings. In open court, he told those of us who testified before it we had the best solicitor, sheriff, and judicial system in the state, and if we didn't like the way it was run we could leave. After witnessing the disgraceful, shameless manner in which he conducted the hearing in Bishopville, the day he threw Mrs. Carrie LeNoir in jail, it is hard for me to place any value on any personal opinion he might have. Even judges have mouth trouble once in awhile, sometimes once too often.

Mr. McLeod is asking the voters of this community to TRUST him and return him to office. He has shown no trust in the people by trying to deceive the public with the old picture he used when he announced his candidacy. Being ill is an uncontrollable factor, but trying to deceive the public is not.

Peg Burleson

The Daily Item — Sumter, SC, June 5, 1982

<u>LETTER TO THE EDITOR</u>

HIGH TIME FOR A CHANGE

Of all the "Letters to the Editor", both pro and con in recent weeks relative to the upcoming election, there have been few concrete reasons as to why one candidate should not be re-elected. We, the voters have been well informed as to why we should re-elect this candidate. However, the average voter, like myself, is relying on what he or she reads in our local newspaper and most of our opinions of the candidate are formed through advertisements, paid for by the candidate or candidate's committee and "Letters to the Editor". Of the two, I think "Letters to the Editor" reveals a broader knowledge of the candidates themselves, both good and not so good. Naturally, the candidates are only printing the good about themselves. Thank goodness for the news media. The Sumter Daily Item — unbiased, straightforward and reliable over the years.

Of the seats up for election, the one I find most questionable is the solicitor. All I hear or see is "Keep Kirk" — "Keep the Best" and "It's Time for a Change". Take "Keep the Best" — was he the best 27 years ago? Any better than the opponent is today? Both candidates come, apparently, well qualified. Since Wade Kolb trained under Kirk McLeod, surely he met with Mr. McLeod's approval.

Now comes the not so good. In my opinion Kirk McLeod has been a good solicitor with the exception of one instance, which comes under article 4* in his political ad which appeared in the Monday, May 31 issue of The Sumter Daily Item, page 3A. Quote: "is dedicated to upholding the law fairly to ensure justice for both the state and the defendant."

I refer to the case of William "Junior" Pierce, which the news media has covered continually. Six times Pierce has appealed for a re-trial hearing, dating back to November 13, 1975, for a 1970 murder in which he was convicted in 1973 that he steadfastly contends he did not commit. His defense attorney, W.F. Jenkinson, III, of Kingstree was quoted as saying, "Junior Pierce didn't kill that girl, and he was found guilty, and that's something a lawyer never forgets." — "We had a case — a very horrible case due to the circumstances — and they wanted to find somebody guilty. It was a legislator's daughter, and there was tremendous pressure" — The Charlotte Observer, May 11, 1982. In that same publication, Solicitor Kirk McLeod was quoted as saying that the investigation was "the most exhaustive and thorough — in the annals of South Carolina law enforcement." Did the solicitor uphold the law fairly to ensure justice for this defendant?"

Finally, on May 3, 1982, Junior Pierce was granted a post-conviction relief hearing by Circuit Judge Ernest A. Finney. What happened to the other five appeals? Who was at fault with regards to the other five appeals?

I ask again, has this solicitor upheld the law fairly to ensure justice for this defendant or does this reek of conspiracy?

Is this solicitor really the best or is it high time for a change?

Susan Hamilton

Note: The hearing Mrs. Hamilton referred to will be covered in a later chapter.

Headlines such as "A BITTER BATTLE FOR THIRD CIRCUIT SOLICITOR", "FEELINGS RUN HIGH IN RACE", "KOLB SAYS HE'LL SEE THAT JUSTICE APPLIED EQUALLY", and "VOTERS TO BE THE JURY" followed; and on June 9, 1982, "KOLB ENDS MCLEOD'S 27-YEAR REIGN". Voters in the four counties — Sumter, Lee, Clarendon, and Williamsburg had decided, almost two to one, that it was indeed high time for a change.

Like an epidemic, troubles spread on over into Williamsburg County. An article by Mike Smith on June 11, 1982, The Item declared: "SAYS DOCUMENTS NOT FILED — PIERCE SUES COURT CLERK": "Convicted murderer William "Junior" Pierce has filed a lawsuit against Williamsburg County Clerk of Court Winnie P. Jones, charging she violated his civil rights by not properly filing documents in his fight for a new trial."

The News — Kingstree, SC, June 17, 1982
by Bob Gorman

William 'Junior' Pierce, who was convicted in Kingstree in 1973 for killing the daughter of a former state legislator, filed the suit from his cell in Jackson, Georgia, through the U.S. Federal Magistrate's office in Columbia.

The legal papers filed by Pierce were served on Mrs. Jones May 26, 1982, by federal marshalls on order from U.S.

Magistrate Charles Gambrell in Columbia. Pierce is seeking $25,000 in punitive damages and $15,000 in compensatory pay. The suit contends that in April 1981, Pierce filed his fourth post conviction relief appeal, seeking to have his 1973 life sentence overturned. On his three previous appeals for a new trial, Pierce has been turned down by state Judge Laney. He contends that Mrs. Jones either destroyed or lost his most recently filed appeal papers, thus violating his constitutional rights.

The case centers around court house employee Elijah Fulton, who picks up mail for all courthouse offices as part of his normal duties. Fulton picked up the envelope sent (by certified mail) to the clerk's office by Pierce and signed for it at the post office. What happened to the envelope after that is where the bone of contention lies. Pierce received his return receipt, contending that the package was delivered by Fulton to the clerk's office and then misplaced or destroyed intentionally. Mrs. Jones contends that the package never reached her office.

County Attorney William Jenkinson, III, who represented Pierce in his murder trial in 1973 and still believes his client was innocent, sides with Mrs. Jones in the recent law suit. "She's (Mrs. Jones) filed all his other appeal papers, so why wouldn't she file this one? She has nothing to gain or lose by destroying the papers."

Irked by weekend newspaper reports about the suit, Mrs. Jones said Monday that neither she nor any employee of her office destroyed "exhibits, motions or evidence" pertaining to the Pierce case or subsequent appeal motions, as the suit alleges. "We haven't destroyed any records," she said Monday. "We didn't receive it (appeal notice from Pierce). This whole thing has been stirred up by Mrs. LeNoir."

Carrie LeNoir, retired postmaster of Horatio, S.C., has been fighting to have Pierce's conviction overturned and questioned Mrs. Jones about the missing papers last August. "I told her that we didn't have the papers, but would be glad to file them if she had copies," said Mrs. Jones. "She had copies and we filed them then." Those familiar with the Pierce case also know the name of Mrs. LeNoir, who has spent the past nine years and several thousands of dollars trying to have his conviction overturned. Mrs. LeNoir said Monday she is "sorry to be the root of all of Mrs. Jones' trouble", but she only wants to see "justice done". She added that she has helped Mr. Pierce through the years because as a convict Pierce is unable to help himself.

The State — Columbia, SC, January 31, 1985

PIERCE DROPS LAWSUIT; SAYS HE'S INNOCENT
by Margaret O'Shea

Insisting after 14 years in prison that he never killed anyone, William "Junior" Pierce has dropped a federal lawsuit charging the Williamsburg County clerk of court with sabotaging his motion for a new trial for the murder of Margaret "Peg" Cuttino. After a three-hour hearing Wednesday before U.S. Magistrate Charles Gambrell, Pierce says he still hopes for a retrial in the Cuttino case, but he no longer believes that Winnie P. Jones deliberately interfered with his efforts to "bring out the truth" about the 1970 murder.

So, Mrs. Jones, relieved that she would not have to pay Mr. Pierce the $45,000 for which he had sued, returned to her work as Clerk of Court. But her peace was to be short lived.

The State — Columbia, SC, September 10, 1986

WILLIAMSBURG OFFICIAL GOES ON TRIAL
by Holly Gatlin

A federal jury began hearing evidence Tuesday to decide whether Williamsburg County Clerk of Court Winnie P. Jones accepted bribes and kickbacks when she bought light bulbs for the county.
Assistant U.S. Attorney John Barton told jurors that the prosecution will show that Mrs. Jones took money from a Pennsylvania janitorial supply company in exchange for ordering light bulbs from the company. She is charged with accepting kickbacks totaling $1,075 from Eveready Maintenance Co. of Rydal, Pa., between July 1981 and August 1982.
But her attorney, Terrell Glenn of Columbia, said Mrs. Jones acted in good faith when she purchased the light bulbs and that she did not intend to violate the law. "It is necessary for the government to prove that, when Winnie Jones acted, she acted with specific intent to violate the law," said Glenn, a former U.S. Attorney. "Winnie may have been negligent in not keeping track of the number of light bulbs she purchased," Glenn told the jurors, "but negligence is not an element of fraud."
U.S. District Judge Clyde Hamilton told the jury that prosecutors must show that Mrs. Jones willfully schemed to defraud Williamsburg County, that she used the U.S. Postal Service to carry out her scheme and that she acted to violate the

law. The first prosecution witness, Samuel S. Persky, former president of the now-defunct Eveready Maintenance Co., testified that he contacted Mrs. Jones and offered her money if she would buy the bulbs.

Persky said he based payments to Mrs. Jones on the size of the order and mailed the payments to her home. "The bigger the order the bigger the gift," he said. He told Barton that he had explained that to Mrs. Jones. He said the amount of the "gift" was figured into the total price of the bulbs. He testified that Mrs. Jones never asked the source of the money or whether it were legal or proper for her to accept it."

The State — Columbia, SC, September 11, 1986

CLERK TELLS JURY
SHE DIDN'T KNOW GIFTS WERE ILLEGAL
by Holly Gatlin

Winnie P. Jones, suspended Williamsburg County clerk of court, told a federal jury Wednesday that she did not know she was breaking the law when she accepted gifts of money from a light bulb supply company. But Mrs. Jones, whose testimony took most of the day, also admitted that she had accepted gifts such as a blender, a hand-held mixer and a black-and-white television from other companies from which she purchased light bulbs for Williamsburg County. The 59-year-old champagne blonde told the jurors that she ordered light bulbs based on what a courthouse janitor named Laurie informed her the needs were. She said Laurie died in October, 1982. Barton asked her to explain why she purchased six cases of light bulbs between Nov. 1, 1980 and Nov. 6, 1980. "I can't remember back that far," she said. The jury is expected to begin its deliberations this afternoon."

The State newspaper, September 12, 1986, announced "CLERK FOUND GUILTY; September 17, 1986, "CONVICTED COURT CLERK RESIGNS"; October 8, 1986, "EX-WILLIAMSBURG COURT CLERK GIVEN $5,000 FINE, PROBATION".

The State — Columbia, SC, December 10, 1986

FUNDS SHORTAGE DETECTED

Kingstree — Williamsburg County authorities have ordered an audit of records in the clerk of court's office to determine the "amount and nature" of a funds shortage, County Supervisor Alex

Chatman said. Although the amount hasn't been determined, the County Council has authorized the transfer from other budget sources of $10,000 to fund operation until the matter is resolved, he said.

Council Vice Chairman Hilton McGill said that officials have been advised not to discuss how the shortage was detected, but he said it involved "old records". Clerk of Court Carolyn Williams said she was unaware until recently of an overdraft that apparently stemmed from the shortage. She took office in September, following the resignation of Winnie Jones.

But the worst blow of all was yet to follow. The Item, November 27, 1990, carried the Associated Press release: "FRAUD CHARGE LEVELED AGAINST FORMER CLERK". The State also carried the story:

The State — Columbia, SC, November 27, 1990

AUTHORITIES ARREST FORMER CLERK OF COURT
by Steve Smith and Holly Gatlin

A former Williamsburg County clerk of court was charged Monday with 47 counts of embezzling public funds and 47 counts of misconduct in office. Winnie P. Jones, 64, of Salters, was booked at the Williamsburg County Jail. She was arrested by State Law Enforcement Division agents after a four-year investigation involving $214,289, SLED spokesman Hugh Munn said. Mrs. Jones was being held Monday night at the Williamsburg County Jail, pending a bond hearing.

In addition to the misconduct counts, Mrs. Jones was charged with 52 counts of embezzlement of public funds in connection with a trust fund account in the clerk's office. She's also charged with five counts of embezzlement of public funds in connection with fines, fees, bonds, commissions, stamps and Family Court fines, Munn said. Munn said investigators believe that she took the money for her own use. The charges stem from various embezzlements from September 1964 to July 1986. Munn said SLED was asked to investigate by the state auditor's office. "The investigation involved thousands of records and documents," Munn said. "Our agents had to track records that didn't seem to exist, to track and locate them." Mrs. Jones was suspended from her $25,000-a-year job in July 1986 after serving as clerk for 22 years.

The State — Columbia, SC, January 30, 1991

64-YEAR-OLD COUNTY CLERK
SENTENCED TO JAIL FOR EMBEZZLEMENT
by Eleanor Foxworth and Margaret N. O'shea

Winnie Powell Jones, who was clerk of court in Williamsburg County for 22 years, was sentenced Tuesday to 25 years in prison for embezzling public money from her office accounts. She has 15 days to pay back $120,037.47 before starting her prison term, but the money is expected to come from a bonding company, not her personal funds.

The 64-year-old Salters woman must serve five years in a state prison before going on probation, but the conviction could mean she goes to federal prison, as well. Jones had not completed a five-year probation for taking kickbacks on light bulbs for the county courthouse. That sentence was handed down in 1986. Jones pleaded guilty Tuesday to multiple embezzlement charges.

CHAPTER TWENTY-ONE

PIERCE'S APPEAL FILED

MAY 4, 1982

You will recall in the previous chapter that Mrs. Jones had failed to file Pierce's earlier appeal, but...

The Daily Item — Sumter, SC, May 4, 1982

PIERCE GRANTED HEARING ON PLEA FOR NEW TRIAL
by Mike Smith

William "Junior" Pierce has been granted a hearing that will determine whether he is entitled to a new trial on charges that he murdered Margaret "Peg" Cuttino, a spokesman for the attorney general's office said today.

Third Circuit Judge Ernest A. Finney, Jr., ordered the post-conviction relief hearing in response to motions filed by Pierce, according to Mark Dillard, public information spokesman in the attorney general's office.

The attorney general's office has opposed granting Pierce the hearing and Third Circuit Judge Daniel F. Laney has turned down several petitions for a new trial filed by Pierce, saying they were "meritless and groundless". No date has been set for the hearing, Dillard said.

Pierce also has asked that he be allowed to undergo a "truth serum" examination in an attempt to show he had no part in the death of Miss Cuttino, a 13-year-old girl found dead in late 1970 after her disappearance.

Pierce, who drew up the legal documents he has filed, also has been appointed an attorney to represent him at the hearing, according to Winnie Jones, clerk of court in Williamsburg County.

Mrs. Jones said Monday she had appointed Gordon B. Jenkins, Williamsburg County public defender, to represent Pierce. She said she acted on instructions from Finney.

A brief review of the case followed.

The State — Columbia, SC, May 5, 1982

PIERCE GETS DAY IN COURT
— POST-CONVICTION RELIEF HEARING

After four years of trying to get a post-conviction relief hearing, William J. Pierce, found guilty of killing a 13-year-old

Page 253

Sumter girl in 1970, will have his day in court. Circuit Judge Ernest Finney has granted Pierce's request for the hearing, called a PCR for post conviction relief, the South Carolina attorney general's office announced Tuesday.

THE HEARING could end 12 years of controversy over the rape and slaying of Peg Cuttino, whose father was a member of the South Carolina House of Representatives at the time.

At his trial, Pierce produced time cards and witnesses showing he had been working in another state on the date he was accused of killing Miss Cuttino. Pierce's past requests for PCR hearings have been denied.

"THE SEEDS we have planted have finally fallen on fertile soil," Sumter County resident Carrie LeNoir said Tuesday. She has been assisting Pierce for several years in his efforts to get a hearing and possibly a new trial...

A review of the case followed.

The Charlotte Observer, May 6, 1982, edition carried the news — "CONVICTED KILLER WINS HEARING IN CUTTINO CASE"; an Associated Press release, similar, but even more in detail of the situation.

May 11, 1982, the Charlotte Observer carried big headlines: "MURDER CASE WON'T DIE DESPITE CONFESSION, CONVICTION", a very detailed article by Sue Anne Pressley; and another lengthy "CONVICTION DIDN'T END S.C. MURDER CASE", also by Ms. Pressley.

Many people were delighted that Mr. Pierce was finally going to get a hearing, but there must have been complaints:

The Daily Item— Sumter, SC, May 17, 1982

NEW HEARING FOR JUNIOR PIERCE
GRANTED TO COMPLY WITH LAW
by Mike Smith

Third Circuit Judge Ernest A. Finney, Jr., said he had no legal recourse but to grant a hearing on convicted murderer William "Junior" Pierce's petition for a new trial. "As I view the law, it says if a person who is incarcerated signs a sworn affidavit setting forth what he perceives to be a violation of some right, I then am mandated or at least required to give him an opportunity to be heard," Finney said in a telephone interview this morning...

Finney said he has no knowledge of other petitions which Pierce has submitted and said it would be inappropriate for him to comment on them. Those petitions for new trials have been opposed by the state attorney general's office, which handles post-conviction relief hearings, and dismissed by Circuit Judge Dan F. Laney, Jr. Finney said no hearing date has been set on

Pierce's latest appeal and that some uncertainty exists on who will represent Pierce in the hearing.

He said Gordon B. Jenkins, a Williamsburg County attorney named to represent Pierce as a public defender, has petitioned the court to be relieved of that duty, citing a possible conflict. "He has some merit to his petition, but I have made no ruling yet," Finney said.

The Daily Item — Sumter, SC, December 6, 1982

HEARING FOR JUNIOR PIERCE DELAYED
by Mike Smith

Third Circuit Judge Dan F. Laney of Bishopville has postponed until at least next March a hearing to determine whether convicted murderer William "Junior" Pierce will get a new trial on the charge of killing a Sumter teenager.

In an order of continuance handed down last month in Williamsburg County Common Pleas Court, Laney also said he would not preside over that hearing. Laney's order says a hearing for Pierce had been scheduled for October 6, but would be continued until the next term of post-conviction relief hearings in the 3rd Judicial Circuit. A spokesman for the state attorney general's office said the circuit's next term of relief hearings is tentatively scheduled for the week of March 21. The attorney general's office will represent the state at that hearing. The order said Laney was removing himself from the hearing because, "This court finds that it has already made a ruling that would effect its opinion in this case." Laney had dismissed Pierce's earlier applications for post-conviction relief without granting him a hearing. Third Circuit Judge Ernest A. Finney, Jr., ordered last spring that Pierce be granted a hearing on the basis of an application Pierce submitted in early April."

The Daily Item — Sumter, SC, March 9, 1983

PIERCE MIGHT BE PRESENT FOR HEARING
by Mike Smith

William "Junior" Pierce may return to Sumter later this month for a hearing that will determine whether he will get a new trial on his 1973 conviction for the murder of Margaret "Peg" Cuttino. Attorney Charles Barr, the Williamsburg County public defender who is representing Pierce, said today, "I am almost certain he will be present for the hearing.

THE HEARING is tentatively scheduled to begin March 23 or 24 before 3rd Circuit Judge Ernest A. Finney, Jr. Pierce filed his own motion. Barr, who was later named to represent Pierce, said some changes may be made in that motion. The attorney general's office will oppose a new trial for Pierce on grounds that his latest motion does not raise any new valid grounds for granting a new trial and that those grounds cited are without merit. Mark Dillard, a spokesman in the attorney general's office, said assistant attorneys general Donald Zelenka and Sally Rentiers will argue against granting Pierce a new trial.

The Daily Item — Sumter, SC, March 22, 1983

PIERCE RETURNING FOR HEARING
by Mike Smith

... Another man, convicted multiple-murderer Donald H. "Pee Wee" Gaskins, once confessed to the Cuttino murder. While being tried on a murder charge in 1976, Gaskins said while on the witness stand that he had murdered the teenager.

But the State Law Enforcement Division, which had been involved in Pierce's arrest for the crime, later said that a truth serum administered to Gaskins showed that he did not commit the murder.

Well, March 24, 1983, finally arrived. In spite of a cold, rainy, stormy day, many of Pierce's supporters crowded into the courtroom, eagerly anticipating the hearing which would finally grant Mr. Pierce a new trial that would certainly overturn his conviction on the Cuttino murder. But it wasn't to be!

The State — Columbia, SC, March 25, 1983

PIERCE'S HEARING DELAYED
by Holly Gatlin

Circuit Judge Ernest Finney delayed a hearing Thursday for William "Junior" Pierce, who is seeking a new trial in the slaying of Peg Cuttino, 13, while lawyers in the case were ordered to submit briefs on technical points.

Finney told attorneys for Pierce and for the state Attorney General's office, which is opposing his request, that they must first decide if Pierce has the right to a hearing. The two sides must also submit briefs to determine if Finney is governed in the case by a law or by a rule of the state Supreme Court, which seemed to be in conflict. The action Thursday was the first time since his conviction in March 1973 that Pierce has received a hearing to air his contention that he was wrongly convicted in the Dec. 18, 1970, sex slaying of Margaret "Peg" Cuttino, daughter of former

Rep. James Cuttino, D-Sumter. Circumstances surrounding the slaying and conviction of Pierce have been a source of unresolved controversy in the Sumter community since the slaying occurred.

Pierce has been denied a hearing four times in the past on the grounds that he is not entitled to a post conviction relief hearing. The state Supreme Court also upheld Pierce's conviction and denied his allegation he was coerced into confessing. "Pierce is a man who's been neglected by the system," his attorney, Charles Barr, argued Thursday in the hearing. "He's been neglected by the system. It's time that the state gave Mr. Pierce his opportunity to present whatever evidence he has that he's not guilty."

But Assistant Attorney General Don Zelenka disagreed. Referring to Pierce, Zelenka said, "This petitioner, more than any other inmate in South Carolina, has come to court for redress of his grievances. I think it's time for these allegations to stop." Zelenka argued that Finney didn't have the jurisdiction to overturn the ruling of other judges who turned down Pierce's appeal. Zelenka also argued that because Pierce's conviction had been affirmed he must receive permission from the Supreme Court to receive a hearing on his contention he has discovered new evidence to prove his innocence after his conviction.

Pierce was not allowed to talk to reporters afterward, but he sat at the courtroom table with his lawyer and his supporter, Carrie LeNoir. Mrs. LeNoir, former Horatio postmaster, has worked for nearly 10 years to clear Pierce of the Cuttino murder.

Mike Smith, in The Item of the same date, elaborated more in detail under the headline: "JUDGE DELAYS PIERCE HEARING ON RE-TRIAL REQUEST". So, we waited and waited...

The Daily Item — Sumter, SC, June 8, 1983

ATTORNEY HASN'T FILED ARGUMENTS
by Holly Hamer

Seventy-six days after convicted multiple-murderer William "Junior" Pierce had a hearing in Sumter, his attorney still has not filed written arguments in Pierce's bid for a new trial. Judge Ernest A. Finney, Jr., said yesterday that, to his knowledge, briefs he had requested within 30 days of the March 24 hearing had not been filed...

More details followed.

CHAPTER TWENTY-ONE

The Daily Item — Sumter, SC, June 10, 1983

PIERCE WANTS NEW ATTORNEY
by Holly Hamor

... In a letter dated June 7, Pierce asked Sumter County Clerk of Court O.V. Player to request that Judge Ernest A. Finney, Jr., "withdraw Mr. Charles David Barr, Attorney, from representing my case due to his failure to file the brief in my behalf that Finney requested March 24...

June 23, 1983, The Item ran the headline: "ATTORNEY FOR PIERCE ASKS TO BE RELIEVED", by Cylinda Scruggs. Mrs. LeNoir commented, "I was not surprised, because after the hearing in Sumter on March 24, Mr. Barr told me he was afraid, not only for his own life, but for his family also. He asked me if I wasn't afraid. When I told him 'No,' he said, 'You'd better be. We're not dealing with cotton pickers.'"

CHAPTER TWENTY-TWO

PIERCE FINALLY GETS A HEARING

MAY 4, 1983

Now, we were waiting, but not very patiently. Attorney Barr still had not filed his arguments, as requested by Judge Finney at the March 24th hearing; and it appeared that someone might be putting the pressure on Judge Finney. I had questioned several people about getting a copy of the transcript of the trial of Donald H. "Pee Wee" Gaskins in Newberry County in April, 1977, but no one seemed to have it.

So, on May 4, 1983, Susan Hamilton and I took off for the Newberry Court House in search of that transcript. Of course, we were interested in the part in which he said that he killed Peg Cuttino. The first person we talked to said it would be in Georgetown. I asked why. She said she didn't know, but someone would be coming back into the Clerk of Court's office that might know. We waited for the next person, who said it would probably be in Williamsburg County. We then asked for the name of the Court Reporter, which was Charlotte C. Smith, of Greenwood. A call to her home told that she was working in Greenwood that day.

We thanked them and headed for Greenwood. The harder Susan drove, the harder I prayed that our trip would not be in vain. We pulled into the parking lot at the Court House, and met a lot of people leaving. On the way in, we met what appeared to be a lawyer, and asked if he knew Charlotte Smith, and if she was in the Court House. He said Court had adjourned, but that we might be able to catch her. We walked in just as she was picking up her things to leave for lunch! She said she thought she still had a copy — she would check when she got home that night. I asked her to call me collect when she found out and, thank God, she had it. She said the cost would be $125, so I put a money order in the next mail to her, as she was leaving town on the 7th, and would be gone for two weeks.

Although attorney Barr had filed a brief on June 14, at the same time he asked to be relieved from this case, we were not very optimistic, due to his great fear for his and his family's safety. We had earlier given him a tape of the conversation between Pee Wee Gaskins and Dr. Charles King of Atlanta. During one of our visits to his office in Kingstree, he told us that his car had been broken into, the tape stolen. We often wondered if he might have thrown it into the Wateree River, as he commuted from Columbia to his Kingstree office.

The Item, June 27, 1983, said "BRIEF ASKS FOR HEARING FOR PIERCE", by Cylinda Scruggs. In the brief (filed June 14), Barr chronologically outlines the history of the case and argues that, if Pierce was tortured into making the confession of Miss Cuttino's murder, his constitutional rights were violated and, therefore, he deserves another trial.

The Item, July 20, 1983, told "LAWYER APPOINTED FOR 'JUNIOR' PIERCE", by Holly Hamor: "In a court order issued yesterday, Judge Ernest A.

Finney, Jr., appointed T.H. Davis, III, as Pierce's public defender and gave the attorney until September 15 to file briefs on Pierce's behalf, arguing for a hearing on whether Pierce is entitled to a new trial. Davis said this morning that he received the order yesterday afternoon, but that he has not had time to review Pierce's file. 'Primarily;, I'm picking up in the middle of a post-conviction relief procedure,' he said. 'It'll be interesting. In a way, I look forward to learning things about the case that I didn't know.'"

So, Mrs. Hamilton and I immediately took the Newberry trial transcript to Mr. Davis.

The Item, September 15, 1983, reported "PIERCE'S ATTORNEY GETS MORE TIME TO FILE BRIEF", by Cylinda Scruggs: "... Davis said yesterday that he had requested the extension because of several delays. The most important, he said, was that he had amended the application for a post-conviction relief hearing. Pierce filed the application in his own behalf."

The Item, September 27, 1983, read "HEARING FOR PIERCE REQUIRED, LAWYER SAYS", by Mike Smith: "U.S. and South Carolina Supreme Court rulings require that William 'Junior' Pierce be granted a hearing in his effort to overturn his conviction for the murder of Margaret 'Peg' Cuttino. Pierce's court-appointed attorney says. Attorney T.H. Davis, III, argues in a brief filed yesterday that Pierce has charged that his constitutional rights were violated and that 'This issue raises a question of fact that can only be resolved by an evidentiary hearing.' Davis also argues that the existence of a confession to the crime by another person — one of the grounds on which Pierce is seeking a new trial — has never been considered by a judge when reviewing Pierce's earlier petitions for post-conviction relief."

The Item, October 12, 1983, told "ATTORNEY GENERAL SAYS PIERCE NOT DUE NEW HEARING", by Cylinda Scruggs. "South Carolina Attorney General Travis Medlock says the issues raised by convicted murderer William 'Junior' Pierce's court-appointed attorney have already been raised and responded to in previous court proceedings and that Pierce is not entitled to an additional post-conviction relief hearing. Medlock said Davis' reference to a confession was not sufficient to justify another post-conviction relief hearing because Davis did not include 'the identity of the alleged confessor, the date when the alleged confession was made, and the substance, if any, of such a confession. With arguments now presented on both sides of the issue, Judge Ernest Finney, Jr., is expected to decide whether to grant Pierce an evidentiary hearing or to hear additional arguments on whether he is due a hearing."

The Item, January 4, 1984, broke the news, "JUDGE DENIES NEW TRIAL FOR PIERCE", by Cylinda Scruggs: "Judge Ernest Finney, Jr., has denied William 'Junior" Pierce's petition for a new trial but has suggested that the South Carolina Supreme Court should properly consider them. Pointing out that Pierce had appealed his conviction to the Supreme Court, Finney said that Supreme Court Rule 24 states that the circuit court loses jurisdiction over a case after a defendant appeals to the Supreme Court. 'The appellate court retains jurisdiction even after the appeal is concluded,' the order said. Finney did say that the record indicates that Pierce has never been granted a hearing on the voluntariness of his confession. But, he said, Judge Dan Laney ruled in 1980 that the petition containing this and other allegations was successive and therefore barred from consideration. 'In view of the fact that the status of the petitioner's allegations have been previously determined by a court of competent jurisdiction, this court is bound by the earlier ruling,' Finney said, adding, 'If the applicant feels that his prior or present petitions are not successive, his proper remedy would be appeal to the Supreme Court.'"

Holly Gatlin, in The State, January 6, 1984, wrote, "JUDGE: HIGH COURT MUST DECIDE ON NEW EVIDENCE IN MURDER", and she brought many good points in Pierce's favor in a very lengthy article. "... Pierce is seeking a new trial on the grounds that vital information was withheld from him by the prosecution during his 1973 trial and that former Solicitor Kirk McLeod, who prosecuted Pierce, made prejudicial statements to the jury in his closing arguments.

"Court records indicate that McLeod told the jury that one element supporting Pierce's guilt was the fact that since Pierce was arrested in March of 1971 no other girls in South Carolina were murdered in the same manner as Miss Cuttino. The statement was inaccurate, although there was no evidence at Pierce's trial to refute the Solicitor's argument. In 1974, the S.C. Supreme Court ruled that because Pierce's lawyers failed to object during the trial they lost their right to complain on appeal."

Gatlin pointed out that, among other murders, "A month after Pierce was jailed in Appling County, Ga., a 19-year-old Lexington County woman, Patricia Oswalt Cannon, was sexually assaulted, beaten and strangled to death with a pillowcase in her West Columbia home."

Then, The Item, January 9, 1984, brought good news — "JUDGE MAY RECONSIDER PIERCE APPEAL", by Cylinda Scruggs: "Judge Ernest A. Finney, Jr., says that he may reconsider an order in which he denied Pierce's petitions for a new trial in the death of Margaret 'Peg' Cuttino. Finney ruled last week that he could not grant one, but a Supreme Court ruling in late 1983 held that the particular rule Finney cited in his order does not apply in cases involving the state's Uniform Post Conviction Procedure Act. Sumter attorney T.H. Davis, III, said today that the Supreme Court ruling could affect Pierce's case."

The Item, January 12, 1984, stated, "FINNEY TO RECONSIDER PIERCE APPEAL", by Cylinda Scruggs. In part, the article said, "In an order filed this morning in Williamsburg County, Finney vacated his order dated January 4 that denied Pierce's petitions. Attorney Davis said, 'He's vacated his prior order, and, as I understand it, he's reconsidering the entire matter.

"Davis said he talked on the telephone with Pierce yesterday 'and he was naturally elated and enthusiastic over this latest development.'"

At long last, the good news arrived. Holly Hamor, in The Item, April 16, 1984, told "JUDGE RULES FOR HEARING FOR PIERCE": "William J. Pierce has won new ground in his attempt to overturn his conviction for the 1970 Cuttino murder. Judge Finney yesterday ordered an evidentiary hearing on Pierce's allegations that convicted murderer Pee Wee Gaskins confessed to the Cuttino murder. The hearing on evidence could lead to Pierce's being granted a new trial. Pierce's attorney T.H. Davis, III said 'I'd say it's probably the first good news that Pierce has had in ten or twelve years. I have not been able to reach Mr. Pierce yet, but I'm sure he will be elated to hear this.'

"Davis said the hearing probably will be scheduled for the next term of post-conviction relief hearings — April 25, 26, and 27; but that he would probably ask for a continuance on Pierce's hearing, due to his heavy case load as public defender."

Holly Gatlin, in The State, April 16, 1984, submitted a full page under the heading: "TRIED, CONVICTED, SENTENCED — BUT IS HE GUILTY?" She wrote an in-depth article on many facts supporting Pierce's innocence.

The Item, January 3, 1985, carried the article by Jeff Johnson — "HEARING SET FOR PIERCE": "After a delay of almost nine months, William Pierce will receive his hearing the week of January 28. 'I'm trying to get him here for the hearing, but it almost takes an act of God to get a prisoner brought in from out of state.' Davis said he intends to present the case whether Pierce is present or not."

However, I had no doubt that Pierce would be brought to Sumter for the hearing, as I had already visited the Governor's office, and had full assurance that he would be brought in.

Jeff Johnson, in The Item, January 12, 1985, released "ARRANGEMENTS BEING MADE TO BRING PIERCE TO HEARING": "Arrangements are being made through Gov. Dick Riley's office to have William J. Pierce transported to Sumter County for his hearing scheduled for January 29 and 30."

We were delighted when, after obtaining a schedule for Post-Conviction Relief Hearings, we found that January 28, 1985, had been set aside to hear nine appeals, while January 29 and 30 had been set up for the Pierce appeal.

January 28, 1985, The Item carried another article by Jeff Johnson — "LONG-SOUGHT HEARING FOR PIERCE OPENS TOMORROW", with many details pertaining to the case. "Sumter County Sheriff Hazel Reeves, who is responsible for security at the courthouse, said extraordinary security measures will be taken during the hearing. 'We will beef up security and have a lot more men there than we usually do,' he said. 'We will have metal detectors and check everyone coming into the courtroom. And we will check the entire courthouse early in the morning,' he said.

"Tomorrow at 9:30 a.m. in the Sumter County Courthouse, Judge Finney will begin hearing two days of arguments and make a ruling on the issue. What makes this latest act in the bizarre and controversial drama so unusual is that, for the first time, Junior Pierce and Pee Wee Gaskins will be together in the same courtroom.

Gaskins and his attorney, Jack Swerling, have been subpoenaed by Davis, also Joe McElveen, Pierce's original court-appointed attorney, the court reporter who took Gaskins' confession in Newberry, and some of Gaskins' former co-workers.

Jeff reviewed the case briefly, pointing out that Pierce's attorney first moved for a new trial on April 5, 1973, a little more than a month after the conviction, but Judge Louis Rosen, who presided at the original trial, denied the motion. While Pierce's attorneys were preparing their next appeal, his supporters had enough momentum to force a Sumter County Grand Jury investigation into law enforcement's handling of the case, an almost unheard-of circumstance that also could have led to a new trial. But on July 27, 1973, after three days and 31 witnesses, the Grand Jury ruled the investigation had been conducted properly.

October 7, 1975, Pierce filed a petition with the United States District Court, but District Judge Sol Blatt, Jr., dismissed the appeal." (If you remember, it was Sol Blatt, Sr., whose office filed the three-million-dollar suits against The Item, Verna Moore and me.) Then, Jeff told of the number of times Judge Dan Laney had dismissed his appeals.

The State, January 29, 1985, carried a lengthy article by Jan Tuten — "JUDGE TO STUDY RETRIAL FOR MAN CONVICTED IN GIRL'S 1970 DEATH".

The Item, January 29, 1985, gave the front page headline "PEE WEE GASK-INS REFUSES TO TESTIFY", with pictures by Bruz Crowson captioned: "Donald H. Pee Wee Gaskins covered face with stocking cap — His confession in 1977 to Cuttino murder prompted today's hearing", and "Junior Pierce acknowledges Sheriff Reeves in Passing — Pierce was brought into courthouse this morning for hearing." The account of the events was written by Jeff Johnson and Bob Redding. Their first few paragraphs covered usual court proceedings, then told that:

> *Pierce and Gaskins, who are appearing together in hearing for the first time, were brought to the Sumter County Courthouse this morning under tight security. In his preliminary statement, Finney said he thought the extra security was necessary based on information he had received. He also said it was needed to ensure impartiality and to protect those who would appear at today's hearing.*
>
> *When Pierce entered the courtroom at 10:45 this morning, he paused to shake hands with Carrie LeNoir, who has waged a personal campaign for Pierce to have his day in court. About 40 spectators, six witnesses, and media representatives attended the hearing, but more than 40 people were turned away from the courthouse, including media representatives from out of town.*
>
> *Sumter County Sheriff Hazel Reeves said security included a surveillance helicopter that followed the two cars carrying Pierce and Gaskins. They arrived at 9:25 a.m. under heavy guard. The two men were kept apart throughout the preliminary maneuverings between their attorneys. As attorneys interviewed one convict in a holding cell, the other was held in a conference room that was guarded by a police officer inside and another outside the window. Reeves said, "Pee Wee is the most dangerous of the two. At a trial in Florence, he jumped out of a window and escaped."*
>
> *Fourteen deputies from the Sheriff's Department, 16 SLED agents, four city policemen and two firemen were among those maintaining security at the courthouse. Before anyone was allowed on the second floor, where the courtrooms are located, a SLED dog sniffed them for explosives. As people went upstairs to attend the hearing, a SLED agent used a metal detector to search them and personal belongings.*

The Columbia Record, January 29, 1985, carried headlines "GASKINS CON-FESSION WOULD HAVE EXONERATED PIERCE, ATTORNEY SAYS", by Brian Duncan, which gave details of the proceedings the earlier part of the day.

The News and Courier, Charleston, SC, January 30, 1985, carried pictures by

AP Laserphotos, showing "Gaskins, Pierce enter Sumter County courthouse for hearing." The account of the previous days were reported by Leverne Prosser in "PIERCE CITED GASKINS CONFESSION IN BID TO OVERTURN MURDER VERDICT".

The State, January 30, 1985, displayed front page pictures by Associated Press, captioned: "Subpoenaed — Head covered, Donald "Pee Wee" Gaskins is led into court at Sumter", and "Seeking new trial — William J. Pierce was convicted in the 1970 slaying of Margaret Cuttino." The article, "CONFESSION CALLED REASON TO GRANT PIERCE A NEW TRIAL", by Jan Tuten, was an extensive report.

Florence Morning News, January 30, 1985, with John Monk reporting, said "GASKINS IN WINGS, BUT DOESN'T TESTIFY IN PIERCE APPEAL". He pointed out:

> *There were some revelations at the hearing. Former Sumter County Sheriff Byrd Parnell, sheriff there from 1953 to 1981, admitted on the witness stand that he had taken some investigative documents concerning the Cuttino killing home with him after he left office. Parnell said he kept them in his attic. Current Sumter County Sheriff Hazel Reeves, in an interview Tuesday, likened Parnell's action to withholding evidence and said investigative files are the property of the sheriff's office.*
>
> *A detailed and lengthy 1978 confession by Gaskins, in which he admitted killing 13 persons and in return was granted life sentences, was apparently not a sworn statement as law officials believed. Former prosecutor Ken Summerford, who testified Tuesday, said he thought Gaskins was sworn in when he gave the statement. However, court records show Gaskins isn't recorded as being sworn in when the statement was made. In that 1978 statement, Gaskins, who law enforcement officials had given a truth serum, denies killing Cuttino. All reporters said that Gaskins, subpoenaed by Pierce's attorney, refused to testify after he arrived in Sumter and never appeared in the courtroom. SLED officers kept close watch on him in a nearby holding cell.*

The Columbia Record, January 30, 1985, headlined "PIERCE RELIEF HEARING EVIDENCE CASTS DOUBT ON GASKINS' CONFESSION", by Brian Duncan.

The Item, January 30, 1985, carried the headlines: "GASKINS' CREDIBILITY WAS BOTTOM LINE AT HEARING", by Jeff Johnson. All reporters' accounts told of a letter former Sumter County Sheriff Byrd Parnell received from Gaskins in July, 1978, in which he denied having killed Miss Cuttino. Pierce's attorney, T.H. Davis, III, countered with a letter dated March 16, 1978, in which Gaskins claimed that SLED agent Tom Henderson, who investigated the Gaskins murders, threatened him. In the letter addressed to Mrs. Carrie LeNoir, a 64-year-old church organist who has championed Pierce's innocence for 12 years, Gaskins wrote: "Well anyway, he (Henderson) made it clear I was going to say I had nothing to do with the Cuttino or Horry County cases. I am supposed to agree with them on what they say and nothing else if I want to survive." Henderson testified the accusation was not true.

Attorney Davis questioned employees of Fort Roofing and Sheet Metal Works, who testified Gaskins was working there on the day Miss Cuttino disappeared. Co-worker Thomas Christmas testified he was with Gaskins all day, except for lunch hour. During that day, Christmas said, he and Gaskins worked at a school district warehouse about a block from where Miss Cuttino was last reported seen.

Remember the Court schedule gave two full days, January 29 and 30, 1985, for Mr. Pierce's hearing, but, strangely enough, on the 29th, Judge Finney announced to the attorneys they would have to wrap it up that afternoon, as he would have to be in Columbia the next morning. Many people wondered why — was he threatened with the possibility of losing his position as leading candidate for the upcoming Supreme Court appointment? Or was too much unfavorable light showing up, such as Sheriff Parnell taking the Cuttino file home and putting it in his attic?

But we had confidence in Judge Finney, who, being black, had probably experienced, or at least heard about some of the injustices that occur in the courtrooms. He had certainly heard that no one could account for Gaskins' whereabouts during his lunch hour, which was the crucial time; and that he was working nearby Miss Cuttino's last reported location. Also, he should have been familiar with Mr. Pierce's alibis, which placed him many miles from Sumter. If, indeed, either of them murdered Miss Cuttino, it would most probably be Gaskins, because of the timing with Patty Alsbrooks, Clyde, and possibly others being killed in the Sumter area.

Anyway, The Columbia Record, January 31, 1985, carried a big headline: "JUDGE FINNEY'S ELEVATION LOGICAL STEP", by Kent Krell. The first paragraph read: "It is fitting and logical that Ernest Adolphys Finney, Jr., should be the first black to sit on the South Carolina Supreme Court," followed by a history of his struggles and achievements through the years.

An editorial in The Item the same day was titled "FINNEY MOVES UP": "The virtual assurance that 3rd Judicial Circuit Judge Ernest A. Finney, Jr., will soon become the first black since Reconstruction to be appointed to the S.C. Supreme Court is a well-deserved honor for the Sumterite." A later paragraph stated, "During his eight years on the bench, Judge Finney has carried out his duties with a rare combination of compassion and diligent pursuit of justice, both qualities strengthened by fairness. His performance as a judge has earned him the respect of all who've appeared in his court."

All this praise made us feel better, and very optimistic about a new trial for Mr. Pierce, at which he would be exonerated of the Cuttino murder.

But our optimism was short-lived. The Item, February 21, 1985, headlined the story, "JUDGE DENIES NEW TRIAL FOR PIERCE", by Jeff Johnson:

> *Once again, William J. Pierce has been denied a new trial in his 11-year effort to have his conviction for the 1970 murder of Margaret "Peg" Cuttino overturned. Circuit Judge Ernest A. Finney, Jr., denied Pierce's motion for a new trial because Pierce "... has fallen short of his burden of proof on the issue." The decision was released late this morning.*

During a hearing before Finney January 29, Pierce's attorney, T.H. Davis, III, argued that a 1977 confession to the murder by Donald H. "Pee Wee" Gaskins was sufficient evidence of Pierce's possible innocence. In his order, Finney said Gaskins' confession, made while he was on trial for another murder in Newberry County "lacked any critical information about how the murder was allegedly accomplished, where it was done, when it was done, or any accomplices in the crime. Finney went through the testimony in his order and, based on that, said Gaskins was not in a position to commit the crime during the critical period of Miss Cuttino's disappearance.

"While it is undisputed that Gaskins was working in Sumter on December 18, 1970 (the day of Miss Cuttino's disappearance)," Finney wrote, "his April, 1977, statement is not 'as such as would probably change the result if a new trial was had,' nor 'is material to the issue of guilt or innocence." In this court's opinion, the evidence presented at the January 29, 1984, hearing was insufficient to warrant the relief (Pierce) requested."

Davis said the next step would be to file an appeal. "We've got 10 days to file a notice of appeal and serve it on the state," he said. "It will probably go to the appellate court." Davis said the appellate court could either dismiss it completely without giving a reason, or issue an opinion affirming or overturning Finney's order. Davis' appeal could take from six to eight months."

The State, February 22, 1985, carried an account by Jan Tuten, "GASKINS CONFESSION WON'T GET NEW TRIAL FOR CONVICTED KILLER".

The Item, February 22, 1985, announced "PIERCE'S LAWYER TO FILE APPEAL FOR NEW TRIAL", from staff and wire reports.

The State, March 2, 1985, had an account by Jan Tuten, "PIERCE TO APPEAL RETRIAL DENIAL".

The Item, March 5, 1985, stated "PIERCE ATTORNEY STARTS APPEAL OF DECISION TO DENY NEW TRIAL", with details by Jeff Johnson.

The Item, March 6, 1985, carried "FINNEY HEARING TOMORROW": "The Senate Judiciary Committee will conduct a public hearing tomorrow on 3rd Circuit Judge Ernest A. Finney, Jr.'s bid to become the first black on the state Supreme Court since Reconstruction. The public hearing will begin at 9:30 a.m. tomorrow in the Senate conference room in the State House, according to a spokeswoman for House Speaker Ramon Schwartz, D-Sumter. The General Assembly elects state judges, and Schwartz said he expects Finney to be elected by acclamation."

Meanwhile, Pee Wee Gaskins was again making news, with such headlines as: "PEE WEE ON HUNGER STRIKE BECAUSE OF MAIL", "GASKINS ASKS TO GO TO DESERTED ISLAND", and "GASKINS' EXECUTION SET, BUT STAY LIKELY".

On July 23, 1985, Jeff Johnson, in The Item, wrote "ATTORNEY SEEKS NEW APPEAL IN PIERCE CASE":

The court-appointed attorney for William J. Pierce has asked the state Supreme Court to consider hearing an appeal of a circuit judge's refusal to grant Pierce a new trial in connection with the 1970 murder of Margaret "Peg" Cuttino of Sumter. The latest stage in Pierce's quest for a new trial came yesterday when Sumter attorney T.H. Davis, III, filed a petition for a writ of certiorari with the Supreme Court.

The petition in effect asks the high court to consider hearing formal arguments over then-3rd Circuit Judge Ernest A. Finney's February 21 denial of a motion for a new trial by Pierce during a post-conviction relief hearing January 29. Pierce's post-conviction relief hearing was originally granted to determine if the 1977 confession of Donald "Pee Wee" Gaskins to the Cuttino murder would be likely to change the outcome of a new trial for Pierce if one were held.

Finney refused to grant a new trial, saying the evidence presented "wasn't sufficient to warrant the relief Pierce requested." In his petition, Davis asserts Finney may have committed errors in law at a number of points in the hearing. First, Davis argued Finney was in error when he ruled Gaskins' confession was not material to Pierce's guilt or innocence. The ultimate issue, Davis said, is who in fact committed the murder. A confession by a third party bears directly on the issue of guilt or innocence, he said.

Second, Davis said Finney erred when he ruled Gaskins' confession probably wouldn't change the result if a new trial were held for Pierce. Even though the credibility of newly discovered evidence is to be determined by a judge, it must be viewed in light of the probable result on the minds of a jury, he said. At the January hearing, Davis presented affidavits from 40 Sumter residents, including Sumter County Sheriff Hazel Reeves, all of whom said they believe a new trial based on Gaskins' confession would result in Pierce's acquittal. In his refusal to grant a new trial, Finney said Gaskins' confession was unsubstantiated because his whereabouts were known during the critical time of Miss Cuttino's abduction, which Finney determined to be between 12:30 p.m. and 2:30 p.m. December 18, 1970.

But Davis argued in the petition that no one knew where Gaskins was between noon and 12:45 that day. Gaskins, who then worked at Fort Roofing and Sheet Metal, was on his lunch break during that time. "The record is devoid of any evidence to support the finding of the lower court that Mr. Gaskins' whereabouts were documented throughout the critical time of the Cuttino abduction."

At the post-conviction relief hearing, Gaskins' confession, which was made under oath while he was on trial in Newberry County for another murder, was admitted without objection. But the state tried to impeach the confession by introducing evidence to contradict it. Davis argued in the petition that Finney erred in admitting the state's evidence. The evidence, which amounted to Gaskins' recanting the confession, was in the form of letters and telephone calls. Davis said since these communications from Gaskins were made out of court, they were hearsay and, therefore, inadmissible.

"Since the state failed to object to the introduction of the transcript of Gaskins' confession, it waived any right to thereafter impeach Gaskins' statement, if Gaskins was not personally called to stand as a witness, and he was not," Davis wrote.

Finally, Davis argued in the petition that Finney "abused his discretion" in ruling that Gaskins' confession was not credible. While the credibility of evidence is for the judge to determine, and that determination can't be set aside unless there is an error in law or abuse in discretion, it must be viewed through the eyes of a jury. Davis said Finney's ruling was a personal opinion, not one made in light of the probable result on the minds of the jury.

"Although it might be argued that the credibility of a mass murderer is suspect," Davis wrote, "we believe that the fact that Gaskins is a convicted mass murderer would lend weight to his confession that he had, in fact, added Miss Cuttino to his list of victims."

The state will have 30 days to file an answer to Davis' petition. If the court issues the writ Davis requested, the matter will be reviewed entirely and more detailed arguments will be presented.

The Citizens for Justice were very pleased with the appeal Mr. Davis had submitted, and were optimistic that it would bring good results. But our hopes soon turned to despair, as The Item, August 27, 1985, published the story by Jeff Johnson, "PIERCE APPEAL REQUEST LACKS MERIT, STATE SAYS":

"The state has answered William J. Pierce's latest appeal of a denial for a new trial by trying to tear the struts out of a petition filed by Pierce's attorney. The 25-page document filed Friday is the latest legal salvo in Pierce's 12-year fight for a new trial on charges of murdering Peg Cuttino. The state's reply is that evidence presented in the hearing failed to meet the criteria and asks the court to dismiss the petition.

"On December 20, 1985, Mr. Davis received a letter from The Supreme Court of South Carolina Re: William J. Pierce, Jr. v. State of South Carolina: Dear Mr. Davis — The Court has issued the following Order on your Petition for Writ of Certiorari in the above matter: 'Petition for Writ of Certiorari denied.' (Signed J.B. Ness, for the Court, Associate Justice Ernest A. Finney, Jr., not participating.)

Well, we were very disappointed, but not really surprised! Remember how the news media, back in 1981, took special note of Justice Julius B. "Bubba" Ness, a former state senator, and a product of the "Good ole boy" school of politics in this state, where one of the things one learns in this school is loyalty to one's friends and allies. So, it would seem, no way could Ness betray his newest Associate Justice, Ernest A. Finney, Jr. There again, we felt that Pierce was a victim of the political system.

Justice Ness appeared to possess an obsession which impelled him to maybe use his heart instead of his head where matters involved his friends.

The Item, May 21, 1987, published an article by David Reed, Associated Press writer, which stated: "Ness thinks he was forced to retire." One paragraph revealed: "On Tuesday, Ness talked at length about the importance of loyalty to friends and associates in remarks to newly sworn attorneys. 'Choose your friends and associates carefully, very carefully,' Ness said. 'You can best judge a man by observing the way he treats those he has considered his friends. I do not believe I have any true friends who could ever say that I was not loyal to them. A carefully chosen friend can be more devastating to you than an entire army of enemies. The blow of an enemy is expected and recovery is anticipated. However, the betrayal of a friend cuts more deeply and its effect can never be overcome,' Ness said."

The State, February 25, 1988, published "CHIEF JUSTICE SAYS GOOD-

BYE", by Margaret O'shea:
"It was a farewell address for Ness, who retires Saturday on his 72nd birthday. Ness says he plans to practice law in federal courts. He'll also teach at the University of South Carolina law school, and serve on the bench when he's asked."
(I hope he will remember to stress that Justice in the courts should take priority over loyalty to friends.)
The article continued, "He spoke to an assembly that included his family and fellow justices, including in-coming Chief Justice George Gregory, and in-coming Justice Jean Toal. Ness spoke highly of both. He called Gregory perceptive, wise and deliberate. 'Chief Justice Gregory will bring to his new role a stability and calm that may sorely be needed after the storm of the 'Ness Administration' has moved out to the sea,' he said. 'Certainly not the least of his gifts is his ability to keep his name out of the newspaper, a trait I have wished many times he had taught to me.'
"Of Mrs. Toal, Ness said he was glad to see a woman on the state's high court, 'and I look forward with great interest to the contributions Jean will undoubtedly make to the judicial system of this state.' Mrs. Toal won the Supreme Court seat after Circuit Judge Rodney A. Peeples withdrew from the race. He'd held the pledges to win election until it was revealed that he apparently had lied in court to hide his interest in the outcome of a lawsuit. It involved a will that named Peeples' daughters as heirs.
"Peeples was for many years considered a friend and protege of Ness, as well as a shoo-in for the state's high court. Ness, however, allegedly blamed Peeples for engineering his forced retirement so that the younger judge could make an earlier move for the Supreme Court.
"His withdrawal gave new impetus to a proposal that South Carolina change its procedure of giving legislators sole authority to choose the state's judges. Among the alternative methods mentioned is direct election of judges by the state's voters. But Ness warned the legislators to leave well enough alone. Alluding to Peeples, without saying his name, Ness said, 'recent events should not sway lawmakers toward making bad law... I urge you, I strongly urge you, to exercise caution before making any change to the judicial selection process in this state,' Ness said. 'It is my earnest belief that South Carolina's method for selecting judges, while not perfect, is better than any other method in place in other states in the nation.'
"He spoke most forcefully against suggestions that judges be elected directly, saying that it opened judges up to political influence because of the need to build a campaign chest."
(I'm sure he realized that some of his judge friends would have been replaced, if the citizens could have had a vote on their elections.)
O'shea continued, "In closing, Ness said the desire for excellence and unending loyalty to friends had been the most important lessons he'd learned on the bench." Nowhere were the words Justice or Truth mentioned as being important issues for a judge to consider. "'If they put anything on my tombstone when I die, it will be that 'He was loyal to his friends,' Ness said. Afterward, reporters asked the chief justice if his friends had stood by him. Ness turned his back to the questioner and asked: 'You want to take that knife from me right there? I don't think that all of my friends have been equally loyal, but I think a big majority of my friends have been equally

loyal.'"

The Citizens for Justice believe that this staunch loyalty and friendship among the judges were conflicts of interest where a friend was involved, and clouded their judgment, resulting in some very questionable decisions. I rest my case!

Believe it or not — The Item, March 4, 1987, stated, "PIERCE FILES MOTION TO HAVE MURDER CONVICTION OVERTURNED", by Jeff Johnson:

"William J. Pierce, convicted 15 years ago for the 1970 murder of Peg Cuttino, has filed yet another motion in a long list of legal maneuvers to have his conviction overturned. In the latest motion, filed in his handwriting and on his own behalf, Pierce contends that his last appearance before a judge on the case, in January, 1985, was a 'farce and a mockery of justice', because the court accepted 'hearsay (sic), unsworn statements, uncertified court documents and manufactured false evidence.' The 1985 hearing, held before Ernest A. Finney, Jr., now a state Supreme Court justice, was to determine if a confession to Miss Cuttino's murder made in 1977 by Donald 'Pee Wee' Gaskins was sufficient to warrant a new trial for Pierce. Finney ruled that it wasn't.

"Gaskins' confession, made in Newberry County while he was on trial for another murder, was ruled to be invalid, because, Finney said, though Gaskins was working in Sumter at the time of the Cuttino murder, he didn't have the opportunity to commit it. But Pierce says the state conspired to discredit Gaskins' confession because of the embarrassment it would cause.

"In the 1985 hearing, Tom Henderson, SLED agent, said he put 'very little validity in what Gaskins said,' and did nothing about the confession. Pierce says the state has put great validity in what Gaskins has said on other occasions. Gaskins, he said, has led authorities to the bodies of three women he confessed to killing. Pierce questions how the state can believe Gaskins one time and dismiss him the next and how his confession to the Cuttino murder can be discounted if not to keep the state from being embarrassed. The potential embarrassment, Pierce contends, is the motive for the alleged conspiracy to discredit Gaskins and keep Pierce in prison.

"Pierce also says in his motion that still another statement made by Gaskins, this one in 1978 in Florence County, was unfairly used against him in 1985. In that statement, Gaskins repudiated his confession to the Cuttino murder. Pierce claims Gaskins was forced to repudiate it, and that testimony made under duress or as the result of a deal is inadmissable.

"In his motion, Pierce also recounts the history of his arrest, repeating his claim that he was beaten and tortured while in jail in Georgia to confess to murders he didn't commit.

"The motion was filed in Sumter County. It is not known when a judge will rule on it."

We heard nothing further on this matter until Mr. Pierce sent me the letter he received from the Supreme Court, dated November 1, 1989 — William J. Pierce, Jr., Petitioner, v. State of South Carolina, Respondent — ORDER —

"Petitioner has filed a petition for writ of certiorari following his denial of his application for post-conviction relief. Petitioner's counsel asserts the petition is without merit and requests permission to withdraw from further representation. Petitioner has not filed a pro se petition. After careful consideration of the entire record as required by Johnson v. State, 294 S.C. 310, 364 S.E. 2d 201 (1988), we deny the petition and grant counsel's request to withdraw. Signed — George T. Gregory, Jr., Chief Justice — Associate Justice Finney, not participating.

"We assume that Mr. T.H. Davis, III, was the attorney asking to withdraw. But, according to the March 4, 1987, news release, Mr. Pierce had filed his pro se petition. It just seems that nothing on this earth will persuade the South Carolina judges to give Mr. Pierce a new trial, because they know that no jury, with the evidence we have supporting his innocence would ever uphold his conviction. However, Mr. Pierce can look forward to the day when he can be judged on the final judgment day. If, indeed, these judges have acted within the law, it is long overdue that some changes be made.

Meanwhile, The State, May 29, 1988, carried "CORONERS AGREE RECORDS ARE PUBLIC", an Associated Press story from Greenville. "Many county coroners say they already keep their records open to the public, concurring with an attorney general's opinion that a new state law closing death certificates to the public does not include coroners' records. The General Assembly passed a bill in February exempting death certificates from the state Freedom of Information Act. The bill was recommended by officials in the Department of Health and Environmental Control, who cited the confidentiality of AIDS patients. Attorney General Travis Medlock on Thursday ruled that records and inquisition reports kept by county coroners are open to the public even if they reflect the same or similar cause of death contained in the death certificate. The opinion means inquisition reports made for every case investigated by the coroner are open to the public along with the records on cause of death, general autopsy results and blood alcohol levels, said Jim Burnett, the Spartanburg County coroner who asked for Medlock's opinion. Greenville County Coroner Charlie Garrett said he has always kept records open and the opinion will not change his policy.

CHAPTER TWENTY-THREE

PEE WEE GASKINS' LAST DAYS

Pee Wee Gaskins knew that his time was getting short, so in early 1991, he started trying any means to extend his life. An article in The State, February 24, 1991, by John Allard, stated "CONDEMNED OPPOSE WAR SERVICE PLAN; INMATES SAY PETITION BY GASKINS OPPOSED": "Some inmates on South Carolina's Death Row said Saturday that they want no part of Pee Wee's petition to have them fight in the Persian Gulf in return for having their sentences reduced to life in prison. Michael Torrence telephoned The State after reading about Gaskins' petition, which he said had been signed by 25 inmates. Torrence doubted he had gained that much support. 'It's a question of an out-of-shape 55-year-old trying to steal the limelight,' Cecil Lucas said, 'You give Pee Wee a bowie knife, a can of water and set him loose in the desert and what the hell is he going to do?' Gaskins' petition is unrealistic, because convicted killers cannot be freed from Death Row, state Department of Corrections spokesman Francis X Archibald said.

The State, June 15, 1991, carried the Associated Press article, "PRISON PUTS GASKINS UNDER 24-HOUR WATCH": "Corrections officials have Gaskins under 24-hour guard as his death sentence appeals progress, a spokeswoman said Friday. Gaskins has been in a cell by himself with a guard posted outside the door since the U.S. Supreme Court rejected his appeal June 3, said Robyn Zimmerman, spokeswoman for the Department of Corrections. He hasn't caused a commotion. The watch is just to make sure everything stays status quo. She said officials weren't afraid that Gaskins might hurt himself or anyone else, but because of a gut feeling, and considering his personality and past record, the 24-hour watch was instituted."

News reports on Gaskins followed almost daily, and The State, August 28, 1991, revealed "CELL DIDN'T STOP GASKINS FROM PLOTTING KIDNAP-PING", by John Allard: "A plot to kidnap the daughter of the prosecutor who put Gaskins on Death Row was just the latest criminal orchestrated by Gaskins, authorities said. The most dangerous criminal mastermind in South Carolina has never let prison walls interfere with scheming, said 5th Circuit Solicitor Dick Harpootlian. 'He's always plotting', said Harpootlian, who got a death sentence for Gaskins in 1983 for blowing apart a fellow inmate with an explosive device. 'I'm not a homici-dal maniac, so it's hard for me to figure out Pee Wee's thought patterns and not know whether there is sufficient evidence to charge Gaskins' son in the kidnapping plot.'

"Donald Lee Gaskins was arrested Monday night on unrelated burglary and drug charges. The lawyer who represented Gaskins during his death-penalty trial was appalled by the kidnapping plot. 'Based on what I've heard, the allegations are outrageous," said Jack Swerling, Gaskins' original attorney and Harpootlian's close friend. 'If this is true, it causes me to lose any empathy I may have had for Pee Wee.'"

Gaskins' most ingenious and daring plot was getting Death Row inmate Rudolph Tyner to take a plastic prison cup packed with plastic explosives into his cell. He told Tyner the cup was an intercom and had Tyner put it to his ear when he triggered Tyner's explosive death.

The story of how Gaskins accomplished that feat is a tale that shocked his original attorneys and prosecutors. The most notorious mass murderer in South Carolina was the unquestioned king of Cell Block Two at the Central Correctional Institution. The cell block was reserved for Death-Row inmates and other prisoners convicted of violent offenses. Gaskins was the maintenance man for the cell block and kept tools and electrical equipment in his cell to make repairs. Gaskins also controlled the delivery of inmates' meals, had freedom to go where he pleased and earned money by running errands for inmates and fixing their appliances. Harpootlian said Gaskins used his position to get the 'pick of the litter for homosexual favors'. The most dangerous inmate in a South Carolina prison even made loans, ran a small-scale pawn shop and sold coffee and sandwiches to fellow inmates. Corrections officials have testified that Gaskins got the maintenance job because he had been on the cell block longer than most other inmates and was a good handyman.

Harpootlian said Gaskins reveled in irritating authorities. Gaskins drove a hearse around his native Prospect during the period in which he has admitted killing nine people, and also used soap to write taunts on police car windows. "Pee Wee would have gotten away with Tyner's murder, except for his massive ego that made him tape-record conversations with co-conspirators," Harpootlian said. "The challenge of killing thrills him."

Murrells Inlet bricklayer Richard Anthony "Tony" Cimo asked Gaskins to kill Tyner. Cimo wanted revenge for the murders of his mother and stepfather, Myrtle and Bill Moon, during the armed robbery of their general store in Horry County.

Gaskins will continue to see visitors once a week and make a telephone call once a day, despite the kidnapping plot, said Robyn Zimmerman, spokeswoman for the state Department of Corrections. "He has not eaten since Monday, and is drinking only water and coffee," she said. She said Gaskins, who previously has gone on hunger strikes, apparently lacks an appetite as he focuses on the specter of execution."

The Item, September 4, 1991, carried the Associated Press story from Florence, "GASKINS' SON SAYS HIS FATHER IS 'READY FOR IT TO BE OVER'": "Donald H. 'Pee Wee' Gaskins' son said Tuesday he hopes to 'live a normal life' after his father's execution. 'I hate it's going to happen,' 20-year-old Donald L. Gaskins told the Florence Morning News in an interview at the Florence County Detention Center. 'But maybe after it happens, I can live a normal life.' The son said that his father 'might have done a life sentence in the penitentiary, but we've also done one out here.' He said his father has been in jail for too long waiting for the execution. 'I think he's ready for it to be over,' the younger Gaskins said. 'I know our family is ready. But I still love him, and what makes it so bad is I can't be with my family."

The Item, September 5, 1991, carried a big "GASKINS ON WAY TO EXECUTION", by Bonnie L. Blackburn:

"In Carrie LeNoir's living room stands a bronze statue of the goddess of Justice, her scales unbalanced. LeNoir says she won't straighten those scales until she sees justice done. The ghost of Margaret 'Peg' Cuttino still haunts the retired Horatio postmaster, who for 21 years has been trying to determine who murdered Cuttino.

LeNoir doesn't believe that a Georgia man, William 'Junior' Pierce, who was convicted of the 13-year-old's murder in 1973, actually killed the girl. And recent letters LeNoir's received from doomed mass murderer Pee Wee Gaskins have convinced her the whole truth has yet to come out about Sumter County's most notorious murder."

Blackburn reviewed the history of the case under the subhead, "A Search Ends in Tragedy". Then, "What Does Pee Wee Know": "Despite four letters in five months from Gaskins asking LeNoir to come and hear 'the truth of that matter', South Carolina Department of Corrections officials denied LeNoir's request to meet with Gaskins before he is electrocuted Friday morning. LeNoir is convinced that if Gaskins didn't kill the daughter of the former state representative, he knows who did. 'I don't want anyone to think I'm some friend of Pee Wee's,' LeNoir said. 'I just want to see justice done. But they don't want me to ask Pee Wee any of those questions.'"

Blackburn reviewed Gaskins' confession during questioning by then-Assistant Solicitor Kenneth Young, Jr., "I killed Peg Cuttino": "Young replied at the time, 'You'd like to take credit for that — it might be more royalties for you,' referring to a book that was being written about Gaskins' murder spree during the trial. I. Byrd Parnell, Sumter County's Sheriff at the time, also discounted Gaskins' confession, saying, 'Pee Wee Gaskins did not kill Peg Cuttino. Junior Pierce killed that girl, and I'm ready to meet my God on that.' Parnell admitted that Gaskins had been investigated when Cuttino first disappeared. A worker with a roofing company in Sumter, Gaskins had been in town the day Cuttino disappeared. But both Parnell and former Sumter Police Chief L.W. Griffin said they ruled out Gaskins after interviewing his supervisor and co-workers, who accounted for Gaskins' whereabouts on the day Cuttino disappeared."

Under another subhead, "Gaskins Letters": "Gaskins, who will become the fourth person to die in the state's electric chair since the death penalty was reinstated in South Carolina in 1977, has written LeNoir several letters this year asking her to visit him in jail before he is electrocuted. 'I know who all was involved because I did see her on the very same night that she left the school that day,' Gaskins wrote in a March 22 letter to LeNoir. 'I was at that school the day she left there and I saw her get into a car that day, and it was not with Junior Pierce that she was with. — But where she went after leaving the school and how she got to the place she was is still a mystery to a lot of people, and who took her there and under what conditions no one knows but me.'

"Kenneth Young, who is now in private practice in Sumter, said he doesn't believe Gaskins killed Cuttino. But he also doubts Pierce killed her. Young was on Pierce's original defense team when the Georgia man was indicted for the murder. Ed Atkinson had been appointed to defend Pierce, and Young was an attorney in Atkinson's firm at the time. But Atkinson's firm was forced to withdraw from the case because it had represented the Cuttino family in other legal matters. Before they withdrew, Young said, he and Atkinson had developed a strong alibi defense for Pierce, finding witnesses who would swear later that Pierce had been at work in Georgia when Cuttino disappeared — a fact Young said is verified by time cards and a cancelled paycheck issued to Pierce and cashed the same day. 'That's where I, shall we say, developed the feeling that Junior Pierce had a good alibi and was in

Georgia at the time of the commission of the Peggy Cuttino case,' Young said Tuesday.

"State Representative Joe McElveen of Sumter, along with Kingstree attorneys James Connor and Bill Jenkinson, were later appointed to represent Pierce and used the same alibi witnesses for Pierce's defense. McElveen said he, too, believes Pierce was convicted wrongly. 'Junior Pierce is not an innocent man in my view, but I don't believe he killed anyone in Sumter County,' McElveen, a Sumter attorney, said. 'I don't think he was guilty of what he was convicted of, and I think we presented ample proof of that. There was at least a reasonable doubt.' McElveen said. 'It bothers me because I think there was a miscarriage of justice that was a disservice to this community and to the family.'

"On Tuesday, Central Correctional Institution Head Warden George Martin refused LeNoir's request to talk with Gaskins, saying, 'It's too close to the execution,' according to Zimmerman, spokesperson for the South Carolina Department of Corrections. Despite her disappointment over the denial, LeNoir said her quest for the truth won't die with Gaskins."

The news media went wild with stories — "GASKINS TRIES TO CHEAT HANGMAN", "DEATH PENALTY FOES PRAY, HOLD VIGIL", "SUICIDE TRY, LAST-MINUTE APPEALS FAIL", "GASKINS DESERVES EXECUTION, DEATH PENALTY SUPPORTERS SAY", "STATE'S MOST NOTORIOUS KILLER TO DIE AT 1 A.M.", etc.

"Four hours before PeeWee was to be executed, the flashing sign outside the Rock City bar off Percival Road was drawing a crowd thirsty for beer and vengeance." "Pee Wee Party", the sign said, reported Pat Butler in The State, September 6, 1991. "Inside, manager Al Kane was serving up miniature Pee Wee burgers. 'Every body here feels he deserves it,' Kane said. 'We wish they would show it live on TV. We're just sorry we've got to pay for the 10,000 volts to kill him.'"

Across town, "The voices were few but fervent Thursday night at College Place Methodist Church, where opponents of capital punishment began their death watch with prayer and song," according to Jennifer Nicholson and Lori D. Roberts in The State, September 6, 1991. "Participants read psalms aloud, meditated silently and listened to mournful folk songs performed by soloist Lynne Moldenhauer. The only time Gaskins was mentioned was during a brief testimony by Kathryn Kidd, a volunteer therapist for Death Row inmates. Kidd said Gaskins knew he would spend the rest of his life in prison, but he wanted to die a natural death. 'He wanted to die a death with dignity, rather than to be executed,'" she said.

"After the service, many participants drove to the Governor's Mansion for a candlelight vigil organized by Amnesty International. There, 'The Death Penalty is Wrong' was spelled out with candles outside the mansion, where security guards kept their own watch on the crowd. Carl Maas, state student coordinator for Amnesty International, was at the Governor's Mansion for the atmosphere. 'I don't want to be down there with the circus down at CCI. It's barbaric,' he said."

But many people did gather at the roped-off area off Broad River Road to celebrate. Bonnie Blackburn recounted in The Item, September 6, 1991, "GASKINS TERROR IS OVER": "The two-decade crime spree of Donald 'Pee Wee' Gaskins ended at 1:04 this morning, when more than 2,000 volts of electricity rushed through South Carolina's most notorious killer's body to the cheers of 'Burn in hell' from hundreds of spectators. Gaskins was pronounced dead at 1:10 a.m. — four minutes after South Carolina Department of Corrections officials stopped the current. His head shaven and smeared with conductive jelly, Gaskins was escorted into the room by four correctional officers and strapped into the state's electric chair at 12:58 a.m. Officials began the electrical current at 1:04 a.m. and stopped it two minutes later. 'We have carried out this execution with as much humanity and dignity as possible. Our equipment functioned as it was designed to function, and our people carried out their responsibilities under the law,' Doug Catoe, deputy commissioner of operations at Broad River Correctional Institution, announced immediately after the execution.

"Witnesses said Gaskins appeared nervous as he entered the room, but flashed a thumbs-up sign to his attorney, Kelly Branham of the South Carolina Death Penalty Resource Center, and reportedly mouthed the words, 'It's all right, it's all right,' to her.. Another witness, WPDE-TV reporter Sue Abrams, said Gaskins 'looked like he could be someone's kindly old grandfather when he was led in. He looked very vulnerable. You had to keep reminding yourself that he was a notorious killer.' Florence Sheriff William Barnes, who represented the victims' families as a witness, said that in the end, Gaskins did not try to avoid his punishment. 'He had said he would take it like a man, and in my opinion, he didn't fight or do anything but just that.'"

Among the many pictures The State carried were "Nine satellite trucks from Carolinas showed up," and "The body of Pee Wee Gaskins is taken to the morgue at Richland Memorial Hospital after he was executed in South Carolina's electric chair early Friday morning." The Item, September 6, 1991, showed a picture by Micheline Phelan of masses of people with raised arms, many with posters reading "Pee Wee Is Now Toast", etc., with the caption: "Death penalty supporters, above, cheer as they learn that Donald 'Pee Wee' Gaskins has been executed in the electric chair in Columbia," ... And below that an AP photo of a beautiful, sad looking young lady — "USC student Tracy Burkett, right, of Sumter, participates in a candlelight vigil in opposition to the death penalty held at the Governor's Mansion earlier in the evening."

The State, September 7, 1991, gave an AP release, "Gaskins: 'Ready to Go.'": "Donald 'Pee Wee' Gaskins left only two sentences with his attorneys as his final statement. 'I'm ready to go. Where I'm going has to be better than where I've been,' Gaskins wrote, according to John Blume of the South Carolina Death Penalty Resource Center. The article stated, "Sources told The Florence Morning News that Gaskins' body will be cremated and his ashes scattered at a later date."

CHAPTER TWENTY-FOUR

END OF AN ERA?

Pee Wee Gaskins was dead, but that did not stop the news media from meditating on his life. The September 6, 1991, Item published an editorial: "PEE WEE GASKINS MAY BE GONE, BUT HIS DEEDS WON'T BE FORGOTTEN". Bill McDonald in The State, September 12, 1991, devoted his entire column to "ONLY GASKINS KNEW ANSWERS".

Excerpts quoted Zeb Osborne, a former inmate who is a Southern Baptist minister in Columbia, and conducts a prison ministry. "Gaskins was at his best when he was doing favors for people," said Osborne. "If you put Pee Wee out in a desert with a frog and a cactus, within a couple of weeks he'd know something that the other needed, and he's get it for them. Truly, if he'd been straight, and was a business person, he'd have been a genius."

The State, October 23, 1991, published "POLITICIZING THE DEATH PENALTY", by Bruce L. Pearson, a professor at the University of South Carolina, specializing in language and culture. He is a volunteer for Amnesty International and is president of the South Carolina Coalition to Abolish the Death Penalty. He gave some good points, including, "Will the death of Gaskins be an example to other potential murderers? Yes, but not in the way one might suppose... The details of these murders will entertain the public, and the cycle of violence is guaranteed to continue."

John Allard in The State, December, 1991, wrote, "FLORENCE AREA WANTS TO FORGET PEE WEE", and The Item, March 2, 1992, showed a picture by Steve Bohnstedt, "Death of a hearse": "A hearse that belonged to Donald "Pee Wee" Gaskins is now just a piece of scrap metal. Timmons Motors sent the car packing to a steel shredder in Lexington County last week. Gaskins, a mass murderer who once lived in Sumter, was executed last year." Shown with the hearse were employees Butch Tolson, Bobby Ires and Christine Timmons. So, this should end the era, but will it?

Now, I'd like to share some personal thoughts on the Pee Wee Gaskins era. I try to read The Item and The State every day as thoroughly as possible, but had not taken a lot of interest in the Gaskins news which was being published about the Prospect murders in the mid-seventies, as I was a very busy person, but my life took a different path after I received a phone call. On the night of April 25, 1977, while preparing supper, Jerry Adams (then an Item reporter) called to ask if I had heard "the news". "What news?", I replied. "There's been a confession on the Peg Cuttino murder," he excitedly told me. I was in a state of shock briefly, then gained control to ask questions. He related the Gaskins confession while on the stand in Newberry. April 27, 1977, I received a letter written by William J. Pierce, Jr.:

Dear Mrs. LeNoir,
I am excited at the Good News I received from Mr. Joseph T.

McElveen, Jr., by telephone on Tuesday afternoon. He informed me that Miss Cuttino's real killer had been identified, and that he had been working in Sumter, S.C., during December 18, 1970. Mr. McElveen gave me his name, but I was so proud of the news that I forgot it later on. I was filled with joy at receiving this news, and knew that our Lord Jesus Christ had answered our prayers..."

On February 20, 1978, William Pierce wrote to Donald Gaskins: "Dear Mr. Gaskins, I pray that you will take time to read my letter in regards to the case of Miss Margaret 'Peg' Cuttino, which I'm serving a life sentence. I am aware of your confession in open court, and feel that it was an Act of God's Great Work, due to the Praying for His Holy Help through Jesus Christ. In 1971, I was charged with the murder of Miss Cuttino, but only after I was beat, burned, and tortured by the law officers of Georgia..."

On February 21, 1978, William Pierce, Jr., wrote:

Dear Mrs. Burleson,
I received your most welcome letter this past Friday, and was pleased to hear from you... I just wrote to Chief Deputy Sheriff, Mr. T.L. McJunkins who plans to study for the Ministry, and requested his help in bringing forth the 'REAL TRUTH' in the Cuttino case. He is in a position to get direct answers, and open doors that would otherwise be closed concerning this case. I can only Pray that he will help me since Mr. Parnell refused. I also wrote to Mr. Gaskins, and 'Thank You' for sending me his address in Columbia, S.C. I know he will welcome any letters as I do, and maybe through the Grace of God, the Real Truth will come out.

On February 26, 1978, Donald Gaskins wrote:

Dear Mr. Pierce,
Will answer your letter that I received on Friday. I have been expecting you to write for some time. I had word that your attorneys wanted to talk with me .

March 9, 1978, Mr. Pierce wrote to me:

Dear Mrs. LeNoir,
I received a letter from Mr. Donald H. Gaskins, Columbia, S.C. and he sent me some information on the Cuttino murder case...

I sent his letter to my attorney, Mr. Joseph T. McElveen, Jr., for his files and record, and requested for him to show you his letter if you wished to see it. Mr.

Gaskins stated that...

On March 14, 1978, I wrote: "Dear Mr. Gaskins, We think about you, and discuss your situation very often, and hope that we might be able to talk with you soon. I was glad to hear from William J. Pierce, Jr., in a letter yesterday, that you two are corresponding now...".

I received a letter, written March 16, 1978, from Donald H. Gaskins: "Dear Mrs. LeNoir, Received your letter today. I did write to Mr. Pierce, and since then I have received some pressure letting me know that I had better lay off the Cuttino matter. This past Tuesday Agent Tom Henderson came to see me. ... Well anyway, he made it clear that I am to say I had nothing to do with the Cuttino Case and the Horry cases. I am supposed to agree with them on what they say and nothing else if I want to survive. I'm sorry at this time that things are working like this, and by the way, he accused you and me of writing to each other. This was on Tuesday, March 14, 1978. At that time you had not sent no letter to me as far as I know...".

I cite the above letters, and call your special attention to the dates, which are very important. The State, April 18, 1978, told "GASKINS PLEADS GUILTY TODAY — AVOIDS POSSIBLE DEATH SENTENCE", by Jerry Dyer: "Donald Henry 'Pee Wee' Gaskins, Monday issued a four-page eight-point statement which said Gaskins 'would enter a guilty plea if the State of South Carolina would not seek the death penalty against him'. Gaskins who already is serving two life sentences for murder, was given the truth serum sodium amytal Monday at a Florence hospital and interrogated by Summerford, Florence County Sheriff William C. Barnes and agents of the South Carolina Law Enforcement Division. The truth serum, administered by a local psychiatrist and sanctioned by Gaskins and his attorneys Grady Query and John K. Grisso, was used so that officials could determine whether previous statements made by Gaskins were true. 'We believe we have the truth,' Query said, and Grisso nodded in agreement. Earlier Summerford and Barnes noted that they too were satisfied the lengthy sessions with Gaskins in conference and under the sodium amytal had reached the bottom line in the twisted Gaskins case.

"According to Summerford, their questioning revealed that Gaskins had no part in the death of Margaret 'Peg' Cuttino, daughter of a former state legislator, or that of some others he had named in previous court hearings were actually accomplices in murders with which he had been charged. 'I'm sold on this sodium amytal,' Summerford said."

The State, April 20, 1978, carried "LAWMAKER WANTS PLEA BARGAINING INVESTIGATION", by The Associated Press: " A state lawmaker said Wednesday he will seek an investigation of the plea bargaining that allowed Donald H. 'Pee Wee' Gaskins, a confessed mass murderer, to receive life prison terms. Rep. Ralph K. Anderson, a Democrat whose Florence County district is not far from the area where most of the killings occurred, said he was dismayed that 'the death penalty law now in effect in this state was simply ignored' by Solicitor T. Kenneth Summerford. Anderson, an attorney, said in an interview the case was a classic example of a person who has exhibited a vicious attitude against society but escapes the death penalty'. Anderson said he will introduce a resolution to ask the state attorney general's office to investigate the negotiations between Gaskins' attorneys and Summerford.

"'The prosecutor should have sought the death penalty in order to test the state's new capital punishment law, which was passed last June,' the legislator said. 'Other persons charged under the law later will point to the Gaskins case as proof that South Carolina does not apply the death penalty evenly,' he argued."

That sounded good, and we expected to hear something positive on his investigation on what we considered to be questionable court procedures. However, before this was accomplished, he was awarded a Circuit Court Judgeship!

Excerpts from the "TRUTH SERUM" which Gaskins underwent, as recorded by Peggy C. Fowler, Court Reporter, follow:

> *...And I figured by going out and saying a lot of that would get a lot of the pressure off of me and everything...*
> *Q. You said pressure was on you, by whom?*
> *A. Well, different people.*
> *Q. You better come across.*
> *A. Well, uh, it could do no good either way. It could only maybe cause hardships.*
> *Q. That's for us to decide. Tell me why you said that you killed the Cuttino girl and you didn't do it.*
> *A. Well, I felt that if I went into it and said I killed her and everything, that would take some pressure off of Pierce. Pierce was wanting to get out from under that and uh...*
> *Q. Did you talk with Pierce?*
> *A. I got letters from him.*
> *Q. Did you save letters?*
> *A. I think I got one of them still up there. Yeh, I know I got some.*
> *Q. In one letter he asked you to take the blame?*
> *A. No, in that letter he just said that he heard that I had copped out to it, and one thing and another.*
> *Q. Copped what?*
> *A. Pled guilty in doing that and everything.*
> *Q. You got the letter then after you said you'd done it?*
> *A. I got two letters but I tore them and destroyed them.*
> *Q. You never tore up anything in your life Pee Wee.*
> *A. Yes, I have too. I get rid of a lot of stuff.*
> *Q. Now, tell me why and lets quit beating around the bush.*
> *A. Well, Mr. Summerford, some things that...*
> *Q. You ain't in a position to hold back some things. Now, lets get it straight. You ain't in no position to hold back nothing.*
> *A. Well, I told you I'm not guilty of it. I had nothing to do with the Cuttino.*
> *Q. I didn't ask you that. I want to know why you did it.*
> *A. I figured it would help me.*
> *Q. Why?*
> *A. Well, I figured if I come up with enough to put it in there to make it look like it do, why I could make some kind of deal. I just felt that if I come up with something strong enough that I*

could make some kind of a deal.

Q. *All right, let me ask you then. Did you hear from Pierce, did he ask you to do it?*

A. *Mr. Summerford, I wish I had brought the letters and let you look at them.*

Q. *Just answer my question.*

A. *I got letters from Mr. Pierce.*

Q. *Did he ask you to do it?*

A. *In one of them, yes.*

Q. *And you tore it up?*

A. *Yes sir, I destroyed it.*

Q. *Why?*

A. *Because if it got out it would have blew everything that I was hoping to work out.*

Q. *Well, why did you keep one letter?*

A. *To show that I had received something from Mr. Pierce and that letter there, why it stated about the Cuttino case and everything.*

Q. *All right, sir, same thing true down to the death in Horry County?*

A. *That's right.*

Q. *Did you get a letter from that man too?*

A. *No sir.*

Q. *Did anybody ask you...*

A. *I talked with him.*

Q. *You talked with him personally?*

A. *Yes.*

Q. *They let you get to him and talk with him?*

A. *Yes sir.*

Q. *And let him talk to you?*

A. *Yes sir.*

Q. *At CCI?*

A. *Yes sir.*

Q. *All right, now how about the police officer in Sumter County?*

A. *I have already told Mr. Henderson and them that that was just a made up statement.*

Q. *Why?*

A. *Well, I just made it up.*

Q. *Well, you must have had a reason. What was your thinking?*

A. *Well, I had quite a few enemies in the police force over there, I figured enemies.*

Q. *That's the reason you did it? That's the only reason?*

A. *Well, like I say, I had some that I figured didn't treat me right over there. But I come back to Mr. Henderson and told Mr. Henderson since then that all that was wrong, that there wasn't nothing to it.*

Q. Well, really and truly now, when you get down to it Pee Wee, you really haven't told us as much today then as you told me the two days that we were in my office. Isn't that correct? Isn't that a fair statement?

A. A lot of the stuff I told you in there wasn't true.

Q. Why did you not tell me the truth then?

A. Because I didn't intend to go through with it.

Q. Why not?

A. Under the circumstances that we was under, I didn't figure that you was gonna go through with what you said. Now, I'm being honest with you there. I didn't figure you'd do it. I figured you was lying to me. Now, to be honest about it. That's exactly what I figured that you was lying to me.

Q. Well, are you involved, either directly or indirectly, in any other killings or murders in the State of South Carolina other...

But, we knew that Gaskins was not telling the truth, even if he was supposed to be under the influence of the truth serum law officers claimed to have so much confidence in. We've always figured it was only a trick to get Gaskins to deny the Cuttino murder.

The Item, April 18, 1978, told "McLEOD UNSURE OF PROSECUTIONS": "Despite 12th Circuit Solicitor T. Kenneth Summerford's insistence that Donald H. Gaskins will never face the death penalty in South Carolina, 3rd Circuit Solicitor R. Kirk McLeod is not so sure he agreed to such a deal. At a press conference in Florence Monday afternoon, Summerford said he had conferred with McLeod and two other solicitors to get their assurance that Gaskins would not get the death penalty if he told all about his involvement in South Carolina murders. ' discussed the matter at length with each of these Solicitors, because they had to participate because of the proposition that we would not seek the death penalty,' Summerford said in a prepared statement. McLeod acknowledged he talked with Summerford last week, but he said he has not been appraised of recent negotiations. 'I couldn't tell you a thing about it except what I saw in the paper this morning,' he said. McLeod said he and Summerford have not discussed specific cases and he has not seen or issued any arrest warrants. He indicated he would contact Summerford in the next day or so to see what has transpired since they first discussed the deal. Summerford said at the press conference that Gaskins would be charged in connection with the deaths of three Sumter County women — Patricia Ann Alsbrook, Janice Faye Kirby and a yet unidentified body found beside a drainage ditch in southeastern Sumter County.

The State, June 15, 1978, told the news "Twelfth Circuit Solicitor T. Kenneth Summerford of Florence, abandoning the courtroom in a bid for the legislature, was defeated by D. Malloy McEachin of Florence, son of a family court judge. Summerford was directly involved in the controversial plea bargaining arrangement in which Donald Henry 'Pee Wee' Gaskins received seven consecutive life sentences in return for guilty pleas to the Prospect mass murders."

Well, "law enforcement" thought they had played it smart to get Gaskins to deny the Cuttino murder while under the truth serum, but we knew he lied about William Pierce asking him to confess, as that confession was made April 25, 1977; and the aforementioned letters prove there was no communication between those two prior to February 20, 1978. Don Zalenka, of the Attorney General's office, even accused me of asking Gaskins to make the confession, but I had absolutely no communication with Gaskins until months after the confession.

I can remember, as a child, hearing my mother say several times:

There is so much good in the worst of us,
And so much bad in the best of us,
That it ill behooves any of us
To find fault with the rest of us.

(author unknown)

The poem is listed in my book of poems under the heading "Charity", and we can't extend much charity to Gaskins, but I do want to give special credit.

On June 26, 1978, he wrote: "Dear Mrs. LeNoir, I'm sorry not to have wrote to you sooner, but there have been some things that has kept me from doing so. As you will recall back in March of this year, I wrote you a letter concerning a certain agent coming to see me and letting me know what I had better do about certain things. Well as it turned out I did as I was told, and I got from under the death penalty. Mrs. LeNoir I have no choice but to do as I have been told to do. Because if I don't I can be tried for the death penalty and believe me I don't want that. By the way here is the first letter that I received from Mr. Pierce and it was in February of 1978. I would like to get this back or a copy of it at least. This will show anyone that when we first started to write to each other..."

I really appreciated Gaskins' honesty with me, and I believe he would have told me the truth, if I could have talked with him before his execution. Too bad we didn't get to talk!!

CHAPTER TWENTY-FIVE

HOW INVOLVED WAS GASKINS?

Although Solicitor T. Kenneth Summerford thought that questioning Gaskins under influence of "truth serum" and his denial of the Cuttino murder would end the matter, it only added fuel to the fire of discontent with Sumter County citizens. What right did he have to be interfering with the legal affairs of 3rd Circuit Solicitor McLeod when he was 12th Circuit Solicitor? Was it a deal between the two solicitors? McLeod acknowledged that he talked with Summerford the week before, and what would be his concern with the Prospect murders. Anyway, Gaskins was honest enough to admit that he had lied about the Cuttino murder while under the "truth serum", as shown in his letter of June 26, 1978.

And then, when Mr. Pierce finally got a hearing on January 29, 1985, on the Gaskins confession to the Cuttino murder, Judge Ernest A. Finney, Jr., presiding judge, Third Circuit, issued his Order of Dismissal on February 21, 1985. "This Court finds that the Applicant's presentation failed to meet his burden. While it is undisputed that Gaskins was working in Sumter on December 18, 1970, his April, 1977 statement is not 'as such as would probably change the result if a new trial was had,' nor 'is material to be the issue of guilt or innocence.' The testimony of Christmas, as corroborated by the work records, reveals that Gaskins was working or was at the shop during the critical time of the Cuttino abduction."

But the transcript, as recorded by Nancy T. Wilkes, circuit court reporter, tells a different version:

CROSS EXAMINATION BY MR. DAVIS:

Q. Mr. Christmas, did you see Mr. Gaskins with all the people that he killed?

A. I never saw him kill no one that I know of.

Q. Mr. Christmas, that day, December 18th, you went to lunch at what time?

A. 12 o'clock.

Q. Are you saying that from here?

A. No, uh huh. I always went to lunch from 12 to 1.

Q. Okay, so as far as the times that you went to lunch and the times you went to School District #17 and McLaughlin Ford, you just telling that from memory. That's not on those records you looking at, right?

A. No Sir, the best I can remember. See, the first record, which is McLaughlin Ford, the first half hour I was in the shop, and 2 hours at McLaughlin Ford. Then we came back to the shop after we left McLaughlin, we came back in the shop.

Q. 8335 is back in the shop?

A. No, 8335 is where we went to the school district after we came back to the shop. We worked in the shop the balance of the morning. I remember that. Then we went to school district warehouse the first thing that afternoon.

Q. Okay, so that all of this isn't on there, so that doesn't mean anything?

A. No.

Q. So you didn't necessarily go, yours is different from Pee Wee's?

A. He kept his pretty well in order.

Q. Okay, yours starts with 8405, both of you leaving, he goes to 1138 and you go to 8335, right?

A. He was working on one job in the shop; and we was working on another job.

Q. Okay, so y'all wouldn't have necessarily been with each other at that point, would you?

A. Well, both of us was in the shop, I could see all the fellows at the shop.

Q. And then he goes to 8335 and you go to 8414 and he goes to 8414 and you go to 1138?

A. Well, 1138, we were both working on the same jobs.

Q. So, what I am saying is the order that these are mentioned on these little old cards doesn't mean anything?

A. Well, Pee Wee listed his jobs pretty well, he kept his in his pocket and kept up with it pretty well.

Q. And you are testifying then that as far as the times and where you went out of what you recall or your memory, right?

A. The best I can remember.

Q. Do you remember where y'all went on December 17, 1970?

A. We worked part of the day at Campbell Soup and we were working a lot of work at Campbell Soup Factory.

Q. How about November 17, 1970?

A. I don't remember back there. I don't remember everything about where we worked.

Q. How about December 28, 1970?

A. No, I probably wasn't even working, I might have been hunting then.

Q. And you knocked off at least an hour earlier or a half hour earlier on the 18th than Pee Wee Gaskins did, is that correct?

A. Yes sir.

Q. And you left at 3:30 and Pee Wee stayed at Fort Roofing?

A. Right.

Q. You don't know how long he stayed as far as your own personal knowledge of whether he stayed there or not?

A. No, I sure don't.

*Q. You don't know where he went when you knocked off work that
day, do you?*
A. No, I sure don't.
Q. Or where he was that night?
A. No.
Q. Or where he was while you were at lunch, do you?
A. No.

MR. DAVIS: Thank you sir.

Also, Mr. William T. Fort, general manager of Fort Roofing and Sheet Metal
Works, Inc., testified:

CROSS EXAMINATION BY MR. DAVIS

*Q. So there is a half hour there that these records would show
that Mr. Christmas and Mr. Gaskins were not together, is that
correct?*
A. Yes sir.

Attorney T. H. Davis, III, filed a very impressive Petition for Writ of Certiorari
in March, 1985, in the Supreme Court in Mr. Pierce's behalf; but, of course, it was
denied. Chief Justice J. B. Ness signed it, with the notation "Associate Justice
Finney, Not participating". It would be inconceivable that Justice Ness could do
otherwise, or he would not be practicing what he preached — Loyalty to Friends —
and, after all, Judge Finney was the newest member of the South Carolina Supreme
Court.

But, in spite of all the efforts to uphold William Pierce's conviction and keep
Gaskins' reputation clean in the Cuttino murder, we strongly believe he was
involved. Rumor has it that he said he got the body while it was still warm, and
disposed of it. We have evidence to support that rumor. We don't believe that
Gaskins had her on December 18, 1970, nor for several days thereafter. We believe
that she was in and out of Pauline Graber's mobile home near Manchester State
Forest, in back of retired Sheriff's Deputy Sidney Geddings' home. Mr. Geddings
told me that cars were going in and out regularly to that mobile home during the
holidays, although Mrs. Graber had gone to England, and left her home with a real
estate agency, in hopes of getting some rent from it while she was gone. On the day
Peg's body was found, it was discovered that the home had been broken into -- beer
cans scattered, blood on the wall, etc.

Mrs. Graber went to England in September, 1970, and when she returned in
January, 1971, she had to order new mattresses. In an affidavit, signed by Samuel T.
Dees, he stated:

*I do hereby certify that during January, 1971, I was employed by
Unclaimed Freight of Sumter, S. C. and did deliver to the mobile
home of Pauline Graber, Wedgefield, S. C., two sets of double bed*

mattresses. On my arrival I found Mrs. Graber and her sister burning mattresses which had been removed from the beds. Upon entering the trailer I found that a panel had been cut from one of the walls, and that dusting material was on the telephone and parts of the trailer. In answer to my question, Mrs. Graber stated that this was left by law enforcement officials who were investigating the Peg Cuttino murder case and which could have had a connection.

That mobile home was in the vicinity of where Peg's body was found on December 30, 1970.

Here, I want to review portions of Earl Williams' testimony. Mr. Earl Williams, being first duly sworn, testified as follows:

DIRECT EXAMINATION BY SOLICITOR McLEOD

Q. *Now, Earl, speak out so all these ladies and gentlemen on the jury and the defense council can hear what you've got to say. Your name is Earl Williams?*

A. *Yes, sir.*

BY THE COURT: *Talk loud.*

Q. *Now you'll have to talk a little louder.*

BY THE COURT; *The gentleman in the corner must hear you, Sonny. See the gentleman in that corner over there?*

BY WITNESS; *Yes, sir.*

BY THE COURT; *Well talk loud enough for him to hear you.*

Q. *Where do you live, Earl?*

A. *Wedgefield.*

Q, *That's in Sumter County?*

A. *Yes, sir.*

Q. *Calling your attention to December of 1970, were you in Sumter County?*

A. *Yes, sir.*

Q. *Where were you and what were you doing?*

A. *I was out, me and my father was out in the woods, and I was shooting at a squirrel nest, and he was cutting wood.*

Q. *What did he have with him, if anything?*

A. *He had an axe.*

Q. *And you had what?*

A. *Twenty-two rifle.*

Q. *And did you see anything that caught your attention while you were there?*

A. *Yes, sir, I seen a white station wagon and thought it was a game warden, but my father said it was alright, so I went ahead and started shooting; and I saw a guy standing up behind the station wagon.*

Q. *And who was that guy?*

A. *That one sitting over there (indicating).*

Q. *The defendant, William J. Pierce, Jr.?*

A. *Yes, sir.*

CROSS EXAMINATION BY MR. McELVEEN

Q. *Earl, how old are you now?*

A. *Fourteen.*

Q. *Fourteen?*

A. *Yes, sir.*

Q. *So at the time this occurred, you were twelve years of age, is that correct, sir?*

A. *Yes, sir.*

Q. *And I believe you stated on direct examination that the car that you saw was a white station wagon?*

A. *Yes, sir.*

Q. *Do you know the make of that car?*

A. *It was a Ford.*

Q. *Ford?*

A. *Yes, sir.*

Q. *Now do you recall what day of the week it was that you happened to see, make this observation?*

A. *Saturday.*

Q. *It was Saturday?*

A. *Yes, sir.*

Q. *Are you certain of the day?*

A. *It was the 19th.*

Q. *You are sure it was a Saturday?*

A. *I —*

Q. *Now I talked with you previously about this matter, have I not?*

A. *Yes, sir.*

Q. *At that time did you not tell me that it was either Saturday or Sunday; you didn't know, you weren't sure?*

A. *Yes, sir.*

Q. *And, of course, you weren't approached about this matter for some time, were you?*

A. *Yes, sir.*

Q. *How long was it before the police came to question you about the observation which you made?*

A. *About a week later, not much, not too long, maybe not quite a week.*

So, Earl Williams was a very important witness for the state, even if his testimony was in direct conflict with Sheriff Parnell's testimony on Pierce's confession to the murder while driving a maroon Pontiac. As God would have it, soon after our investigation started, we were given a document:

"CHANGE OF AUTOMOBILE ENDORSEMENT. This endorsement is for attachment to Policy No. AR 715348, issued to Donald Henry Gaskins by United States Fire Insurance Company. In consideration of the adjustment of premiums herein stated, it is understood and agreed that the following automobile is included in the coverage of this policy effective 12:01 A.M. 4-11-72. A 1965 Olds., serial number 35269E172559 and 1962 Sta. Wag., serial number 2 A 22V165884. ASSIGNED RISK dw was on the paper, and was signed by Authorized Representative George G. Saudy."

The 1965 Oldsmobile was the black hearse Gaskins was driving at that time. I took pictures of it after I got a call telling me where it was, and the last license plate issued by the Highway Department was in 1972. This was after the Prospect murder era, and when I went, there were only what appeared to be black bags of trash inside, but when I took an Item reporter out a few days later to see it, he jumped "about a foot high." I got out to look, and someone had placed a couple inside — a blond mannequin with her head cut off, and a man in military uniform.

The 1962 station wagon really "opened a can of worms" for us. We obtained a book to decipher the serial number code, and found the "2" designates model year 1962; the "A" designates the assembly plant, Atlanta; the third and fourth digits designate series and body type, Falcon four-door station wagon.

Earl Williams had told that the station wagon had round tail lights, so I searched my old magazines until I found what we were looking for — a Ford ad in a late-1961 *LIFE Magazine*. The picture of the Falcon Squire showed the round tail lights, and the ad stated: "The Falcon Squire combines the elegance of the Country Squire with Falcon savings — the only compact wagon of its kind." This clue seemed to be an answer to prayer, and Bernard Shirar began a search for the history of this particular car. His search revealed that Ford Motor Company sold the car on June 20, 1962, to McInnis Motor Sales, Inc., Rockingham, North Carolina, who sold it to Witcher Frank Burton, Route 1, Laurel Hill, North Carolina, on July 14, 1962. Certificate of Title was issued to Earl Wayne Freemen on Feb. 7, 1967, and on September 17, 1970, the white Ford station wagon was brought into Sumter, South Carolina. Beside the signature on Assignment of Title from North Carolina was written Donald H. Gaskins. So Gaskins apparently brought the car down for Irick Motors, on Manning Avenue. On May 7, 1971, Irick Motors sold the station wagon to John Kolb, who then sold it to Richard S. Bartlett the same day. Certificate of Title was issued to Donald H. Gaskins, 417 Manning Avenue, Sumter, South Carolina, on March 23, 1972. On July 19, 1972, Donald H. Gaskins signed Assignment of Title to Marion C. Broadway. On May 25, 1984, Gladys S. Taylor, Motor Vehicle Manager, Title Section, wrote, "To whom it may concern: Copy of Certificate of title #6113688 is on film at the Department of Highways and Public Transportation, and may be located in Box #78. This title covers a 1962 Ford, Serial

Number 2A22U165885."

Why have we gone to all this trouble to do this research? We believe this was the white Ford station wagon Earl and his father saw. Remember, he said either Saturday or Sunday, which probably was December 26th or 27th, which would coincide with the autopsy report: "It is the opinion of these prosecters with the information found in this protocol that the deceased had been dead at least five days prior to the discovery of her body." A theory is that Gaskins stopped between picking up and delivering the car, and had an extra switch key made, and living nearby, could use the car any time he desired, with or without permission. Theory also dictates that the burns on Peg's body were caused by hydro fluosilicic acid, the label of which carried the warning: "Toxic, irritating, corrosive material. Causes severe burns on skin and mucous membranes." This label was found in Gaskins' house, and given to us. Rumor is that he volunteered to dispose of waste acid from Fort Roofing and Sheet Metal works.

I'm inclined to agree with Kenneth Young in a statement to Bonnie Blackburn as recorded in The Item September 5, 1991, "... said he doesn't believe Gaskins killed Cuttino. But he also doubts Pierce killed her." Who, then, did it? Names of several young men from prominent families have continued to float around through the years as being involved, and this is a terrible injustice to the innocent, as they can't all be guilty, if, indeed, any of them are. Too bad Gaskins was not allowed to talk to us in his final days.

CHAPTER TWENTY-SIX

EARL WILLIAMS

Earl Williams' testimony at the Cuttino murder trial apparently helped convict William J. Pierce for the crime, but it seemed for a while that he might have had second thoughts about the trial. Two girls from Wedgefield, who said they were friends of Earl came to my house the early part of 1976, and said Earl wanted to talk with me. I told them I'd be glad to talk with him at any time — just give me a call. He called once, but called back to cancel before we met. A few weeks later, my husband and I were out riding on Sunday afternoon on our way to Poinsett State Park, and saw Earl in his yard. We stopped, and he came over to the car. I asked if he'd like to talk, and all he would say is, "That case is closed." So, we continued on our way. A few weeks later, I got another call that he wanted to talk, so I picked up an acquaintance in Manning, Chip Gettys, who went into the garage on Mill Street, where he was working, and Earl came out to the car. I had pictures of Gaskins and Pierce side by side, and said, "Earl, if you had seen pictures of both of these men before the trial, could you have sworn that it was Pierce you saw in the woods that day?" We compared similarities in the way their hair was combed, and facial features, and he said, "I don't know, to tell you the truth."

I didn't hear anything else from Earl until February, 1979. Ray and Sue Hamilton had met him in a Manning restaurant, and they started talking about the Cuttino case. He told them he'd like to talk with me, so they arranged for us to meet at their house on the Wedgefield Road on Saturday, February 10, at 2:00 pm. I went, but Earl didn't show up. They saw him again the next week. He said he couldn't make it that Saturday, but wanted to meet the next Saturday, February 17, 3:30 pm, at the Hamilton home. Saturday morning, I received a collect call from Earl, 435-2994, wanting to change the meeting place to the old Williams store on highway 261, south of Wedgefield. I agreed to that. A few minutes later, I got another collect call, wanting to know how much we were going to pay him. "We're not paying you anything," I replied. "Mr. Hamilton said you'd pay me," he said. "Oh, no, I'm sure Mr. Hamilton didn't promise you any pay," I said. "Well, just forget it then," he said, and hung up. I was later told by a law enforcement man that I was lucky I didn't get caught in that scheme. It was a set-up to try to catch me giving a bribe. Earl was to be wired, and a SLED cameraman was to get pictures of our meeting.

Well, the Hamiltons had seen Earl in the Manning restaurant several weeks prior to this, and he told them about the reward money he received for solving the Cuttino murder. They asked how much he got, and who gave it to him. He said he got enough to buy a used pickup, and put the rest in the bank to save until he got married. He said he went down the street in Sumter in front of the hospital, and if you made a left turn, you'd go by the Post Office, but you didn't go by the Post Office, but go a little further on down the street. He said the lawyer's name was something like a mule. On March 22, 1979, I went in to talk with Art Bahnmuller of the Bryan Bahnmuller King Goldman and McElveen Law Firm at 17 East Calhoun. Art knew nothing about a reward, but called to see if the firm had a file on Earl Williams. He cautioned me that there could be another Earl Williams. But, when he opened the file folder and saw the detective magazines, he knew that was what we were looking for. He discovered that Howard P. King had handled the transaction, so I made an appointment to meet with King the next day, as he was in court in Manning at that time. King told me that the reward money, $5,000, was paid November 8, 1976, by one man, and it came through the Sheriff's office. King got $1,250 (25%) for handling the transaction. Mrs. Nettie Geddings told me that Earl got converted during that time, and asked the Reverend Harold Kirkland, of First Baptist Church, to pray for him. I have not seen or heard anything from Earl since then.

CHAPTER TWENTY-SEVEN

THE "PEG" COAT

At an April 5, 1973, hearing in Sumter to determine whether or not William J. Pierce, Jr., would get a new trial on the Cuttino murder conviction, Solicitor Kirk McLeod asked, "As a result of talking to them (the LeNoirs), did y'all pursue any further investigation in the neighborhood?" Detective Tommie Mims responded, "We did. The remainder of the afternoon, we interviewed other people in the Horatio area, and checked all known clubhouses that the young people usually congregated at, as well as abandoned farmhouses." "And you found nothing?" the solicitor asked. "Nothing. No, sir," Mims stated.

That was Sunday, December 20, 1970, and they certainly would have searched Horatio Community Center, the area's only clubhouse. However, some interesting news followed. The following is an affidavit by Laura Shannon and Frances Perry:

> We do hereby certify that we have been working in the Horatio Community Building almost every month since it was built in 1950. Soon after Horatio Grange was organized, also in 1950, we were hired to clean the building, cook, and serve the Grange supper, and clean up afterwards, for each meeting. We further certify that on January 19, 1971, when we went in to clean the building, we found a large girl's blue coat in a chair on the stage. We did not move it, but when Mrs. S.G. LeNoir, Director of Women's Activities for the Grange, and under whose direction we were working, came in, we called her attention to the coat. She said she did not know to whom it belonged, but it must have been left by someone who was at the Grange Christmas Party, which was held on December 15, 1970. As there were 4-H boys and girls, Junior Grangers, and Boy Scouts at that party, we also thought that someone would come back and pick it up. We are also positive that it was not there when we cleaned up for the Christmas Party. It stayed on the stage from then on, and was there when we last served supper for the Grange in November, 1974. Mrs. LeNoir told us that she has taken the coat in for investigation, as it was discovered that PEG was on the lapel.

An affidavit signed by W.M. LeNoir follows:

> I do hereby certify that the enclosed coat has been in the Horatio Community Building ever since I was appointed Magistrate for this district in 1971. Since it is blue, and the Boy Scouts meet in the building each Monday night, I assumed that it belonged to one of them. As I am remodeling the building, I called the coat to

the attention of Carrie B. LeNoir, custodian for the building, so that the owner might be contacted, if possible. Upon close inspection, it was discovered that the coat has PEG monogrammed on the lapel. Mrs. LeNoir took the coat for further investigation.

I contacted Jack Truluck and Hugh Munn, reporters for The State newspaper, who were doing a grand job in keeping the public informed on developments in this very bizarre case. They, along with a State photographer, came over and worked on a news article that we expected to be released in due time. They volunteered to take the PEG coat on to the Sheriff's office, so I gave it to them. Nothing was published, and we heard nothing further. So, after a lapse in time, I contacted The State, and Hugh Munn told me that they didn't publish the article because we all were going to be sued. Meanwhile, they said that Sheriff Parnell said that the coat did not belong to Peg Cuttino, so I asked for the coat. They said that Sheriff Parnell wanted to keep it for evidence, but I insisted that if they said it was not Peg Cuttino's coat, I wanted it back. It took a court order from Judge Frank Epps for the return of the coat. So, in April, 1977, I ran a big ad in The Item and The Sumter News:

WANTED: The girl named 'PEG' who left her coat in Horatio Community Center between December 20, 1970, and January 19, 1971, to come pick it up. By a Court Order, we got it back from the Sheriff's Office, and owner may claim it by proof of ownership and paying for this ad. Mrs. S.G. LeNoir, 'Four Oaks', Horatio, S.C. Phone 499-4023.

On October 27, 1980, during depositions prior to the three million dollar suit James Cuttino had filed against The Item, Verna Moore, and me — after a gruelling session of questions directed to me — I had my chance to question Mr. Cuttino.

EXAMINATION BY MRS. LENOIR

Q. Mr. Cuttino, are you aware that Earl Williams, State's witness for the trial of William Pierce, Jr., received $5,000.00 to testify in this trial?

MR. RICE (Cuttino's Attorney): I object and instruct the witness not to answer the question — it's totally irrelevant and has absolutely nothing to do with this case.

Q. My point is to prove that my story is connected with my activities and is not fraud. I think this is very relevant to the case because certainly it is a — in fact, I have several more questions in that category I would like to ask. They are relevant in the case.

MR. RICE: Mrs. LeNoir, would you agree to read those questions as you have them down and we'll —

Q. Yes. Are you aware that Earl Williams that testified at the

William Pierce, Jr., trial received $5,000.00 for his testimony? Did you consider this hush money or a reward? Did you pay this money? If you did not, do you know who did or his name, and why was it not paid after Pierce's conviction instead of waiting until 1976, November 8th? And why did Earl have to bring a suit to collect it and using over $1,200.00 of it for legal fees to Howard P. King? Are you aware that Earl said his conscience bothered him that he had helped to convict an innocent man?

MR. RICE: I'm going to instruct him not to answer any of those questions.

Q. I've heard rumors to the effect that you've been told you'll be killed if you reveal who really killed Peg. Is this true?

MR. RICE: Answer the question.

A. My life has never been threatened by anybody. And I know who killed Peg.

Q. Have your lawyers received a copy of the 1977 Grand Jury hearings?

A. I have no knowledge of whether they have or not.

Q. Also, we have received information that you have received monies from authors of various stories in national detective magazines, is this true?

A. That is as fallacious as a lot of other things.

Q. That's the very reason I asked the question. And I have one final question and I'll be through. Have you seen this coat before?

A. My daughter would not have come within twenty feet of that coat, because of its filth. I've seen it. They brought it into my office. And that is not her coat. And I can tell you it's not her coat. I've answered that question a dozen times.

MRS. LENOIR: That's all I have.

But others had different recollections of the blue coat. In an affidavit signed by Mattie M. Logan, she states:

I do hereby certify that I am the mother of Jessie Ruth Logan Judy, one of the victims of the Prospect Murders in which Pee Wee Gaskins, James Knox Judy, and LeRoy Neeley were involved. I further certify that Peg Cuttino was a friend of Jessie Ruth's, and had visited in my home, when I lived on the Boulevard Road near Britton's Siding, several times prior to her death. Also, my daughter, Jessie Ruth, told me prior to her disappearance on June 20, 1974, that Pee Wee Gaskins had told her that he killed Peg Cuttino and Patty Allsbrooks. She also said she witnessed the murder of Dorene Hope Dempsey Geddings. I tried to get Jessie Ruth to stop seeing Pee Wee Gaskins, but she would not listen to me. I also believe that the blue coat with PEG on it which was found in Horatio Community Center belonged to Peg Cuttino, as she had worn the blue coat to my house.

Also, an affidavit by Darlene Floyd Logan:

I do hereby certify that I was a friend of Peg Cuttino at Alice Drive Junior High. We were in the same study hall, and we talked frequently. I have seen the blue coat with PEG on it, and definitely remember it as belonging to Peg Cuttino.

Some time soon after the coat, which had been laid aside at the back of the Community Center stage and was discovered to have the PEG monogram, Joy Reis, whom I knew as a beautician who worked in a shop I patronized, called just to chat and to ask how "the Cuttino Case" was coming along. She was aware that we were trying to get a new trial for Pierce. I told her about the PEG coat, and she immediately said she remembered the coat quite well. She worked at the Broad Street Pharmacy during the 60's and 70's, so when I got the coat back, I called for an appointment to talk with her. Before I took the coat out of the bag, she started talking and describing the coat — "Now, it didn't have flat buttons, like on my blouse here, but rounded, either plastic or wood, with a design on them." The minute I showed her the coat, she said, "That's it." She said Peg frequently walked from her home on Mason Croft to the Drug Store, located in the vicinity of Highland Avenue and Willow Drive, on Broad Street. I asked if she would give us an affidavit. She said that her husband was afraid for them to get involved, so I said no more.

She and her husband, William A. Reis, later separated, and he moved to Columbia. About 11:45 a.m. on August 7, 1987, he was stabbed to death as he apparently attempted to fend off two robbers, police said. At his Gold and Silver Exchange on Rosewood Drive, he suffered cuts to his face, head, neck, hands, and chest. "There was a lot of blood all over the place," Coroner Frank Barron said. "He put up a fight. A lot of things were turned over, coins scattered."

That was a horrible death for Mr. Reis, at the early age of 47. I happened to see Joy Reis recently, for the first time in many years, and the Cuttino murder was discussed. She said she would no longer be afraid to make a statement about the PEG coat, as she realizes that no one can hide from danger.

CHAPTER TWENTY-EIGHT

UPDATE ON CHIEF CHARACTERS AND EVENTS

The Moving Finger writes; and having writ,
Moves on; nor all your Piety nor Wit
Shall lure it back to cancel half a Line,
Nor all your Tears wash out a Word of it.

— Omar Khayyam

The Fate of the main characters in this real life drama has been extremely varied. Jack Levon Truluck, 62, award-winning journalist, died March 13, 1982. Known for his disarmingly low-key questioning and his easy access to news sources, he was with The State newspaper from 1949 (most of the time) until 1982, when he became public information director at the South Carolina Criminal Justice Academy.

The passing of J.P. "Pete" Strom was called the end of an era and the death of an institution. By any measure, Strom's death Monday, December 14, 1987, at the age of 69 left a void in the State Law Enforcement Division, which he headed through more than 30 years and eight governors. He died of a heart attack.

Richard Kirk McLeod, a Third Circuit solicitor for 28 years, died at his home on December 28, 1987. McLeod, 66, served as solicitor from 1954 through 1982 and was described as one of South Carolina's most fiery, aggressive and fair prosecutors.

Ira Byrd Parnell, Sr., a veteran law enforcement officer who served 28 years as Sumter County Sheriff, died October 9, 1989, at the age of 74. "His goal was to raise the level of professionalism in law enforcement," said Sumter County Sheriff Tommy Mims, who was an officer under Parnell for 13 years.

Judge Louis Rosen, 79, died December 29, 1989, at the Regional Medical Center of Orangeburg and Calhoun Counties. He was the Judge at the March, 1973, trial of William J. Pierce, Jr., for the Cuttino murder, and at the April hearing for a new trial.

Donald Henry "Pee Wee" Gaskins was electrocuted September 6, 1991, at age 58. His death penalty came as a result of his involvement in the explosive death of Death Row inmate Rudolph Tyner.

State Law Enforcement Division spokesman Hugh Munn left The State newspaper as a reporter in 1975. He often worked with Jack Truluck, especially on the Cuttino murder investigation.

Judge Dan Laney retired from the bench in 1991, to work with a Columbia Law Firm. "I want to represent any type of person who's been wronged by someone else," Laney, age 60, was quoted as saying.

Holly Gatlin is a Novitiate at Pecos Benedictine Monastery in Pecos, New Mexico.

Former South Carolina Supreme Court Chief Justice Julius "Bubba" Ness died November 12, 1991, at the age of 75, after a bout with cancer. Third Circuit Court Judge David McInnis said Ness was "refreshing" at a time when public officials didn't show their true feelings about others. Sumter County Clerk of Court O.V. Player said, "If he was your friend, he'd do anything for you."

Former Appling County, Georgia, Sheriff J.B. "Red" Carter is serving time in a Federal Prison after receiving a 35-year sentence, plus a $150,000 fine, for his conviction of racketeering and drug dealing charges. "He came to prominence in the early 1970's after capturing William 'Junior' Pierce, who later was found guilty of the murder of Margaret 'Peg' Cuttino of Sumter. Pierce later charged that Carter tortured him to force him to confess to the Cuttino slaying," an AP wire story stated on February 3, 1982.

Former Williamsburg Clerk of Court Winnie P. Jones is serving her sentence in the Kingstree Jail, after being sentenced to 25 years for embezzling public money from her office accounts. She must serve five years before being eligible for probation.

And William J. Pierce, Jr., is still in prison in Valdosta, Georgia, still filing appeals, which are still being denied, but he still hopes to be exonerated of the Cuttino murder one day.

Although Mr. Pierce has not been successful in having his conviction in the Cuttino murder overturned, he has had good luck in other murder cases that Sheriff "Red" Carter said Pierce confessed to. An article in a Charleston, West Virginia, newspaper in July, 1974, stated:

CONFESSION IN MURDER QUESTIONED

Governor Moore said Thursday a preliminary investigation indicates a Georgia prison inmate, who insists he killed two West Virginia University coeds, was in prison at the time the murders were committed in 1970. Moore identified the prisoner as William J. Pierce, an inmate of the Georgia State Prison at Reidsville, who has confessed to a total of 18 murders. Moore quoted the Georgia Bureau of Investigation at Statesville that Pierce declared he was responsible for the deaths of Karen Ferrell and Mared Malarik, who disappeared from the WVU campus on January 19, 1970.

The State newspaper, January 20, 1980, carried a UPI story from Morgantown, West Virginia:

MURDERS CASE HITS 10 YEARS

Friday was the 10th anniversary of the slayings of two West Virginia coeds who were raped, shot and beheaded. The victims were Mared Malarik and Karen Ferrell, both 19. Eugene P. Clawson, now 40, confessed to slaying them six years later. At the time of his confessions he was in a county jail in Camden,

N.J., on unrelated sexual assault charges. He said he had been having nightmares and 'could hear them, you know, begging, and they just tortured me'.

The State, December 19, 1979, printed a report by Holly Gatlin:

PIERCE RULED OUT AS GIRL'S KILLER

Nine years after her 17-year-old niece was murdered in a sex crime, Lucille Jackson of Lexington is not upset that charges have been dropped against the accused killer. Lexington Sheriff James R. Metts announced in a press conference Tuesday that William 'Junior' Pierce, who is in jail in Georgia for other crimes, is no longer branded with the death of Kathy Jo Anderson. Mrs. Jackson said in an interview she was pleased, "because I've known all along he didn't do it." "New information proves that the convicted murderer did not kill Miss Anderson despite his alleged confession nine years ago," Metts said.

Also, the charges against Pierce in the Beaufort, South Carolina, slaying of James L. Sires, whom Sheriff Carter said Pierce confessed to killing have been dropped, because of lack of evidence of guilt.

Why, then, have South Carolina court systems steadfastly refused to listen to Pierce's pleas in the Cuttino murder? I have watched court cases very carefully since being involved, and often see news releases such as the following, which appeared in The State newspaper April 14, 1982:

SANTEE SLAYING TRIAL FAULTY

The S.C. Supreme Court has awarded a new trial for James Anthony Butler, who was convicted of murder in the death of a Santee motel keeper and the beating of his wife. The court agreed with Butler that both the circuit solicitor and the presiding judge had made reversible errors in the original trial. Butler was convicted in March 1981 for the murder of Thakor Patel and assault and battery with intent to kill Mrs. Patel, who was wounded. Judge John H. Smith sentenced Butler to death on the jury's recommendation. On appeal, Butler argued the solicitor had injected his personal opinion into the jury's deliberations and improperly influenced them. Butler also contended that the solicitor's closing argument was such as to make a fair trial impossible.

How about Solicitor Kirk McLeod's closing remarks to the Cuttino trial jurors? "I'll tell you what we've got here," began Solicitor McLeod in the state's final argument, "is a dead little girl and a man who admitted killing her and that's the facts of the case — Are you going to believe these men (law enforcement officials), or are you going to believe this man and his friends? All I know is that since he's been locked up, I don't know of another little girl who's been killed in South Carolina." Yet the Supreme Court has denied Pierce a new trial. Is this fair and equal treatment? I think not!

The State newspaper, March 4, 1982, carried an article by Charles Pope, headed:

MURDER TRIAL JUDGE'S ERROR EARNS DEFENDANT NEW TRIAL

The South Carolina Supreme Court Wednesday unanimously awarded a new trial to convicted killer Angela Z. Stewart, ruling that the conduct of a courtroom spectator may have hindered her right to a fair trial. Justice C. Bruce Littlejohn, writing for the majority said: "We think it was an error for the trial judge to overrule the motion for a mistrial without having first explored the improper conduct of the spectator and without having first determined whether or not there was prejudice."

In a companion opinion, Justice Julius B. Ness questioned the state's reliance on circumstantial evidence to convict Mrs. Stewart. " I concur in the majority opinion that prejudicial error was committed at trial," Ness wrote. "I also believe the evidence is insufficient to support the conviction." Ness wrote that the "proof offered by the state to establish the time of death... is insufficient to support the conviction."

Well, compare that one to the Cuttino trial. The arrest warrant Magistrate O.L. Hogan, Jr., signed on April 30th, 1971, specified that William J. Pierce, Jr., committed the Cuttino murder on December 18, 1970. Then, the Indictment For Murder was signed the first Monday of November, 1972, using December 18, 1970, as the murder date. At the Preliminary Hearing, no one questioned the date of the murder. At the Inquest on February 8, 1973, Solicitor Kirk McLeod took over and conducted it, rather than Coroner Howard J. Parnell. Mr. McLeod questioned the pathologist, Dr. Joel Sexton, only as to the cause of death:

Solicitor McLeod:	*In other words, in your opinion, the death was either caused by strangulation or a blow to the head, but not by any other means?*
Dr. Sexton:	*That is correct.*
Solicitor McLeod:	*This is an Inquest into the death of Margaret (Peggy) Cuttino. This is not a trial. This is to determine the cause of death. The Preliminary Hearing has been held. And the full extent of that Preliminary Hearing was offered to the attorneys for the Defendant. Come down,*

	Doctor.
Mr. McElveen:	The position of The State is we have no right to be heard, is that correct?
Solicitor McLeod:	That is correct.
Mr. McElveen:	That is your ruling, your Honor?
Coroner Parnell:	Yes, sir.

Next followed examination of Sheriff Parnell by Solicitor McLeod. At the conclusion, the following exchange occurred:

Solicitor McLeod:	Thank you, Sheriff, you can come down. That is all that we have at this time.
Mr. McElveen:	We once again request that we be given the right to question the witness. This is in the nature of a public hearing.
Coroner Parnell:	This is an Inquest. We are here to determine the cause of death.
Mr. McElveen:	Your Honor, this man has already been indicted.
Coroner Parnell:	You will have an opportunity — he has a right to testify if he would like to testify.
Mr. McElveen:	He does not wish to testify. We still request our rights to cross-examine the witness.
Solicitor McLeod:	They have no rights whatsoever under the Constitution of this State. That is all The State presents at this time.
Mr. McElveen:	Is that your ruling on my question?
Coroner Parnell:	Yes.
Mr. McElveen:	And I am not allowed to question?
Coroner Parnell:	Yes. Is there anyone else that you want to put up?
Solicitor McLeod:	No, sir, that will do.

Funny thing Solicitor McLeod didn't know that the Law Book says an Inquest should determine how, where, at what time, and by what instrument the deceased was killed. I believe that Coroner Parnell knew better, but seemed to be under great pressure.

Anyway, he had conducted an Inquest in the death of a boy who had drowned in our pool several months prior to the Cuttino Inquest, and he was very generous in allowing everyone — all the lawyers and jurors, to ask as many questions as they wanted from any of the witnesses. This boy drowned "as a result of his own negligence." Yet Peg Cuttino was brutally slain, and never were any jurors told — during the Grand Jury Hearing, the Coroner's Inquest, or even the trial, that the autopsy report stated that Peg had been dead at least five days prior to the discovery of her body, although she was missing twelve days. Surely, the Sheriff and Solicitor should have had access to the pathologists' report, and certainly the jurors should have been informed. But they knew William J. Pierce would never have been convicted, and their scapegoat would never be convicted, if these facts were told. This is one of life's saddest eras, when we learn that we cannot trust our elected officials and law enforcement personnel whom we pay to protect us.

CHAPTER TWENTY-NINE

LOSING FAITH IN OUR FELLOW MAN

If anyone wants to give credit or blame for the upset of the status quo of Sumter County Law Enforcement, all the honors go to then-Detectives Tommy Mims and Hugh Mathis. They were really good detectives, and I had cooperated with them on several occasions prior to the Cuttino murder. You may recall, in an earlier chapter, this testimony:

DIRECT EXAMINATION OF MR. MIMS BY SOLICITOR MCLEOD

Solicitor McLeod:	As a result of talking to them (the LeNoirs), did y'all pursue any further investigation in the neighborhood?
Mr. Mims:	We did. The remainder of the afternoon, we interviewed other people in the Horatio area, and checked all known clubhouses that the young people usually congregated at, as well as abandoned farmhouses.

Sounds like they believed us. Why else would they waste an afternoon in Horatio? Following cross-examination by Mr. Connor:

REDIRECT EXAMINATION OF MR. MIMS BY SOLICITOR MCLEOD

Solicitor McLeod:	Did Mrs. LeNoir make any statement about Mr. LeNoir's statement?
Mr. Mims:	Yes, sir, she did. She stated that — something to the effect, I'm not, this is not word for word, that she doubted that he could remember what he saw, if he saw the girl.

DIRECT EXAMINATION OF HUGH MATHIS BY SOLICITOR MCLEOD

Solicitor McLeod:	What did she say, if anything, about the, about Mr. LeNoir's statement?
Mr. Mathis:	She said she didn't think he knew what he was talking about. He had seen this thing in the paper.

CROSS-EXAMINATION OF MR. MATHIS BY MR. MCELVEEN

Mr. McElveen:	Mr. Mathis, do you recall the conversation that you had with Mrs. LeNoir when you approached her at the church, I believe it was?
Mr. Mathis:	Yes, sir.
Mr. McElveen:	Do you recall the first thing you said to her?
Mr. Mathis:	Probably hello.
Mr. McElveen:	After that?
Mr. Mathis:	Well —
Mr. McElveen:	Let me refresh your memory. How about, "Mrs. Lenoir, I've come to tell you that I expect J. Edgar Hoover will be drafting you most any time to serve with the F.B.I." Is that the statement you made?
Mr. Mathis:	I wouldn't doubt it, or something to that effect.
Mr. McElveen:	In a subsequent conversation after the trial, I believe you told me that if the LeNoirs told me something, I could put it in my pipe and smoke it; is that not correct?
Mr. Mathis:	That has been my experience with the LeNoirs.

Although the ugly, untrue remarks Tommy Mims and Hugh Mathis made about my husband and me hurt, I never really blamed them, however, as I felt that they were coerced by higher authorities to testify in order to try to discredit our testimony. As a matter of fact, it made them look pretty stupid, as just minutes earlier, Tommy Mims had testified that as a result of talking to us, they spent the rest of the afternoon in Horatio looking for Peg. I've been asked by several people recently if I have forgiven Tommy and Hugh for their remarks. I replied that I probably have forgiven, but certainly can't forget.

It was bad enough to hear these false statements about us from the Law Enforcement agencies, but much more surprising and mysterious to hear them from James Cuttino, Peg's father. During the depositions prior to the Three Million Dollar suit trial, he referred to me: "Yes, and the perpetrated fraud that this woman has tried to put over on Sumter County." He accused me of showing pictures of Peg's body on Election Day, when, in fact, I was clerk of poll managers, opened the building, along with other managers, at 6:30 a.m., and other than a brief lunch period, was on duty all day, helped count ballots, and went with other poll managers to take ballot boxes in that night. He named people to whom I'd supposedly shown the picture, so I decided to contact them. The following letter is self-explanatory:

LETTER TO MRS. WALTER SANDERS FROM MRS. LENOIR
DATED AUGUST 6, 1980

Dear Maude,

I need to know the date (or approximate date) I showed you the picture of Peg Cuttino's body. Please fill in, sign, and return to me as quickly as possible. Am enclosing addressed, stamped envelope for your convenience. Thanks.

Sincerely yours,
Carrie B. LeNoir

MRS. SANDERS' REPLY TO MRS. LENOIR

Dear Carrie,

You never showed me the picture that you referred to. If you will recall, when this first started, I told you that I was a friend of the Myers and you and that I didn't want to discuss it with either party. You both respected my wishes and I deeply appreciated it.

Maude

He hurled some terrible accusations, but probably his most ridiculous statement was while being questioned by The Item's attorney, William Pope:

Mr. Pope: *How about Marilyn Abergast?*
Mr. Cuttino: *Marilyn Abergast was the girl that testified*
                 that she was the girl that admitted that she
                 had been to Carrie LeNoir's store with the
                 two boys.

Apparently, he didn't know that I saw Marilyn as an infant a few days after Julian Nunnery brought her home and later adopted. I watched Marilyn grow from infancy into a beautiful blonde teenager, as she came into our store often, and even visited in our home. I saw her regularly, as I was a local 4-H Leader and Junior Grange matron. She belonged to both organizations. Certainly, there was no way to mistake the identity of Peg Cuttino and Marilyn Nunnery Abergast.

Chapter Thirty

Inspiration & Encouragement from Many Sources

Of course, all these developments were aggravating, but I never lost sight of my goal to try to help William J. Pierce, Jr., in his attempts to be exonerated of the Cuttino murder. One of the most inspiring thoughts are given in Dear Abby's column at regular intervals, and I always clip and save each one:

I Didn't Speak Up
by Martin Niemoeller, a German Lutheran Pastor

In Germany, the Nazis first came for the communists, and I didn't speak up because I wasn't a communist. Then, they came for the Jews, and I didn't speak up because I wasn't a Jew. Then they came for the trade unionists, and I didn't speak up because I wasn't a trade unionist. Then they came for the Catholics, and I didn't speak up because I was Protestant. Then they came for me, and by that time there was no one left to speak for me.

During the terrible ordeals of the depositions prior to the law suit, when the Barnwell lawyers went into a huddle, I pulled my little "Day by Day" from my purse, and fervently prayed "For Today"...

O God: Give me strength to live another day;
Let me not turn coward before its difficulties
or prove recreant to its duties;
Let me not lose faith in other people;
Keep me sweet and sound of heart,
in spite of ingratitude, treachery, or meanness;
Preserve me from minding little stings or giving them;
help me to keep my heart clean, and to live
so honestly and fearlessly that no outward
failure can dishearten me or take away the joy
of conscious integrity;
Open wide the eyes of my soul that I may
see good in all things;
Grant me this day some new vision of thy truth;
Inspire me with the spirit of joy and gladness;
and make me the cup of strength to
suffering souls; in the name of the strong
Deliverer, our only Lord and Savior, Jesus Christ.

Since I couldn't afford to hire a lawyer for "The Three Million Dollar Suit," I felt all alone, and often thought I could imagine how Daniel must have felt in the Den of Lions; but God did hear, and He answered my prayers, and I never lost my Faith. Also, my loved ones and friends, some old and some new, gave me wonderful support throughout the entire ordeal. My nephew was Headmaster of a boys' military academy. I'd like to share a letter I received from him while I was incarcerated at the Sumter Correctional Center, awaiting transfer to the State Women's Prison to serve my 90-day sentence for refusing to obey Judge Dan Laney's order:

31 August, 1977

Aunt Carrie —

I have always wanted to be on the front page of The State paper and have failed, but you are the next best thing. I hope this letter finds you in good spirits. Seriously speaking, if there is anything I can do to help you and your family, please let me know. I admire your courage, guts and determination in this matter. Standing up for what you believe appears to be diminishing in our power controlled society, but your actions have been an inspiration to me. So many unethical, immoral acts go undetected and unchallenged these days that in the near future we may find ourselves in great difficulty. Everyone should attempt to strive for truth and justice and I know that is exactly what you are doing. Remember — you are not alone. I am involved in education and can see through my students our need to "get back to basics." I told my students about your "perils" and the price you are paying. If there is anything I can do, please let me help. If you have a chance, drop me a line and let me know your current situation.

Love —
Dean

I must point out, however, that on the fourth day of my incarceration, attorneys Werber Bryan and Joe McElveen met with South Carolina Supreme Court Chief Justice Woodrow Lewis and asked for and received an Order of Supersedes, so I could get out of prison on Friday and play the organ in Church on Sunday morning. I was very grateful that Mr. Bryan and Mr. McElveen followed that with an appeal to the Supreme Court, which voted in my favor, and my criminal records had to be destroyed.

I'd also like to share another letter, which I have been given permission to use:

June 18, 1980

Mrs. Carrie LeNoir
Horatio

Dear Mrs. LeNoir,
You may think it odd that I am writing you but please let me explain:

Many years ago, I wrote a poem about Peg Cuttino and lost it. It was during the "second investigation" of the case when Mr. Howard Parnell was Coroner and he gave you and your "Citizens for Justice" group a hearing. I was hopeful then, that the facts would be known and brought to light and that "justice would be done." It felt, to me, like Peg was somewhere watching, hoping, with baited breath — and I wrote the poem down. When the hearing was concluded, and "no further action" would be taken and it became a "closed" issue with nothing new resolved, I put the poem away and forgot it.

Now — one week after (Hazel) Reeves is elected as our new Sheriff — I find the poem. Just like that. I was not looking for it. In fact, I had to jog my memory when I did find it, to remember the circumstances of its origin. I write poetry all the time and can not even remember them unless I keep them in my files.

The irony of finding it now made me feel as if I should send it to you. Here is a copy. (The "original" was too messy and smudged.) I hope you like it. I feel as if it shows the oppression that we were under as far as our law enforcement system went back then.

It is for you and your justice group to keep and perhaps it is a "good omen" that I found it when I did.

Maybe, just maybe, the truth will be found out with a new administration at the helm.

Let's hope.
I hope you like it.

Sincerely,
Mrs. Charlotte Partin
(Julian's wife)

To Peg, In Heaven

Hang in there, Peg —
We will catch the man...
The Evil one
Who ripped you loose
From carefree days...
Who — under threatening gaze
made you submit.
And then threw back his head
And laughed at it!

Hang in there, child...
Look down from Heavenly perch.
Watch us try
To overcome the obstacles...
And Power.
Now, it is the Hour —
The pieces are being drawn
— magnet like —
Towards a central core.
We know things now
That we never knew before!

You can sit back, Peg
    And breathe free —
It won't be long now...
You can play amongst the clouds
And kiss the moon —
Justice will be done
The Mighty House of Cards will fall
And soon...

Goodnight, sweet child...
Keep your fingers crossed!

— Mrs. Charlotte Partin

CHAPTER THIRTY-ONE

IN RETROSPECT

Perhaps If — Magistrate O.L. Hogon, Jr. had not issued an Arrest Warrant for William J. Pierce, Jr., on April 30, 1971, at the request of Sheriff I. Byrd Parnell, who had no signed nor taped confession from Mr. Pierce; and said oral confession was in direct conflict of report of Earl Williams and his father; and

Perhaps If — Solicitor R. Kirk McLeod had presented a few more facts to the Grand Jury on November 1, 1972, in seeking Indictment For Murder, the jurors would not have found him guilty; and,

Perhaps If — at the Preliminary Hearing on November 2, 1972, when Attorney Edward Atkinson requested a polygraph test be given Mr. Pierce, and the Sheriff and Solicitor had granted that request, Magistrate Lang Hogon would not have found probable cause for the case to be sent up for trial in the Court of General Sessions; and,

Perhaps If — at the Inquisition on February 8, 1973, Coroner Howard Parnell and solicitor Kirk McLeod had allowed Attorney Joseph McElveen to ask questions of Dr. Joel Sexton, as to how, where, at what time, and by what instrument the deceased was killed, Pierce would not have been held for further action; and

Perhaps If — at the Pierce trial in Kingstree on March 1st and 2nd, 1973, where the testimony conflicts were numerous as to time of death, car Pierce was driving, etc., Solicitor McLeod had not charged the jurors thus — "I'll tell you what we've got here," began Solicitor McLeod in the state's final argument, "is a dead little girl and a man who admitted killing her and that's the facts of the case. Are you going to believe these men (law enforcement officials) or are you going to believe this man and his friends — All I know is that since he's been locked up, I don't know of another little girl who's been killed in South Carolina", I doubt that the jurors would have found Pierce guilty of the Cuttino murder.

And I'm very sure that if Tommie Mims and Hugh Mathis could "have remembered", and testified truthfully as to our conversation at Ascension Church on the afternoon of December 20, 1970, I would never have become so deeply involved. I'm satisfied that an honest accounting of what I told them would have resulted in Judge Louis Rosen granting a new trial for William J. Pierce, at the hearing on April 5, 1973 and he would have been exonerated of the Cuttino murder back in 1973.

Perhaps If — Judge Ernest Finney had listened more carefully, or studied the court reporter's transcript, he would have discovered that no witness could account for Pee Wee Gaskins during the "crucial time", and he would have ordered a new trial, which would surely have cleared Pierce of this conviction.

This brings to mind a recent article which appeared in numerous papers, and I quote The Item, April 17, 1992 — "House debates changing judge selection process" — "Members of the state House want the public to know the judiciary is more than a private club of ex-lawmakers. At the heart of the debate on Thursday was the perception — some have said a reality — that a legislator running for judge has a virtual lock on winning the seat despite qualifications of other candidates. Most judges on circuit courts or higher have served in the Legislature. Several others have ties to leading lawmakers. 'The problem is that it looks like a closed system. The problem is it looks like you can't get it unless you have legislative connection', said House Democratic leader Joe McElveen of Sumter.

Under McElveen's proposal, the House and Senate each could elect three members, with the governor appointing the other three, but none could be legislators. Five members could be lawyers, but the remaining five would have to come from outside the legal ranks. The panel would investigate judicial candidates and rate them highly qualified, qualified, or not qualified."

This plan sounds better than the present method, but the best plan would be to have Judges elected by all the people. This method might curtail the "Loyalty To Friends" philosophy which the late Judge "Bubba" Ness preached and practiced.

And finally, if the Attorney General and his staff were allowed to search for and promote the truth in cases, rather than defend The State of South Carolina and its officials, regardless of what mistakes they might have made, Justice could more readily prevail. This case reminds me of a garment being buttoned. If the first button is put into the wrong buttonhole, and the process is followed, the garment will be crooked right on through. Until someone is willing to unbutton the top button and start over, there's no hopes for Justice for Pierce.

CHAPTER THIRTY-TWO

IN DEEP GRATITUDE

Yes, we're very grateful to everyone who supported us in any manner, whether with financial contributions, or just a smile or handshake, but there are two gentlemen that must be singled out. The first one was Attorney William James, who sent me "It is a fundamental doctrine of law that a party whose personal rights are to be affected by a personal judgment must have a day in court, or opportunity to be heard; without due notice and opportunity to be heard the court has no jurisdiction to adjudicate such personal rights A personal judgment by a court without jurisdiction of both the parties and the subject matter is a nullity and must be so treated by the courts whenever and for whatever purpose it is presented and relied on." Although I felt that I had legal rights in refusing to obey Judge Dan Laney's August 12, 1977, order, this information from Attorney William James added starch to my courage when I appeared before Judge Laney for the hearing on August 29, 1977.

Another hero for our cause was Attorney Herb Buhl, of The American Civil Liberties Union in Columbia, S.C. By the time I was served with the Three Million Dollar Law Suit — James Cuttino, Jr. against Carrie LeNoir, Verna Moore and The Sumter Daily Item, on October 24, 1978, our legal funds were getting very low, and I did not want to go in debt. A visit to Mr. Buhl provided free legal counsel so that I was able to successfully defend myself in that suit. We shall always be in deep gratitude to these kind gentlemen.

Just as the doubts seems to increase on the Cuttino murder case, so do the doubts linger on the 1932 Lindbergh baby kidnapping and murder; and the 1963 President John F. Kennedy assassination. The State, April 2, 1992, carried a Dallas Morning News headline: "Doctor: Oswald didn't kill JFK"

A doctor who worked at Parkland Memorial Hospital when President John F. Kennedy and Lee Harvey Oswald were killed says Kennedy's fatal head wound "had to have come from the front."

Dr. Charles Crenshaw, director and chairman of the surgery department at John Peter Smith Hospital in Fort Worth, is breaking his 29-year silence on the subject by talking to two national television shows, ABC's "20/20" on Friday and the syndicated "Now It Can Be Told".

Crenshaw also tells of receiving a call from President Lyndon Johnson, who demanded a "deathbed statement" from Oswald after he was shot by Jack Ruby. Oswald made no known statements in his dying minutes.

According to transcripts, Crenshaw tells "20/20" that he looked at Kennedy's wounds before "we placed him in the coffin." I wanted to know and remember this for the rest of my life. And the rest of my life I will always know he was shot from the front." The Warren Commission concluded that Oswald was the only assassin and fired from behind the motorcade.

Our prayer is that someone who knows who killed Peg Cuttino will soon break the silence and tell the truth.

I quote Ecclesiastes 12, verses 13 & 14 — "Let us hear the conclusion of the whole matter; Fear God, and keep his commandments; for this is the whole duty of man. For God shall bring every work into judgment, with every secret thing, whether it be good or whether it be evil."

I believe that all the foregoing facts will prove BEYOND REASONABLE DOUBT that William J. Pierce, Jr., is innocent of the Cuttino murder. I apologize to anyone I might have offended, and sympathize to all who have suffered pain and grief; but I feel that this account of events should be recorded, in hopes that similar mistakes will not be made in the future. Repetition was unavoidable at times, as events were reported; and yet, it seems, we've only "touched the tip of the iceberg."

Again, I wish to express gratitude, apologies, and sympathy to everyone whose life has been touched by this very sad event. And in closing, I'd like to share a poem which was given to me on August 26, 1973. I feel very humble, but it has been an inspiration to me during some of the darkest days.

> During our lifetime we meet very few totally unselfish and courageous people. This poem, however amateurish it may be, is written for a lady whom we believe to be one of the truly beautiful people — Mrs Carrie Lenoir.

> *I believe in myself only —*
> *for what I am reflects the world around me.*
> *I cannot shrink inside myself and say that what will be must be.*
> *What is my life worth if I touch no one along the way?*
> *And who'll remember when I'm gone?*
> *What will there be to say?*

> *Don't ask me to travel thoroughfares —*
> *if a sideroad holds one soul in distress.*
> *I have the time to detour — and I have no regrets.*
> *I've touched the hand of many — and wiped the tears of some.*
> *And even though the road is long, I know the end must come.*

> *Someday, through each cloud, the sun must show its rays.*
> *I have held the hand of God through many cloudy days.*
> *Some beautiful sunlit morning-when no clouds shall mar the sky,*
> *I'll set my shoulders — lift my head — and look God in the eye.*

> *Peggy Green*
> *8/26/73*